CONQUER THE QUESTION ASKED 80-85% ON
"AS A PROJECT MANAGER WHAT WOULD Y

PASS THE NEW JAN 2021 PMP EXAM NOW

INFRASTRUCTURE TECHNOLOGY

ALL-IN-ONE
PMP
EXAM PREP KIT

TECHNICAL PROJECT MANAGEMENT EDITION

1300 QUESTIONS, ANSWERS, AND EXPLANATIONS
FIVE MOCK EXAMS

240 plus Flashcards, Templates and Pamphlet

DARRON CLARK, PMP, EMBA, BSEET, BSCS
Author of PMP Exam Prep: Technical Project Manager
BASED ON PMBOK 6TH EDITION UPDATED FOR JAN 2021 EXAM

Library of Congress Control Number: 2020921961
Independent Publishing Platform, North Charleston, SC

PMBOK® is a registered trademark of Project Management Institute. Project Management Professional and PMP® are registered trademarks of Project Management Institute.
Oracle®, Real Application Clusters, and Data Guard are registered trademarks of the Oracle Corporation.
Strayer University is a registered trademark.

Credits

This coursebook follows the PMBOK® Guide, Sixth Edition.
PMI®, PMBOK® Guide, Project Management Professional, PMP®, Certified Associate in Project Management (CAPM)®, PMI Agile Certified Practitioner (PMI-ACP)®, and PMI-ACP® are registered trademarks of the Project Management Institute, Inc.

Oracle® is a registered trademark of the Oracle Corporation GPM LLC® is a registered trademark.

* Note that PMI reserves the right to test on materials not contained in the PMBOK® Guide. See exam content outline at www.pmi.org under certifications (PMP)®.

PMP Exam Prep:

Technical Project Manager

Contents

Acknowledgments

I thank my mom, daughter, family, friends, and colleagues for the many things they have taught me, the love they have given me, the genuine connections we have forged, and the knowledge they have shared over the years. Without all of them, this book would not have been possible.

Dear Reader,

Thank you for choosing PMP® Exam Prep, a PMBOK®, Sixth Edition preparation guide.

As of August 2019, there are 932,720 active PMP certified individuals and 300 chartered chapters across 218 countries and territories worldwide. Already most companies will not interview even the most successful and experienced project manager without PMP certification. The exam will only get trickier moving forward. The time to get PMP certified is now.

This book is unique because it teaches, guides, and prepares the reader to pass the PMP exam the way we naturally learn. Through diagrams, repetition, and exam questions using IT infrastructure projects and technical project management as primary examples, you will achieve the following objectives:

» Effectively use all 49 project management processes

» Master PMBOK® terminology

» Understand how internal and external environments influence projects

» Utilize tools and techniques effectively to plan, manage, and monitor projects

» Learn to develop and monitor a schedule and budget

» Employ various risk management strategies and methods for managing projects

PART I:

About the PMP® Exam

The PMP® is difficult—one of the hardest project management exams. Be prepared to study beyond PMBOK® and the classroom material.

The exam tests substantive and reading comprehension skills. Some questions are long and wordy, and you'll need to filter through irrelevant information to find critical facts for answering the question correctly.

What Can I Expect on the PMP® Exam?

» Scenario-based questions

» Long, wordy questions

» More-than-one-answer questions

» Common sense versus *PMBOK® Guide* answers

» Mathematical problems

» Long and complicated critical path diagrams

» Answers that are correct, but for a different question

» An innovative approach to a known topic

Current Exam Content Outline

Domain	Percentage of Items on Test
I. Initiating	13%
II. Planning	24%
III. Executing	31%
IV. Monitoring and Controlling	25%
V. Closing	7%
Total	100%
Total Number of Scored Questions	175
Total Number of Unscored (Pretest) Questions	25
Total Number of Questions	200

Exam Content Outline updated for January 2021

Project Management Professional (PMP)® For January 2021 Exam Update[1]

The last day for candidates to take the current version of the PMP exam is before January 31, 2020.

The PMP examination is a necessary part of the activities leading to earning a professional certification; thus, the PMP examination must reflect precisely the practices of the project management practitioner.

PMI retained Alpine Testing Solutions to develop the global *PMP Examination Content Outline*. Alpine Testing Solutions provides psychometric, test development, and credential management solutions to credentialing and educational programs. The task force members were given responsibility for outlining critical job tasks of individuals who lead, and direct projects based on their experience and related resources.

---

1   "PMP® Exam Change is Moving to June 2020," https://www.pmi.org/update-center/certification-changes/pmp.

Mapping Domains to Project Processes

The following table identifies the proportion of questions from each domain that will appear on the examination.

Domain	Percentage of Items on Test	Number of Exam Questions
I. People	42%	84
II. Process	50%	100
III. Business Environment	8%	16
Total	100%	

About half the examination will represent predictive project management approaches, and the other half will represent agile or hybrid approaches. Predictive, agile, and hybrid approaches will be found throughout the three-domain areas listed above and are not isolated to any particular domain or task.

Domains, Tasks, and Enablers

In this document, you will find an updated structure for the *PMP Examination Content Outline*. Based on feedback from customers and stakeholders, we have worked on simplifying the format so that the *PMP Examination Content Outline* is easier to understand and interpret.

On the following pages, you will find the domains, tasks, and enablers as defined by the Role Delineation Study.

» Domain: Domain is defined as the high-level knowledge area that is essential to the practice of project management.

» Tasks: Tasks are the underlying responsibilities of the project manager within each domain area.

» Enablers: Illustrative examples of the work associated with the task. Please note that enablers are not meant to be an exhaustive list but instead offer a few examples to help demonstrate what the task encompasses.

Domain I	People—42%	How it maps to PMBOK 6
Task 1	Manage conflict » Interpret the source and stage of the conflict » Analyze the context for the conflict » Evaluate/recommend/reconcile the appropriate conflict resolution solution	9.5 Manage Team 9.6 Control Resources
Task 2	Lead a team » Set a clear vision and mission » Support diversity and inclusion (e.g., behavior types, thought processes) » Value servant leadership (e.g., relate the tenets of servant leadership to the team) » Determine an appropriate leadership style (e.g., directive, collaborative) » Inspire, motivate, and influence team members/stakeholders (e.g., team contract, social contract, reward system) » Analyze team members and stakeholders' influence » Distinguish various options to lead various team members and stakeholders	4.2 Develop Project Charter 4.3 Develop Project Management Plan 4.4 Direct and Manage project 4.5 Monitor and Control Project
Task 3	Support team performance » Appraise team member performance against key performance indicators » Support and recognize team member growth and development » Determine appropriate feedback approach » Verify performance improvements	9.1 Plan Resource Management 9.5 Manage Team 9.6 Control Resources
Task 4	Empower team members and stakeholders » Organize around team strengths » Support team task accountability » Evaluate demonstration of task accountability » Determine and bestow level(s) of decision-making authority	9.1 Plan Resource Management 9.3 Acquire Resources
Task 5	Ensure that team members/stakeholders are adequately trained » Determine the required competencies and elements of training » Determine training options based on training needs » Allocate resources for training » Measure training outcomes	9.1 Plan Resource Management 9.4 Develop Team 9.6 Control Resources
Task 6	Build a team » Appraise stakeholder skills » Deduce project resource requirements » Continuously assess and refresh team skills to meet project needs » Maintain team and knowledge transfer	9.1 Plan Resource Management 9.3 Acquire Resources
Task 7	Address and remove impediments, obstacles, and blockers for the team » Determine critical impediments, obstacles, and blockers for the team » Prioritize critical impediments, obstacles, and blockers for the team » Use the network to implement solutions to remove impediments, obstacles, and blockers for the team Reassess continually to ensure impediments, obstacles, and blockers for the team are being addressed	Agile Project Management

Task 8	Negotiate project agreements	4.1 Develop Project Charter
	» Analyze the bounds of the negotiations for an agreement	5.5 Validate Scope
	» Assess priorities and determine the ultimate objective(s)	
	» Verify objective(s) of the project agreement is met	
	» Participate in agreement negotiations	
	Determine a negotiation strategy	
Task 9	Collaborate with stakeholders » Evaluate engagement needs for stakeholders	13.2 Plan Stakeholder Engagement
	» Optimize alignment between stakeholder needs, expectations, and project objectives	13.3 Manage Stakeholder Engagement
	Build trust and influence stakeholders to accomplish project objectives	13.3 Monitor Stakeholder Engagement
Task 10	Build a shared understanding	9.5 Manage Team
	» Break down situation to identify the root cause of a misunderstanding	9.6 Control Resources
	» Survey all necessary parties to reach consensus	
	» Support outcome of parties' agreement	
	Investigate potential misunderstandings	
Task 11	Engage and support virtual teams	9.5 Manage Team
	» Examine virtual team member needs (e.g., environment, geography, culture, global, etc.)	9.6 Control Resources
	» Investigate alternatives (e.g., communication tools, colocation) for virtual team member engagement	
	» Implement options for virtual team member engagement	
	Continually evaluate the effectiveness of virtual team member engagement	
Task 12	Define team ground rules	9.6 Control Resources
	» Communicate organizational principles with team and external stakeholders	10.1 Plan Communication Management
	» Establish an environment that fosters adherence to the ground rules	10.2 Manage Communications
	Manage and rectify ground-rule violations	
Task 13	Mentor relevant stakeholders	10.3 Monitor Stakeholders
	» Allocate the time to mentoring	13.3 Manage Stakeholder Engagement
	Recognize and act on mentoring opportunities	
Task 14	Promote team performance through the application of emotional intelligence	9.5 Manage resources
	» Assess behavior through the use of personality indicators	9.6 Control resources
	Analyze personality indicators and adjust to the emotional needs of key project stakeholders	

Domain II	Process—50%	How it maps to PMBOK 6
Task 1	Execute project with the urgency required to deliver business value » Assess opportunities to deliver value incrementally » Examine the business value throughout the project » Support the team to subdivide project tasks as necessary to find the minimum viable product	4.1 Develop Project Charter 4.3 Direct and Manage Project 5.4 Create WBS
Task 2	Manage communications » Analyze communication needs of all stakeholders » Determine communication methods, channels, frequency, and level of detail for all stakeholders » Communicate project information and updates effectively » Confirm communication is understood and feedback is received	10.1 Plan Communication Management 10.2 Manage Communications 10.3 Monitor Communications
Task 3	Assess and manage risks » Determine risk management options » Iteratively assess and prioritize risks	11.1 Plan Risk Management 11.2 Identify Risks 11.3 Perform Qualitative Risk Analysis 11.4 Perform Quantitative Risk Analysis
Task 4	Engage stakeholders » Analyze stakeholders (e.g., power interest grid, influence, impact) » Categorize stakeholders » Engage stakeholders by category » Develop, execute, and validate a strategy for stakeholder engagement	13.1 Identify Stakeholders 13.2 Plan Stakeholder Management 13.3 Manage Stakeholders
Task 5	Plan and manage budget and resources » Estimate budgetary needs based on the scope of the project and lessons learned from past projects » Anticipate future budget challenges » Monitor budget variations and work with the governance process to adjust as necessary » Plan and manage resources	7.1 Plan Cost Management 7.2 Estimate Costs 7.3 Determine Budget
Task 6	Plan and manage schedule » Estimate project tasks (milestones, dependencies, story points) » Utilize benchmarks and historical data » Prepare schedule based on the methodology » Measure ongoing progress based on the methodology » Modify schedule as needed, based on the methodology Coordinate with other projects and other operations	6.1 Plan Schedule Management 6.2 Define Activities 6.3 Sequence Activities 6.4 Estimate Activities 6.5 Develop Schedule 4.6 Perform Integrated Change Control Program/Portfolio Management/Project Management Office
Task 7	Plan and manage quality of products/deliverables » Determine quality standard required for project deliverables » Recommend options for improvement based on quality gaps Continually survey project deliverable quality	8.1 Plan Quality Management 8.2 Manage Quality 8.3 Control Quality
Task 8	Plan and manage scope » Determine and prioritize requirements » Break down scope (e.g., WBS, backlog) Monitor and validate scope	5.1 Plan Scope Management 5.2 Collect Requirements 5.3 Define Scope

Task 9	Integrate project planning activities
	  » Consolidate the project/phase plans
	  » Assess consolidated project plans for dependencies, gaps, and continued business value
	  » Analyze the data collected
	  » Collect and analyze data to make informed project decisions
	Determine critical information requirements
		Program/Portfolio Management/Project Management Office

Task 10	Manage project changes
	  » Anticipate and embrace the need for change (e.g., follow change management practices)
	  » Determine a strategy to handle change
	  » Execute change management strategy according to the methodology
	Determine a change response to move the project forward
		4.5 Monitor and Control Project Work
		4.6 Perform Integrated Change Control

Task 11	Plan and manage procurement
	  » Define resource requirements and needs
	  » Communicate resource requirements
	  » Manage suppliers/contracts
	  » Plan and manage procurement strategy
	Develop a delivery solution
		9.1 Plan Resource Management
		9.6 Control Resources
		10.2 Manage Communications
		13.3 Manage Stakeholder Engagement

Task 12	Manage project artifacts
	  » Determine the requirements (what, when, where, who, etc.) for managing the project artifacts
	  » Validate that the project information is kept up to date (i.e., version control) and accessible to all stakeholders
	Continually assess the effectiveness of the management of the project artifacts
		4.6 Perform Integrated Change Control
		5.6 Control Scope
		13.3 Manage Stakeholder Engagement

Task 13	Determine appropriate project methodology/methods and practices
	  » Assess project needs, complexity, and magnitude
	  » Recommend project execution strategy (e.g., contracting, finance)
	  » Recommend a project methodology/approach (i.e., predictive, agile, hybrid)
	Use iterative, incremental practices throughout the project life cycle (e.g., lessons learned, stakeholder engagement, risk)
		4.2 Develop Project Plan
		4.3 Direct and Manage Project Work

Task 14	Establish project governance structure » Determine appropriate governance for a project (e.g., replicate organizational governance) Define escalation paths and thresholds	4.1 Develop Project Charter 4.2 Develop Project Plan 9.1 Plan Resource Management

Task 15	Manage project issues
	  » Recognize when a risk becomes an issue
	  » Attack the issue with the optimal action to achieve project success
	Collaborate with relevant stakeholders on the approach to resolve the issues
		11.6 Implement Risk Responses
		11.7 Monitor Risks
		13.3 Manage Stakeholder Engagement

Task 16	Ensure knowledge transfer for project continuity	4.3 Direct and Manage Project Work
	» Discuss project responsibilities within the team	4.4 Manage Project Knowledge
	» Outline expectations for the working environment	
	Confirm approach for knowledge transfers	
Task 17	Plan and manage project/phase closure or transitions	4.2 Develop Project Plan
	» Determine criteria to successfully close the project or phase	4.3 Direct and Manage Project Work
	» Validate readiness for transition (e.g., to operations team or next phase)	4.7 Close Project or Phase
		5.5 Validate Scope
	Conclude activities to close out project or phase (e.g., final lessons learned, retrospective, procurement, financials, resources)	

Domain III	**Business Environment—8%**	**How it maps to PMBOK 6**
Task 1	Plan and manage project compliance	4.1 Develop Project Charter
	» Confirm project compliance requirements (e.g., security, health and safety, regulatory compliance)	
	» Classify compliance categories	
	» Determine potential threats to compliance	
	» Use methods to support compliance	
	» Analyze the consequences of noncompliance	
	» Determine the necessary approach and action to address compliance needs (e.g., risk, legal)	
	» Measure the extent to which the project is in compliance	
Task 2	Evaluate and deliver project benefits and value	4.1 Develop Project Charter Statement of Work Business Need
	» Investigate that benefits are identified	Business Case
	» Document agreement on ownership for ongoing benefit realization	
	» Verify measurement system is in place to track benefits	
	» Evaluate delivery options to demonstrate the value	
	» Appraise stakeholders of value gain progress	
Task 3	Evaluate and address external business environment changes for impact on the scope	Enterprise External Factors
	» Survey changes to external business environment (e.g., regulations, technology, geopolitical, market)	
	» Assess and prioritize impact on project scope/backlog based on changes in the external business environment	
	» Recommend options for scope/backlog changes (e.g., schedule, cost changes)	
	» Continually review the external business environment for impacts on project scope/backlog	
Task 4	Support organizational change	Organizational Process Assets
	» Assess organizational culture	
	» Evaluate the impact of organizational change to project and determine required actions	
	» Evaluate the impact of the project on the organization and determine required actions	

What Do I Need to Know About the Application Process?

Price

- » Member: US $405
- » Non-member: US $555

Prerequisites

- » A secondary degree (high school diploma, associate degree, or the global equivalent)
- » 7,500 hours leading and directing projects
- » 35 hours of project management education

or

- » Four-year degree
- » 4,500 hours leading and directing projects
- » 35 hours of project management education

Tips

- » When filling out the application to register for the exam, your résumé should be in language PMI understands. Use key terms such as *deliverables*, *objectives*, *planning*, *initiating*, *executing*, *monitoring*, *controlling*, and *closing*. (See the sample project descriptions below.)
- » PMI does not care whether you submit 1 or 100 projects if you meet the criteria.
- » It is not necessary for you to have managed a project from initiation to closing.
- » You must have experience in all 5 process groups.
- » PMI only contacts you if there are issues with your application.
- » Audits are completely random. If you should get audited, the PMI team will look to verify your degree or diploma, project management experience, and 35 hours of continuing PM education.

Sample Project Description (Poor)

» Darron Clark built an impressive record of:

» Achievements deploying and enhancing Oracle environments.

» Training and mentoring teams on Oracle technologies.

» Project management and administration best practices and

» Leading the delivery of strategic projects and resolving critical issues for clients within the financial services, entertainment, manufacturing, and telecommunications industries.

Sample Project Description (Better)

» This project benefited the managing director.

» In the **initiating** phase, my team determined the **stakeholders** that would be affected by this new project, which was to automate a data replication environment to be faster.

» In the **planning** phase, my team met to gather all requirements and determine **deliverables**.

» In the **executing** phase, the team members executed their roles and responsibilities.

» In the **monitoring and control** phase, I contacted team members to ascertain the status.

» In the **closing** phase, the reporting scripts were **delivered, accepted**, and **validated**.

PART II:

Project Management Fundamentals

» What Is a Project?

» Project Integration

» Operations versus Projects

» The Project Manager's Role

» Programs

» Portfolios

» Project Management Office (PMO)

» Enterprise Environmental Factors

» Organizational Process Assets

» Project Life Cycle

» Project Phases

» Sequential Phase Relationship

» Overlapping Phase Relationship

» Predictive Life Cycles

» Iterative Life Cycles

» Adaptive Life Cycles

» Stakeholders

» Project Team versus Project Management Team

» Operational Influences

» Project Selection Methods

» Project Selection Methods (Examples)

» Project Selection Method on the PMP Exam

» Summary of Project Management Fundamentals

What Is a Project?

PMBOK® defines a project as "a temporary endeavor undertaken to create a unique product, service or result. A project is temporary in that it has a defined begin and end time, and therefore defined scope and resources."[2]

For example, when Andrew Carnegie, the steel magnate, was inspired to build the first bridge made of steel—the landmark Eads Bridge project across the Mississippi River in Saint Louis, Missouri—he and his team of engineers planned it, executed it, monitored its progress, controlled all activities, and eventually closed the project successfully. The project had a start date and an end date: 1867 and 1874, respectively. The project did not go as planned, but when completed, the desired result, the proof of the concept of steel technology, was confirmed after a few quality tests.

A project can be the start and completion of a bridge, building, software or hardware implementation, data migration, infrastructure design, or many other tasks. What does it take to understand and manage projects? Let us start with project integration and how it all works, then delve into the components of project management, such as scope, schedule, costs, quality, resources, communication, risks, procurement, and stakeholders' engagement.[3]

Project Integration

Project management is the application of knowledge, skills, tools, and techniques to complete project activities to meet project requirements. Project management is the appropriate application and integration of the 49 logically grouped project management processes and is further organized into five process groups.[4] The five process groups are initiating, planning, executing, monitoring and controlling, and closing and are discussed in more detail later in this book.

Managing a project typically includes the following tasks: identifying constraints and risks, establishing quality, addressing the needs and concerns of stakeholders, establishing and maintaining stakeholder communications, and determining how long it will take to complete the project and the budget. These are a few things that a project manager and project team must uncover to determine the feasibility of

---

3   *A Guide to the Project Management Body of Knowledge (PMBOK® Guide),* Sixth Edition (Newtown Square, PA: Project Management Institute, Inc., 2017), 4

4   EPDF, *A Guide to the Project Management Body of Knowledge,* accessed June 19, 2018, https://epdf. tips/a-guide-to-the-project-management-body-of-knowledge.html.

the project and then perform the necessary functions to implement and complete the project to the customer's satisfaction.

However, as a project manager, it is paramount that you meet stakeholder project requirements, create project deliverables to satisfy the customer's needs, and successfully close the project. There are many more cases in which a project is not managed properly, all the requirements are not delivered as promised, or the project is not on schedule or at the budget than there are cases in which the customer takes delivery and is satisfied.

As a project manager, you must balance competing project constraints, such as scope, quality, schedule, budget, resources, and risks.

Operations versus Projects

In any organization, only two aspects of work exist—projects and ongoing operations. Projects are defined as unique, temporary endeavors with a specific beginning and end, whereas operations constitute an organization's ongoing, repetitive activities, such as accounting or production.

For example, when starting a restaurant business, all steps that require setting up the infrastructure, from breaking ground to the restaurant owner accepting delivery of the finished work, would be considered the "project." Once the project is completed and the doors open for business, the day-to-day activities of the restaurant are now considered "ongoing operations."

Since all work and efforts performed within an organization are either operations or projects, all the costs of an organization are allocated for either operations or projects.

Projects are initiated by organizations for a variety of reasons, such as to meet a business need, attain a strategic objective, or meet market demand.

For example, Henry Ford began developing his famed Model T because he had a fresh idea for building cars faster, more cheaply, and of better quality. His idea was called an assembly line, and this new way of car building and distribution met a business need that got the automotive industry moving and never looking back. In the project phase, deliverables were established, requirements discovered, schedules defined, costs established, and quality tests performed. Once all quality tests were successful, the Model T was rolled out for production. Once the Model T was in production, the operations phase began, as the car was then continuously assembled and made available for public purchase. The operations phase was ongoing until a new model was required or demanded by the consumer, at which point, a new project was started.

The Project Manager's Role

A *project manager* is a person who has the overall responsibility for the successful initiation, planning, design, execution, monitoring, controlling, and closure of a *project*. The project manager has the responsibility of leading and managing the project throughout its entire life cycle.

The project manager is assigned the role after the approval of the project charter (discussed later in this book); however, the project manager may also play a role with the sponsor and senior management in creating the project charter. Furthermore, project managers are the first point of contact for any issues or discrepancy arising among the heads of various departments in an organization before the problem escalates to higher authorities.

As a project manager, I have assisted with and written project charters. I have planned both the high-level requirements in the project charter and the detailed requirements in the project plan. Upon approval of the project plan, I have managed and monitored, and controlled all aspects of the project. Upon completion of the project, I made sure all accepted deliverables were approved by the stakeholder, all documents were received and signed off, and all resources were released for an orderly closure of the project.

The project manager's role includes but is not limited to:

- » managing the project from start to finish.

- » keeping the project within scope, on schedule, and under budget.

- » controlling quality and minimizing risks.

- » making changes to the customer's satisfaction; and

- » delivering the product, service, or results of the project.

Project managers are not responsible for whether the project, once delivered, makes the desired profit the customer expects.

Programs

A *program* in PMBOK is a group of related projects, subprograms, and program activities managed in a coordinated way to obtain benefits not available from managing them individually.[5]

An organization can have several projects going on at the same time or at separate times in which each project has its deliverables, requirements, schedules, and costs. However, all projects are created to support one program. The projects will have specific project managers or the same project manager controlling efforts. However, the program these projects support will have a *program manager* directing all efforts of the projects and project managers.

---

5   *PMBOK Guide*, Sixth Edition, 12.

Portfolios

In PMBOK, a *portfolio* refers to projects, programs, subportfolios, and operations managed as a group to achieve strategic objectives. The projects or programs of the portfolio may not necessarily be interdependent or directly related

As you can see in the figure above, a portfolio manager can manage programs, projects, and components of programs and projects, such as separate phases or process groups. The projects and programs need not be dependent on each other.

Project Management Office (PMO)

The project management office (PMO) is the natural liaison between the organization's portfolios, programs, and projects and the corporate measurement systems. There are three types of PMOs: supportive, controlling, and directive.

Supportive—Supportive PMOs *provide a consultative role* to projects by supplying templates, best practices, training, access to information, and lessons learned from other projects. This type of PMO serves as a project repository.

Controlling—Controlling PMOs *provide support and require compliance* through various means. Compliance may involve adopting project management frameworks or methodologies; using specific templates, forms, and tools; or conforming to governance.

Directive—Directive PMOs take control by *directly managing the project.*

In organizations I have worked with, the PMOs coordinated the many projects in the company and managed the "lessons learned" documents, archive documents, templates, best practice documents, project charters, project plans, and any other documents associated with projects.

Enterprise Environmental Factors

Enterprise environmental factors, or EEFs, refer to conditions not under the control of the project team, which influence, constrain, or direct the project.

EEFs include but are not limited to:

- » organizational culture, structure, and governance
- » government or industry standards and infrastructure
- » personnel administration
- » company work-authorization systems
- » marketplace conditions
- » stakeholder tolerances
- » political climate

Anything internal or external to the project that could have an impact on the project but is not in the project manager's or project team's control is considered an enterprise environmental factor.

Organizational Process Assets

Organizational process assets, or OPAs, are the plans, processes, policies, procedures, and knowledge specific to and used by the performing organization.

OPAs are divided into two areas—processes and procedures—and may include:

- » guidelines and specific organization standards such as policies and templates

- » change control procedures, financial control procedures, and issues and defect management procedures

- » project closure guidelines and requirements

- » corporate knowledge

OPA is the knowledge base for storing and retrieving information on configuration management; financial information such as labor costs, budgets, or project overruns; historical information; issue and defect status results; process measurement information; and project information from previous projects.[6]

Project Life Cycle

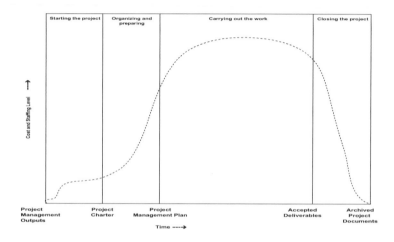

This graph illustrates from left to right the life cycle of the average project from inception to completion.

1. A project starts with an idea, a need, or a want from the project sponsor that will benefit the organization and that will become a business case and eventually a statement of work (SOW).

2. Once the statement of work is completed by the project sponsor, the project charter is created by the project manager or the project sponsor. The project charter will include the contents of the SOW.

3. Next, with an approved project charter, a project manager is authorized, and the project

---

6   *PMBOK Guide*, Sixth Edition, 557.

plan will be developed with all the instructions needed to manage the project.

4. After the project plan is approved, a kickoff meeting is held, and the team begins carrying out the work, which is more formally called "executing the project plan."

5. Now that the project is in the execution phase, the project team immediately begins to monitor the progress of the project. Should anything in the project need to be corrected, the project team will *control* the project, making the necessary adjustments to scope, schedule, quality, resources, risks, communications, or procurements via a change request.

6. Finally, when all deliverables are completed and accepted by the project sponsor, the project can be closed.

The project sponsor starts the project by stating objectives in the SOW, and the project sponsor ends the project by accepting the deliverables that were implemented by the project team.

Project Phases

A project may be divided into any number of project phases. A project phase is a collection of logically related project activities that culminates in the completion of one or more deliverables. Project phases are typically completed sequentially but can overlap in some project situations.

All phases have similar characteristics:

» The work has a distinct focus that differs from any other phase.

» Achieving the primary deliverable or objective of the phase requires controls or processes unique to the phase or its activities.

» The closure of a phase ends with some form of transfer or hand off of the work product produced as the phase deliverable.

Below is an example of a single-phase project with no overlapping objectives. All five process groups are visited, and you can see the loop that represents the integration between planning and executing. This iteration represents the collection requirements in the planning stage before continuing to the executing stage. As requirements are gathered, additional information about the project is discovered, and the earlier knowledge areas (scope, time, cost, quality, HR, risk, communication, and procurements) must be revisited until uncertainties or risks have been minimized or addressed to the project team's satisfaction.

Sequential Phase Relationship

In a sequential phase relationship, one phase starts once another phase is completed.

When I had my house built, the project had a start date of May 1992 and an end date of August 1993; however, there were phases within the construction of the house:

1. I chose a housing design and location.

2. The construction digging team dug a big square hole for the foundation.

3. The foundation team installed the iron rods and poured the concrete.

4. The skeleton of the house was built.

5. The wiring and plumbing were fitted.

6. The roof was completed.

7. The walls were installed.

8. After each phase, a land, building, plumbing, and/or wiring inspector signed off on the work.

9. At the end, I was given a walk-through to request fixes before signing off on the project.

Overlapping Phase Relationship

In the overlapping phase relationship, a phase starts before the completion of the previous one. Overlapping phase relationship is sometimes applied when the project team is using schedule compression techniques and fast-tracking, both of which are discussed more in the project planning section in schedule management.

For example, during the building phase of my house, there were also overlapping phases, which were primarily external to the house, such as putting up the fence and installing the grass. These are phases that could have been performed in parallel while the house was in its finishing stages.

Predictive Life Cycles

Predictive life cycles are fully plan driven. In a predictive life cycle, the three major constraints of the project—the scope, time, and cost—are determined ahead of time, not just at a high level but in detail in the planning stage, and the project is split up into phases that can be either sequential or overlapping.[7]

Now the planning can be done for the entire project at a detailed level in iterations also known as *progressive elaboration*—starting at project integration management and continuing to project risk management and going back again to project integration management until all requirements are collected and risks are identified and strategized for. Alternatively, one can do what is referred to as *rolling wave planning*.

In the rolling wave planning method, the high-level planning is done for the entire project, but the detailed planning is done only for the work that needs to be done in the near future. Then, as that work is completed, more detailed planning is done for the work to be completed after that.[8]

Iterative Life Cycles

In an iterative life cycle, the scope is not determined ahead of time at a detailed level but only for the first iteration or phase of the project. Once that phase is completed, the detailed scope of the next phase is worked out, and so on.

In iterative life cycles, project phases or iterations intentionally repeat one or more project activities as the project team's understanding of the product increases. Iterations develop through a series of repeated

---

7   *PMBOK® Guide*, Fifth Edition, Web, June 19, 2018.

8   *PMBOK® Guide*, Fifth Edition, Web, June 19, 2018.

cycles, while increments successively add to the functionality of the product. These life cycles develop both iteratively and incrementally.

At the end of each iteration, a deliverable or set of deliverables will be completed. Future iterations may enhance those deliverables or create new ones.[9] Each iteration incrementally builds the deliverables until the exit criteria for the phase are met, allowing the project team to incorporate feedback.

Adaptive Life Cycles

Adaptive life cycles are agile—sometimes the processes within their iterations can be going on in parallel. Adaptive life cycles are used in application areas such as IT where there is rapid change.

As in the iterative and incremental life cycles, the detailed scope is only determined ahead of time for the current iteration or phase of the project. The phases or iterations are more rapid than in the iterative and incremental life cycles, however, and usually have a duration of two to four weeks. During the iteration, the scope is decomposed into a set of requirements (deliverables), and the work to be done to meet those requirements (often called the *product backlog*) is prioritized. At the end of the iteration, the work on the product is reviewed by the customer, and the feedback from the customer is used to set the detailed scope of the *next* iteration.[10]

GPM LLC®

9   Course Hero, "Predictive Life Cycles Are Generally Preferred When…," accessed June 20, 2018, https://www.coursehero.com/file/pl1ctu5/Predictive-life-cycles-are-generally-p.

10   *PMBOK® Guide*, Fifth Edition, Web, June 19, 2018.

Stakeholders

A stakeholder is an individual, group, or organization that may affect, be affected by, or perceive itself to be affected by a decision, activity, or outcome of a project.

Stakeholders include all members of the project team as well as all interested entities that are internal or external to the organization.

Examples of stakeholders:

» sponsors

» project team

» project management team

» customers and users

» sellers

» business partners

» organizational groups

» functional managers

In an IT infrastructure project, a stakeholder can be the sponsor, senior management, functional managers, a department, owners of applications, and users who will be negatively or positively affected by the project. For example:

» Sponsors and senior management are the reason for the project.

» Functional managers provide resources to the project.

» Other applications share the same environment as the project.

Project Team versus Project Management Team

For the PMP exam, there are two types of teams that you must know: project team and project management team.

The *project team* is defined as a set of individuals (such as the project management team, the sponsor, and senior management) who support the project manager in performing the work of the project to achieve its objectives.[11]

The *project management team* are members of the project team who are directly involved with project management activities. In other words, the project management team is a subset of the project team and may include project management staff, project staff, supporting experts, customer representatives, sellers, business partners, and so on.

Operational Influences

As you can see from figure 1, the project manager has no authority in a functional matrix but has high authority in a strong matrix and almost total authority in a projectized matrix. Likewise, the project manager has a part-time role in a functional matrix and a full-time role in a strong and projectized matrix.

Functional Matrix. This is the practice of managing individuals with more than one reporting line.[12]

Weak Matrix. In this form of organization, the functional manager retains most of the power; they "own" the people and resources. In a weak/functional matrix, the project manager is not very powerful. Usually, they carry out an administrative or coordinating role and rely on the functional manager to get things done.[13]

Balanced Matrix. A two-dimensional management structure (matrix) in which employees are assigned to two organizational groups: a functional group based on skill sets, which has a functional manager (vertical), and a specific project group, in which employees report to a product manager (horizontal).[14]

11   *PMBOK Guide*, Sixth Edition, Glossary Flashcards.

12   *Wikipedia, The Free Encyclopedia*, s.v. "Matrix Management," https://en.wikipedia.org/wiki/Matrix_management.

13   Global Integration, "Strong, Project, Horizontal, or Balanced Matrix?" http://www.global-integration.com/blog/strong-matrix-project-matrix-horizontal-matrix-or-balanced-matrix-organization/.

14   Business Dictionary, s.v. "Balanced Matrix Organization," http://www.businessdictionary.com/definition/balanced-matrix-organization.html.

Strong Matrix or **Project Matrix.** The project manager has most of the power, resources, and control over the work. The functional manager is there to add support and technical expertise and to look after HR issues.[15]

Organization Structure / Project Characteristics	Functional	Matrix			Projectized
		Weak Matrix	Balanced Matrix	Strong Matrix	
Project Manager's Authority	Little or None	Low	Low to Moderate	Moderate to High	High to Almost Total
Resource Availability	Little or None	Low	Low to Moderate	Moderate to High	High to Almost Total
Who manages the project budget	Functional Manager	Functional Manager	Mixed	Project Manager	Project Manager
Project Manager's Role	Part-time	Part-time	Full-time	Full-time	Full-time
Project Management Administrative Staff	Part-time	Part-time	Part-time	Full-time	Full-time

Figure 1. Influences of Organizational Structures on Projects

It is paramount to understand as a project manager where you are in the projectized matrix to provide correct answers on the PMP exam.

Project Selection Methods

Project selection methods offer a set of time-tested techniques based on sound logical reasoning to arrive at a choice of project and filter out undesirable projects with a very low likelihood of success. Project selection methods are important to both practicing project managers and the organization.

15   Global Integration, "Strong, Project, Horizontal, or Balanced Matrix?" http://www.global-integration. com/blog/strong-matrix-project-matrix-horizontal-matrix-or-balanced-matrix-organization/.

Consider a scenario in which the organization you are working for has been handed several project contracts. However, due to resource constraints, the organization cannot take up all the projects at once. Therefore, a decision must be made as to which project needs to be taken up to maximize profitability.

These economic models will be covered briefly. However, they are beyond the scope of this book. PMBOK and PMP focus on the following economic model for the exam:

» Benefit-cost analysis

» Payback period

» Discounted cash flows

» Net present value

» Internal rate of return (IRR)

Benefit-Cost and Cost-Benefit Analysis

Project managers use cost-benefit analysis in project initiation to demonstrate the value of doing a project. When a new project is initiated, the sponsor and project manager must justify the project to obtain organizational approval to spend the money. The cost-benefit analysis compares the project costs to the business value it will deliver.[16] Cost-benefit ratio, as the name suggests, is the ratio of the present value of inflow or the cost invested in a project to the present value of outflow, which is the value of return from the project. Projects that have a higher benefit-cost ratio or lower cost-benefit ratio are generally chosen over others.

Payback Period

The payback period is the ratio of the total cash to the average per period inflow cash. In simpler terms, it is the time necessary to recover the cost invested in the project.

When the payback period is being used as the project selection method, the project that has the shortest payback period is the preferred method since the organization can regain the original investment faster.

There are, however, a few limitations to this method:

» It does not consider the time value of money.

16   SimpliLearn, "Project Selection Methods for Project Management Professionals," accessed June 20, 2018, https://www.simplilearn.com/project-selection-methods-article.

» The benefits that occur after the payback period are not considered. Thus, it focuses more on liquidity while profitability is neglected.

» The risk involved in the individual project is neglected.

Discounted Cash Flow / Inflation

It is known to the world that the value of an amount of money today is different from what it will be in the future. For example, the value of $20,000 will not be the same after 10 years as it is today—it will be much lower than the current value.

Thus, during calculations of cost investment and return on investment (ROI), one must consider the concept of discounted cash flow.

Internal Rate of Return

The internal rate of return (IRR) is the interest rate at which the net present value (NPV) is zero. This state is attained when the present value of outflow is equal to the present value of inflow.

It is defined as "annualized effective compounded return rate" or "discount rate that makes the net present value of all cash flows (both positive and negative) from a particular investment equal to zero."[17] The IRR is used to select the project with the best profitability.

When using the IRR as the project selection criteria, it must not be used exclusively to decide among projects that need undertaking but only for a single project that must be invested in. This is because a project with a lower IRR might have a higher NPV, and, assuming there is no capital constraint, the project with the higher NPV should be selected as this increases the shareholders' wealth.

When selecting a project, the one with the higher IRR is chosen.

Net Present Value

The net present value is the difference between the project's current value of cash inflow and the current value of cash outflow. The NPV must always be positive. When selecting a project, the one with the higher NPV is a recommended option.

---

17 Investopedia, "What Is the Difference Between Stated Annual Return and Effective Annual Return?" https://www.investopedia.com/ask/answers/04/031804.asp.

The advantage of considering the NPV over the payback period is that it takes into consideration the future value of money.

However, there are limitations to the NPV:

» There is no accepted method of deriving the discount value used for the present value calculation.

» The NPV does not provide any picture of profit or loss that the organization can make by embarking on a certain project.

Opportunity Cost

The opportunity cost is a cost that is being given up when choosing another project. During project selection, the project that has the lower opportunity cost is selected.

Project Selection Methods (Examples)

Economic Models

Benefit-Cost Analysis

This method compares the project benefits to the costs to derive a ratio from which a decision can be made. For example, if a project generates $150,000 in benefits and costs $50,000, the benefit-cost ratio would be 3 (also written as 3:1) because the project produces 3 times the benefits.

Payback Period

This method is the number of periods required to recover a project's cost. For example, if a project costs $1 million and will generate revenue of $200,000 per year, then the payback period would be 5 years.

Note: The PMP exam will also express payback periods in weeks and months.

Discounted Cash Flows

This method calculates in today's terms what the value of a project would be given cash inflows and outflows over a period of time.

Present Value (PV)

This method will appear on the exam several times. It is a formula that calculates the value today of a future cash flow. If you will receive a cash flow in 3 years of $1,157.62, what would that be worth today if the interest rate is 5%?

$$PV = FV/(1 + I)^n$$

$$PV = \$1,157.62 / (1 + .05)^3$$

$$PV = \$1,157.62 / (1.05)^3$$

$$PV = \$1,157.62 / ((1.05)(1.05)(1.05))$$

$$PV = \$1,000.00$$

You will have to calculate the PV several times during the PMP exam.

Net Present Value (NPV)

The NPV is a sum of a series of discounted future cash flows, offset against initial investment.

On the PMP exam, I was not asked to calculate the NPV.

Internal Rate of Return (IRR)

The discount interest rate when NPV equals zero—it is stated on the exam this way.

On the PMP exam, you will not be asked to calculate the IRR.

Always choose the project with the highest positive IRR; reject the negative one—it is stated on the exam this way.

Assume that cash flows are reinvested at the IRR value.

Which Project Selection Method to Choose on the Exam

High Value

- » Benefit-cost analysis
- » Discounted cash flows
- » Net present value (NPV)
- » Internal rate of return (IRR)

Low Value

- » Opportunity costs
- » Payback period

Pick the selection method with the highest value.

Exam Alert!

1. Assume a project costs $10,000 today and will return $2,500 per year for five years. Your required return on investments is 10%. Should you do the project?

   a) No, because the project will make a great profit.

   b) No, because payback period is four years.

   c) No, because the required return on investments is 10%.

   d) Yes, because the project meets the organization's strategic goals.

Answer c. No, because "the required return on investments is 10%."

Let's look more closely at the math:

- » Benefit-cost ratio will be 1.25 or 5:4.
- » Payback period is 4 years.
- » Net present value will be -$523.03.
- » IRR will be 7.93%.

2. Senior management is attempting to decide in which project to invest. Which one would you recommend?

   a) Has a present value of $1,157.00.

   b) Payback period is 4 years.

   c) Net present value will be -$523.03.

   d) IRR will be 7.93%.

Answer *d*. IRR will be 7.93%.

On the PMP exam, you should always choose the project with the highest return. In this example, answer *a* only gives a dollar value. Answer *b* is just a payback period, which yields no return. And answer *c* is in the negative range.

PART III:

Project Management Group Processes

Section 1: Overview

Managing large, complex projects from beginning to end can be a challenge for even the most seasoned project manager. However, the widely accepted *Project Management Body of Knowledge Guide* (PMBOK®, Sixth Edition) can assist a project leader in effectively managing intricate projects one step at a time. The information is arranged sequentially in *process groups*, which are collections of processes that have been grouped into five categories:

1. Initiating processes

2. Planning processes

3. Executing processes

4. Monitoring and controlling processes

5. Closing processes

Understanding the process groups is fundamental to knowing project management at a high level because it helps you understand where you are in the project when certain questions occur on the exam.

Initiating Process Group

The initiating process group is the first of the five PMBOK-defined project process groups. The initiation processes formalize the authorization to start a project or phase. Keep in mind that the process groups can apply to a project or a specific phase within a project. Look at the project life cycle reference section for more information.

At the start of a project, the project could be separated into multiple phases. For example, if the project is a complex one with many moving parts, it could be broken into phases that bring up the core functions. Then future functions could be incorporated as budget, schedule, and resources permit. Breaking a project into phases helps avoid the complete release and reduces project risk in general.

The project charter document is created by the *develop project charter* process. It includes:

» SOW—contains objectives necessary to complete the project
  • The factors affecting the project are external and internal to the project and organization, such as weather, inflation, people, or processes outside the project team's control.
» High-level requirements
» High-level constraints
» High-level risk
» Initial stakeholders

Planning Process Group

The planning process group consists of those processes performed to establish the total scope of the effort, define and refine objectives via progressive elaboration, and develop the course of action required to attain those objectives.[18]

Overview of the Processes

Unlike the other process groups, the planning process group has processes from each knowledge area. The following section provides a brief description of each process in the planning process group. When studying the planning process group section, remember that the order defined in the section below is the order you must remember for the exam.

---

18 *PMBOK Guide*, Sixth Edition.

I found it a good idea to remember the project knowledge areas this way because I knew I would be asked questions about the sequence of processes on the PMP exam. There are several questions asking the correct order of project knowledge areas in planning process groups. **Memorize this section**.

1. Integration—develop project charter, develop project plan, manage and direct work, monitor and control, and close

2. Scope—plan scope management, collect requirements, define scope, and create work breakdown structure

3. Schedule—plan schedule management, define activities, sequence activities, estimate activity duration, and develop schedule

4. Cost—plan cost management, estimate costs, and determine budget

5. Quality—plan quality management

6. Human resources—plan human resource management and estimate activity resources

7. Communication—plan communication management

8. Risk—plan risk management, identify risks, perform qualitative risk analysis, perform quantitative risk analysis, and plan risk responses

9. Procurement—procurement management plan

10. Stakeholder—plan stakeholder engagement and identify initial stakeholders

The planning process group can be the most complicated one, as it contains processes from every knowledge area. However, this stage is critical to the success of your project because by gathering all requirements, identifying and sequencing activities correctly, determining the most accurate time and costs (with the appropriate quality measures), minimizing risks, and finally informing all affected stakeholders of what is planned, you can increase the likelihood of a project's success to the customer's satisfaction. After the creation of a project management plan and other outputs of this process group, you will have a clear and actionable road map for project delivery.

Executing Process Group

The executing process group occurs after the approval of the project plan and the kickoff meeting for the project. The executing process group is when the activities in the project plan are executed and managed until completion.

For project managers in the process of setting new projects into motion, the executing process group can work as a checklist to help make sure the project is off to a strong start.

The overall goal of the executing process group is to get the teams situated properly so that the work is done efficiently and effectively, and the project stays on target regarding the scope and previously agreed-upon goals. Teams are set in place to complete work according to stakeholder specifications. At this stage in the work cycle, any areas of risk or concern are mitigated, and change requests are addressed.

Across the industry, the executing process group entails the following core tasks:

» Direct and manage project work. This process executes new activities and approved change requests.

» Manage project knowledge. This process manages the collection of material during the project.

» Manage quality. The quality process is performed according to the quality plan.

» Acquire resources. This may be done via internal or external channels, advertisements, or negotiations with other departments.

» Develop team. This is the process that provides the necessary training to team members.

» Manage team. This is the process than manages the individual and overall team activity and project work.

» Manage communications. This is the process to manage communications, such as email, shared storage, or virtual communications.

» Implement risk responses. This process executes the risk response strategy when risks arise and is implemented according to the risk response plan.

» Conduct procurements. This process manages vendors' performance on the project.

» Manage stakeholder engagement. During this process, the project manager and the project team send appropriate reports to stakeholders.

All the above processes will be discussed in more detail as we progress through the book.

Monitoring and Controlling Process Group

Once the executing process has begun, the project team immediately begins monitoring the progress of the work and controlling the work. We hope that enough preventive measures have been designed into the process to prevent problems; however, some unforeseen issues do occur. Then a correction is necessary, which may result in changes. In the planning process, we *plan* the work. In the executing process, we *work* the plan.

The monitoring and controlling process entails the following core tasks:

» Monitor and control project work. This process monitors new activities and approved change requests.

» Perform integrated change control. This process manages change control activities.

» Validate scope. This process inspects deliverable completeness to the scope baseline.

» Control schedule. This process monitors schedule performance to the schedule baseline.

» Control costs. This process monitors cost performance to the cost baseline.

» Control quality. This process includes inspecting deliverables for correctness.

» Control resources. The project manager observes team and individual performance.

» Monitor communications. The project team checks that emails, storage, and virtual communications are operational.

» Monitor risks. Are risk complete, in progress, new risks, or residual risk.

» Control procurements. Check that vendors and contractors are completing assignments.

» Control stakeholders. Monitor stakeholders engaged in the project process.

We check the work to make sure that it is indeed going according to plan. And if it is not, and changes need to be made in either the work or the plan, those requests for changes are input into another process—the second on the list, perform integrated change control—which will be discussed later in the book.

Closing Process Group

The purpose of the closing process group is to conclude all activities across all project management process groups and formally complete the project, phase, or contractual obligations.

A key word in this definition is *formally*, which means that the conclusion of the project must be documented. (Whenever you see the word *formally*, think "in writing.")

The phrase contractual obligations cover two sets of obligations:

1. If the organization doing the project is a buyer receiving some component from a supplier to make the finished product, the contractual obligation to the supplier is to compensate the supplier according to the agreed-upon terms of the procurement contract.

2. If the organization doing the project is providing the finished product to a customer, the contractual obligation to the customer is to provide the customer with the finished product according to the agreed-upon criteria for acceptance.

Exam Alert!

Memorize this section! You must know the precise order of closing a project. Closing Process Group

1. Obtain acceptance by customer or sponsor.

2. Conduct post-project or phase-end review.

3. Record impacts of tailoring to any process.

4. Document lessons learned.

5. Apply appropriate updates to OPA.

6. Archive all relevant project documents in the project management information system (PMIS) to be used as historical data.

7. Close out all procurement activities, ensuring termination of all relevant agreements.

8. Perform team members' assessments and release project resources.

AGAIN: Knowing the order of closing a project is extremely important on the exam.

The process groups consist of:

1. Initiating processes

2. Planning processes

3. Executing processes

4. Monitoring and controlling processes

5. Closing processes

We will discover which processes belong to which process group in subsequent sections of the PMP guidebook.

Let us begin our study of the 49 processes that comprise the 5 process groups we just discussed. The numbers in this chart correspond to where process can be referenced in the PMBOK guide.

Project Management Process Groups

	Initiating	Planning	Executing	Monitoring and Controlling	Closing
[4] Project Integration Management	4.1 Develop Project Charter	4.2 Develop Project Management Plan	4.3 Direct and Manage Project Work 4.4 Manage Project Knowledge	4.5 Monitor and Control Project Work 4.6 Perform Integrated Change Control	4.7 Close Project or Phase
[5] Project Scope Management		5.1 Plan Scope Management 5.2 Collect Requirements 5.3 Define Scope 5.4 Create WBS		5.5 Validate Scope 5.6 Control Scope	
[6] Project Schedule Management		6.1 Plan Schedule Management 6.2 Define Activities 6.3 Sequence Activities 6.4 Estimate Activity Durations 6.5 Develop Schedule		6.6 Control Schedule	
[7] Project Cost Management		7.1 Plan Cost Management 7.2 Estimate Costs 7.3 Determine Budget		7.4 Control Costs	
[8] Project Quality Management		8.1 Plan Quality Management	8.2 Manage Quality	8.3 Control Quality	
[9] Project Resource Management		9.1 Plan Resource Management 9.2 Estimate Activity Resources	9.3 Acquire Resources 9.4 Develop Team 9.5 Manage Team	9.6 Control Resources	
[10] Project Communications Management		10.1 Plan Communications Management	10.2 Manage Communications	10.3 Monitor Communications	
[11] Project Risk Management		11.1 Plan Risk Management 11.2 Identify Risks 11.3 Perform Qualitative Risk Analysis 11.4 Perform Quantitative Risk Analysis 11.5 Plan Risk Responses	11.6 Implement Risk Responses	11.7 Monitor Risks	
[12] Project Procurement Management		12.1 Plan Procurement Management	12.2 Conduct Procurements	12.3 Control Procurements	
[13] Project Stakeholder Management	13.1 Identify Stakeholders	13.2 Plan Stakeholder Engagement	13.3 Manage Stakeholder Engagement	13.4 Monitor Stakeholder Engagement	

Darron's Process Chart

When questions such as "As a project manager, what would you do next?" dominate the exam, this chart becomes your best friend. You must know exactly where you are at all times in the project during the exam.

Why you should use Darron's Process Chart

1. It helps you understand the overall project management process beyond the PMBOK guide.

2. It helps you understand why each activity is in a specific column.

3. It helps you replicate the order of the processes and understand what happens and when it happens.

4. It helps you understand the project management process from initiating to closing.

5. It helps you see why project management is an iterative process.

6. It helps you find the gaps in your knowledge before the PMP exam.

Darron's Process Chart				
Initiating	**Planning**	**Executing**	**Monitoring and Controlling**	**Closing**
	Plan each knowledge area.	Perform all work according to the plan.	Track and review project and report project work.	Finalize all project phases and contract activities.
		Implement the approved change requests.	Compare progress of work to the performance objectives.	
		Perform knowledge transfer in the value of project management.	Manage change requests.	

Determine external and internal factors that will influence the project.	Plan how scope will be collected and documented.		Verify deliverables.	Obtain customer acceptance.
	Gather non-procurement and procurement requirements.		Manage changes to the scope baseline.	
	Determine equipment and people necessary to perform the work.		Manage changes to the schedule baseline.	
			Manage changes to the cost baseline.	
	Determine which requirements will be performed and not performed.		Accept completed deliverables.	
	Decompose requirements into deliverable and work packages.			
Determine policies, processes, and procedures that may affect the project.	Determine how the schedule will be managed.			Conduct post-project or phase review.
	Create the activity list.			
	Sequence activities in the order they will be executed.			
	Determine how long it will take to perform each activity.			
	Create a network diagram.			

Divide large projects into phases.	Estimate costs of activities and goods.			Record the impact of tailoring to any process.
	Determine the budget.			
Understand the business case.	Define the quality metrics.	Manage the quality process.	Manage fixes and issue appropriate changes if necessary. Make appropriate corrections.	Document lessons learned.
Determine assumptions, constraints, and risks.	Estimate resources.	Acquire resources.	Manage resources to meet performance, quality, and deliverable objectives. Make appropriate corrections.	Apply updates to OPA.
		Develop team.		
		Manage team.		
Determine if the project is feasible.	Define communication.	Manage team, management, and stakeholder communication.	Monitor team, management, and stakeholder communication. Make appropriate corrections.	Archive documents.
Create measurable objectives.	Identify risks, probability of risks occurring, cost should risks occur, and strategy to resolve risks.	Implement risks to the agreed-upon response plan.	Track and identify existing and new risk. Make appropriate corrections.	Close out procurements activities.
Develop the project charter	Define plan to acquire external resources.	Obtain seller response.	Monitor procurement relations, contract performance, and change requests. Make appropriate corrections.	Perform individual and team assessments.
		Select a seller.		
		Award a contract.		
Identify stakeholders and determine their expectations and influences.	Define plan to engage all stakeholders.	Communicate with stakeholders to meet their needs and expectations and address any issues.	Monitor stakeholder relationships and tailor strategies to engage stakeholders.	Release resources.
	Finalize baselines.			
	Finalize procurement plan.			
	Finalize project plan.			
	Kick off project.			

Section 2: Initiating Group Processes

Initiating Group Processes
4.1 Develop Project Charter
13.1 Identify Stakeholders

4.1 Develop Project Charter

According to PMBOK, this is the process of developing a document that formally authorizes the existence of a project and provides the project manager with authority to apply organizational resources to project activities.[19]

The project always begins with an idea from senior management, a sponsor, or a customer. The project will be initiated either for a business need, a customer need, market demand, or technological enhancement.

Case Study— IT Infrastructure Project in the Role of Technical Project Manager

Whether it was senior management, a sponsor, or a customer who wanted to keep up with innovative technology to take advantage of the added security, performance, and reliability of new systems that are on the market today, as the technical project manager, it was my responsibility to understand their objectives in the SOW, prepare a project charter, and determine the feasibility of the project.

In this case, senior management, the sponsor, or a customer wants a system that

a) is unbreakable and never goes down.

b) always performs at its best; and

c) has the latest and greatest security features.

These will be the project objectives stated by the sponsor and included in the statement of work (SOW).

Is this system possible or feasible? As a technical project manager, you will need to understand the following:

- » How will internal and external factors out of your control influence this idea?
- » How will the organization's procedures, practices, and policies affect this idea?
- » What are the high-level assumptions, constraints, and risks?
- » What is the initial cost of implementing this system?
- » What team must you assemble to successfully bring this idea to life with exceptional quality? What will that team cost?
- » What timeline will you require to complete the work with exceptional quality?

---

19 *PMBOK Guide*, Sixth Edition, 76.

Figure 2. Create project charter in project plan

Let us start by applying the 49 processes to this idea. We start with the *develop project charter* process because it is always the starting point. This process consists of the following inputs, tools and techniques, and outputs.

Process	Inputs	Tools and Techniques	Outputs
4.1 Develop Project Charter	Business documents Agreements Organizational process assets Enterprise environmental factors	Expert judgments Data gathering Interpersonal skills Meetings	Project charter Assumptions log

Inputs

The *business documents* describe the necessary information from a business standpoint and whether the expected outcomes justify the investments.

Agreements are the intentions for the project (Service Level Agreement [SLA], Memorandum of Understanding [MOU], letters of intent, verbal agreements, contracts, or emails).

Organizational process assets are the policies, procedures, and practices of the organization. Examples are best practices, templates, and organizational procedure documents. OPA are used to produce the most successful project within the organization's guidelines.

Enterprise environmental factors are the things out of the project team's control. Examples are war, weather events, and economic conditions.

Tools and Techniques

Expert judgments are considerations provided by an individual or group with specialized knowledge or training available for many resources. Expert judgments can come from consultants, customers, or sponsors; professional or technical organizations; industry groups; subject matter experts (SME); and PMO.

Data gathering includes brainstorming, problem-solving, and meeting management, to give a few examples.

Interpersonal skills are used in conflict management, facilitation, and meeting management.

Outputs

The *project charter* document is created by process 4.1, develop project charter. The project charter contains the objectives of the project, which are part of the statement of work (SOW). The project charter also contains the high-level risks and constraints, initial stakeholders, and things external to the organization that might have an impact on the project. The project charter will also have information such as policies, procedures, processes, and templates that can be used to assist the project manager as well as the project team.

A project charter may state any or all of the following:

» Project purpose or justification

» Measurable project objectives and related success criteria

» High-level requirements

» Assumptions and constraints

» High-level risks

» Summary milestone schedule

» Summary budget

» Stakeholder list

- » Project approval requirements

- » Assigned project manager

- » Name and authority of sponsor authorizing the project charter

Important Note

High-level, strategic operation assumptions and constraints are part of the project charter. Low-level activity and task assumptions will be developed in the project plan.

The *assumptions log* is a document used to record all assumptions and constraints in the project's life cycle.

Example of a Project Charter Template

Project Charter				
Project Name				
Project Description				
Project Manager		**Date Approved**		
Project Sponsor		**Signature**		
Business Case		**Expected Goals/Deliverables**		
Team Members				
Name	**Role**			
Risks and Constraints		**Milestones**		

Exam Alert!

1. David is a new project manager for Razor LLC. David wants to get off to the best start in understanding the project, people, and environment. Interpersonal and team skills is a tool and technique of which process?

   a) Meetings

   b) Develop project charter

   c) Organizational process assets

   d) Planning

Answer: *b. Develop project charter* is the only process on this list. *Meetings* is a tool and technique for many processes. *Organizational process assets* are an input to many processes, and *planning* is a process group.

2. All the following are inputs to the develop project charter process except

   a) SOW

   b) Enterprise environmental factors

   c) Organizational process assets

   d) Data gathering

Answer: *d. Data gathering* is a tool and technique, not an input.

3. You are a new project manager for an existing project with issues. What document do you need to determine the project goals, high-level risks, and high-level constraints?

   a) Communication plan

   b) Project management plan

   c) SOW

   d) Project charter

Answer: *d.* The communication plan is a document for planning communication of the project. The project management plan plans the overall activities of the project and contains detail requirements of the project. The SOW is the statement of work, which includes the objectives of the project. The project charter contains the high-level requirements of the project.

13.1 Identify Stakeholders

According to PMBOK, this "is the process of identifying project stakeholders regularly and analyzing and determining relevant information regarding their interests, involvement, interdependencies, influence, and potential impact on project success."[20]

> ### Case Study— IT Infrastructure Project in the Role of Technical Project Manager
>
> The sponsor and senior management will be the initial stakeholders of the project. After that, the project manager or, in this case, the technical project manager is assigned. The project may also have a predefined resource such as a particular database administrator (DBA) who must be assigned to the project because this DBA is the only person in the company who understands and can implement the database system the sponsor is requesting.
>
> The sponsor or senior management will be responsible for the two most important aspects of the project: support and financial backing.
>
> Management support gives the project importance and credibility, without which the project may not be taken seriously and may not get the necessary resources. Also, without financial backing, the project will not get the necessary physical or people resources to be completed successfully, and the project will eventually starve from lack of funding. When the project is starved for funding, then the project manager will be asked to close the project. As project manager, when management requests that the project be closed, then start the closing process stated earlier immediately. **As a project manager you are not to negotiate keeping the project open or reopening the proje**ct.

Process	Inputs	Tools and Techniques	Outputs
13.1 Identify Stakeholders	Project charter PMP » communications management plan » stakeholder engagement plan Business documents Project documents Agreements Enterprise environmental factors Organizational process assets	Expert judgments Data gathering Data analysis Data representation Meetings	Stakeholder register Change requests PMP updates Project documents updates

---

20 *PMBOK Guide,* Sixth Edition, 507.

Inputs

The *project charter* will name the first stakeholders, such as the project sponsor and the project manager, as well as high-level constraints and high-level assumptions.

The charter also states the business case and benefits management plan. The benefits management plan is a document outlining the activities necessary for achieving the planned **benefits**. It shows a timeline and the tools and resources necessary to ensure the **benefits** are fully realized over time.

The *project management plan* has the *communications management plan* and the *stakeholder engagement plan*. The communications management plan is the how-to guide that explains what type of communication technology, communication models, and communications methods will be used to engage stakeholders. Likewise, the stakeholder engagement plan is used to understand the stakeholder communications requirements, level of stakeholder engagement, and level of stakeholder participation.

Business documents will contain the business case and the benefits management plan. The benefits case contains the project's objectives, and the benefits management plan will describe the expected plan for realizing the benefits that are claimed in the business case.

Project documents will hold other information about stakeholders, such as project team assignments, resource breakdown structure, resource calendar, team charter, and stakeholder register.

Agreements identify stakeholders in contracts and other legal documents.

Enterprise environmental factors will have information about external and internal stakeholders affected by the project.

Organizational process assets will contain information about policies, practices, and procedures established by the PMO.

Tools and Techniques

Expert judgments are considerations from those with specialized knowledge, skills, training, and experience who should be consulted to work on the project.

In *data gathering*, questionnaires and surveys like the Delphi technique are used. The Delphi technique is used to solicit information anonymously and gather honest feedback by eliminating intimidation from other team members. Brainstorming sessions among the project team members bring ideas to the project to solve problems and issues affecting the project.

Data analysis includes the stakeholder analysis of its interests, legal rights, ownership, knowledge, and contribution. It may also include analyzing documents from previous projects.

Data representation is an exercise in which the stakeholders are represented in a model such as a power/interest grid, a power influence grid, or an impact/influence grid. (See the figure below.)

Table 1 Power Interest Grid

POWER		
High	Keep satisfied	Manage closely
Low	Keep informed	Monitor
	INTEREST	
	High Low	

- » Keep satisfied = high interest, high power

- » Manage closely = low interest, high power

- » Keep informed = high interest, low power

- » Monitor = low interest, low power

Outputs

The *stakeholder register* contains information about stakeholders such as their names, profiles, and interest.

Stakeholder register			
Stakeholder Name	Title	Power	Interest

Change requests hold information such as new stakeholders and additional information about stakeholders.

Project management plan updates are those made to the requirements management plan, communications plan, risk management plan, and stakeholder engagement plan.

Project documents updates are those made to the assumptions log, issue log, and risk register.

Exam Alert!

1. All are inputs to the identify stakeholders process except

   a) Project charter

   b) EEF

   c) Expert judgments

   d) Organizational process assets

Answer: *c. Expert judgments* is a tool and technique.

2. If a stakeholder has high interest but low power, what is the best way to manage the stakeholder?

   a) Keep satisfied

   b) Manage closely

   c) Keep informed

   d) Monitor

Answer: *c.* Keep informed.

3. Which document would the project manager use to achieve the plan benefits of timeline, tools, and resources to ensure benefits are fully realized?

   a) Project management plan

   b) Benefits management plan

   c) Projects documents

   d) OPA

Answer: *b.* The benefits management plan is a document outlining the activities necessary for achieving the planned **benefits**. It shows a timeline and the tools and resources necessary to ensure the **benefits** are fully realized over time.

Section 3: Planning Group Processes

Planning Group Processes	
4.2 Develop Project Management Plan	8.1 Plan Quality Management
5.1 Plan Scope Management 5.2 Collect Requirements 5.3 Define Scope 5.4 Create WBS	9.1 Plan Resource Management 9.2 Estimate Activity Resources
6.1 Plan Schedule Management 6.2 Define Activities 6.3 Sequence Activities 6.4 Estimate Activity Durations 6.5 Develop Schedule	10.1 Plan Communications Management
7.1 Plan Cost Management 7.2 Estimate Costs 7.3 Determine Budget	11.1 Plan Risk Management 11.2 Identify Risks 11.3 Perform Qualitative Risk Analysis 11.4 Perform Quantitative Risk Analysis 11.5 Plan Risk Responses
	12.1 Plan Procurement Management
	13.2 Plan Stakeholder Engagement

4.2 Develop Project Management Plan

According to PMBOK, the *develop project management plan* process lays out what needs to be done to define, prepare, and coordinate all subsidiary activities to produce a document that defines the project. This document will be the project management plan.[21]

---

21 *PMBOK Guide,* Sixth Edition, 82.

Case Study— IT Infrastructure Project in the Role of Technical Project Manager

Once a project manager is authorized via the project charter, the project team is assembled. The project team will be paramount in developing a project management plan, taking into account all the necessary deliverables, requirements, activities, budget, and quality with communication and the necessary procurements.

To develop the project management plan for our example IT infrastructure project, initially we need a system architect or system engineer, as well as hardware, software, and database experts. We'll need their input in meetings, focus groups, and one-on-one interviews. Alternative fresh ideas and brainstorming are encouraged. (A project manager with great interpersonal skills is key to the development process because of the varying personalities and personal agendas.)

After several iterations of developing a detailed plan, the risks are discovered, and appropriate response strategies are designed. Constraints are real, both internal and external to the project. Assumptions are made, and issues are encountered. All will be dealt with in this process through progressive elaboration or rolling wave techniques.

Process	Inputs	Tools and Techniques	Outputs
4.2 Develop Project Management Plan	Project charter Outputs from other processes EEF OPA	Expert judgments Data gathering Interpersonal and team skills Meetings	Project management plan

Inputs

The *project charter* contains the objectives of the project. The objectives are part of the statement of work (SOW).

Outputs from other processes are the subsidiary plans and baselines that will be used to create the project management plan.

Enterprise environmental factors are the internal and external factors the project manager and project team have no control over but are identified in the project plan, such as organizational structure, culture, management policies, and sustainability.

Organizational process assets are the policies, practices, and procedures documents that are included in the project management plan. Other documents to be used are templates, monitoring and reporting methods, lessons learned documents, and historical information.

Tools and Techniques

Expert judgments are provided by an individual or group with specialized knowledge or training and are available from many resources.

Data gathering techniques include brainstorming, writing checklists, and holding focus groups and one-on-one interviews.

Interpersonal and team skills will include conflict resolution methods, facilitation, and meeting management.

Meetings are organized by the project manager, either as leader, facilitator, or participant only. If the meeting is to gather requirements, the project manager is definitely the leader; however, if the meeting is very technical and beyond the project manager's expertise, the project manager participates, taking minutes or notes to share with stakeholders later. The project manager is the organizer, leader, manager, creator, and coordinator of meetings.

Outputs

The *project management plan* is a how-to guide on how the project will be designed, managed, monitored and controlled, and closed. The project management plan starts with the high-level information contained in the project charter. It also includes:

» Scope baseline, which acts as a reference point for which requirements are included and which are not. It has several components. These include the project scope document, the WBS itself, and the WBS dictionary.

» Schedule baseline, which is the approved version of a schedule that can be changed only through formal change control procedures and is used as a basis for comparison to actual results.

» Cost baseline is a basis against which to measure, monitor, and control overall cost performance on the project.

The chart below shows how software can be used to plan the infrastructure project plan.

Figure 3. Develop project plan in project management plan

Exam Alert!

1. The output of the develop project management plan process is

   a) Project charter

   b) Enterprise environmental factors

   c) Project management plan

   d) Organizational process assets

Answer: *c*. Project charter, EEF, and OPA are all inputs to the process.

2. The following are tools and techniques for the develop project management plan process except

   a) Meetings

   b) Project management plan

   c) Interpersonal and team skills

d) Expert judgments

Answer: *b*. The project management plan is the output of the process, not a tool and technique.

3.   Which of the following is an input to develop the project management plan?

a) Data gathering

b) Project management plan

c) Inspection

d) Project charter

Answer: *d*. The project charter contains the objectives and other information needed to create the PMP. Data gathering and inspection are tools and techniques. The project management plan is the output of the process.

5.1 Plan Scope Management

According to PMBOK, the *plan scope management* process documents how the project and product scope will be defined, validated, and controlled throughout the project.[22] All requirements are collected by the project team; however, not all the requirements will be necessary. Some of the requirements will not fit because of budget, technological constraints, risk to quality, or scheduling problems. The rules used to determine which requirements are necessary will be established here.

---

22 *PMBOK Guide,* Sixth Edition, 134.

Case Study— IT Infrastructure Project in the Role of Technical Project Manager

Now that objectives are established in the infrastructure project, the project team can establish how requirements for the infrastructure project will be defined, validated, and controlled.

Experts with knowledge, experience, and training, such as the system architect or system engineer, will be paramount in this process and the creation of a scope management plan and requirements management plan documents.

As a leader of the infrastructure project, you are responsible for planning what is required to take concepts and turn them into something tangible.

You'll put together a rule book of how to gather what is required, how it is required, and how it will be validated and controlled for the IT infrastructure project.

The rule book created in the plan scope management process is the scope management plan.

Process	Inputs	Tools and Techniques	Outputs
5.1 Plan Scope Management	Project charter Project management plan Quality management plan Project life cycle description Development approach EEF OPA	Expert judgments Data analysis Alternative analysis for collecting requirements Meetings	Scope management plan Requirements management plan

Inputs

The *project charter* contains the objectives of the project. The objectives are part of the statement of work (SOW).

The deliverable information contained in the project charter will be decomposed into requirements in the *project management plan*.

The *quality management plan* contains policies and procedures on how quality policy, methodologies, and standards are executed on the project.

The *project life cycle description* determines the phases a project passes through from one inception to another.

The *development approach* defines the approach used in the project management plan: waterfall, iterative, adaptive, agile, or hybrid.

"The waterfall model is a relatively linear sequential design approach as progress flows in largely one direction through the phases of conception, initiation, analysis, design, construction, testing, deployment, and maintenance".[23]

Enterprise environmental factors are the internal and external factors the project manager and project team have no control over but are identified in the project management plan, such as organizational structure, culture, management policies, and sustainability.

Organizational process assets are the policies, practices, and procedures documents that are included in the project management plan. Other documents to be used are templates, monitoring and reporting methods, lessons learned, and historical information.

Tools and Techniques

Expert judgments refer to input received from experienced parties.

Data analysis can be *alternative analysis for collecting requirements*. Alternative analysis is the evaluation of the different choices available to achieve a particular project management objective. It is an analytical comparison of different factors like operational cost, risks, and effectiveness as well as the shortfalls in an operational capability.[24]

Meetings are necessary to develop the scope management plan.

---

23   Wikipedia, The Free Encyclopedia, s.v. "Waterfall Model," https://en.wikipedia.org/wiki/Waterfall_model.

24   Project Management Knowledge, "Alternative Analysis," https://project-management-knowledge.com/definitions/a/alternative-analysis/.

Outputs

The *scope management plan* documents what will be used to prepare the project scope statement, the creation of the WBS, the scope baseline, and formal acceptance of the deliverables.

The *requirements management plan* is used to document the information required to efficiently manage the project requirements from their definition through traceability to delivery. It will also explain how configuration management (change requests) will be initiated, how requests will affect analysis, and what is required to approve changes. Lastly, it will define the process for prioritization—what we do first, then second, then third, and so on.

Exam Alert!

1. The _____ are influences out of the project manager's control.

    a) Enterprise environmental factors

    b) Organizational process assets

    c) Evolution environmental factors

    d) Extreme environmental factors

Answer: *a.* Enterprise environmental factors are influences outside the project manager's control. Organizational process assets are factors within the organization's and project team's control. And *c* and *d* are not part of the project management plan.

2. Susan is a project manager with many years of experience. Susan's current project is especially difficult because of problems with the timeline gettin g extended many times. This could be because the scope may not be well defined, and the delays are causing increases in cost because of increased hours of work on the project for fixes. All are found in the project charter except

    a) Project purpose

    b) High-level requirements

    c) Detailed requirements

    d) Key stakeholder list

Answer: *c.* The project charter does not contain detailed information of any type. Detailed information is found in the project management plan.

Note: This is a typical PMP exam question. The problem has nothing to do with the answer. Focus on the "ask" which All is *are found in the project charter except*.

3.   Which of the following are outputs to *the plan scope management* process?

    a)   Scope management plan and requirements management plan

    b)   Project charter and project management plan

    c)   Quality management plan and process improvement plan

    d)   Risk management plan and risk response plan

Answer: *a.* Scope management plan and requirements management plan are outputs to plan scope management process. The project charter and project management plan are outputs of earlier stages. Answers *c* and *d* are plan quality management and plan risk management, respectively.

5.2 Collect Requirements

According to PMBOK, the *collect requirements* process determines, documents, and manages stakeholder needs and requirements to meet project objectives.[25] What resources and tools are necessary to perform and complete the project?

---

25   *PMBOK Guide*, Sixth Edition, 138.

Case Study— IT Infrastructure Project in the Role of Technical Project Manager

When collecting requirements as technical project manager, you are looking at everything, including things that are not necessary but considered legitimate requirements. Therefore, in our IT infrastructure example, you would ask the following questions:

- » What is needed to meet the objectives?
- » What is necessary because of government regulations, organizational standards, or security protection?
- » What is necessary for business use?
- » What is necessary for system storage, which includes growth of data for the next 3 to 5 years?
- » What is necessary to fulfill the best practices for a more efficient and protective system?
- » What is necessary for customer satisfaction?

So, for our IT infrastructure project, we might need the following:

- » 3 computers for primary systems
- » 3 computers for standby systems
- » Public networks for internet access
- » Duplicate high-speed interconnect to manage data between the computers
- » 100 TB primary storage
- » 100 TB secondary storage
- » Load balancer that manages and distributes traffic
- » Firewall that allows and rejects access to the system
- » Trackball for easier and faster navigation
- » Software games (?)
- » Operating systems license (always necessary)
- » Cluster management software that manages communication between servers
- » Database software that manages data
- » Application software that manages the application

Not all the requirements will be necessary, but the define scope process, which we'll discuss next, will filter out unnecessary requirements.

There are many ways to categorize information for clarity. The example below is the way I categorize which resources are people and which resources are not people, such as equipment and software.

Non-people resources:	People resources:
6 servers (3 primary, 3 secondary)	Hardware engineers
Load balancers	Network administrators
100 TB shared storage	Storage administrators
Interconnect	System administrators
Public network connection	Database administrators for HA and DG systems
Operating system software	Application administrators
Cluster software	
Application software	
Game software	
Game controllers	
Seibel	
Goldengate	
Enterprise business system	

Process	Inputs	Tools and Techniques	Outputs
5.2 Collect Requirements	Project charter Project management plan Project documents Business documents Agreements EEF OPA	Expert judgments Data gathering Benchmarking Data analysis Document analysis Decision-making Voting Multicriteria analysis Data representation Affinity diagram Mind mapping Interpersonal and team skills Context diagram Prototypes	Requirements documentation Requirements traceability matrix

Inputs

The *project charter* contains the objectives of the project. The objectives are part of the statement of work (SOW).

The *project management plan* includes the scope management plan, the requirements management plan, and the stakeholder engagement plan.

Project documents include the assumptions log, lessons learned, and the stakeholder register.

Business documents hold the business case.

Agreements are the intentions for the project (SLA, MOU, letters of intent, verbal agreements, contracts, or emails).

Enterprise environmental factors are the internal and external factors the project manager and project team have no control over but will be identified in the project plan, such as organizational structure, culture, management policies, and sustainability.

Organizational process assets are the policies, practices, and procedures documents included in the project management plan. Other documents to be used are templates, monitoring and reporting methods, lessons learned, and historical information.

Tools and Techniques

Expert judgments include information from subject matter experts and consultants that helps determine the entire scope of the project and define the necessary requirements.

Data gathering at this stage includes *benchmarking*. Benchmarking is defined as a comparison with a standard business process or product.

Data analysis at this stage includes *document analysis*, which is a process of inspecting, cleansing, transforming, and modeling data with the goal of discovering useful information, informing conclusions, and supporting decision-making.

Decision-making at this stage includes such activities as *voting* and *multicriteria analysis*. Multicriteria analysis is a method of assigning weighted scores for a more qualitative evaluation method of which resource to choose. For example, when choosing a project team member, which criteria is most important among availability, cost, experience, ability, knowledge, skills, attitude, and international factors?

Data representation includes the *affinity diagram* and *mind mapping*. The affinity diagram is a business tool used to organize ideas and data. *Mind mapping* is a technique that is used to collect and consolidate ideas created through brainstorming sessions with the team members.

Affinity Diagrams

The affinity diagram organizes ideas with the following steps:

1. Record each idea on cards or notes.
2. Look for ideas that seem to be related.
3. Sort cards into groups until all cards have been used.

Once the cards have been sorted into groups, the team may sort large clusters into subgroups for easier management and analysis.[26]

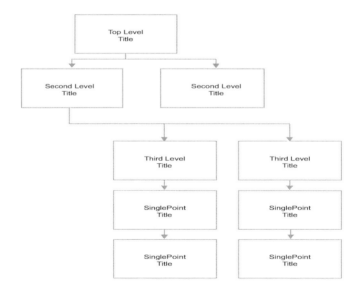

Figure 4. Affinity diagram

26 *Wikipedia, The Free Encyclopedia*, s.v. "Affinity Diagram," https://en.wikipedia.org/wiki/Affinity_diagram.

Mind Mapping

Mind maps are great tools for project managers and their teams. The most important benefit they provide is a way of expressing ideas visually and communicating these ideas to the rest of the team members.[27]

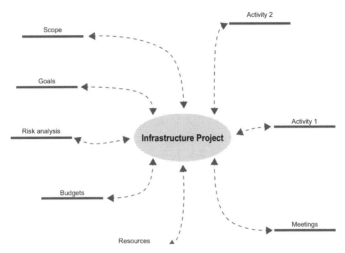

Figure 5. Mind mapping diagram

Interpersonal and team skills are used to communicate effectively with team members, sponsors, and others either face to face or via email or other communication methods.

A *context diagram* is a visual tool that depicts the scope of the product, showing the business system and how it relates to and interacts with the other systems as well.

Prototypes are project management tools that are used in getting early feedback related to the project requirements. This is done by providing a working model of the product even before building it.

Outputs

The *requirements documentation* contains all the requirements that are necessary to achieve deliverables and the objectives of the project. Some unnecessary requirements will be filtered out in the next process, define scope.

---

27   Project Management Knowledge, "Idea/Mind Mapping," https://project-management-knowledge. com/definitions/i/ideamind-mapping/.

» Requirements include both procurements and non-procurement requirements, or people and non-people, respectively.

» The requirements may start out at a high level and become progressively more detailed as more about the requirements is revealed.

The *requirements traceability matrix* links product requirements from their origins to the deliverables that satisfy them.

Example: Requirements Traceability Matrix

Project Name									
Cost Center									
Project Description									
ID	Associate ID	Requirements Description	Business Needs	Project Objectives	WBS deliverables	Project Design	Product Development	Test Cases
001	1.0							
	1.1							
	1.2.1							
002	2.0							
	2.1							
	2.2.1							

Figure 6. Requirements traceability matrix

The requirements traceability matrix is filled in later in the planning stage.

Exam Alert!

1. The following are tools and techniques used to collect requirements except

    a) Data analysis

    b) Decision-making

    c) Organizational process assets

    d) Interpersonal skills and team skills

Answer: *c. Organizational process assets* is an input. But *a*, *b*, and *d* are all tools and techniques.

2. The following are inputs to collect requirements except

   a) Project management plan

   b) Communication management plan

   c) Project documents

   d) EEF

Answer: *b.* The communication management plan is not an input to collect requirements. The communication management plan is a guide on how the project team will send, receive, distribute, store, and dispose of communication material.

3. Which of the following is an output of the collect requirements process?

   a) OPA

   b) Requirements traceability matrix

   c) Project management plan

   d) Data analysis

Answer: *b.* The OPA and project management plan are inputs. Data analysis is a tool and technique.

5.3 Define Scope

According to PMBOK, the *define scope* process involves developing a detailed description of the project (what it includes and excludes) and its products.[28] This process determines what is and is not in scope. By excluding unnecessary requirements, we save on time, cost, and the complexity of the project.

In the collecting requirements process, we listed the total of all requirements that can be performed for the project. During the define scope process, we select the final project requirements from the requirements documentation.

Preparations of a detailed project scope build on the major project deliverables, assumptions, and constraints that are documented during the project initiation process.

---

28 *PMBOK Guide*, Sixth Edition, 150.

Case Study— IT Infrastructure Project in the Role of Technical Project Manager

What is defined scope for the IT infrastructure project? For the system imagined in the statement of work of the project charter, the total requirements would be:

- » 3 primary servers
- » 3 secondary servers
- » High-speed interconnect for the primary server
- » High-speed interconnect for the secondary servers
- » Public connections
- » 100 TB storage each for the primary and secondary server
- » Operating system software, database software, cluster software, security software, and tuning tools
- » Game software, joystick, and tracking ball
- » Application software
- » Firewall
- » Load balancer
- » Cloud environment for development environment
- » Virtual environment for testing

You will also need people, such as hardware engineers, software administrators, database administrators, network administrators, and storage administrators, who are qualified to do the work at a reasonable cost with the necessary effort and produce high-quality results.

When defining scope, the project team must decide what in this long list is to be included in the project and what is to be excluded because it is not necessary for the project's success. Try determining inclusion and exclusion with questions like:

1. What is mandatory for the system to work?
2. What is the best practice?
3. What are government regulations?
4. What are industry standards?
5. What are corporate policies and procedures?
6. What must be done to meet customer expectations?

When you take another look at the list above while asking these questions, it's now clear that all requirements will be included in this project except the game software and joystick or trackball.

Process	Inputs	Tools and Techniques	Outputs
5.3 Define Scope	Project charter	Expert judgments	Project scope statement
	Project management plan	Data analysis	Project document updates
	Scope management plan	Alternative analysis	
	Project documents	Decision-making	
	EEF	Multicriteria decision analysis	
	OPA	Interpersonal and team skills	
		Facilitation	
		Product analysis	

Inputs

The *project charter* contains the objectives of the project. The objectives are part of the statement of work (SOW) for which the scope will be defined.

The *project management plan* contains the *scope management plan*. The scope management plan explains how the project scope will be defined, developed, and verified.

Project documents contain the assumptions log, requirements documentation, and risk register about the scope.

Enterprise environmental factors are the internal and external factors the project manager and project team have no control over but will be identified in the project plan, such as organizational structure, culture, management policies, and sustainability.

Organizational process assets are the policies, practices, and procedures documents that will be included in the project management plan. Other documents to be used are templates, monitoring and reporting methods, lessons learned, and historical information.

Tools and Techniques

Expert judgments include information from subject matter experts and consultants that helps determine the entire scope of the project and define the necessary requirements.

Data analysis at this stage includes an *alternative analysis* of the scope provided by the sponsor, experts, consultants, team members or publication articles or gathered by performing an internet search for others who have performed the same or a similar project and completed it successfully.

Decision-making at this stage includes *multicriteria analysis*, which is a method of assigning weighted scores for a more qualitative evaluation method of which resource to choose. For example, when choosing a project team member, which criteria is most important among availability, cost, experience, ability, knowledge, skills, attitude, and international factors?

Under the category of *interpersonal and team skills*, at this stage, *facilitation* becomes very important. Facilitation is a skill all project managers must have to drive meetings according to that meeting's agenda.

Product analysis is a tool that is used to define the scope of the product. It basically means that when analyzing the product through its scope, questions can be asked about it.[29]

Outputs

The *project scope statement* provides detailed descriptions of the project deliverables, such as the project scope, major deliverables, assumptions, and constraints. The project scope statement will include all work that will need to be done and exclude the work that will not need to be done. If work is done that is outside the scope of the project and suggested by the sponsor, senior management, or a stakeholder other than a project team member, that work is called scope creep. Work performed outside the scope but suggested by the project team is called gold-plating. Scope creep and gold-plating are discussed in more detail in the control scope section.

While the project charter contains information about project objectives at a high level, the project scope statement will contain information about deliverables at a detailed level.

Also, at this stage, *project document updates* will be needed as follows:

>> Assumption logs are updated with the additional assumptions or constraints occurring during the defined process.

>> Requirements documentation is updated with additional requirements or changed requirements during the defined process.

>> Requirements traceability matrix is updated to reflect updates in the requirement documentation.

>> Stakeholder register is updated with additional information on existing or new stakeholders.

---

29 Project Management Knowledge, "Product Analysis," https://project-management-knowledge.com/definitions/p/product-analysis/.

Exam Alert!

1. Which best describes the define scope process?

    a) The process of developing a detailed description of the project and product

    b) The process of creating a scope management plan that documents how the project and product scope will be defined, validated, and controlled

    c) The process of subdividing project deliverables and project work into smaller, more manageable components

    d) The process of monitoring the status of the project and product scope and managing changes in the scope baseline

Answer: *a.* Answer *b* describes the plan scope management process. Answer *c* describes the create WBS process, which we will discuss next. Answer *d* best describes monitoring and controlling a process.

2. Work performed that is outside the scope of the project but is demanded by a sponsor, senior management, or stakeholders other than the project team is called _____.

    a) Gold-plating

    b) Work that is necessary

    c) Work that is unnecessary

    d) Scope creep

Answer: *d.* Gold-plating is work outside the scope of the project but deemed necessary by the project team. Answers *b* and *c* are general concepts that help narrow down the scope of the project.

3. The work performed outside of scope and suggested by the project team is called _____.

    a) Gold-plating

    b) Work that is necessary

    c) Work that is unnecessary

    d) Scope creep

Answer: *a.* Gold-plating is when project team member(s) makes unnecessary and unwanted changes to the project.

5.4 Create WBS

According to PMBOK, the *create work breakdown structure (WBS)* process subdivides project deliverables and project work into smaller, more manageable components.[30] The WBS decomposes work information into work packages. This decomposition helps the project manager identify risks, resource assignments, and estimate resources; gets team buy-in; prevent changes; and improve quality. Decomposition can also identify what procurements are necessary for the success of the project. The WBS gives the project manager greater control of the project.

Case Study— IT Infrastructure Project in the Role of Technical Project Manager

For example, a client asked if I, as an infrastructure project manager, would design an unbreakable system with high availability, instant recovery, no downtime, and multiple levels of redundancy. I told them this type of system requires a primary system, a backup system, a redundant network system and storage redundancy, duplicate operating systems on each machine, duplicate cluster software, and duplicate database software as well as anything the project team considered necessary to complete the project successfully.

The project deliverables are:

Non-people resources:	People resources:
6 servers: 3 primary, 3 secondary	Hardware engineers
Load balancers	Network administrators
100 TB shared storage	Storage administrators
Interconnect	System administrators
Public network connection	Database administrators for high availability and standby database systems
Operating system software	Application administrators
Cluster software	
Application software	

As a project manager, you may be assigned to build bridges, tunnels, buildings, or computer infrastructures; however, each of these components needs decomposition to decide what potential effort will be needed to deliver the result.

30   *PMBOK Guide*, Sixth Edition, 570.

Here are some important terms that will help you understand the create WBS process. These will definitely be on the exam.

» *Code of account identifier.* This is a project management tool that assigns a code of numbers, letters, or a combination of the two to every item on the work breakdown structure of a project.

» *Chart of account.* This is a listing of all accounts used in the general ledger of an organization.

» *Control account.* This is the control point where the integration of scope, budget, actual cost, and schedule takes place and where the measurement of performance will occur.

WBS Architecture Example

Process	Inputs	Tools and Techniques	Outputs
5.4 Create WBS	Project management plan	Expert judgments	Scope baseline
	Scope management plan		Project scope statement
	Project documents	Decomposition	WBS
	Project scope statement		Work package
	Requirements document		WBS dictionary
	EEF		Planning package
	OPA		Project document updates

Inputs

Within the *project management plan* is the *scope management plan.* The scope management plan is the how-to document that defines how the WBS will be created from the project scope statement.

Project documents contain the *project scope statement* and *requirements document*. The project scope statement describes work that is performed and work that is excluded. The requirements document describes the detailed requirements and how these requirements meet the business needs of the project.

Enterprise environmental factors may include industry standards that may influence the WBS.

Organizational process assets that may influence the WBS are the policies, practices, and procedures of the organization as well as lessons learned and other project files from earlier projects.

Tools and Techniques

Expert judgments include information from any individual or group with knowledge of or experience on similar projects.

Decomposition is the technique for dividing and subdividing the project scope and project deliverables into smaller, more manageable components. There are 5 steps to decomposition:

1. Find deliverables and work.

2. Organize the WBS.
3. Decompose deliverables into lower-level components called work packages.
4. Assign the code of account identifier.
5. Verify that the WBS is correct.

Outputs

The *scope baseline* is the approved version of a project scope statement, WBS, and WBS dictionary. The scope baseline can only be changed with formal change control procedures.

The *project scope statement* contains the project scope, major deliverables, assumptions, and constraints.

The *WBS* is the decomposition of the total scope. The *work package* is the lowest level of the WBS and has a unique identifier associated with it called the code of account identifier. The identifier will contain summation of costs, schedule, and resource information. The work package is part of the control account.

The *WBS dictionary* holds detailed deliverable, activity, and scheduling information. The WBS dictionary may include a code of account identifier, description of work, assumptions and constraints, responsible organization, milestones, schedule activities, the resources needed, cost estimates, quality requirements, acceptance criteria, technical references, and agreement information.

A *planning package* is above the work package but below the control account and has known work content but does not have detailed schedule activities.

Project document updates will include the assumptions log and requirements documentation for the create WBS process.

Exam Alert!

1. Which are number systems in the WBS dictionary and the WBS, respectively?

    a) Code of account identifier and (1.0, 1.1, 1.1.1)

    b) Chart of accounts and (a, ab, abc)

    c) Control chart and (1, 2, 3)

    d) All the above

Answer: *a.* Code of accounts identifier is listed in the WBS dictionary on page 162 of PMBOK and 1.0, 1.1, 1.1.1 best exemplifies the tier of the WBS.

2. The scope baseline consists of

    a) The process of developing a detailed description of the project and product

    b) The project scope statement, the WBS, the WBS dictionary, and the planning package

    c) The process of subdividing project deliverables and project work into smaller, more manageable components

    d) The process of monitoring the status of the project and product scope and managing changes in the scope baseline

Answer: *b.* Choice *a* describes project management plan, and *c* is create WBS.

6.1 Plan Schedule Management

According to PMBOK, the *plan schedule management* process establishes the policies, processes, and documentation for planning, developing, managing, executing, and controlling the project schedule. This process provides guidance and direction on how the project schedule will be managed throughout the project.[31]

Once deliverables have been established and decomposed, the project manager and project team then define activities, sequence activities, estimate how long each activity will take to complete, and develop a schedule model.

---

31   *PMBOK Guide*, Sixth Edition, 179.

Process	Inputs	Tools and Techniques	Outputs

6.1 Plan Schedule Management	Project charter
	
	Project management plan
	  » Scope management plan
	
	Development approach
	
	EEF
	
	OPA
		Expert judgments
		
		Data analysis
		  » Alternative analysis
		  » Rolling wave
		
		Meetings
			Schedule management plan

Inputs

The *project charter* contains the objectives of the project. The objectives are part of the statement of work (SOW), which later is decomposed into activities; later, the activities can be sequenced.

The *project management plan* contains the scope management plan. The *scope management plan* has information on how the scope will be defined. The scope management plan, in turn, will determine how the schedule will be developed.

The *development approach* can be an estimating technique, scheduling approach, or tools and techniques for controlling the schedule.

The *enterprise environmental factors* are the things outside the project manager's and project team's control, such as the organizational culture and structure, available scheduling software, commercialize databases, and standardized estimating tools.

The *organizational process assets* are the policies, practices, procedures, templates, and lessons learned and how these influence the project schedule.

Tools and Techniques

Expert judgments are the knowledge and experience of those who have scheduled similar projects.

Data analysis may include *alternative analysis* for which scheduling methods to use or may involve combining different scheduling methodologies. This may also include the *rolling wave* scheduling method, which is used to capture detailed information on near-term activities. (For far-term activities, the project team will capture that information when it is available or when the activity is closer to occurring.)

Meetings are held to develop the schedule management plan.

Outputs

The *schedule management plan* is the document used in developing, maintaining, and communicating schedules for time and resources.

Exam Alert!

1. As a project manager, you are planning the activities in the project schedule. What is the output of plan schedule management?

    a) Collect requirements, define scope, and create WBS

    b) Identify risks, perform qualitative risk analysis, perform quantitative risk analysis, and plan risk responses

    c) Create the schedule management plan

    d) Estimate costs and determine the budget

Answer: c. Option *a* describes scope management, *b* describes defining risk management, and *d* is cost management.

2. The inputs to the plan schedule management process are

    a) Project charter, project management plan, scope management plan, development approach, EEF, and OPA

b) Perform qualitative risk analysis, perform quantitative risk analysis, and plan risk responses

c) Project management plan, project documents, approved change requests, EEF, and OPA

d) Project charter, project management plan, quality management plan, project life cycle development, EEF, and OPA

Answer: *a*. Choice *b* describes plan risk management, and *c* describes direct and manage projects. As stated earlier, knowing the sequences of the planning group in all knowledge areas is crucial to passing the PMP exam.

6.2 Define Activities

According to PMBOK, the *define activities* process identifies and documents the specific actions to be performed to produce the project deliverables.[32] Now that a plan is established on how activities will be defined, the project manager and project team can decompose the work packages in the WBS further into activities.

Case Study— IT Infrastructure Project in the Role of Technical Project Manager

For example, in the IT infrastructure project for which I was technical project manager, the project team and I defined what was necessary to install and configure the hardware and software from the deliverables in the work breakdown structure in the create WBS section.

---

32 *PMBOK Guide*, Sixth Edition, 183.

Requirement	Activity	Deliverable
Hardware	Install Configure Test	Dev (cloud)
Software	Install Configure Test	QA test (virtual)
Database	Install Configure Test	Production (physical)
Application	Install Configure Test	Production only
Load balancer	Install Configure Test	Production only
Firewall	Install Configure Test	Production only
Obtain project team	Acquire team Develop team Manage team	
Download software	Operating system	
Install software	Operating system	
Configure software	Operating system	
Download software	Database software	
Install software	Database software	
Configure software	Database software	
Download software	Application software	
Install software	Application software	
Configure software	Application software	
…more		
…more		

Process	Inputs	Tools and Techniques	Outputs
6.2 Define Activities	Project management plan » Schedule management plan » Scope baseline EEF OPA	Expert judgments Decomposition Rolling wave planning Meetings	Activity list Activity attributes Milestone list Change requests PMP updates » Schedule baseline » Cost baseline

Inputs

The project management plan contains the *schedule management plan* and the *scope baseline*.

> » The schedule management plan contains the method of scheduling that will be used, the duration of rolling wave planning, and the level of detailed work necessary to manage the work.

> » The scope baseline acts as a reference point for which requirements are included and which are not. It has several components. These include the project scope document, the WBS itself, and the WBS dictionary.

Enterprise environmental factors are the factors outside the project team's control, such as organizational culture, project management information systems used, and published commercial databases and how they influence the define activities process.

Organizational process assets are the lessons learned, templates, policies, practices, and procedures and how they influence the define activities process.

Tools and Techniques

Expert judgments are information from those who are familiar with defining activities for similar projects.

Decomposition is the process of creating WBS work packages into activities.

Rolling wave planning is a technique wherein work to be completed in the near term is planned in detail, while work further in the future is planned at a higher level.

Meetings may be held with team members or experts to define activities needed to complete the work. The meetings can be face to face or virtual and informal or formal.

Outputs

The *activity list* includes scheduled activities needed for the project.

Activity attributes will contain sequenced information along with predecessor and successor information. It also defines the duration of the activity, lead, lag, and logical relationships.

The *milestone list* is a list of significant points or events in a project. It is important to remember that milestones have zero duration because they are significant points or events.

Change requests may be necessary if you find that some activities were not initially discovered through progressive elaboration.

Project management plan updates are made to the *schedule baseline* and *cost baseline*.

Exam Alert!

1.   Which of the following depicts the order of activities in schedule management?

   a) Collect requirements, define scope, and create the WBS

   b) Identify risks, perform qualitative risk analysis, perform quantitative risk analysis, and plan risk responses

   c) Plan schedule management, define activities, sequence activities, estimate activity durations, and develop schedules

   d) Estimate costs and determine budget

Answer: *c.* Option *a* describes scope management, *b* defines risk management, and *d* is cost management.

2.   In the define activities process, work is decomposed into which of the following?

   a) Work packages

   b) WBS

   c) Activities

   d) WBS and activities

Answer: *c.* Decomposition into activities occurs in the define activities process. Decomposition into work packages occurs in the create WBS process. Answer *d* is a typical PMP exam trick to trip you up because it combines processes like WBS and activities.

6.3 Sequence Activities

According to PMBOK, the *sequence activities* process identifies the relationships among project activities.[33] Once all requirements are gathered, the order of implementation is necessary for a faster, more orderly, and higher-quality product, service, or result. For example, you cannot install software before the necessary equipment is in place.

Case Study— IT Infrastructure Project in the Role of Technical Project Manager

Once activities have been defined for the infrastructure project, the order of installation can be established. For example, all physical and people resources must be ordered or hired, respectively, if not already in house. Once all physical and people resources are in place and correctly sequenced, the next phase of the project is to create the project schedule network diagram.

Process	Inputs	Tools and Techniques	Outputs
6.3 Sequence Activities	Project management plan » Schedule management plan » Scope baseline Project documents EEF OPA	Precedence diagramming method (PDM) Dependency determination and integration » Mandatory dependency » Discretionary dependency » External dependencies » Internal dependencies Leads and lags PMIS	Project schedule network diagram Project documents updates

Inputs

The *project management plan* contains the *schedule management plan* and *scope baseline*.

» The schedule management plan defines information on the level of accuracy used and other criteria required for sequenced activities.

» The scope baseline includes the project scope document, the WBS and the WBS dictionary, all of which are considered when sequencing the activities.

33 *PMBOK Guide*, Sixth Edition, 187.

Project documents have information on the activity attributes, activity list, assumptions log, and milestone list.

Enterprise environmental factors are things outside the project team's control that could influence sequence activities, such as government or industry standards, PMIS, or scheduling tools.

Organizational process assets will contain portfolios, programs, lessons learned, policies, practices, procedures, and templates that may influence sequence activities.

Tools and Techniques

Precedence Diagramming Method (PDM)

There are four types of PDM relationships:

1. Finish to start (FS)

2. Finish to finish (FF)

3. Start to finish (SF)

4. Start to start (SS)

Finish to start (FS) is a logical relationship in which a successor activity cannot start until a predecessor activity has finished. For example:

> Activity A is "hardware setup and configuration."
>
> Activity B is "installing the operating system."
>
> Installing the operating system cannot begin until the hardware setup and configuration is finished.
>
> Finish to start is the most commonly use

Finish to start is the most commonly used.

Start to finish (SF) is a logical relationship in which a successor activity cannot finish until a predecessor activity has started. For example:

> Activity A is "execute."

Activity B is "kickoff."

The execute project stage cannot start until the kickoff has finished.

Start to finish is very rarely used.

Start to start (SS) is a logical relationship in which a successor activity cannot start until a predecessor activity has started. For example:

Activity A is "execute."

Activity B is "monitor and control."

Monitoring and control cannot start until execution starts.

Finish to finish (FF) is a logical relationship in which a successor activity cannot finish until a predecessor activity has finished. For example:

Activity A is "deliverables have been completed, all documents archived, lessons learned collected, and resources released."

Activity B is "project finish (close)."

Dependency determination and integration: Dependencies are defined as relationships among tasks that determine the sequence in which project management activities need to be performed. These tasks may be multiple preceding tasks, which mean that two tasks can be applicable at the same time.

» *Mandatory dependency* refers to tasks that are stipulated in the contract; thus, they are inherent in the project. Failure to deliver the task involves a certain level of penalty. In the IT infrastructure project, to make the system unbreakable, you absolutely must have a redundant system at every tier or level, such as at least one primary and standby server, redundant network systems, and redundant storage system.

» *Discretionary dependency*, also referred to as preferred logic, is established based on knowledge of best practices. A best practice could be an industry standard or vendor product standard. For example, in an IT infrastructure project, a best practice might be to go with an industry leader in high availability and disaster recovery systems, such as Oracle software. Real Application Clusters is an Oracle high availability product. Data Guard is the Oracle disaster recovery product.

» *External dependencies* involve the relationship between project activities and those that are not related to the project. They are usually beyond the control of the project team. Examples of external dependencies include government environment hearings before a construction project can begin and software testing. An external dependency in an IT infrastructure project that is government standard might be protecting the company's data with encryption and security with accepted security practices.

» The *internal dependencies* involve the relationship between different project activities that are within the control of the project team. This includes internal testing of product components before assembling the entire product. Determining which activities are performed and in what order is within the project team's control.

The process of dependency determination requires the project manager or the project management team to assign tasks to the team members and also inform the stakeholders. Moreover, it is easier to arrange the task if the dependencies are all identified.

A *lead* is the amount of time a successor can be advanced with respect to a predecessor activity. For example, prior to the project planning completion, the project manager can begin assembling the project team. This gives the project a good head start and needed subject matter experts who will be doing the actual work.

A *lag* is the amount of time a successor activity will be delayed with respect to a predecessor activity. For example, the IT infrastructure technical writing team can be editing the draft 2 weeks before writing the document.

PMIS is project management scheduling software such as Microsoft® Project.

The project cannot finish unless all deliverables have been completed, all documents have been archived, all lessons learned have been collected, and resources have been released.

Outputs

The *project schedule network diagram* is a graphical representation of relationships between project activities, also referred to as dependencies. The project schedule network diagram can be created either manually or using project management software.

Project documents updates are made to the activity attributes, activity list, assumptions log, and milestone list.

Exam Alert!

1. Jason is a new project manager who is currently in the planning phase of a project. Jason has defined the activities—what should he do next?

    a) Sequence activities

    b) Estimate costs

    c) Collect requirements

    d) Identify risks

Answer: *a.* The question clearly states that Jason is still in the planning process, so what process occurs after sequence that in in the list of choices and part on the planning process group. Define activities, sequence activities, estimate activity duration, et cetera. Knowing the order of processes in planning process group is crucial to passing the exam. *Memorize the order of processes in the planning process group!*

2. Jason is a new project manager who is currently in the planning phase of a project. Jason has defined the activities. As a project manager, what did Jason do before defining the activities?

    a) Sequence activities

    b) Estimate costs

    c) Plan schedule management

    d) Identify risks

Answer: *c.* See the order of processes in the planning process group.

3. Of the four types of PDM relationships, which is used least often?

    a) Finish to start (FS)

    b) Finish to finish (FF)

    c) Start to finish (SF)

    d) Start to start (SS)

Answer: *c.* Start to finish (SF) is very rarely used.

4. Of the four types of PDM relationships, which is used most often?

    a) Finish to start (FS)

b) Finish to finish (FF)

c) Start to finish (SF)

d) Start to start (SS)

Answer: *a.* Finish to start (FS) is the most commonly used.

6.4 Estimate Activity Durations

According to PMBOK, the *estimate activity durations* process estimates the number of work periods needed to complete activities with the estimated resources.[34] From start to finish, how long will it take to complete the IT infrastructure project? This is accomplished by totaling how long it takes to complete each activity.

Case Study— IT Infrastructure Project in the Role of Technical Project Manager

Continuing with our infrastructure example, once the requirements are collected, the scope defined, the activities defined, and the sequence ordered, the next step is to figure out how long each activity will take to complete. There are several approaches to determining how long it will take to complete individual activities, such as historical or archived project plans, PERT formulas, and software tools.

For example, the approach we used was a combination of analogous, parametric, and expert judgments. I asked the project manager for a company whose services we procured how long a migration would take. Their project manager responded, "In the past, migrations have occurred with other projects in as little as 3 days, as long as 7 days, and on average 5 days."

The procured project manager and team represented expert judgments. When the project manager mentioned "in the past," it represented a parametric estimating technique, but the comment of "as little as 3 days, as long as 7 days, and on average 5 days" represented a three-point estimating technique.

---

34 *PMBOK Guide*, Sixth Edition, 195.

Process	Inputs	Tools and Techniques	Outputs
6.4 Estimate Activity Durations	Project management plan Project documents » Activity attributes, activity list, assumption log » Lessons learned register » Milestone list » Project team assignments » Resource breakdown structure (RBS) » Resource calendars » Resource requirements » Risk register EEF OPA	Expert judgments Analogous estimating Parametric estimating Three-point estimating Bottom-up estimating Data analysis » Alternative analysis » Reserve analysis Decision-making Meetings	Duration estimates Basis estimates Project documents updates Activity attributes Assumption log Lessons learned register

Inputs

From the *project management plan*, once the activities are sequenced, a schedule can be developed, and cost of the project can be estimated.

From *project documents*, the following inputs are used:

» activity attributes, activity list, assumptions log

» lessons learned register

» milestone list (the events reached to measure project progress)

» project team assignments (owners of the activities)

» resource breakdown structure (RBS) (a hierarchical graphical chart of resources, which will be covered later)

» resource calendars with information on the availability of resources

» resource requirements (resources necessary for the success of the project)

» risk register (the list of risks, the status of risks, and owners of risks)

Enterprise environmental factors are the external or internal factors outside the project team's control and how they influence the process.

Organizational process assets are the policies, practices, and procedures as they influence the process.

Tools and Techniques

Expert judgments are information from those whose knowledge and experience can give immediate insight into how long an activity may take.

Analogous estimating is the historical estimating from a very similar or same-size project.

Parametric estimating is also the historical estimating from a very similar project; however, it is from a project of a different size.

Three-point estimating is more of an exact science using a tested formula to estimate activity duration. (See expanded explanation of this method below.)

Bottom-up estimating is the most exact way to determine activity duration. Bottom-up estimating gets analysis information from the lower-level components of the WBS. Bottom-up estimating takes longer but is the most accurate method for schedule and cost estimation.

Data analysis:

» *Alternative analysis* is a diverse way of capturing duration information whether the analysis is manual or automatic.

» *Reserve analysis* is used to figure out the amount of contingency and management reserve necessary for the project. The contingency reserve is associated with knowns-unknowns. Management reserve is associated with unknowns-unknowns.

Decision-making allows team members to vote to show the level of support. If a team member is not in favor of a decision, that team member can explain why.

The project team holds *meetings* to estimate activity durations.

What Is Three-Point Estimating (PERT)?

Three-point estimating originated with the program evaluation and review technique (PERT). Using three-point estimating helps define an approximate range for an activity's duration. PERT uses three estimates to define an approximate range for an activity's duration:

Most likely (M) is the realistic expectation of the duration.

Optimistic (O) is the best-case scenario for the duration.

Pessimistic (P) is the worst-case scenario for the duration.

The formulas for PERT are:

Triangular Distribution = (O + M + P) / 3 or simple average

Beta Distribution = (O + 4M + P) / 6 or PERT formula

Standard Deviation = (P - O) / 6

Note: Beta distribution is more accurate than triangular distribution.

PERT Three-Point Estimate or Beta Distribution Example

For Activity A:

M = 8 hours

O = 4 hours

P = 16 hours

Using the estimates above for Activity A, calculate the estimate:

E = (4 + 4(8) + 16) / 6

E = 52 / 6

E = 8.7 hours

Using the estimates above for Activity A, calculate the standard deviation:

SD = (16 - 4) / 6

SD = 12 / 6

SD = 2 hours

PERT Three-Point Estimate Results for Activity A:

6.5h–10.5h: Confidence level in E value +/- SD is 68.2%.

5.4h–12h: Confidence level in E value +/- 1.645 × SD is 90%.

4.7h–12.7h: Confidence level in E value +/- 2 × SD is 95%.

2.7h–14.7h: Confidence level in E value +/- 3 × SD is 99.7%.

Information systems typically use the 90% confidence level (i.e., E Value + 1.645 × SD) for all project and task estimates.

Outputs

Duration estimates are how long each activity will take to complete. How long the project will take to complete will be known when all activity durations are known.

Basis estimates are how the durations originated—the tools and techniques that were used to identify or compute duration.

Project documents updates are made to the activity attributes, assumptions log, and lessons learned register.

Exam Alert!

1.   As a project manager, you are planning the activities in the project schedule. Which of the following depicts the order of activities in cost management?

   a) Collect requirements, define scope, and create WBS

   b) Identify risks, perform qualitative risk analysis, perform quantitative risk analysis, and plan risk responses

   c) Plan schedule management, define activities, sequence activities, estimate activity resources, estimate activity costs, and develop schedule

   d) Estimate costs and determine budget

Answer: *d*. Option *a* describes scope management, *b* defines risk management, and *c* is schedule management.

2.   Which is not a tool and technique used in the estimate activity durations process?

   a) Analogous estimating

   b) Bottom-up estimating

   c) Three-point estimating

   d) Duration estimates

Answer: *d*. Analogous, bottom-up, and three-point estimating are tool and techniques for estimate activity process.

3.   Using the PERT beta distribution formula, how long will it take Mary to complete the project if most likely = 32, optimistic = 20, and pessimistic = 50?

   a)   44

   b)   33

   c)   34

   d)   32

Answer: *b*. $(P+(4(M)+O)/6=(20 + 32(4) + 50) / 6 = 33$

4.   Using the triangular distribution method, how long will it take Mary to complete the project if most likely = 32, optimistic = 20, and pessimistic = 50?

   a)   44

   b)   33

   c)   34

   d)   32

Answer: *c*. $(P+M+O)/3= (32 + 20 + 50) / 3 = 34$

6.5 Develop Schedule

According to PMBOK, the *develop schedule* process analyzes sequences, durations, resource requirements, and schedule constraints to create a project model for project executions, monitoring, and controlling.[35] Knowing requirements will help identify deliverables of the project, but knowing the schedule of when activities start and finish gives the project manager the best control of the project. When you must report the status of a project to the sponsor, senior manager, or other stakeholders, they are most likely asking the status on the completion of the project or when a resource will be needed or available. The well-defined schedule provides the project manager with this information.

---

35   *PMBOK Guide*, Sixth Edition 205.

Case Study— IT Infrastructure Project in the Role of Technical Project Manager

Now that the durations for each activity have been defined, the IT infrastructure project manager can forecast when resources will be needed and expected to complete their task. Putting together an infrastructure project can take a few days, a few weeks, or a few months depending on the complexity of the project and resource availability. With the develop schedule process, the project manager identifies resource availability to coincide with the project activities.

With this process we put together a road map that is a visual way to better manage and control the project.

Process	Inputs	Tools and Techniques	Outputs
6.5 Develop Schedule	Project management plan » Schedule management plan » Scope baseline Project documents » Activity attributes, activity list, assumption log » Basis of estimates » Duration estimates » Lessons learned register » Milestone list » Project schedule network diagrams » Project team assignments » Resource breakdown structure (RBS) » Resource calendars » Resource requirements » Risk register » Agreements EEF OPA	Schedule network analysis » Critical path method » Resource optimization Data analysis » What-if scenario analysis » Monte Carlo simulation Leads and lags Schedule compression PMIS Agile release planning	Schedule baseline Project schedule » Schedule data » Project calendars » Change requests Project management plan updates » Schedule management plan » Cost baseline Project documents updates » Activity attributes, activity list, assumption log » Duration estimates » Lessons learned register » Resource requirements » Risk register

Inputs

The *project management plan* contains the *schedule management plan* and the *scope baseline*.

> » The schedule management plan identifies the scheduling method and scheduling tool to be used to create the schedule and determine how the schedule is calculated.

» The scope baseline acts as a reference point for which requirements are included and which are not. It has several components. These include the project scope document, the WBS itself, and the WBS dictionary.

Project documents include:

» Activity attributes, activity list, and assumptions log

» Basis of estimates

» Duration estimates

» Lessons learned register

» Milestone list

» Project schedule network diagrams

» Project team assignments

» Resource breakdown structure (RBS)

» Resource calendars

» Resource requirements

» Risk register

Agreements are the inputs that vendors have, including the project schedule and the details of how they will perform their work.

Enterprise environmental factors are the external and internal factors such as organization structure and culture and how they influence the project schedule.

Organizational process assets are the policies, practices, procedures, and lessons learned as they influence the develop schedule process.

Tools and Techniques

Schedule network analysis is the technique used to generate the project schedule for which we use the *critical path method*, *resource optimization*, and other modeling techniques to plan and manage the schedule.

» The critical path is the sequence of activities that represents the longest path through a project, which determines the shortest duration. The critical path method is used to estimate the minimum project duration and determine the amount of schedule flexibility on the logical network paths within the schedule model. The critical path is the path with zero total float. (Total float is the amount of time an activity can be delayed without delaying the project completion date.) On a critical path, the total float is zero.

» *Resource optimization* is used to adjust the start and finish dates of activities to match adjusted planned resource availability. For example, if it is determined that a resource will not be available on the date planned, the start and finish dates of an activity can sometimes be adjusted, extending the time line. Adjusting the schedule for resource optimization includes either resource leveling or resource smoothing.

  • Resource leveling is used when shared or critically required resources are only available at certain times or in limited quantities or are overallocated, such as when a resource has been assigned to two or more projects during the same time. Resource leveling can often cause the original critical path to change, usually by increasing the CP.

  • Resource smoothing does not change the critical path, and the completion date may not be delayed because with resource smoothing, the activities are adjusted on the schedule model so the requirements for resources on the project do not exceed certain predefined resource limits.

Data analysis:

» *What-if scenario analysis* is the process of changing the values in cells to see how those changes will affect the outcome of formulas on the worksheet.

» *Monte Carlo simulation is* a quantitative risk-analysis technique used to identify the risk level of completing the project. The simulation involves taking multiple work packages in the WBS with a diverse set of assumptions, constraints, risks, issue, or scenarios and using probability distributions with the probability of achieving a certain target date.

Lead and *lag* are both used in the development of the project schedule. Lead is an acceleration of the successor activity and can be used only on finish-to-start activity relationships. Lag is a delay in the successor activity and can be found in all activity relationship types.

Schedule compression is used to shorten the schedule duration without reducing the project scope to meet imposed constraints. (For example, a customer states the project must be completed by a certain date.) Schedule compression consists of two types: crashing and fast-tracking.

» Crashing shortens schedule duration by adding resources, such as approving overtime or paying to expedite delivery to activities on the critical path.[36]

» Fast-tracking is when activities normally done in sequence are performed in parallel for at least a portion of their duration. For example, installing application objects before database configuration is completed. Fast-tracking may result in rework and increased risk. Fast-tracking only works if activities can be overlapped to shorten project duration.

PMIS is a scheduling tool such as Excel or Microsoft Project to aid in project management scheduling.

Agile release planning provides a high-level summary timeline of the release schedule (typically 3 to 6 months) based on the product road map and the vision for the product's evolution. Agile release planning also determines the number of iterations or sprints in the release.[37]

Once all activities are arranged in logical order and relationships are set, the logic diagram is ready for the calculation process. The format used to indicate values for each activity is shown in figure 7. TF and FF indicate where to place float values. ES, EF, LS, LF, and the duration indicate where to place their respective values.[38]

Figure 7. Activity node format

36 Course Hero, "6.6.2.7 Schedule Compression," https://www.coursehero.com/file/p7o0grd/6627-Schedule-Compression-Schedule-compr.

37 *PMBOK Guide*, Sixth Edition, "Agile Release Planning," YouTube video, 9:06, Posted January 17, 2018, https://www.youtube.com/watch?v=YmwqmCVKwUw.

38 S. W. Kramer and J. L. Jenkins, "Understanding the Basics of CPM Calculations: What Is Scheduling Software Really Telling You?" (paper presented at PMI® Global Congress 2006—EMEA, Madrid, Spain) (Newtown Square, PA: Project Management Institute, 2006), https://www.pmi.org/learning/library/basics-cpm-scheduling-software-axon-8170.

» Early start (ES): Earliest date the activity can start

» Early finish (EF): Earliest date the activity can finish

» Late finish (LF): Latest date the activity can finish without causing a delay to the project completion date

» Late start (LS): Latest date the activity can start without causing a delay to the project completion date

» Free float (FF): The maximum number of days the activity can be delayed without delaying any succeeding activity

» Total float (TF): The maximum number of days the activity can be delayed without delaying the project completion date

Example: CPM

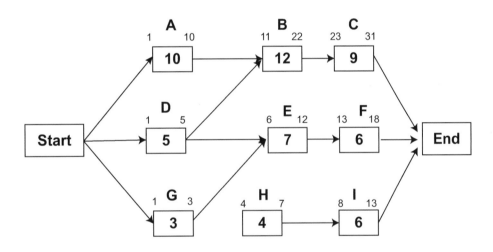

The network diagram above has 5 paths. The paths and their duration are as follows:

Start -> A -> B -> C-> End, duration: 31 days

Start ->D -> E ->F -> End, duration: 18 days

Start -> D -> B -> C -> End, duration: 26 days

Start -> G ->H ->I -> End, duration: 13 days

Start -> G -> E ->F -> End, duration: 16 days

Example: CPM—The Forward Pass

The forward pass is the critical path method technique for calculating the early start and early finish dates by working forward through the schedule model from the project start date or a given point in time.

> Early start of activity A = 1 (since this is the first activity of the path)
>
> Early finish of activity A = ES of activity A + activity duration -1 = 1 + 10 -1 = 10
>
> Early start of activity B = EF of predecessor activity + 1 = 10 + 1 = 11
>
> Early finish of activity B = ES of activity B + activity duration - 1 = 11 + 12 - 1 = 22
>
> Early start of activity C = EF of predecessor activity + 1 = 22 +1 = 23
>
> Early finish of activity C = ES of activity C + activity duration - 1 = 23 + 9 - 1 = 31

Example: CPM—The Backward Pass

The backward pass is a critical path method technique for calculating the late start and late finish dates by working backward through a schedule model from the project end date.

On a critical path, early start and early finish dates will be the same as late start and late finish dates

> Late start of activity E = LF of activity E - activity duration + 1 = 25 - 7 + 1 = 19
>
> Late finish of activity D = LS of successor activity - 1

If you look at the network diagram, you will notice that activity D has two successor activities, B and E. So, which activity will you select?

You will select the activity with the lower late start date. Here, late start of activity B is 11, and late start of activity E is 19. Therefore, you will select activity B, which has the lower late start date.

Therefore:

> Late finish of activity D = LS of activity B - 1 = 11 - 1 = 10
>
> Late start of activity D = LF of activity D - activity duration + 1 = 10 - 5 + 1 = 6

Outputs

The *schedule baseline* is the approved version of the scheduled start and end dates that can only be changed through formal change control procedures. It is used for comparison to the actual results. The schedule baseline can keep the project manager aware of the performance of the project by determining if the project is ahead of or behind schedule for the planned end date.

The *project schedule* is the output of the schedule mode with linked activities of planned dates, durations, milestones, and resources.

- » *Schedule data* is the raw start date, end date, and schedule milestones along with activity attributes, schedule activities, and all identified constraints and assumptions.
- » *Project calendars* are the working days and shifts that are available for the scheduled activities.
- » *Change requests* can occur with modifications to the scope or schedule activities.

Project management plan updates are made to the *schedule management plan* and *cost baseline*.

Project documents updates are made to:

- » Activity attributes, activity list, assumption log
- » Duration estimates
- » Lessons learned register
- » Resource requirements
- » Risk register

Exam Alert!

1. Which of the following depicts the order of activities in schedule management?

   a) Collect requirements, define scope, and create WBS

   b) Identify risks, perform qualitative risk analysis, perform quantitative risk analysis, and plan risk responses

   c) Plan schedule management, define activities, sequence activities, estimate activity durations, and develop schedule

   d) Estimate costs and determine budget

Answer: *c. a* is plan scope management, *b* is plan risk management, and *d* is plan cost management.

2. The following are tools and techniques of the develop schedule process except

a) Schedule compression

b) Data analysis

c) Project documents

d) Critical path method

Answer: *c.* Project documents are inputs.

7.1 Plan Cost Management

According to PMBOK, the *plan cost management* process defines how the project cost will be estimated, budgeted, managed, and monitored and controlled.[39] The schedule is now set, so it is time to determine the budget and how much this project could potentially cost. The project manager must put together a document called a *cost management plan*, which states how the cost will be determined.

Case Study— IT Infrastructure Project in the Role of Technical Project Manager

As project manager, when creating the cost management plan document, ask the following questions:

1. Where will the funds for the IT infrastructure project come from?
2. How much will the project cost?
3. How will its cost be estimated?

Your cost management plan answers these questions.

» The project charter contains information on the initial funding or the preapproved budget for the project.

» The project plan contains information on how the schedule was conceived and the risk plan, along with organizational policies, procedures, and external and internal factors to effectively manage the IT infrastructure project.

---

39 *PMBOK Guide*, Sixth Edition, 235.

Process	Inputs	Tools and Techniques	Outputs

7.1 Plan Cost Management	Project charter
	
	Project management plan
	» Schedule management plan
	» Risk management plan
	EEF
	OPA
		Expert judgments
		
		Data analysis
		» Alternative analysis
		  • Self-funding
		  • Funding with equity or debt
		  • Making resources
		  • Purchasing resources
		  • Renting resources
		  • Leasing resources
		Meetings
			Cost management plan
			» Units of measure
			» Level of precision
			» Level of accuracy
			» Control threshold
			Strategic funding choices
			Procedures for fluctuations in currency
			Procedure for project cost recording

Inputs

The *project charter* contains the preapproved financial resources from which detailed project costs were developed.

The *project management plan* contains the *schedule management plan* and the *risk management plan.*

> » The schedule management plan is the document developing, maintaining, and communicating schedules for timeline and resources.

> » The risk management plan is the document a project manager prepares to foresee risks, estimate impacts, and define responses to issues.

Enterprise environmental factors are things outside the project manager's and project team's control that can influence cost estimation.

Organizational process assets are the policies, practices, procedures, and lessons learned documents that can influence cost estimation.

Tools and Techniques

Expert judgments include information from those who can offer insight into cost estimation, such as PMOs, consultants, and those with expertise in cost estimation.

Data analysis techniques that can be used in the estimate costs include:

» Alternative analysis

» Self-funding

» Funding with equity or debt

» Making resources

» Purchasing resources

» Renting resources

» Leasing resources

Meetings are held to develop the cost management plan. Attendees include the project team, sponsor, selected stakeholders, and anyone responsible for plan costs.

Outputs

The *cost management plan* is the document planning and controlling the budget of a project. Some factors noted in the plan are:

» The recommended units of measure, such as hours, days, or weeks, for the project.

» The level of precision used in cost estimates, such as rounding up or down. For example, $995.59 would be rounded up to $1,000.

» The level of accuracy of the estimates (for example, +10%).

» Organizational procedure links. WBS performs framework for cost management plan.

» The control threshold—the percentage of deviations.

» Rules of earn value management (EVM) performance.

» Reporting formats (look and feel, how often, recipients, and how much information).

» Additional details:

- Strategic funding choices

- Procedures for fluctuations in currency

- Procedures for project cost recording

Exam Alert!

1. Which of the following depicts the order of activities in cost management?

    a) Collect requirements, define scope, and create WBS

    b) Identify risks, perform qualitative risk analysis, perform quantitative risk analysis, and plan risk responses

    c) Plan schedule management, define activities, sequence activities, estimate activity resources, estimate activity costs, and develop schedule

    d) Estimate costs and determine budget

Answer: *d*. Option *a* describes scope management, *b* defines risk management, and *c* is schedule management.

2. Which is a tool and technique of the plan cost management process?

    a) Alternative analysis

    b) Project documents

    c) Project plan updates

    d) Rolling wave technique

Answer: *a*. *Project documents* is an input, *project plan updates* is an output, and *rolling wave technique* is a technique in another process.

7.2 Estimate Costs

According to PMBOK, the *estimate costs* process develops an approximation of the monetary resources needed to complete project activities.[40] This process determines the cost to complete the project work. Here we put the cost plan to work in estimating the costs of the project.

Terminology you will need to know for the exam:

»   Fixed costs

    • Business expenses not dependent on the level of goods or services produced, such as rent paid by the month

---

40 *PMBOK Guide*, Sixth Edition, 240.

- » Variable costs

  - Expenses that change in proportion to the level of activity of a business, such as the purchase of more or less raw material

- » Direct costs

  - Costs related to the production of specific goods: for example, employee wages.

- » Indirect costs

  - Costs not related to a particular project, such as heat or lighting (overhead).

Case Study— IT Infrastructure Project in the Role of Technical Project Manager

For our example IT infrastructure project, we are estimating the costs of the IT infrastructure, the components, the resources, the schedule, and the contingency reserve.

- » Resources are the physical items, such as the computers, the 100 TB of storage, the network, and the cables, as well as people (the project team deemed necessary and documented in the project scope statement, work breakdown structure, and work breakdown structure dictionary).

- » The schedule is the total time it takes to complete the project. which is the total of all activities durations in the project plan.

- » The cost baseline for the IT infrastructure project can be determined from previous projects or via a formula called PERT. The contingency reserve comes from the risk management analysis, which states the time and effort necessary to resolve a risk.

Process	Inputs	Tools and Techniques	Outputs
7.2 Estimate Costs	Project management plan » Cost management plan » Quality management plan » Scope baseline » Project scope statement » WBS » WBS dictionary Project documents » Lessons learned » Project schedules » Resource requirements » Risk register EEF OPA	Expert judgments Analogous estimating Parameter estimating Bottom-up estimating Three-point estimating Data analysis » Alternative analysis » Reserve analysis » Cost of quality PMIS Decision-making » voting	Cost estimates » Quantitative assessments » Contingency amounts » Basis of estimates Project documents updates » Lessons learned » Project schedule » Risk register

Other terminology you need to know for the PMP exam:

» *Rough order of magnitude:* When a project is at or near its birth stage and someone asks what it may cost for the project, the project manager may give the sponsor or senior management a rough order of magnitude, which is -25% to + 75%.

» *Definitive estimate:* After project initiation, you may check for the cost of past projects using analogous or parametric estimating. Once you apply a formula (PERT) to information discovered about the project, you'll get a definitive estimate, which is a more accurate answer of -5% to +10%.

Case Study— IT Infrastructure Project in the Role of Technical Project Manager

For example, in another migration project, I had a situation like this when I was asking another project manager how long a migration might take. Her project team responded, "Anywhere from four hours to four days." I asked her for a more accurate answer. I wanted the earliest time the migration could complete, the average time, and the worst case her team had seen based on

prior migrations. That was the answer I placed in my project management plan. The migration for both the development environment and subsequent deployment to production took eleven hours.

Inputs

The *project management plan* includes the *cost management plan*, the *quality management plan*, and the *scope baseline*.

» The cost management plan contains information on how costs will be estimated, the methods used, and the precision and accuracy required.

» The quality management plan defines the activities and resources necessary for the project management team to achieve the quality objectives of the project.

» The scope baseline contains the following:

  • *Project scope statement*—the requirements that will be used.

  • *WBS* relationship among deliverables.

- *WBS dictionary*, which has detailed descriptions of deliverables and work involved for each deliverable.

Project documents include:

» *Lessons learned* in earlier phases of the project that can be applied to the current phase with regard to developing cost estimates.

» *Project schedules* that help determine what type and quantity of team resources will be needed and for what amount of time those resources will be active.

» *Resource requirements* that describe how many and the type of resources required for each work package activity.

» *Risk register* that contains the details of individual project risks that have been identified and prioritized.

Enterprise environmental factors are the internal and external influences out of the project team's control that may affect cost estimates.

Organizational process assets are the policies, practices, procedures, and lessons learned as to how they will influence cost estimates.

Tools and Techniques

Expert judgments include information from consultants, individuals, and groups with specialized knowledge or training or similar or previous project experience in estimating costs.

Analogous estimating is cost estimating based on a previous project similar to the current one.

Parametric estimating uses a similar previous project with a statistical relationship between historical data and variables. For example, if a previous project building a 15,000-square-foot structure took 5 days to complete, then a 45,000-square-foot structure would take 15 days to complete.

Bottom-up estimating is the most accurate way to estimate costs because each work package in the WBS is analyzed.

Three-point estimating uses a formula based on most likely, optimistic, and pessimistic time estimates.

Data analysis:

» The *alternative analysis* considers buying versus making a deliverable.

» *Reserve analysis* estimates include contingency reserves. As more information becomes available through progressive elaboration, the contingency reserve is changed, reduced, and possibly eliminated.

» *Cost of quality* is the additional cost that includes conformance versus nonconformance.

Conformance is how well a product, service or result meets a specific standard. Nonconformance is the failure to comply with a requirement, standard or procedure.

PMIS is a project management software tool that can be used to estimate costs.

Decision-making:

» *Voting* is used to select for best response involving project team members when discussing cost estimates.

Example: PERT Three-Point Estimating

For Activity A:

o = $4

p = $16

m = $8

Using the estimates above for Activity A, calculate the estimate:

E = (4 + 4(8) + 16) / 6

E = 52 / 6

E = $8.70

Example: Triangular Distribution Method

For Activity A:

o = $4

p = $16

m = $8

Using the estimates above for Activity A, calculate the estimate:

$$E = (4 + 8 + 16) / 3$$

$$E = 28 / 3$$

$$E = \$ \, 9.333333333333333$$

Outputs

When performing *cost estimates*, the estimates can be presented in summary or detailed form, depending on the audience.

» The cost estimates include *quantitative assessments* and *contingency amounts* for identified risks. The estimates include direct labor, equipment, services, facilities, and information technology as well as the cost of financing, inflation allowance, exchange rates, or a cost contingency reserve.

» The *basis of estimates* is necessary to support the estimated costs. A basis of estimates might include how estimates were developed, how assumptions were made, known constraints, identified risks, the range of costs for the estimate, and your level of confidence in the estimates.

Project documents updates will include:

» lessons learned

» project schedule

» risk register

Exam Alert!

1. Which of the following depicts the order of activities in estimate costs?
   a) Collect requirements, define scope, and create WBS
   b) Identify risks, perform qualitative risk analysis, perform quantitative risk analysis, and plan risk responses
   c) Plan schedule management, define activities, sequence activities, estimate activity durations, and develop schedule
   d) Estimate costs and determine budget

   Answer: *d*. *a* is plan scope management, *b* is plan risk management. and *c* is plan schedule management.

2. Mary is a new project manager. How much will it cost for Mary to complete the project if most likely = $2,000, optimistic = $1,000, and pessimistic = $3,000, using three-point estimation?
   a) 44

b) 2,000

c) 2,167

d) 32

Answer: ***b.*** 1,000 + 2,000(4) + 3,000 = 12000

12,000 / 6 = 2000

7.3 Determine Budget

According to PMBOK, the *determine budget* process aggregates the estimated costs of individual activities or work packages to establish an authorized cost baseline.[41] Once the sponsor has initiated the project objectives, the requirements and work packages are determined by the project team; the project team also determines the budget. Upon completion of the estimating cost process, the following will be used to determine the budget for the project:

Category of components	Components	Costs
Hardware	6 computers, load balancers, firewalls	
Software	Operating system, security software, cluster software, database software, application software	
Network	Public networks, high-speed interconnect	
Storage	100 TB of shared storage (times 2). Can be SAN, NAS, Raw, etc.	
Designers	System architect or system engineer	
Planners	Project manager	
Implementers	Hardware, software, database, storage, network, and application administrators	
Procurements	Vendors based on contract or PO	
Contingency reserve	Amount determined by risk strategy	
Management reserve	Amount determined by senior management	

41 *PMBOK Guide*, Sixth Edition, 245.

Process	Inputs	Tools and Techniques	Outputs
7.3 Determine Budget	Project management plan » Cost management plan » Resource management plan » Scope baseline Project documents » Basis estimates » Cost estimates » Project schedule » Risk register Business documents » Business case » Benefits management plan Agreements EEF OPA	Expert judgments Cost aggregation Data analysis » Reserve analysis Historical information review » Analogous estimates » Parametric estimates Funding limitation reconciliation Financing	Cost baseline Project funding requirements Project documents updates » Cost estimates » Project schedule » Risk register

Inputs

The *project management plan* contains the *cost management plan*, *resource management plan*, and *scope baseline*.

» The cost management plan is the how-to document that determines how costs will be structured.

» The resource management plan has information about how the rates of resources and contingency reserves will be determined.

» The scope baseline acts as a reference point for which requirements are included and which are not. It has several components. These include the project scope document, the WBS itself, and the WBS dictionary.

Project documents:

» *Basis estimates* support how the cost estimates were determined.

» *Cost estimates* are determined for activities within a work package.

» *Project schedule* is the planned start and end dates of the activities.

» *Risk register* has information on the aggregated costs of foreseen risk.

Business documents:

» The *business case* describes why the project is necessary and includes information on funding the project.

» The *benefits management plan* includes the target benefits of the project, such as net present value calculations and the time frame for realizing the benefits.

Agreements contain information on costs related to products, services, or results that have been purchased that are added to determine the budget.

Enterprise environmental factors are the internal and external factors outside the project team's control that may affect budget processes, such as exchange rates and fluctuations of currencies.

Organizational process assets are the policies, practices, procedures, and lessons learned that may affect this process. The assets may include budgeting tools, reporting methods, and templates.

Tools and Techniques

Expert judgments include information from those with experience and specialized knowledge in determining the budget for the project or activity.

Cost aggregation is defined as summing up the **cost** for the individual work package to control the financial account up to the entire project level.[42]

» Cost is aggregated or rolled up based on work packages in WBS.

» Cost is aggregated ultimately to the entire project.

Data analysis:

» *Reserve analysis* refers in this case to the management reserves for the project to address unknowns within the scope of the project. Management reserves are not part of the cost baseline; however, they are part of the overall project funding.

Historical information review:

» *Analogous estimates* are used to determine costs for the budget.

» *Parametric estimates* are used to determine costs for the budget.

Funding limit reconciliation can result in the rescheduling of work to level out the rate of expenditure.

Financing means obtaining funding for the project.

---

42   Project Victor, "Knowledge Base/Cost Management/Cost Aggregation," https://projectvictor.com/knowledge-base/cost-aggregation/.

Outputs

The *cost baseline* is the approved version of the time-based project budget.

Project funding requirements are derived from the cost baseline.

Project document updates include

» cost estimates

» project schedule

» risk register

Exam Alert!

1. The following are tools and techniques that can be used to determine budget except

   a) Expert judgments

   b) Historical information review

   c) Funding limit reconciliation

   d) Business documents

Answer: *d.* Expert judgments, historical information review, and funding limit reconciliation are all tools and techniques that can be used to determine spending budget.

2. Which is an output of the determine budget process?

   a) Cost baseline

   b) Alternative analysis

   c) Project management plan

   d) Voting

Answer: *a.* Options *b*, *c*, and *d* are not outputs.

8.1 Plan Quality Management

According to PMBOK, the *plan quality management* process identifies quality requirements and standards for the project and its deliverables and documents how the project will demonstrate compliance with quality requirements.[43]

When determining quality standards, here are three things to be aware of:

1. Quality versus grade
2. Precision versus accuracy
3. International Organization Standardization (ISO) quality standards

Quality is the degree of performance to which a deliverable will fulfill requirements.

Grade is a category assigned to a deliverable having the same functional or technical use.

Precision is a measure of exactness.

Accuracy is an assessment of correction.

International Organization Standardization (ISO) is intended to provide generic guidance and explain core principles and what constitutes good practice in project management.

Planning quality management means managing and tracking three things in any project: the quality process, the prevention of quality issues, and the correction of quality issues. You can deliver something, you can deliver something fast, or you can deliver something that does what the customer expects it to do.

---

43   *PMBOK Guide*, Sixth Edition, 277.

Case Study— IT Infrastructure Project in the Role of Technical Project Manager

For example, an electronics engineer first checks quality during the design of a product, then checks to see if the correct procedures and processes are in place and being performed on the product, and later checks for correctness of the product to be delivered.

The engineers or technicians will use various tools to measure the expected results based on the manufacturer's claims in the specification sheets. For example, the hardware engineer will check computer hardware for memory correctness, number of CPUs, and storage. The database software will be checked for program correctness and the recovery and downtime capabilities, respectively, during disaster recovery and high availability.

Metrics such as memory size, CPUs, and storage capacity must be first established in the quality management plan. Then there are metrics established for the database operation, failover capabilities, and recovery time when managing high availability and disaster recovery.

Customer satisfaction—meeting the customer's expectations—is what the project manager and project team must strive toward. Even if everything is done correctly, if the customer is not satisfied, the project is a failure.

Process	Inputs	Tools and Techniques	Outputs
8.1 Plan Quality Management	Project charter Project management plan » Requirements management plan » Risk management plan » Stakeholder engagement plan » Scope baseline Project documents » Assumptions log » Requirements documentation » Requirements traceability matrix » Risk register » Stakeholder register OPA EEF	Expert judgments Data gathering » Benchmarking » Brainstorming » Interviews Data analysis » Cost-benefit analysis » Cost of quality Data representation » Flowcharts » Logical model » Matrix diagrams » Mind mapping » Decision-making » Multicriteria analysis » Test and inspection Meetings	Quality management plan PMP updates » Risk management plan » Scope baseline Quality metrics Project documents updates » Lessons learned register » Requirements traceability matrix » Risk register » Stakeholder register

Inputs

The *project charter* contains the sponsor-defined deliverables for the project. The objectives are part of the statement of work (SOW), and the project team must determine how quality will be applied and delivered to these deliverables. The project charter also contains the high-level risks and constraints, initial stakeholders, and things external to the organization that might have an impact on what kind of quality can be designed and applied to the deliverables on the project.

The *project management plan* states how the project will be designed, managed, monitored and controlled, and closed. For the plan quality management process, the project management plan focuses on the *requirements management plan*, *risk management plan*, *stakeholder engagement plan*, and *scope baseline*.

> » The requirements management plan provides a way to identify, analyze, and manage the requirements that the quality management plan and quality metrics will reference.

> » The risk management plan is a document that a project manager prepares to foresee risks, estimate impacts, and define responses to issues.

> » The stakeholder engagement plan provides a method for documenting the stakeholders' needs and expectations.

> » The scope baseline acts as a reference point for which requirements are included and which are not. It has several components. These include the project scope document, the WBS itself, and the WBS dictionary.

The *project documents* used for this process include the *assumptions log*, *requirements documentation*, *requirements traceability matrix*, *risk register*, and *stakeholder register*.

Organizational process assets are the policies, practices, procedures, and lessons learned that may affect this process. The assets may include budgeting tools, reporting methods, and templates.

Enterprise environmental factors are the internal and external influences out of the project team's control that may affect the process.

Tools and Techniques

Expert judgments include information from consultants, the PMO, and those with expertise in quality management and quality metrics, quality assurance, quality control, and quality systems.

Data gathering:

- » *Benchmarking* is a process of measuring the performance of a company's products, services or results against those of another business considered to be the best in the industry.

- » *Brainstorming* uses the combined creative efforts of the project team, experts, and consultants to develop the quality management plan.

- » *Interviews*—informal, formal, implicit, and explicit—can help create a quality project plan.

Data analysis:

- » The cost-benefit analysis determines strengths and weaknesses and measures the cost and benefits of the quality activities individually.

- » The cost of quality associated with the project determines what happens when quality procedures are followed and when they are not.

Cost of Conformance	Cost of Nonconformance
Preventive Costs	**Internal Failure Costs**
Training	Rework
Document processes	Scrap
Equipment	
Time to do it right	**External Failure Costs**
Appraisal Costs	Liabilities
Testing	Warranty work
Destructive testing loss	Lost business
Inspections	

Cost of quality (COQ) refers to the total costs needed to bring products or services up to standards defined by project management professionals. To determine the cost of quality, combine the costs of conformance and the costs of nonconformance.[44]

---

44 Magoosh, PMP Blog, "Cost of Quality: PMP Topics to Learn for the Exam," https://magoosh.com/pmp/cost-of-quality-pmp/.

Data representation:

> » *Flowcharts* or process maps display the sequence of steps and the branching possibilities that exist that transform one or more inputs into one or more outputs. (See "The Seven Basic Quality Tools.")

> » *Logical data model*

> » *Matrix diagrams*

> » *Mind mapping*

> » *Decision-making*

> » *Multicriteria analysis* is a tool that is used to identify key issues and suitable alternatives, which are prioritized as a set of decisions for implementation. Decide which criteria in quality management are important in this project. Then prioritize the criteria. Give each criterion a numerical score. Now a mathematical score can be obtained for each alternative.

> » *Test and inspection* can be from industry, company, or corporate standards.

Seven Basic Quality Tools

Cause-and-effect diagram, Fishbone, Ishakawa is a tool that can help you perform a cause-and-effect analysis for a problem you are trying to solve. This type of analysis enables you to discover the root cause of a problem.

In the figure below, we attempt to determine a problem by

1. First checking if the equipment is okay. If the equipment is the problem, then we order replacement equipment or have the equipment repaired.

2. If the equipment is okay, we check the process such as was the installation, upgrade, or migration performed correctly. If not, we perform the process again.

3. If the installation, upgrade, or migration is okay, we then check if materials(components) are okay.

4. If the materials check okay, then we investigate the people.

Figure 8 Cause-and-effect diagram, Fishbone, Ishakawa

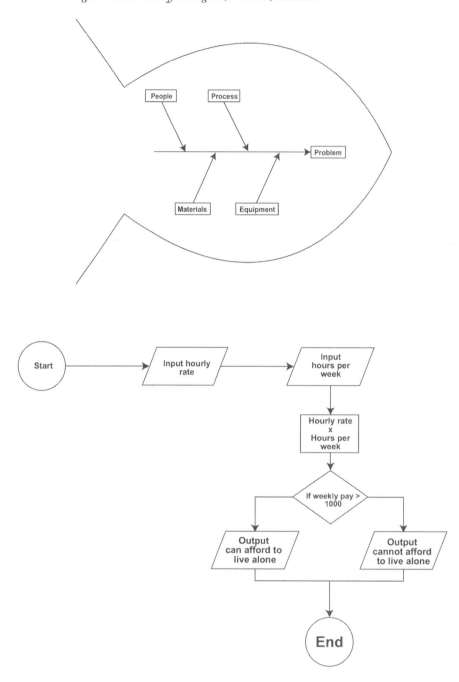

Flowcharts provide visual representations of project processes. The flowchart below has a start and end point stating the hourly and weekly rate and is used to determine whether someone can afford to live alone based on if their weekly pay rate is above $1000 per week.

Check sheets are simple tally sheets that are used to gather data. Use this template when categorizing how often a problem occurs.

Defect	Tallies	Total
Defect 1	//// /// —	8
Defect 2	///	3
Defect 3	//// —	5
Defect 4	//// //// /// — —	13

A *pareto diagram* is a chart that consists of a vertical bar and sometimes a bar-and-line graph. The vertical bar represents the frequency of defects from most to least, and the line represents a cumulative percentage of the defects.

A *histogram chart* is a bar graph that illustrates the frequency of an event occurring using the height of the bar as an indicator.

A *control chart* is a graphic display of process data over time and against established control limits that has a centerline that assists in detecting a trend of plotted values toward either control limit.[45]

Scatter diagrams allow you to analyze the relationship between two variables.

A *SIPOC* (suppliers, inputs, process, outputs, customers) diagram is a visual tool for documenting a business process from beginning to end.

45   Xbar chart for a paired xbar and R chart.svg, https://en.wikipedia.org/wiki/File:Xbar_chart_for_a_paired_xbar_and_R_chart.svg.

Meetings are set up to create a quality management plan.

Outputs

A *quality management plan* is the main output of the plan quality management process. The quality management plan is a subsidiary plan of the project management plan and may contain quality standards for the project, quality objectives for the project, and roles and responsibilities for the quality. The quality management plan may also include project deliverables subject to quality review, quality control planned for the project, and major procedures important to the project, such as nonconformance, corrective action, and continuous procedures.

Project management plan updates contain the *risk management plan* and *scope baselines* and how risk and scope may change due to introduction or changes in quality.

Project documents updates:

» *Lessons learned register* contains the challenges encountered in the quality process.

» *Requirements traceability matrix* contains all quality requirements encountered in the process.

» The *risk register* includes new risks identified during the quality process.

» The *stakeholder register* is updated with additional information on existing and new stakeholders.

Exam Alert!

1. What is the output of the plan quality management process?

   a) Project management plan

   b) Project documents

   c) Risk management plan

   d) Quality management plan

Answer: *d*. Option *a* is the output for develop project plan, *c* is the output for plan risk management, and *b* is not the output for the plan quality management process.

2. Which best describes the plan quality management process?

a) The process of identifying quality requirements and standards for the project and its deliverables and documenting how the project will demonstrate compliance with quality requirements and standards

b) The process of monitoring and recording the results of executing the quality management activities to assess performance and ensure the project outputs are complete, correct, and meet customer requirements

c) The process of translating the quality management plan into executable quality activities that incorporate the organization's quality policies into the project

d) None of the above

Answer: *a.* Option *b* is monitoring quality. Option *c* is managing quality, and *d* is not the answer.

9.1 Plan Resource Management

According to PMBOK, the *plan resource management* process defines how to estimate, acquire, manage, and use team resources. The resources can be either physical (like equipment) or people.[46]

Case Study— IT Infrastructure Project in the Role of Technical Project Manager

In the IT infrastructure project, the physical resources are the computer systems, the operating system, the database systems, the storage systems, and the application system.

A people resource, such as a hardware, software, or storage administrator, will be necessary to own the implementation of each physical resource such as hardware, software, and storage.

Also, system administrators, application administrators, and database administrators are necessary for the responsibilities of installation, upgrading, migrations, and management.

These resources will need to be acquired or developed and managed and, in the case of people resources, may need to be hired or trained.

46 *PMBOK Guide*, Sixth Edition, 312.

A best practice is to look for qualified resources within the organization first because it may be cheaper and/or a known commodity and HR approval, background checks, security, and funds approval may be simpler.

If going outside the organization, ask team members about professionals they know and have worked with who can do the work.

Lastly, advertise to find qualified candidates, narrow the list, then vet qualified candidates based on the criteria identified for the position. If all things are equal for candidates based on criteria on a résumé and the interviews, then it will come down to who is most cost efficient. Someone who is local is likely to be more cost efficient than someone who must travel because of expenses incurred such as airfare, housing, and meals.

Process	Inputs	Tools and Techniques	Outputs
9.1 Plan Resource Management	Project charter Project management plan » Quality management plan » Scope baseline » Project documents » Project schedule » Requirements documentation Risk register Stakeholder register OPA EEF	Expert judgments Data representation » Hierarchical charts » Responsibility assignment matrix » Text-oriented formats » Organizational theory Meetings	Resource management plan Team charter PMP updates » Assumption log » Risk register

Inputs

The *project charter* contains designated resources and project objectives.

The *project management plan* includes

» Quality management plan

» Scope baseline

» Project documents

- » Project schedule

- » Requirements documentation

The *risk register* is the list of known risks for the project.

The *stakeholder register* is the list of stakeholders for the project.

Organizational process assets are the procedures, policies, practices, and lessons learned that influence resource planning.

Enterprise environmental factors are the external and internal factors out of the project team's control that influence resource planning.

Tools and Techniques

Expert judgments are considerations provided by sources that have expertise in planning resources for a project like this one.

Data representation: Hierarchical charts include the WBS, the organizational breakdown structure (OBS), or the resource breakdown structure (RBS). OBS can be defined as a model that is structured to help identify which employees will be responsible for specific parts of a project.[47]

- » The *responsibility assignment matrix* shows the resources assigned to each work package in the WBS. It is a tool used for the assignment of roles and responsibilities.

- » *Text-oriented formats* are also used to described team member roles and responsibilities.

Organizational theory provides information on the way that people, teams, and organizational units behave. Organizations are defined as social units of people that are structured and managed to meet a need or to pursue collective goals.

Meetings can be held when planning resource management.

---

47   Study.com, "Organizational Breakdown: Definition & Example," https://study.com/academy/lesson/organizational-breakdown-structure-definition-example.html.

Requirements Traceability Matrix									
Project Name	IT HA, DR, Upgrade/Migration Project								
Cost Center	6007								
Project Description	Build Unbreakable System								
ID	**Associate ID**	**Requirements Description**	**Business Needs**	**Project Objectives**	**WBS Deliverables**	**Project Design**	**Product Development**	**Test Cases**	
001	1.0	Primary	Continuous service	Build 24 x 7 system	Primary system	Oracle® RAC	Production	Previous Prod Environment	
	1.1	Database Creation							
	1.2.1	Oracle® Real Application Clusters (RAC)							
002	2.0	Secondary	Backup system	Disaster Recovery	Secondary system	Oracle® DG	Production	Previous Prod Environment	
	2.1	Database Creation							
	2.2.1	Oracle® Data Guard (DG)							

Figure 9. Requirements traceability matrix

Outputs

The *resource management plan* is a component of the project management plan that guides how project resources will be acquired, developed, allocated, managed, and released.

The *team charter* is a document that establishes team values, team agreements, and operating guidelines for the team. The team charter will contain information on how to handle conflict resolution, decision-making, and communication.

The *project management plan updates* are made to the *assumption log* and the *risk register* for known resource-related issues.

Exam Alert!

1. The process of defining how to estimate, acquire, manage, and utilize physical and team resources fits which process?

    a) Develop team

    b) Plan resource management

    c) Organizational theory

    d) Team charter

Answer: *b.* The key word here is how, which describes plan. In this case plan resource management.

9.2 Estimate Activity Resources

According to PMBOK, the *estimate activity resources* process estimates team resources and the quantity of materials, equipment, and supplies necessary to perform project work.[48] Before implementing the project, the project manager wants to know how much it will cost in equipment and labor. This process can accurately or broadly determine the estimate, depending on which tool or technique is used.

> ### Case Study— IT Infrastructure Project in the Role of Technical Project Manager
>
> In the IT infrastructure project, I used the project management plan to guide me on how the project would be designed, managed, monitored and controlled, and closed. To determine the cost of a resource, first I looked at historical documentation. Second, I looked at what the market would bear for the resource. Third, I factored on how long it would take to accomplish a task and used expert judgment and the PERT formula to determine the cost.
>
> What you paid for a resource on a prior project is a wonderful place to start. Also, advertisement for specific resources with pay rates for appropriate skill levels for the region is needed. If candidates are not responding in abundance, then adjust your advertising tactics to find more qualified candidates.

---

48 *PMBOK Guide*, Sixth Edition, 320.

Process	Inputs	Tools and Techniques	Outputs
9.2 Estimate Activity Resources	Project management plan » Resource management plan » Scope baseline Project documents » Activity attributes » Activity list » Assumption log » Cost estimates » Resource calendars » Risk register OPA EEF	Expert judgments Analogous estimating Parametric estimating Three-point estimating Bottom-up estimating Data analysis » Alternative analysis PMIS Meetings	Resource requirements Basis estimates Resource breakdown structure (RBS) Project document updates » Activity attributes » Assumption log » Lessons learned register

Inputs

The *resource management plan* and *scope baseline* are subsidiary plans of the *project management plan* used as a guide to acquire, develop, and manage resources. And the scope baseline will have information on the project and project scope necessary to meet the project objectives.

Project documents include the *activity attributes, activity list, assumptions log, cost estimates, resource calendars,* and *risk register.*

Organizational process assets are the procedures, policies, practices, and lessons learned that influence the process.

Enterprise environmental factors are the external and internal factors out of the project team's control that influence the process.

Tools and Techniques

Expert judgments are considerations provided by experts that give immediate insight into how long an activity may take.

Analogous estimating is the historical estimating from a very similar project of the same size for cost estimation.

Parametric estimating is also the historical estimating from a very similar project, though one that is different in size.

Three-point estimating is more of an exact science, using a tested formula to estimate activity duration.

Bottom-up estimating is the most accurate way to determine activity duration. Bottom-up estimating gets analysis information from the lower-level components of the WBS. Bottom-up estimating takes longer but is the most accurate way of schedule and cost estimation.

Data analysis includes *alternative analysis*, which is a diverse way of capturing duration information whether the analysis is manual or automatic.

PMIS is project management software that helps manage the project more effectively. When tasks are properly entered, time, costs, and resources can be automatically managed even when changes to the project plan are made.

Meetings to plan resources estimates are strongly encouraged.

Outputs

Resource requirements identify the types and amounts of resources necessary for the project.

Basis estimates are the details that support how the resource requirements were determined and what tools and techniques, assumptions, range of estimates, confidence levels, and documentation were used.

The *resource breakdown structure (RBS)* is a list of necessary people, equipment, and supplies by category.

Project documents updates are made to the *activity attributes*, *assumption log*, and *lessons learned register*.

Exam Alert!

1.   Theodore is a new project manager with minimal experience in acquiring proper resources to do the necessary work. The following tools and techniques can assist Theodore to estimate resources except

   a) Bottom-up estimating

   b) Analogous estimating

   c) Parametric estimating

   d) Resource breakdown structure (RBS)

Answer: *d. a, b,* and *c* can help in estimating resources.

10.1 Plan Communications Management

According to PMBOK, the *plan communications management* process develops an approach and plan for project communications activities based on the information needs of each stakeholder and the project.[49] Communication is the most important process when managing a project, because as a project manager, you are managing people, what work they are doing, when they are doing the work, how long it will take them to complete the work, and conflict resolution.

> For the IT infrastructure project manager, planning communication was based on stakeholder information needs. We combined communications types, such as:
>
> » communication technology
>
> » communication models
>
> » communication skills
>
> These methods are explained in this section.

Process	Inputs	Tools and Techniques	Outputs
10.1 Plan Communications Management	Project charter Project management plan » Resource management plan » Stakeholder engagement plan Project documents » Requirements documentation » Stakeholder register OPA EEF	Expert judgments Communications requirements analysis Communication technology Communication models Communication skills PMIS Project reporting Interpersonal and team skills » Communication styles assessment » Political awareness » Cultural awareness Data Representation » Stakeholder engagement assessment matrix Meetings	Communications management plan PMP updates » Stakeholder engagement plan Project documents updates » Project schedule » Stakeholder register Organizational process assets updates

---

49   *PMBOK Guide*, Sixth Edition, 366.

Inputs

The *project charter* will have information such as policies, procedures, processes, and templates that can be used to assist the project manager and project team on project communication.

The *project management plan* is a how-to guide on how the project will be designed, managed, monitored and controlled, and closed. The project management plan contains the *resource management plan* and the *stakeholder engagement plan*.

» The resource management plan is the guide to how resources will be allocated, acquired, developed, managed, and released. Team members may have communication requirements that have been defined in the communications management plan.

» The stakeholder engagement plan contains the communication management strategies identified to engage stakeholders.

Project documents include the *requirements documentation* and the *stakeholder register*.

Organizational process assets are the policies, practices, procedures, templates, and lessons learned that influence the communications management plan.

Enterprise environmental factors are the internal and external factors that are out of the project team's control that influence the communications management plan.

Tools and Techniques

Expert judgments are considerations provided by those with expertise and specialized knowledge in planning communications management.

The *communications requirements analysis* combines communications types and formats as needed to maximize the value of the information for project stakeholders. A list of project stakeholders can be found in the stakeholder register. The communications requirements analysis also includes an organization chart showing the power and influence level of stakeholders, the development approach, and the number of communication channels. Analysis can also include legal requirements and logistics of how many persons will be involved in the project and at which locations.

The number of communication channels can be calculated using the formula

$$N(N - 1) / 2; \text{ where } N = \text{ the number of people}$$

For example:

Joleen is a new project manager for World Force Inc. Joleen's team consists of 6 members including Joleen. Two new members have just been added. What is the number of channels of communication?

a) 13

b) 12

c) 15

d) 28

Answer: *d.*

The communication channel formula is n (n + 1) / 2

$$6 + 2 = 8$$

$$8(7) = 56$$

$$56 / 2 = 28$$

Communication technology includes shared portals, video and conferencing, chats, databases, social media, email, and websites.

Communication models include encoding, which is transmitting the message, and decoding, which is receiving the message. For example, someone wants to deliver a message and have it read and understood by the receiving person or audience. The letter would be carefully written and formatted based on the perceived audience (encode). The letter would then be placed in an envelope and mailed. Once the letter reaches the receiver or audience, the letter would be opened and read (decode). Hopefully, the message will be understood as intended. The same happens whether we communicate with others via phone, conference, email, or document.

Communication methods are interactive (multidirectional conversations), push (emails), and pull (shared storage, portals, or websites).

Project reporting for the project team, stakeholders, sponsor, and senior management is strongly recommended for stakeholder engagement. Project team members want a status so they know when their involvement is needed, stakeholders want to be informed on how the project affects them, the sponsor wants to know the status and how the project is progressing, and senior management want a summary and the percent completion of the project.

Interpersonal and team skills needed are *communication styles assessment, political awareness,* and *cultural awareness.* Communication styles assessment of the stakeholder engagement plan defines what additional tailoring of communication methods or communication technology is needed for the stakeholder. Political awareness is understanding the organizational and political environment and recognizing power and relationships, both formal and informal, within the organization because no project operates in a vacuum. Cultural awareness is understanding the differences between themselves and people from other countries or other backgrounds, especially in attitudes and values. Being culturally aware can improve work relations with people from different backgrounds Better work relations can mean better collaboration or compromise and improve performance on the job.

Data representation is a *stakeholder engagement assessment matrix* that can identify gaps between current and desired engagement levels of individual stakeholders.

Meetings, whether virtual or face to face, are also used to develop the communications plan.

Outputs

Effective communication is the key to successful project management. The *communications management plan* is the guide to effective project communications. The communications management plan defines who should be given specific information, when that information should be delivered, and what communication channels will be used to deliver the information. The communications plan also describes how project communications will be planned, structured, implemented, and monitored for effectiveness.

Project management plan updates are made to *the stakeholder engagement plan* to reflect any processes, policies, procedure, tools, and techniques that affect the engagement of stakeholders in project decisions and execution.

Project documents updates are made to the *project schedule* and *stakeholder register*. There may also be *organizational process assets updates*.

Exam Alert!

1.   Which is a tool and technique of plan communications management?

   a)   Change log

   b)   Project management plan

c) Manage quality

d) Interpersonal and team skills

Answer: *d.* Option *b* is an input, *c* is process, and *a* is an output.

2.   Which answer below best fits the tools and technique of plan communication management?

a) Change log

b) Project management plan

c) Manage quality

d) Communication technology

Answer: *d.* Change log and project management plan are never a tool and technique. Manage quality is a process.

3.   Conversations and meetings are part of which tool and technique?

a) Communications analysis

b) Communications technology

c) Communications model

d) Communications method

Answer: *b.* Communications analysis describes what is needed to maximize the value of information of project stakeholders. Communications technology includes shared portals, emails, and databases. Communications model is the encoding and decoding of messages. And communication method is the interaction of information such as one way or multidirectional conversations.

11.1 Plan Risk Management

According to PMBOK, the *plan risk management* process defines how to conduct risk management activities.[50] Risks are the events that have been foreseen as possible, so it is wise to have a risk plan. Ask yourself the following questions:

1. What is the probability something can happen?

2. What will be the cost and time impact on the project if the risk does occur?

3. What is the response strategy to handle individual risk?

Case Study— IT Infrastructure Project in the Role of Technical Project Manager

There will always be assumptions, constraints, and risks in projects. Assumptions are the things we believe are true; for example, a database administrator (DBA) believes the hardware (HW) and software (SW) are set up properly when handed over from the HW and SW teams, and the DBA may proceed with their tasks. Constraints are the limits placed upon a project: for example, a schedule, funds, government regulations, or having a sole resource for one or more of the activities.

When we put in an order for the hardware, then we assume the vendor will send what we ordered. However, if the vendor says that the product is out of stock, then a risk response strategy is to have an alternate vendor ready to deliver.

Process	Inputs	Tools and Techniques	Outputs
11.1 Plan Risk Management	Project charter Project management plan » All subsidiary plans Project documents » Stakeholder register EEF OPA	Expert judgments Data analysis Meetings	Risk management plan » Methodology » Roles and responsibilities » Funding » Timing » Risk categories Probability and impact matrix Revised stakeholder tolerances Tracking

---

50   *PMBOK Guide*, Sixth Edition, 401.

Inputs

The *project charter* contains the high-level risks and constraints, initial stakeholders, and things internal and external to the organization that might have an impact on the project.

The *project management plan* is a how-to guide on how the project will be designed, managed, monitored and controlled, and closed, including how risks are planned for, implemented, and controlled. *All subsidiary plans* may involve some risks.

Project documents needed as input include the *stakeholder register.* The stakeholders will have risk tolerance. Risk tolerance is the specified range of acceptable results.

Enterprise environmental factors are the internal and external factors that are influenced by project risks.

Organizational process assets are policies, practices, procedures, and lessons learned that are influenced by project risks.

Tools and Techniques

Expert judgments are considerations provided by those with experience or specialized knowledge in creating a risk management plan.

Data analysis is used to determine the communications type, models, and technology needed to communicate risk management for this project and the stakeholders.

Meetings are held to create the risk management plan. Meetings can be either face to face or virtual.

Outputs

The *risk management plan* includes the risk strategy, which is the general approach to managing the risk. *Methodology* is the approaches, tools, and data sources to perform risk management, the *roles and responsibilities* of risk management team members; *funding* to perform risk management tasks from contingency and management reserves; *timing* on when risk management will be performed throughout project life cycle; and *risk categories* usually structured with a risk breakdown structure (RBS). RBS is a hierarchal structure of potential resources to risk.

Figure 10 Example: Risk Breakdown Structure

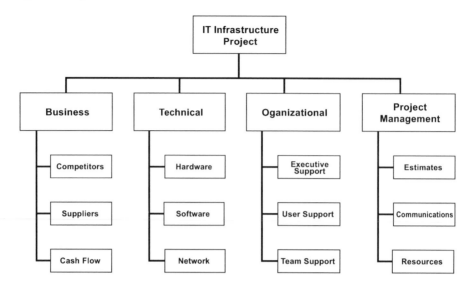

Exam Alert!

1.   Which of the following depicts the order of activities in plan risk management?

    a) Collect requirements, define scope, and create WBS

    b) Identify risks, perform qualitative risk analysis, perform quantitative risk analysis, and plan risk responses

    c) Plan schedule management, define activities, sequence activities, estimate activity resources, estimate activity costs, and develop schedule

    d) Estimate costs and determine budget

Answer: *b.* Only b describes plan risk management.

2.   Which is a tool and technique of plan risk management?

    a) Stakeholder analysis

    b) Project documents

    c) Decomposition

    d) Project management plan updates

Answer: *a*. *Project documents* is an input, *decomposition* is a tool and technique of create WBS and define activities, and *project management plan updates* is an output of other processes.

11.2 Identify Risks

According to PMBOK, the *identify risks* process identifies individuals' risks as well as sources of overall project risks and documents their characteristics.[51] Identifying risks, assessing the risk probability of those outcomes, quantifying the loss because of a risk occurring, and designing a risk response strategy are all very important parts of project management. The more requirements and information that are discovered, the more the risk is eliminated or at least reduced and made manageable.

Identified Risks in the IT Infrastructure Project	
Categories of risk	Individual risk
Technical	Hardware, software, network, application, database
Business	Competitors, suppliers, cash flow
Organizational	Executive support, user support, team support
Project management	Estimates, communication, resources

These are just a few of the risk categories to consider. Each risk category will be further decomposed into individual risks.

---

51   *PMBOK Guide,* Sixth Edition, 409.

Process	Inputs	Tools and Techniques	Outputs
11.2 Identify Risks	Project management plan » Requirements management plan » Schedule management plan » Cost management plan » Quality management plan » Resource management plan » Risk management plan » Scope baseline » Schedule baseline » Cost baseline Project documents » Assumptions log » Cost estimates » Duration estimates » Issues log » Lessons learned register » Requirements documentation » Stakeholder register Agreements Procurement documents EEF OPA	Expert judgments Data gathering » Brainstorming » Checklists » Interviews Data analysis » Root cause analysis » Assumption and constraint analysis » SWOT analysis » Document analysis Interpersonal and team skills Facilitation Prompt lists Meetings	Risk register Risk report Project documents updates » Assumption log » Issues log » Lessons learned register

Inputs

The *project management plan* is a how-to guide on how the project will be designed, managed, monitored and controlled, and closed, including risk planning.

» The *requirements management plan* indicates project objectives that are at risk.

» The *schedule management plan* indicates areas of the schedule that could be at risk.

» The *cost management plan* indicates areas of cost that may be at risk.

» The *quality management plan* may indicate areas of quality that may be at risk.

» The *resource management plan* may identify areas of resources that may be at risk due to constraints and assumptions.

» The *risk management plan* is a document that a project manager prepares to foresee risks; estimate impacts; and define responses to issues, roles, and responsibilities.

» The *scope baseline* acts as the reference point through the project life. It has several components.

These include the project scope document, the WBS itself, and the WBS dictionary.

» The *schedule baseline* is the approved version of a schedule that can be changed only through formal change control procedures and is used as a basis for comparison to actual results.

» The *cost baseline* is used as an example in which cost performance is measured and monitored to gauge the importance of the project. This cost baseline is created by estimating the costs by the period in which the project would be completed.

Project documents include the *assumptions log, cost estimates, duration estimates, issues log, lessons learned register, requirements documentation, resource requirements,* and *stakeholder register*.

Agreements can be subject to risk because of contract type, milestones, acceptance criteria, threats, and opportunities.

Procurement documents from external resources could contain additional risks when procuring goods and services.

Enterprise environmental factors include published material, academic studies, benchmarking, and similar projects that could influence risks.

Organizational process assets are procedures, processes, and practices that could influence risks.

Tools and Techniques

Expert judgments are considerations provided by those with experience in and specialized knowledge of identifying risks.

Data gathering:

» Project team members use *brainstorming* to identify risks under the guidance of a facilitator.

» Project team members use *checklists* of risks from previous projects.

» Project team members use *interviews* with experienced project participants, stakeholders, and subject matter experts.

Data analysis at this stage may include *root cause analysis*. Root cause analysis is used to discover the underlying cause that leads to a problem and develop a preventive action.

Assumption and constraint analysis

Assumptions and constraints can be anything; they might be related to resources, budget, time or any kind of functionally.[52]

The *SWOT analysis* analyzes the project's strengths, weaknesses, opportunities, and threats. The technique starts with identification of strengths and weaknesses of the organization, the project, or the business. The analysis examines the threats and opportunities that may arise because of weakness or strengths respectively.

Document analysis is where risks are identified.

Interpersonal and team skills are necessary to manage personalities when identifying risks

Facilitation drives the agenda of the meeting, which in this case is identifying risks.

Prompt lists are predetermined lists of categorized risks to help guide meetings.

Meetings are undertaken to discuss risks.

Outputs

The *risk register* is a list of identified risks, risk owners, and potential risks.

The *risk report* includes sources of overall project risks. This report is developed progressively throughout the project risk management process.

Project documents updates are made to the *assumption log*, *issues log*, and *lessons learned register*.

Exam Alert!

1.   The output to identify risk is

   a)   Project management plan

   b)   Procurement plan

   c)   Project documents

   d)   Risk register

Answer: *d.* Answers *a*, *b*, and *c* are inputs to other processes.

2.   Which is an output of the plan risk management process?

   a)   Project management plan

   b)   Communications management plan

---

52   *Assumptions and Constraints in Project Management, https://pmstudycircle.com/2012/10/assumptions-and-constraints-in-project-management/*

c) Data analysis

d) Risk management plan

Answer: *d*. Options *a* and *b* are outputs to develop project plan and plan communication management, respectively; *c* is a tool and technique to other processes.

11.3 Perform Qualitative Risk Analysis

According to PMBOK, the *perform qualitative risk analysis* process prioritizes individual project risks for further analysis by assessing their probability of occurrence and impact as well as other characteristics.[53]

Case Study— IT Infrastructure Project in the Role of Technical Project Manager

When planning risk analysis, I prioritize risk by:

» which risk is most dangerous to the project,

» which risks are most likely to happen, and

» which risks will cost the project the most if they occur.

The risks that occurred most often were during upgrades and migrations of the IT infrastructure project. When upgrading the operating system, cluster software, or database software, we were mostly concerned with whether the application would break afterward. We checked for known issues in release documents, and we tested in development environments and QA test environments before deploying into production environments.

With migrations, there was a possibility of data corruption during conversion, so again we tested in development environments and QA test environments before deploying into production environments.

For both migrations and upgrades, there were always performance issues, which the project team attempted to design in the architecture or fix in development environments and QA test environments, but the overall solution would usually happen once deployed into production environments using live transactions.

---

53 *PMBOK Guide*, Sixth Edition, 419.

Process	Inputs	Tools and Techniques	Outputs
11.3 Perform Qualitative Risk Analysis	Project management plan » Risk management plan Project documents » Assumptions log » Risk register » Stakeholder register OPA EEF	Expert judgments Data gathering » Interviews of » data analysts » Risk data quality assessment » Risk probability and impact assessment » Assessment of other risk parameters Interpersonal and team skills » Facilitation Risk categorization Data representation » Probability and impact matrix » Hierarchical charts	Project documents updates » Assumptions log » Issues log » Risk register » Risk report

Inputs

The *project management plan* is a how-to guide on how the project will be designed, managed, monitored and controlled, and closed, including risk planning. The *risk management plan* is a document that a project manager prepares to foresee risks, estimate impacts, and define responses to issues, which will be used to perform qualitative risk analysis.

Project documents used to perform qualitative risk analysis are the *assumptions log*, *risk register*, and *stakeholder register*.

Organizational process assets and *enterprise environmental factors* are also used to perform qualitative risk analysis because of policies, practices, and procedures as well as those things beyond the control of the project team.

Tools and Techniques

Expert judgments are considerations provided by those with experience in and specialized knowledge of qualitative risk analysis.

Data gathering is done using *interviews of data analysts*, *risk data quality assessment*, *risk probability and impact assessment*, and *assessment of other risk parameters*.

Interpersonal and team skills are important, such as *facilitation* to drive meetings and gather information for performing qualitative risk analysis.

Risk categorization or grouping of risks is usually structured with a risk breakdown structure (RBS). RBS is a hierarchal structure of potential resources to risk. Risk is categorized to determine areas of the project most exposed and common root causes. Grouping risks this way can lead to a more effective risk response plan.

Data representation includes a *probability and impact matrix* showing the likelihood a risk might occur and *hierarchical charts*, such as bubble charts. Essentially, bubble charts are like XY scatter graphs except that each point on the scatter graph has an additional data value associated with it that is represented by the size of a circle or "bubble" centered around the XY point.[54] Bubble charts are often used in business to visualize the relationships between projects or investment alternatives in dimensions such as cost, value, and risk.

Meetings on information gathering and analysis are held for performing qualitative risk analysis.

Example: Probability and Impact Matrix[55]

Probability	Threats					Opportunities				
0.90	0.05	0.09	0.18	0.36	0.72	0.72	0.36	0.18	0.09	0.05
0.70	0.04	0.07	0.14	0.28	0.56	0.56	0.28	0.14	0.07	0.04
0.50	0.03	0.05	0.10	0.20	0.40	0.40	0.20	0.10	0.05	0.03
0.30	0.02	0.03	0.06	0.12	0.24	0.24	0.12	0.06	0.03	0.02
0.10	0.01	0.01	0.02	0.04	0.08	0.08	0.04	0.02	0.01	0.01
	0.05	0.10	0.20	0.40	0.80	0.80	0.40	0.20	0.10	0.05

Probability and Impact Matrix

Impact (numerical scale) on an objective (e.g., cost, time, scope or quality)

Each risk is rated on its probability of occurring and impact on an objective if it does occur. The organization's thresholds for low, moderate or high risks are shown in the matrix and determine whether the risk is scored as high, moderate or low for that objective.

---

54   What Are Bubble Charts, http://www.bubblechartpro.com/content/what_are_bubble_charts.php

55   *PMBOK Guide*, Sixth Edition, 408.

The probability impact matrix is the process of assessing the probabilities and consequences of risk events if they are realized. The results of this assessment are then used to prioritize risks to establish a most-to-least-critical importance ranking.[56]

Outputs

Project documents updates are made to:

» assumptions log

» issues log

» risk register

» risk report

Exam Alert!

1. A tool and technique that can be used in assessing risk impact is

   a) Project management plan

   b) Project document updates

   c) Risk probability and impact assessment

   d) Risk register

Answer: *c.* Risk probability and impact assessment is the only tool and technique in the list of answers. A project management plan is a document, Project documents updates is an output. A risk register is a document.

2. Which is an input to the process perform qualitative risk analysis?

   a) Project management plan

   b) Alternative analysis

   c) OPA updates

   d) EEF updates

Answer: *a.* Project management plan is an input. An alternative analysis is a tool and technique. OPA updates and EEF updates are outputs

---

56 MITRE, *Systems Engineering Guide*, "Risk Impact Assessment and Prioritization" https://www.mitre.org/publications/systems-engineering-guide/acquisition-systems-engineering/risk-management/risk-impact-assessment-and-prioritization.

11.4 Perform Quantitative Risk Analysis

According to PMBOK, the *perform quantitative risk analysis* process numerically analyzes the combined effect of identified individual project risks.[57]

Before we begin, let me say that perform quantitative risk analysis is not required for all projects. This process requires the availability of high-quality data about the project risks and an understanding of the project baseline for scope, time, and costs.

This process also requires information that has been assessed by the perform qualitative risk analysis process as having a significant impact on the project objects.

Case Study— IT Infrastructure Project in the Role of Technical Project Manager

For example, in the IT infrastructure project, the risk items that could have an impact on the project's objects were application malfunction from migrations, upgrades, or performance issues.

Using expert knowledge and skills can provide insight into other approaches that were successful with less risk to the project.

Simulations, such as the Monte Carlo analysis, also use models to evaluate the impact on achieving project objectives by running either cost risk or schedule risk analysis. The output is quantitative risk analysis documents.

Sensitivity analysis is used to determine which project risks have the most potential impact on the project outcome.

---

57   *PMBOK Guide,* Sixth Edition, 428.

Process	Inputs	Tools and Techniques	Outputs
11.4 Perform Quantitative Risk Analysis	Project management plan » Risk management plan » Scope baseline » Schedule baseline » Cost baseline Project documents » Assumption log » Basis of estimates » Cost estimates » Cost forecasts » Duration estimates » Milestone list » Risk register » Risk report » Schedule forecasts OPA EEF	Expert judgments Data gathering » Interviews Interpersonal and team skills » Facilitation Representations of uncertainty Data analysis » Simulations » Sensitivity analysis » Decision tree analysis » Influence diagrams	Project documents updates » Risk report » Assessment of overall project risks » Detail probabilistic analysis of project » Prioritized list of individual project risks » Trends in the quantitative risk analysis results » Recommended risk responses

Inputs

The *project management plan* is a how-to guide on how the project will be designed, managed, monitored and controlled, and closed, including risk planning.

» The *risk management plan* is a document that a project manager prepares to foresee risks, estimate impacts, and define responses to issues identified for performing quantitative risk analysis.

» The *scope baseline* acts as a reference point for which requirements are included and which are not. It has several components. These include the project scope document, the WBS itself, and the WBS dictionary.

» The *schedule baseline* is the approved version of a schedule that can be changed only through formal change control procedures and is used as a basis for comparison to actual results.

» The *cost baseline* is used as an example in which cost performance is measured and monitored to gauge the importance of the project. This cost baseline is created by estimating the costs by the period that the project will be completed.

Project documents used are the *assumption log, basis of estimates, cost estimates, cost forecasts, duration estimates, milestone list, risk register, risk report,* and *schedule forecasts.*

Organizational process assets and *enterprise environmental factors* are also used in this process for policies, practices, and procedures as well as internal and external influences out of the project team's control.

Tools and Techniques

Expert judgments are considerations provided by those who have experience and specialized knowledge in performing quantitative risk analysis.

Data gathering techniques include holding *interviews* to gather information on performing quantitative risk analysis.

Interpersonal and team skills such as *facilitation* are needed. A project manager needs to drive the agenda of meeting—in this case, to perform quantitative risk analysis.

Representations of uncertainty such as representations of risk in duration, cost, or resource requirement use a probability distribution such as triangular, normal, lognormal, beta, uniform, or discrete distributions. What impact would it have on a project if duration, cost, or resource requirements were to change? Outcomes of probability distribution are best seen with simulation techniques such Monte Carlo or PMIS.

Data analysis tools used in this process may include *simulations*, *sensitivity analysis*, *decision tree analysis*, and *influence diagrams*. Those in project management must be aware of the means of modeling risks to their projects. Sensitivity analysis is one such method. It is implemented to analyze the various risks to the project by looking at all aspects of the project and their potential impact on the overall goal.[58]

Example: Tornado Diagram or Sensitivity Analysis

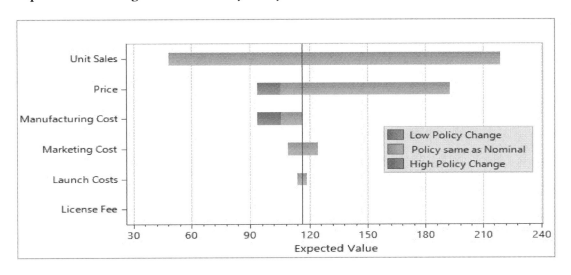

---

58   Project Management Knowledge, "Sensitivity Analysis," https://project-management-knowledge.com/definitions/s/sensitivity-analysis/.

Example: Expected Monetary Value

In the example above, unit sales has the highest sensitivity of risk, with a monetary value slightly above 210, followed by price with a monetary value above 180.

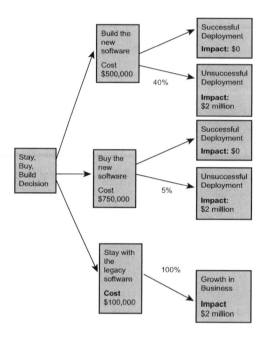

Example: Cost Risk Simulation

In this example of deciding whether to stay, buy, or build, though the legacy system looks tempting because the cost is lower and the impact the same, staying with a legacy system is staying with outdated technology. The real choice is between building and buying the new software. However, if you follow PMP philosophy and logic, then the legacy answer will be the correct answer because it has 100 percent chance of success and impact.

Outputs

The *project documents updates* contain the *risk report document*, *assessment of overall project risks*, *detail probabilistic analysis of the project*, *prioritized list of individual project risks*, *trends in the quantitative risk analysis results*, and *recommended risk responses*.

Exam Alert!

1. Which answer is the best description of perform quantitative risk analysis?

    a) It is the process of numerically analyzing the effect of identified risks on overall project objects.

    b) It is the process by which we identify risks, perform qualitative risk analysis, perform quantitative risk analysis, and plan risk responses.

    c) It is the process by which we plan schedule management, define activities, sequence activities, estimate activity resources, estimate activity costs, and develop schedules.

    d) It involves estimating costs and determining budget.

Answer: *a.* The one key word I always look for in this quesiton is "numerically."

2. Which is both an input and output of the process perform quantitative risk analysis?

    a) Risk report

    b) Analysis report

    c) Rolling wave

    d) Decomposition

Answer: *a.* *c* and *d* are both tools and techniques of other processes. *b* does not exist.

11.5 Plan Risk Responses

According to PMBOK, the *plan risk responses* process develops strategies and actions to address project risk exposure.[59] The best time to manage risk is before the risk occurs. Plan how risk will be managed and identify as many risks for the project as possible through meetings, interviews, and past projects. Determine the likelihood the risk will occur, its impact on the project, and the potential cost. Lastly, take more preventive measures on risk by having a risk response strategy.

After implementing the risk response plan, either secondary risks or residual risks can be created as an aftereffect.

---

59 *PMBOK Guide*, Sixth Edition, 437.

The PMBOK guide defines *secondary risks* as "those risks that arise as a direct outcome of implementing a risk response."[60] In simple terms, you identify risk and have a response plan in place to deal with that risk. Once this plan is implemented, a new risk that may arise from the implementation tactics.

Residual risks are the leftover risks, the minor risks that remain. The PMBOK guide defines residual risks as "those risks that are expected to remain after the planned response of risk has been taken, as well as those that have been deliberately accepted."[61]

Case Study— IT Infrastructure Project in the Role of Technical Project Manager

We established in this project that there were risks regarding applications and database instabilities because of migrations and performance. There may also be database risks due to software or database upgrades. Any unknown risk will be discovered and solved in the development environment; performed again in the QA test environment; and lastly deployed into the production environment where most or all installation, upgrade, and migration risk will have been resolved.

Also, as stated before, we can take preventive measures by performing all planned installations, upgrades, and migrations in development (first) and a QA test environment (second) before deploying them into the production environment.

With this method we minimize and eliminate risks, thereby improving the likelihood of a successful project closing to the customer satisfaction.

---

60   SimpliLearn, "Residual Risk versus Secondary Risk," June 20, 2018, https://www.simplilearn.com/residual-risk-versus-secondary-risk-article.

61   Ibid.

Process	Inputs	Tools and Techniques	Outputs
11.5 Plan Risk Responses	Project management plan » Resource management plan » Risk management plan » Cost baseline Project documents » Lessons learned register » Project schedule » Project team assignments » Resource calendars » Risk register » Risk report » Stakeholder register OPA EEF	Expert judgments Data gathering » Interviews Interpersonal and team skills » Facilitation Data analysis » Alternative analysis Decision-making » Multicriteria decision analysis Contingency response strategies Strategies for overall project risk » Strategies for threats » Strategies for opportunities	Change requests Project management plan updates » Schedule management plan » Cost management plan » Quality management plan » Resource management plan » Procurement management plan » Scope baseline » Schedule baseline » Cost baseline Project documents updates » Assumptions log » Cost forecasts » Lessons learned register » Project schedule » Project team assignments » Risk register » Risk report

Inputs

The *project management plan* is a how-to guide on how the project will be designed, managed, monitored and controlled, and closed, including risk planning and risk response strategy.

» The *resource management plan* is the efficient and effective development of an organization's resources when they are needed.

» The *risk management plan* is a document that a project manager prepares to foresee risks, estimate impacts, and define responses to issues.

» The *cost baseline* is used as an example in which cost performance is measured and monitored to gauge the importance of the project. This cost baseline is created by estimating the costs by the period that the project will be completed.

Project documents used to help generate the risk responses strategy are *lessons learned register, project schedule, project team assignments, resource calendars, risk register, risk report,* and *stakeholder register.*

Organizational process assets and *enterprise environmental factors* are used to help generate risk response strategy for policies, practices, and procedures as well as internal and external influences the project team has no control over.

Tools and Techniques

Expert judgments are considerations provided by those with experience in and specialized knowledge of strategies for threats, strategies for opportunities, contingency response strategies, and strategies for overall project risk.

Data gathering techniques include holding *interviews* around planning risk responses.

Interpersonal and team skills include using *facilitation* techniques to drive the agenda of meetings.

Data analysis in this stage includes *alternative analysis*.

Decision-making techniques may include *multicriteria decision analysis*. Multicriteria decision analysis is a method of assigning weighted scores for a more qualitative evaluation method of which resource to choose. For example, when choosing a project team member, which criteria is most important among availability, cost, experience, ability, knowledge, skills, attitude, and international factors?

Contingency response strategies are designed only if certain events should occur, such as missing milestones or gaining higher priority with the seller.

Strategies for overall project risk are strategies for negative risks or threats.

Strategies for Negative Risks or Threats

Escalate	The threat is beyond the scope of the project or beyond the project manager's authority.
Avoid	Change the plan to eliminate the threat.
Transfer	Shift the threat to a third party.
Mitigate	Reduce the probability of the occurrence of the threat.
Accept	Acknowledge the risk and take no action unless it happens.

Strategies for Positive Risks or Opportunities

Escalate	The opportunity is beyond the scope of the project or beyond project manager's authority.
Exploit	Ensure the opportunity does happen.
Enhance	Increase the chances the opportunity will happen.
Share	Share the ownership with a third party.
Accept	Acknowledge the opportunity and take no action unless it happens.

Outputs

This process could result in *change requests* in case of a change in cost, schedule, or other components of the project management plan.

Project management plan updates:

» *Schedule management plan* is the document developing, maintaining, and communicating schedules for time and resource.

» *Cost management plan* is the document planning and controlling the budget of a business.

» *Quality management plan* defines the acceptable level of quality, which is typically determined by the customer, and describes how the project will ensure this level of quality in its deliverables and work processes.

» *Resource management plan* is the efficient and effective development of an organization's resources when they are needed.

» *Procurement management plan* is the creation of relationships with outside vendors and suppliers for goods and services needed to complete a project.

» Changes in the approved version of the *scope baseline*, *schedule baseline*, or *cost baseline* are incorporated into the scope, schedule, or cost, respectively, in case of implementation of risk response.

Project documents updates can result in changes to the *assumptions log, cost forecasts, lessons learned register, project schedule, project team assignments, risk register,* or *risk report* in case of a risk response implementation.

Exam Alert!

1. All are tools and techniques of the plan risk responses process except

    a) Expert judgments

    b) Interpersonal and team skills

    c) Contingency response strategy

    d) Change requests

Answer: *d.* You can find change requests as an output of all monitoring and control processes.

2. Which is a tool or technique of the plan risk response process?

    a) Interpersonal and team skills

    b) Process improvement plan

    c) Project management plan

    d) Quality management plan

Answer: *a.* *b, c,* and d are never tools and techniques.

12.1 Plan Procurement Management

According to PMBOK, the *plan procurement management* process documents project decisions, specifying the approach and identifying potential sellers.[62]

The best scenario is that all the resources you need to manage and complete the project are colocated and easily accessible. However, the reality is that you'll need to acquire or procure people and/or equipment from outside the organization. A project manager must create a plan for how procurements will be managed.

---

62 *PMBOK Guide*, Sixth Edition, 466.

Case Study— IT Infrastructure Project in the Role of Technical Project Manager

For example, during the planning stage of the IT project, we discovered we needed outside resources, both people and equipment, so we planned to use a cloud environment for the development environment. *Cloud computing* describes a type of outsourcing of computer services, similar to the way in which electricity supply is outsourced.[63]

With cloud computing, we paid an outside vendor for services such as platform as a service (PAAS), service as a service (SAAS), and database as a service (DAAS). Now we had a place to test new installs, upgrades, and migrations for operating systems or databases. We could also test for known issues and devise a strategy for the issues before performing the same install, upgrade, or migration in the QA environment. Because we invested in cloud computing, we were able to deploy in a production environment with confidence.

Also, if professionals were not available within the organization to perform the work, we had a plan to hire outside firms or individuals with the best contract type for the seller and us. That would be fixed price to control cost and time and material when the scope was incomplete.

63   Wikipedia, The Free Encyclopedia, s.v. "Cloud Computing," https://simple.wikipedia.org/wiki/Cloud_computing.

Process	Inputs	Tools and Techniques	Outputs

12.1 Plan Procurement Management	Project Charter
	
	Business documents
	» Business case
	» Benefits management plan
	
	Project management plan
	» Scope management plan
	» Quality management plan
	» Resource management plan
	» Scope baseline
	
	Project documents
	» Milestone list
	» Project team assignments
	» Requirements document
	» Requirements traceability matrix
	» Resource requirements
	» Risk register
	» Stakeholder register
	
	OPA
	
	EEF
		Expert judgments
		
		Data gathering
		
		Market research
		
		Data analysis
		
		    Make or buy analysis
		
		    Source selection analysis
		
		Meetings
			Procurement management plan
			
			Procurement strategy
			
			Procurement statement of work
			
			Source selection criteria
			
			Make-or-buy analysis decision
			
			Independent cost estimates
			
			Change requests
			
			Project documents updates
			» Milestone list
			» Project team assignments
			» Requirements document
			» Requirements traceability matrix
			» Resource requirements
			» Risk register
			» Stakeholder register
			
			OPA updates
			
			Procurement documents
			
			Bid documents

Inputs

The *project charter* contains objectives of the project. The objectives are part of the statement of work (SOW). If there are deliverables that cannot be done with in-house personnel and equipment, then outside resources will be procured.

Business documents includes the *business case* and the *benefits management plan*.

The business case and procurement strategy must be aligned to ensure the business case remains valid. The benefits management plan is a document outlining the activities necessary for achieving the planned **benefits**. It shows a timeline and the tools and resources necessary to ensure the **benefits** are fully realized over time.

The *project management plan* is a guide on how the project will be designed, managed, monitored and controlled, and closed, including how external resources are procured, managed, monitored and controlled, and closed.

» *Scope management plan* is a document that explains how the project scope will be defined, developed, and verified.

» *Quality management plan* defines the acceptable level of quality, which is typically determined by the customer, and describes how the project will ensure this level of quality in its deliverables and work processes.

» *Resource management plan* is the efficient and effective development of an organization's resources when they are needed.

» *Scope baseline acts* as a reference point for which requirements are included and which are not. It has several components. These include project scope document, the WBS itself and the WBS dictionary.

Project documents that are used as inputs to the procurement management plan are the *milestone list*, *project team assignments*, *requirements document*, *requirements traceability matrix*[1], *resource requirements*, *risk register*, and *stakeholder register*.

Organizational process assets and *enterprise environmental factors* may also influence procurement because of procedure, policies, and practices, as well as things out of the project's team control.

Contract Types: Fixed Price Contracts

Firm fixed price contracts (FFP): The FFP is the simplest type of procurement contract because the fee is fixed, and the seller must complete the job for an agreed amount of money and within an agreed amount of time. The seller must pay any cost overruns because of inferior performance or time. This type of contract is mostly used in government or semi-government contracts, in which the scope of work is specified with every detail.

Both parties know the scope of the work and the total cost of the task before the work is started. Any cost increase due to substandard performance of the seller will be the responsibility of the seller.

Fixed price incentive fee contracts (FPIF): In the FPIF, the price is fixed; however, the seller is given an added incentive based on his or her performance.

Example: $30,000 will be paid to the contractor as an incentive if he or she completes the work within two months.

Both parties know the scope of the work and the total cost of the task before the work is started.

This incentive lowers the risk borne by the seller.

Fixed price with economic price adjustment contracts (FP-EPA). Use an FP-EPA for multiyear contracts. Why? Because here you include a special provision in a clause that protects the seller from inflation.

Example: About 3.5% of the cost of the project will be increased after a certain period of time, based on the Consumer Price Index.

Both parties know the scope of the work and the total cost of the task before the work is started.

Purchase order (PO): This type of contract is used to buy commodities.

Example: Buy 10,000 bolts at a cost of $1.00.

Contract Types: Cost-Reimbursable Contracts

Cost plus fixed fee contracts (CPFF): With CPFF, the seller is paid for all the costs he or she incurs plus a fixed fee, which will not change, regardless of his or her performance. This type of contract is used in projects where risk is high, and no one is interested in bidding.

Sometimes this fee will be paid if the seller meets or exceeds the selected project objectives: for example, completing the task before deadline or completing the task with fewer costs than projected.

The seller is reimbursed for completed work plus a fee representing his or her profit. Consider using a CPFF when there is uncertainty about the scope, or the risk is high.

Cost plus incentive fee contracts (CPIF): With a CPIF, the seller is reimbursed for all costs plus an incentive fee based on when performance objectives mentioned in the contract are met.

Example: If the project is completed with fewer costs, 10% of the remaining funds will be given to the seller.

Cost plus award fee contracts (CPAF): With a CPAF, the seller is paid for all his or her legitimate costs plus an award fee. This award fee is based on achieving satisfaction with the performance objectives described in the contract.

Example: If the seller completes the task by meeting or exceeding all quality standards, based on his or her performance, he or she may be given an award of up to $10,000.

Cost plus percentage of cost contracts (CPPC): With a CPPC, the seller is paid for all costs incurred plus a percentage of these costs. This type of contract is generally not preferred because the seller might artificially increase the costs to earn a higher profit.

Example: If the total cost of the project is $10,000, the seller is paid $10,000 plus 20% ($2,000), for a total payout of $12,000.

Time and materials contracts (T&M): T&M is a hybrid of fixed-price and cost-reimbursable contracts. Use this type of contract when the scope is incomplete or not determined. T&Ms are also used when the deliverable is "labor hours."

Example: A technician will be paid $20 per hour.

Tools and Techniques

Expert judgments are considerations provided by those with experience in and specialized knowledge of planning procurement management.

Data gathering for procurement primarily involves market research and studying seller and market capabilities.

Data analysis is used to determine that which is best for the deliverables. *Make or buy analysis* is used to determine whether the project team can accomplish work or deliverables. For example, do we have the necessary professional to perform the work within the organization, or does it make more sense to buy software on the market or write our own code? *Source selection analysis* is based on some or all of the following: least cost, qualifications, quality-based with the highest possible technical score, quality, sole source, and fixed budget.

Meetings are also used to create the procurement management plan.

Outputs

The *procurement management plan* defines activities to be undertaken during the procurement process such as the type of bidding (local, national, or international) and how the project is funded.

The *procurement strategy* is used to determine the project delivery method, type of contract, and how the procurement will move forward through phases.

The *procurement statement of work (PSOW)* is developed from the project scope baseline and defines a part of the project scope and describes the procurement items in sufficient detail to allow prospective sellers to determine if they are capable of providing the products, services, or results. The PSOW should be clear, concise, and complete so the seller or contractor knows what is expected in satisfying each requirement, the physical resources meet all specifications, and deliverables are per the contractual agreement. Each PSOW item requires a SOW; however, multiple products or services can be grouped as one procurement item within a single SOW.

Source selection criteria should offer the best quality of service based on selection criteria such as capability, product cost, life-cycle cost, delivery dates, technical expertise, specific experience, et cetera. The project team or subject matter experts should be relied on heavily in determining selection criteria.

Make-or-buy analysis determines which is best for project needs. As explained before, a make-or-buy analysis is used to determine whether the project team can accomplish work or deliverables. For example, do we have the necessary professional to perform the work within the organization, or does it make more sense to buy software on the market or write our own code?

Independent cost estimates are estimates from a third party that has no stake in the project. Independent cost estimates are said to be more objective or truthful than those generated in house.

Change requests may be submitted for procurement resources.

Project documents updates are made to the following: *milestone list*, *project team assignments*, *requirements document*, *requirements traceability matrix*, *resource requirements*, *risk register*, and *stakeholder register*.

Organizational process assets updates are made to information on qualified sellers.

Procurement documents are used to solicit proposals from prospective sellers in terms such as bid, tender, or quotation. *Bid documents* include the request for information (RFI), request for quotation (RFQ), request for proposal (RFP),[64] tender notice, invitation for negotiation, procurement request, and source selection criteria.

> » Request for information (RFI) is a standard business process to collect written information about the capabilities of various suppliers.

> » Request for quotations (RFQ) is a standard business process to invite suppliers into a bidding process to bid on specific products or services. RFQ generally means the same thing as IFB (invitation for bid).

> » Invitation for bid (IFB) is an invitation to contractors or equipment suppliers to submit an offer

---

64   Alana F. Dunoff, "A Smarter RFP Process: Getting Apples to Apples Conference," http://afdfacilityplanning.com/sitebuildercontent/sitebuilderfiles/RFP101.pdf.

on a specific project to be realized or product or service to be furnished. The IFB is focused on pricing and not on ideas or concepts.

» Request for proposal (RFP) is a document that solicits a proposal from potential suppliers. An RFP is often made through a bidding process by an agency or company interested in procurement of a commodity, service, or valuable asset.

» A tender notice invites bids for a project or to accept a formal offer such as a takeover bid. *Tender* usually refers to the process whereby governments and financial institutions invite bids for large projects that must be submitted by a finite deadline.

» An invitation for negotiation is merely a preliminary discussion or an invitation by one party to the other to negotiate or make an offer.

» Issuing a procurement request to potential sellers to submit a proposal or bid is normally done in newspapers, in trade journals, in public registries, or on the internet.

» Source selection criteria, often included as part of the procurement documents, are used to rate or score seller proposals and can be objective or subjective. Selection criteria can be based on purchase price of an available product from some acceptable sellers.

Exam Alert!

1. The process of documenting project procurement decisions, specifying the approach, and identifying potential sellers best describes which process?

   a) Data analysis

   b) Procurement management plan

   c) Organizational process assets

   d) Plan procurement management

Answer: *b*. Plan procurement management is the process that creates the procurement management plan. Data analysis is a tool and technique. Organizational process assets are input.

2. The output to the plan procurement management process is?

   a) Procurement management plan

   b) Project management plan

   c) Conduct procurement

d) Control procurement

Answer: *a.* Project management plan is the output of develop project management plan process. Conduct and control procurement are part of execute and monitor and control process respectively.

13.2 Plan Stakeholder Engagement

Per PMBOK, the *plan stakeholder engagement* process develops approaches to involving project stakeholders based on their needs, expectations, interests, and potential impact on the project. Involving stakeholders is crucial not only to the success of the project but also to the acceptance of the project by the sponsor.[65] If all project objectives are met and delivered but the customer refuses delivery under any circumstances, then the project is a failure.

Case Study— IT Infrastructure Project in the Role of Technical Project Manager

In the infrastructure project plan, we needed to know what communication method, model, and technology were necessary for stakeholder engagement. Would we communicate formally or informally, by email, presentation, report, or memo? The answer was all. However, the level of detail of the communication would depend on the stakeholder and what information they were privileged to and what information they wanted.

» Senior management and the sponsor wanted high-level *work performance reports*, the issues log, the risk report, and reports on how the project was performing compared to the scope baseline, schedule baseline, and cost baseline. The project manager must be prepared to answer questions on any divergence and how to get the project in good standing.

» The sponsor also wanted high-level *work performance reports* and, if possible, a *work performance information report*.

» Project implementers needed a *work performance information* report and *work performance data* report.

» Other stakeholders needed the issues log and risk reports and how the project now affected their environment.

---

65   *PMBOK Guide*, Sixth Edition, 516.

Process	Inputs	Tools and Techniques	Outputs
13.2 Plan Stakeholder Engagement	Project charter Project management plan Resource management plan Communications management plan Risk management plan » Projects documents » Assumptions log » Change log » Issue log » Project schedule » Risk register » Stakeholder register Agreements OPA EEF	Expert judgments Data gathering » Benchmarking » Data analysis » Assumptions » Constraint analysis » Root cause analysis Data representation » Prioritization/ ranking » Mind mapping » Stakeholder engagement matrix Meetings	Stakeholder engagement plan

Inputs

The *project charter* contains the high-level risks and constraints, initial stakeholders, things external to the organization that might have an impact on the project and project purpose, objectives, and success criteria that can be taken into consideration when engaging the stakeholders.

The *project management plan* is a how-to guide on how the project will be designed, managed, monitored and controlled, and closed.

The *resource management plan* may contain information on the roles and responsibilities of team members and other stakeholders in the stakeholder register.

The *communications management plan* contains information about communication strategies and implementation plans for stakeholder engagement.

The *risk management plan* is a document that a project manager prepares to foresee risks, estimate impacts, and define responses to issues. This plan may contain information on risk attitudes, and risk thresholds can be added to stakeholder engagement matrix. Strategy,

Projects documents that are the linked to or affect stakeholders are the *assumptions log*, *change log*, *issues log*, *project schedule*, *risk register*, and *stakeholder register*.

Agreements are used when planning the engagement of contractors and suppliers.

Organizational process assets and *enterprise environmental factors* can also influence stakeholder engagement via processes, policies, and procedures as well as the internal and external factors the project team has no control over.

Tools and Techniques

Expert judgments are considerations provided by those with experience in and specialized knowledge of planning stakeholder engagement.

Data gathering techniques used are *benchmarking*, *data analysis*, *assumptions*, and *constraint analysis* as well as *root cause analysis*.

> » *Data representation* uses *mind mapping* and the *stakeholder engagement matrix*. Prioritization/ranking is where stakeholder requirements need to be prioritized and ranked, as do the stakeholders themselves. Those stakeholders with the most interest and the highest influence are often prioritized at the top of the list.[66]

Meetings are used to plan stakeholder engagement.

Stakeholder	Unaware	Resistant	Neutral	Supportive	Leading
Stakeholder 1	C			D	
Stakeholder 2			C	D	
Stakeholder 3				D C	

Figure 11. Stakeholders engagement assessment matrix[67]

C represents the current engagement level of each stakeholder; *D* represents desired level of stakeholder engagement to ensure project success. The gap between D and C will direct the communication necessary to engage the stakeholder. Closing the gap between desired and current is essential in monitoring projects.

66   *PMBOK Guide,* Sixth Edition, 521.

67   *PMBOK Guide,* Sixth Edition, 522.

Outputs

The *stakeholder engagement plan* includes strategies formal or informal for engaging stakeholders. The stakeholder engagement plan also contains methods for engaging stakeholders such as face-to-face meetings, status reports, or any communication designed in the communications plan.

Exam Alert!

1. Which answer best describes the stakeholder engagement plan?

    a) The process of developing approaches to involve project stakeholders based on their needs and expectations, addressing issues, and fostering appropriate stakeholder engagement involvement

    b) The process of monitoring project stakeholder relationships and tailoring strategies for engaging stakeholders through the modification of engagement strategies and plans

    c) The process of communicating and working with stakeholders to meet their needs and expectations

    d) The process of not communicating and working with stakeholders to meet their needs and expectations

Answer: *a.* If the question asks for a plan then *b* is not the answer. Answer *d* is not correct because you always want to communicate in project management. Answer *c* is executing the plan. The process of developing is a plan type answer.

2. The output to plan stakeholder engagement is:

    a) Assumption and constraint analysis

    b) Stakeholder engagement plan

    c) Project management plan

    d) Process improvement plan

Answer: *b.* Assumption and constraint analysis is a tool and technique. C and d are outputs of other processes.

Section 4: Executing Execute Process Group

Executing Process Group	
4.3 Direct and Manage Project Work 4.4 Manage Project Knowledge	10.2 Manage Communications
8.2 Manage Quality	11.6 Implement Risk Responses
9.3 Acquire Resources 9.4 Develop Team 9.5 Manage Team	12.2 Conduct Procurements
	13.3 Manage Stakeholder Engagement

4.3 Direct and Manage Project Work

According to PMBOK, the *direct and manage project work* process leads and performs the work defined in the project plan and implements the approved changes to achieve the project objectives.[68] This process starts only when the project charter and project management plan are completed and approved. A kickoff meeting is held to announce the objectives of the project to all involved. It is time for the real work to begin.

In the case of our infrastructure project:

» The equipment and software have been ordered.

» Once the equipment arrives, the software is downloaded and installed as stated per the project plan.

» All work is completed according to the quality expected.

» All activities and risk response strategies have an owner assigned to do the work readily.

» Procurements resources and agreements are part of the direct and manage project work process.

» The project will continue to be managed until all activities are completed and deliverables accepted by the customer.

---

68   *PMBOK Guide*, Sixth Edition, 597.

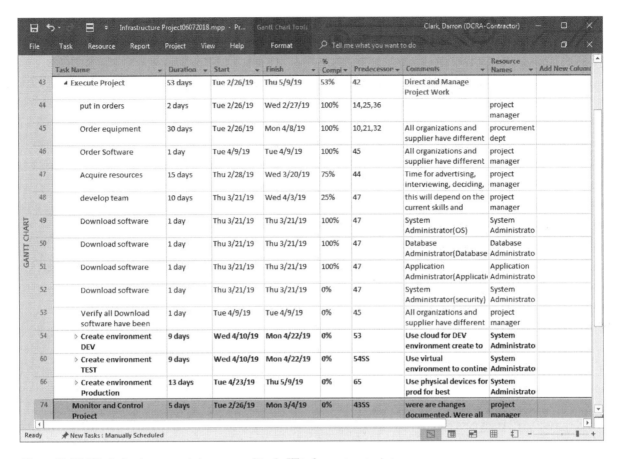

Figure 12. PMIS of what has currently been executed in the IT infrastructure project.

Process	Inputs	Tools and Techniques	Outputs
4.3 Direct and Manage Project Work	Project management plan Project documents » Change log » Lessons learned register » Milestones list » Project communications » Project schedule » Requirements traceability matrix » Risk register » Risk report Approved change requests OPA EEF	Expert judgments PMIS Meetings	Deliverables Work performance data Issues log Change requests PMP updates Project documents updates » Activity list » Assumptions log » Lessons learned register » Requirements documentation » Risk register » Stakeholder register » OPA updates

Inputs

The *project management plan* is a how-to guide on how the project is managed throughout this process. All subsidiary plans are part of this managing process.

The following *project documents* are used during the direct and manage project work process:

- » The *change log* has the status of all change requests.

- » The *lessons learned register* is used to improve performance and avoid repeat mistakes.

- » The *milestone list* has scheduled dates for specific milestones.

- » *Project communications* include performance reports, deliverable status, and other information generated by the project.

- » The *project schedule* has a list of work activities, durations, resources, and planned start and finish dates.

- » The *requirements traceability matrix* links product requirements to the deliverables that satisfy them.

- » The *risk register* has a list of risks along with threats and opportunities that may affect project execution.

- » The *risk report* provides information on overall project risk.

Approved change requests, which are an output to project integrated change control, are executed in this process.

Organizational process assets and *enterprise environmental factors* are the processes, policies, and procedures along with internal and external factors that are not in the project team's control.

Tools and Techniques

Expert judgments are considerations provided by subject matter experts and consultants that help determine the entire scope that is necessary to accomplish the defined deliverables.

A *project management information system (PMIS)*, which is part of the EEFs, includes a scheduling tool, a work-authorization system, a configuration-management system, and an information-collection system.

Meetings are held to discuss, direct, and manage project work process.

Outputs

The outputs include *deliverables*, *work performance data*, *issues log*, *change requests*, and the *project management plan updates*, including managing any project components.

Project documents updates include:

» activity list

» assumptions log

» lessons learned register

» requirements documentation

» risk register

» stakeholder register

» organizational process assets updates

Exam Alert!

1. Deliverables is an output of which process group?

    a) Organizational process assets

    b) Enterprise environmental factors

    c) Final report

    d) Direct and manage project work

Answer: *d.* Organizational process assets and enterprise environmental factors are inputs to many process groups. Final report is an output of the close project or phase process group.

2.   Which of the following is a tool and technique of direct and manage project work?

a) Change requests

b) PMIS

c) Project management plan

d) OPA updates

Answer: *b. a, c,* and *d* are an output to other processes,

4.4 Manage Project Knowledge

According to PMBOK, the *manage project knowledge* process uses existing knowledge and creates new knowledge to achieve the project's objectives and contribute to organizational learning.[69]

Case Study— IT Infrastructure Project in the Role of Technical Project Manager

In the IT infrastructure project, any documents obtained that existed, such a current standard operating procedure (SOP) or architectural diagram of current databases system, were used before, during and after the project to help achieve organizational and project objectives.

Likewise, any new document created, such as lessons learned, risk reports, or installation documents, became part of the project and were used to achieve organizational and project objectives.

---

69   *PMBOK Guide*, Sixth Edition, 98.

Process	Inputs	Tools and Techniques	Outputs
4.4 Manage Project Knowledge	Project management plan Project documents » Lessons learned register » Project team assignments » Resource breakdown structure » Stakeholder register Deliverables OPA EEF	Expert Judgments Knowledge management Information management Interpersonal and team skills » Active listening » Facilitation » Leadership » Networking » Political awareness	Lessons learned register PMP updates OPA updates

Inputs

The *project management plan* is a how-to guide on how the project will be managed which may involve all components.

Project documents

» The *lessons learned register* is used to improve performance and avoid repeat mistakes.

» *Project team assignments* contain information on the project team's skill sets and competencies.

» The *resource breakdown structure* has information on team competencies as well as what knowledge may be missing.

» The *stakeholder register* has information on individual stakeholders and understands the knowledge they may have.

Deliverables are unique and verifiable products, results, or services that are required to be completed.

Organizational process assets and *enterprise environmental factors* are the processes, policies, and procedures along with internal and external factors that are not in the project team's control.

Tools and Techniques

Expert judgments are considerations provided by subject matter experts and consultants to determine the entire scope that is necessary to accomplish defined deliverables.

Knowledge management connects people so they can work together to create new knowledge, share tacit knowledge, and integrate the knowledge of various team members. The connection occurs via networking, practice communities, physical and virtual meetings, shadowing others on the team, workshops, storytelling, fairs, cafés, and training.

Information management is used to connect people to information, such as the lessons learned register, library services, web searches, reading published articles, and PMIS.

Interpersonal and team skills required include *active listening*, *facilitation*, *leadership*, *networking*, and *political awareness*.

Outputs

Lessons learned register may include an impact analysis and recommendation and proposed actions of a situation. The lessons learned register can also record challenges, problems, realized risks, and opportunities.

Project management plan updates include any changes to the project management plan that go through the change control process.

Organizational process assets updates will contain any new knowledge created or existing knowledge modified.

Exam Alert!

1. The following are components of tools and techniques in the manage project knowledge process except

    a) Knowledge management

    b) Information management

    c) Interpersonal and team skills

    d) Lessons learned register

Answer: *d.* The lessons learned register is an input.

2. Which of the following is an input of the manage project knowledge process?

    a) Alternative analysis

    b) Deliverables

    c) OPA updates

    d) Project management plan updates

Answer: *b.* Choice *a* is a tools and techniques of another process; *c* and *d* are outputs to other processes.

8.2 Manage Quality

According to PMBOK, the *manage quality* process translates the quality management plan into executable project activities that incorporate the organization's quality policies.[70]

> ## Case Study— IT Infrastructure Project in the Role of Technical Project Manager
>
> In infrastructure projects, the product, service, or result must do what the project team says it will do. The likelihood of meeting quality objectives will depend greatly on the quality of the design, the quality of the products, the quality of the equipment, the quality of the people who put it all together, and successful quality checks throughout the entire project life cycle.

Process	Inputs	Tools and Techniques	Outputs
8.2 Manage Quality	Project management plan » Quality management plan Project documents » Lessons learned register » Quality control measurements » Quality metrics » Risk report OPA	Data gathering » Checklists Data analysis » Alternative analysis » Document analysis » Process analysis » Root cause analysis Decision-making » Multicriteria decision analysis Data representation » Affinity diagrams » Cause-and-effect diagrams » Flowcharts » Histograms » Matrix diagrams » Scatter diagrams Audits Design for X Problem-solving Quality improvement methods	Quality reports Test and evaluation documents Change requests PMP updates » Quality management plan » Scope baseline » Schedule baseline » Cost baseline Project documents updates » Issues log » Lessons learned register » Risk register

---

70 *PMBOK Guide*, Sixth Edition, 288.

Inputs

The *project management plan* is a how-to guide on how the project will be managed. The *quality management plan* defines the acceptable level of quality, which is typically determined by the customer, and describes how the project will ensure this level of quality in its deliverables and work processes.

Project documents utilized when managing quality are the *lessons learned register*, *quality control measurements*, *quality metrics*, and *risk report*.

Organizational process assets contain the policies, procedures, and practices that are used when managing quality.

Tools and Techniques

Data gathering at this stage includes *checklists*.

Data analysis makes use of either *alternative analysis*, *document analysis*, *process analysis*, or *root cause analysis*.

Decision-making makes use of *multicriteria decision analysis*.

Data representation involves any or all of the following tools:

- » affinity diagrams
- » cause-and-effect diagrams
- » flowcharts
- » histograms
- » matrix diagrams
- » scatter diagrams

Other tools and techniques that are used in quality checks are *audits*, *design for X*, *problem-solving*, and *quality improvement methods*.

Design for X is a set of technical guidelines that can be applied during the design for the optimization for a specific aspect of the design. The X can be for reliability, deployment, assembly, cost, service, usability, safety, or quality. Using design for X can result in a product that has reduced costs, improved quality, better performance, and customer satisfaction.

Outputs

Quality reports can be graphical, numerical, or qualitative. These reports are used by other processes and departments to take corrective actions to achieve quality expectations. Other outputs include *test and evaluation documents* and *change requests*.

The *project management plan updates* include

» Quality management plan

» Scope baseline

» Schedule baseline

» Cost baseline

Project documents updates are performed on documents such as

» Issues log

» Lessons learned register

» Risk register

Exam Alert!

1. Which of the following is an input to the manage quality process?

    a) Quality reports

    b) Quality metrics

    c) Data gathering

    d) Enterprise environmental factors

Answer: *b*. Quality reports is an output; enterprise environmental factors is not an input in this process and data gathering is a tool and technique.

9.3 Acquire Resources

According to PMBOK, the *acquire resources* process obtains team members, facilities, equipment, materials, supplies, and other resources necessary to complete the project work.[71]

---

71 *PMBOK Guide*, Sixth Edition, 328.

Case Study— IT Infrastructure Project in the Role of Technical Project Manager

With the infrastructure project management, the resources will include people, computers, wires, cables, and storage devices. Acquiring resources might also include obtaining application software, database software, network configuring software, and security software.

What resources are needed will be defined in the project management plan, resource management plan, and procurement management plan.

Process	Inputs	Tools and Techniques	Outputs
9.3 Acquire Resources	Project management plan » Resource management plan » Procurement management plan » Cost baseline Project documents » Project schedule » Resource calendars » Resource requirements » Stakeholder register OPA EEF	Decision-making » Multicriteria analysis Interpersonal skills » Negotiation Pre-assignment Virtual teams	Physical resource assignments Project team assignments Resource calendars Change requests PMP updates » Resource management plan » Cost baseline Project documents updates » Lessons learned register » Project schedule » RBS » Resource requirements » Risk register » Stakeholder register EEF updates OPA updates

Inputs

The *project management plan* is a how-to guide on how the project is managed.

» The *resource management plan* is the efficient and effective development of an organization's resources when they are needed.

» The *procurement management plan* is the creation of relationships with outside vendors and suppliers for goods and services needed to complete a project.

» The *cost baseline* is used as an example in which cost performance is measured and monitored to gauge the importance of the project. This cost baseline is created by estimating the costs by the period that the project will be completed.

The *project documents* that are used in this process are the *project schedule*, *resource calendars*, *resource requirements*, and *stakeholder register*.

The *organizational process assets* and *enterprise environmental factors* are also used to create outputs.

Tools and Techniques

Decision-making tools and techniques such as *multicriteria analysis* are used to acquire resources. The multicriteria analysis could be based on years of experience or specialized knowledge, as well as degrees and certifications.

Interpersonal skills, such as *negotiation skills*, are necessary whether acquiring resources from another department or procuring resources.

Pre-assignment of resources will be stated in the project charter. Pre-assignment is a physical or team resource determined in advance before the resource manage plan has been completed.

Virtual teams are resources that are not colocated.

Outputs

Physical resource assignments are the material, equipment, supplies, and location of physical resources that will be used during the project.

Project team assignments contain the project team directory and the roles and responsibilities of team member recorded in the project plan.

The *resource calendar* identifies working days and shifts, start and end of normal business hours, and holidays and vacation for available resources.

Change requests are needed to add or replace resources.

Project management plan updates are made to the *resource management plan* and *cost baseline*.

Project documents updates are made to the *lessons learned register*, *project schedule*, *RBS*, *resource requirements*, *risk register*, and *stakeholder register*.

There are also *enterprise environmental factors updates* and *organizational process assets updates*.

Exam Alert!

1. Pepper is a new project manager for TF Banking Services. Pepper is in the process of acquiring resources. All are tools and techniques Pepper can use to aid in her search except

    a) Virtual teams

    b) Multicriteria analysis

    c) Resource management plan

    d) Negotiation

Answer: *c.* d is an output to another process.

9.4 Develop Team

According to PMBOK, the *develop team* process improves competencies of team members' interactions and the overall team environment to enhance project performance.[72]

Ideally, when you bring someone onto the project team, you want them to have all the experience, skills, and specialized knowledge necessary to do the work they are assigned.

However, in the real world, some training may be necessary, such as bringing someone up to speed on the project and how they fit into it. Or they may understand a specific software but need time to learn a special tool that is part of the same software family.

---

72 *PMBOK Guide*, Sixth Edition, 375.

Case Study— IT Infrastructure Project in the Role of Technical Project Manager

For example, I have on the project team an Oracle database administrator (DBA) that has 20-plus years in the Oracle database software family, which includes Real application clusters and Data Guard; however, if the project also calls for Oracle Goldengate skill, and the DBA on staff does not have this tool in their skill set, my options as a project manager are:

» have the DBA take an Oracle Goldengate training course,

» negotiate with a functional manager for use of a DBA with Oracle Goldengate knowledge and experience, or

» hire an Oracle Goldengate DBA from outside the company.

Process	Inputs	Tools and Techniques	Outputs
9.4 Develop Team	Project management plan » Resource management plan Project documents » Lessons learned register » Project schedule » Project team assignments » Resource calendars » Team charter OPA EEF	Colocation Virtual teams Mixed locations Communication technology Interpersonal and team skills » Conflict management » Influencing » Motivation » Negotiation » Team building Recognition and rewards Training Individual and team assessments Meetings	Team performance assessments Change requests PMP updates » Resource management plan Project documents updates » Lessons learned register » Project schedule » Project team assignments » Resource calendars » Team charter » EEF updates » OPA updates

Inputs

The *project management plan* is a how-to guide on how the project will be designed, managed, monitored and controlled, and closed. The *resource management plan* is the efficient and effective development of an organization's resources when they are needed.

Project documents used in developing the team are the *lessons learned register*, *project schedule*, *project team assignments*, *resource calendars*, and *team charter*.

Organizational process assets and *enterprise environmental factors* are used to help generate outputs.

Tools and Techniques

Colocation, *virtual teams*, and *mixed locations* are a few team structures you can use.

The appropriate *communication technology* must be in place so the team's members can communicate either by email, phone, chat, or conference calls.

Interpersonal and team skills necessary for developing teams are *conflict management*, *influencing*, *motivation*, *negotiation*, and *team building*.

Recognition and rewards are needed to show team members how important they are to the project and to say thanks for a job well done.

Training is necessary for team members very close to the needed skill set but missing a certain tool or discipline.

Individual and team assessments are needed to evaluate performance and to look for areas of improvement or change.

Meetings are necessary to determine the status of individual assignments and to let team members know the project status and status of activities.

Stages of Team Development: Tuckman's Ladder

Tuckman's ladder describes the stages of team formation and development. These stages are:

Forming	The team meets and learns about the project.
Storming	The team begins to address the project work.
Norming	The team begins to work together.
Performing	The team is efficient and works through issues.
Adjourning	The team completes the work and is released.

Outputs

Team performance assessments are the evaluation of how effective the team is with their skills, competencies, staff turnover, and team social interaction.

Change requests may be necessary if corrective action is needed such as training.

Project management plan updates include the *resource management plan*, which has information about how the rates of resources and contingency reserves will be determined.

Project documents updates are made to the *lessons learned register*, *project schedule*, *project team assignments*, *resource calendars*, *team charter*, *EEFs*, and *OPAs*.

Exam Alert!

1.   What is the correct order of Tuckman's ladder?

   a)   Forming, storming, norming, performing, adjourning

   b)   Adjourning, forming, storming, norming, performing

   c)   Performing, forming, storming, norming, adjourning

   d)   Storming, norming, forming, performing, adjourning

Answer: *a.* b,c and d are not in correct order.

9.5 Manage Team

According to PMBOK, the *manage team* process tracks team member performance, provides feedback, resolves issues, and manages team changes to optimize project performance.[73]

> ### Case Study— IT Infrastructure Project in the Role of Technical Project Manager
>
> On the infrastructure project, team and individual performance are measured on the activities' planned start and finish dates versus the actual dates activities started and finished.
>
> The total of activity performance will give indications whether the project is ahead of schedule, on schedule, or behind schedule.

---

73   *PMBOK Guide*, Sixth Edition, 384.

Process	Inputs	Tools and Techniques	Outputs
9.5 Manage Team	Project management plan » Resource management plan Project documents » Issues log » Lessons learned register » Project team assignments » Team charter Work performance report Team performance OPA EEF	Interpersonal and team skills » Conflict management » Decision-making » Emotional intelligence » Influencing » Leadership PMIS	Change requests PMP updates » Resource management plan » Cost baseline » Schedule baseline Project documents updates » Issues log » Lessons learned register » Project team assignments EEF updates

Inputs

The *project management plan* is a how-to guide on how the project will be designed, managed, monitored and controlled, and closed. The *resource management plan* has information about how the rates of resources and contingency reserves will be determined.

Project documents created are the *issues log*, *lessons learned register*, *project team assignments*, and *team charter*.

A *work performance report* is a compilation of work performance information for consumption for some purpose such as status or decision-making.

Team performance is the evaluation of how effective the team is with their skills, competencies, staff turnover, and team social interaction.

Organizational process assets and enterprise environmental factors are policies, practices, and procedures as well as internal and external factors that are out of the project team's control and how they influence managing teams.

Tools and Techniques

Interpersonal and team skills needed in managing people are *conflict management, decision-making, emotional intelligence, influencing,* and *leadership.*

PMIS are software tools with which you can create, manage, and coordinate the project management plan and quickly assess individual and team performance.

Outputs

Change requests are generated because of project work when managing the project team.

Project management plan updates are made to the *resource management plan*, *cost baseline*, and *schedule baseline*.

Project documents updates are made to the *issues log*, *lessons learned register*, and *project team assignments*.

Enterprise environmental factors updates may occur because of project work when managing the project team.

Exam Alert!

1. All of the following are inputs to manage a team except

    a) Project management plan

    b) Project documents updates

    c) Work performance reports

    d) Team performance

Answer: *b*. Project documents updates is an output.

10.2 Manage Communications

According to PMBOK, the *manage communications* process ensures timely and appropriate collection, creation, distribution, storage, retrieval, management, monitoring, and ultimate disposition of project information.[74]

Communication is the most important part of project management. If avoiding people is your style, consider activities that change your behavior, such as dancing, group activities, and giving more presentations. You absolutely will not be able to avoid people in project management. You are leading communication via email, phone, web conference, meetings, and presentations. Get ready for a wonderful ride.

---

74   *PMBOK Guide*, Sixth Edition, 379.

Case Study— IT Infrastructure Project in the Role of Technical Project Manager

Distribution groups were created for all stakeholders of the IT infrastructure project. For example:

» Dist-all, dist-team, and dist-senior-management email distribution groups were created to start communication.

» The contact information for all stakeholders was collected, and conference numbers and WebEx were established for virtual and colocated meetings.

» A shared folder was created as a central repository location for all team and project documents with the appropriate security based on the sensitivity of the information. For example, not all stakeholders needed access to cost or team performance information. Only the appropriate personnel had access to this type of sensitive document as established by the organization policies, procedures, and practices.

Process	Inputs	Tools and Techniques	Outputs
10.2 Manage Communications	PMP » Requirements management plan » Communications management plan » Stakeholder engagement plan Project documents » Change log » Issues log » Lessons learned register » Quality report » Risk report » Stakeholder register Work performance reports OPA EEF	Communications technology Communications methods Communications skills » Communications competence » Feedback » Nonverbal » Presentations PMIS Project reporting Interpersonal and team skills » Active listening » Conflict management » Cultural awareness » Meeting management » Networking » Political awareness Meetings	Project communications PMP updates » Communications management plan » Stakeholder engagement plan Project documents updates » Issues log » Lessons learned register » Project schedule » Risk register » Stakeholder register OPA updates

Inputs

The *project management plan* is a how-to guide on how the project will be designed, managed, monitored and controlled, and closed.

> » The *requirements management plan* is used to document the information required to efficiently manage project requirements.

> » The *communications management plan* describes how project communications will be planned, structured, and monitored and controlled.

> » The *stakeholder engagement plan* describes how the stakeholders will be engaged through the communication strategies chosen for the project.

Project documents that are created or updated are the *change log, issues log, lessons learned register, quality report, risk report,* and *stakeholder register.*

Work performance reports are distributed to stakeholders as defined in the communications management plan.

Organizational process assets and *enterprise environmental factors* can influence how you manage communications because of policies, practices, and procedures as well as internal and external factors out of the project team's control.

Tools and Techniques

The tools used to manage communication come from *communications technology, communications methods,* and *communications skills.* Communications skills consist of *communications competence, feedback, nonverbal,* and *presentations.*

PMIS is a software tool that can be used to distribute communications that state the project status.

Project reporting includes work performance reports, work performance data, and work performance information.

Interpersonal and team skills used to manage communications are *active listening, conflict management, cultural awareness, meeting management, networking,* and *political awareness.*

Meetings are often used to manage communications.

Outputs

Project communications include project reports, deliverable status, progress reports, cost incurred, presentations, and information required by stakeholders.

Project management plan updates are made to the *communications management plan* and *stakeholder engagement plan*.

Project documents updates are made to the *issues log*, *lessons learned register*, *project schedule*, *risk register*, and *stakeholder register*.

Organizational process assets updates are also made because of managing communications.

Exam Alert!

1.   Which best describes the process to manage communications?

    a)   Project management plan

    b)   The process of ensuring timely and appropriate collection, creation, distribution, storage, retrieval, management, monitoring, and the ultimate disposition of project information

    c)   Work performance reports

    d)   Team performance

Answer: *b*. Project management plan describes the project, work performance reports describe status of the project, and team performance is the evaluation of effectiveness of the team.

11.6 Implement Risk Response

According to PMBOK, the *implement risk response* process implements the agreed-upon risk response.[75] When the agreed-upon risk response is implemented, the overall project risk exposure is addressed, threats are minimized, and opportunities are maximized. This process is performed throughout the project.

---

75   *PMBOK Guide,* Sixth Edition, 449.

Case Study— IT Infrastructure Project in the Role of Technical Project Manager

The IT infrastructure project went through a thorough examination by the project team. Through interviews with the sponsor, stakeholders, subject matter experts, suppliers, and project team, we were able to put together a well-planned risk response strategy.

One of the strategies was migrating the data from one database to another. The Oracle software offers several ways to perform a migration; however, we left the final decision up to the person responsible for completing the task. When the task was completed, all the data had to be migrated within a certain time frame. The exactness of the database would be how we measured quality. If the initial method did not work, we had at least two more ways to migrate the data from one system to the other.

1. Oracle Recovery Manager (RMAN) migration is faster, and exactness of data migration is assured.

2. Oracle Data pump migration is slower, but exactness of data migration is also assured.

3. Oracle SQL Loader is also exact but requires more configuration and setup time, but exactness of data migration is also assured.

If the project management plan has gone through a thorough examination (progressively elaborated) and requirements gathering has been maximized, then the number of risks associated with the project have been minimized, and the number of opportunities have been maximized.

For the risks that remain, the project team has risk strategies and owners. When a risk does occur, this process will be used to execute the risk strategy.

Inputs	Tools and Techniques	Process	Outputs
Project management plan » Risk management plan Project documents » Lessons learned register » Risk register » Risk report OPA	Expert judgments Interpersonal skills Influencing PMIS	11.6 Implement Risk Response	Change requests Project document updates » Issues log » Lessons learned register » Project team assignments » Risk register » Risk report

Inputs

The *project management plan* is a how-to guide on how the project will be managed when implementing risk responses. The *risk management plan* is a document that a project manager prepares to foresee risks, estimate impacts, and define responses to issues such as implementing risk responses.

Project documents used in this process are the *lessons learned register*, *risk register*, and *risk report*.

Organizational process assets is used as an input.

Tools and Techniques

Expert judgments are considerations provided by subject matter experts and consultants to determine the entire scope necessary to accomplish defined deliverables.

Interpersonal and team skills are necessary to communicate how risk response will be implemented by the project team and reported to the stakeholders.

PMIS is used to manage schedules, resources, and costs for the agreed-upon risk response plan.

Outputs

Change requests are created when fixes do not go as planned and create residual and secondary risks.

Project document updates are made to the *issues log*, *lessons learned register*, *project team assignments*, *risk register*, and *risk report*.

Exam Alert!

1. Frank is a project manager with Carmon Lip Balm LLC. Frank and his project team meticulously put together a project plan that captured and strategized for many risks. One of the risks has just materialized. As a project manager, what should Frank do next?

    a) Plan risk management

    b) Monitor risks

    c) Use his interpersonal and team management skills

    d) Implement risk responses

Answer: *d*. Plan risk management is a process to first create the Risk management plan document. Interpesonaly skills is a tool and technique. Risks are being monitored to see if any risks occur. If risk do occur the next step as a project manager is to implement the risk response strategy.

2. Debbie is a project manager at Cool Socks, Inc. Debbie is in the planning process for a new project and has completed the sequence activities process. The kickoff of the project occurred 3 months ago. The project team is currently managing the project. As a project manager, what would you do next?

    a) Estimate activity durations

    b) Close the project

    c) Control schedule

    d) Identify stakeholders

Answer: *c*. We are clearly in the execute phase of the project. We have already estimated durations because we have entered the execute phase. There is no mention of project close or cancellation. Identifying stakeholders is going on throughout the life cycle. The best answer is control schedule.

3. Which of the following is an output of the process implement risk response plan?

    a) Change requests

    b) Data analysis

    c) Approved changes

    d) OPA

Answer: *a*. Data analysis is a tool and technique of most processes. Approved changes is an output to performed integrated change control and an input to direct and manage project work. OPA is an input to most processes.

12.2 Conduct Procurements

According to PMBOK, the *conduct procurements* process obtains seller responses, selects sellers, and awards a contract.[76]

Case Study— IT Infrastructure Project in the Role of Technical Project Manager

In the infrastructure project management plan, the project team acquired other qualified team members by advertising or identifying potential sellers, equipment, or people resources. Then a decision was made whether the resources best fit the needs of the project. Lastly, the contract was awarded to the most qualified candidate or equipment.

When selecting a resource, the multicriteria technique is used to determine the most qualified candidate or equipment. For example, when selecting a database administrator to implement a high-availability and disaster-recovery system, the criteria might have been:

» Must know and have performed Oracle's Real application and Data Guard implementation.

» Must also have at least 5 years of experience and have performed at least 10 implementations.

» Must be an Oracle Certified Professional.

Once the resource is selected, the procured resource will then be managed according to the terms of the contract and the organizational policy until either the project completes, or the contract expires or is canceled.

---

76   *PMBOK Guide*, Sixth Edition, 482.

Process	Inputs	Tools and Techniques	Outputs
12.2 Conduct Procurements	Procurement management plan » Scope management plan » Requirements management plan » Communications management plan » Risk management plan » Procurement management plan » Configuration management plan » Cost baseline Product documents » Lessons learned register » Project schedule » Requirements documentation » Risk register » Stakeholder register Procurement documents » Bid documents » Procurement statement of work » Independent cost estimates » Source selection criteria Seller proposals OPA EEF	Expert judgment Advertising Bidder conferences Data analysis » Proposal evaluation Interpersonal and team skills » Negotiation	Select sellers Agreements Change requests Project management plan updates » Requirements management plan » Quality management plan » Communications management plan » Risk management plan » Procurement management plan » Cost baseline » Scope baseline » Schedule baseline Project documents updates » Lessons learned register » Requirements documentation » Requirements traceability matrix! » Resource calendar » Risk register » Stakeholder register OPA updates

Inputs

The *project management plan* is a how-to guide on how the project is managed.

» All subsidiary plans on page 89 of the PMBOK book are part of this managing process.

» The *scope management plan* is a document that explains how the project scope will be defined, developed, and verified.

» The *requirements management plan* is used to document the information required to efficiently manage project requirements.

» The *communications management plan* contains specific instructions on how the team will communicate with sellers.

» The *risk management plan* is a document that a project manager prepares to foresee risks, estimate impacts, and define responses to issues.

» The *procurement management plan* is the creation of relationships with outside vendors and suppliers of goods and services needed to complete a project.

» The *configuration management plan* defines items that are configurable and require a formal change control and the process for controlling changes to the items.

» The *cost baseline* is used as an example in which cost performance is measured and monitored to gauge the importance of the project. This cost baseline is created by estimating the costs by the period that the project will be completed.

Product documents referenced in this process are the *lessons learned register*, *project schedule*, *requirements documentation*, *risk register*, and *stakeholder register*.

Procurement documents used are the *bid documents*, *procurement statement of work*, *independent cost estimates*, and *source selection criteria*.

Seller proposals will have basic information on how a seller is selected.

Organizational process assets and *enterprise environmental factors* will be inputs based on policies, procedures, and practices as well as internal and external factors that influence the conduct procurements process.

Tools and Techniques

Expert judgments are considerations by those individuals and groups who have skills, experience, and specialized knowledge in conducting procurements.

Advertising is a way to reach out to companies or individuals who can perform the work needed.

Bidder conferences are the meetings between buyer and prospective seller prior to proposal submittal.

Data analysis that can be used is *proposal evaluation*. Proposal analyses are evaluated to ensure they are complete and respond in full to bid documents, procurement statement of work, source selection criteria, and other documents that went out in the bid package.

Interpersonal and team skills, such as *negotiation* skills, are needed to reach an agreement and structure the rights and obligations of the parties and terms of the purchases of products or services. The negotiation should be led by the procurement department. The project manager must not lead the procurement negotiations because of the legal language expertise necessary.

Outputs

At the end of this process, procurement *sellers* are selected, and *agreements* are signed.

Change requests must go through the perform integrated change control process.

Project management plan updates may be needed for the *requirements management plan, quality management plan, communications management plan, risk management plan, procurement management plan, cost baseline, scope baseline,* and *schedule baseline.*

Project documents updates may be need for the *lessons learned register, requirements documentation, requirements traceability matrix, resource calendar, risk register,* and *stakeholder register.*

Organizational process assets can be updated too.

Exam Alert!

1.   The process of obtaining seller responses, selecting a seller, and awarding a contract describes which process?

    a)   Plan procurement management

    b)   Conduct procurements

    c)   Control procurements

    d)   Project procurement management

Answer: *b*. According to PMBOK, the *conduct procurements* process obtains seller responses, selects sellers, and awards a contract.

2.   All are tools and techniques to select a seller except

    a)   Advertising

    b)   Bidder conference

    c)   Proposal evaluation

    d)   Asking your best friend

Answer: *d*. If you see a question like asking a friend or family member, it is likely the question that is out of place. Advertising, bidder conference, and proposal evaluation are tools and techniques used to select a seller.

13.3 Manage Stakeholder Engagement

According to PMBOK, the *manage stakeholder engagement* process works with stakeholders to meet their needs, expectations, and interests and communicates the project's potential impacts to them.[77]

In the stakeholders section at the beginning of the book, I provided examples of stakeholders, such as the sponsor, project team, project management team, customers and users, sellers, business partners, organizational groups, functional managers, et cetera.

In my experience, I have seen four categories of stakeholders:	
1. Sponsors and senior management	Initially support and fund the project
2. Project team	Plans, executes, monitors, and controls the project until closing
3. Internal stakeholders	Functional managers and departments affected by the project
4. External stakeholders	Those outside the organization who will be positively or negatively affected by the project

Case Study— IT Infrastructure Project in the Role of Technical Project Manager

Once the kickoff meeting has been completed, the project is ready to begin. The first communication I send out occurs the day before the project begins. I inform all project team members that I have dedicated an email thread to the performance of work being done for the activity currently in progress. This email will continue for that activity until the activity has completed successfully. The next activity will have its own email thread and so on.

The email threads are created to communicate with project team and affected stakeholders, senior management, and the sponsor to keep everyone apprised of the progress of the project.

The same type of separate communication was established for risks, assumptions, constraints, and lessons learned throughout the project.

---

77 *PMBOK Guide*, Sixth Edition, 523.

Process	Inputs	Tools and Techniques	Outputs
13.3 Manage Stakeholder Engagement	Project Management Plan » Communications management plan » Risk management plan » Change management plan » Stakeholder engagement plan Project documents » Change log » Issues log » Lessons learned register » Stakeholder register OPA EEF	Expert judgments Communication skills » Feedback Interpersonal and team skills » Conflict management » Cultural awareness » Negotiation » Observation/ conversation » Political awareness » Ground rules Meetings	Change requests Project management plan updates » Communications management plan » Stakeholder engagement plan Project documents updates » Change log » Issues log » Lessons learned register » Stakeholder register OPA updates

Inputs

The *project management plan* is a how-to guide on how the project will be designed, managed, monitored and controlled, and closed.

> » *Communications management plan* is the guide on how project status will be reported to project stakeholders, what will be reported, and who it will be reported to.

> » *Risk management plan* is a document that a project manager prepares to foresee risks, estimate impacts, and define responses to issues.

> » *Change management plan* guides how changes will be managed through the perform integrated change control board.

> » *Stakeholder engagement plan* is the guide on how to, when to, and where to manage stakeholder engagement.

Project documents used in this process are the *change log, issues log, lessons learned register*, and *stakeholder register*.

Other inputs to this process are *organizational process assets* and *enterprise environmental factors*.

Tools and Techniques

Expert judgments are considerations provided by individuals or groups with experience, skills, and specialized knowledge in managing stakeholder engagement.

Communication skills are the *feedback* received in the manage stakeholder engagement process.

Interpersonal and team skills needed are *conflict management, cultural awareness, negotiation, observation/ conversation, political awareness,* and *ground rules.*

Lastly, *meetings* are where the agenda is managed in the stakeholder engagement process.

Outputs

Change requests for project or product scope can occur as a result of managing this process. All change requests are processed for review or disposition through the perform integrated change control process.

Project management plan updates are made to the *communications management plan* and *stakeholder engagement plan.*

Project documents updates are made to the *change log, issues log, lessons learned register,* and *stakeholder register.*

Lastly, *organizational process assets updates* are made.

Exam Alert!

1.   The process of communicating and working with stakeholders to meet their needs and expectations, address issues, and foster appropriate involvement describes which process?

    a)   Manage stakeholder engagement

    b)   Monitor communications

    c)   Manage communications

    d)   Monitor stakeholder engagement

Answer: *a.* The difference between monitor and manage is that monitor is watching or observing. Manage is an action where you are actually doing something. In this case it is the "process of communicating and working with stakeholders"

Section 5: Monitoring and Controlling Group Processes

Monitoring and Controlling Process Group	
4.5 Monitor and Control Project Work 4.6 Perform Integrated Change Control	7.4 Control Costs
5.5 Validate Scope 5.6 Control Scope	8.3 Control Quality
6.6 Control Schedule	9.6 Control Resources
4.5 Monitor and Control Project Work 4.6 Perform Integrated Change Control	10.3 Monitor Communications
5.5 Validate Scope 5.6 Control Scope	11.7 Monitor Risks

4.5 Monitor and Control Project Work

According to PMBOK, monitor and control project work is the process of tracking, reviewing, and reporting the overall progress to meet performance objectives defined in the project management plan.[78]

---

78 *PMBOK Guide,* Sixth Edition, 105.

Case Study— IT Infrastructure Project in the Role of Technical Project Manager

Continuing with the IT infrastructure project, once the direct and manage work process has started, the monitor and control project work process immediately begins. You check the progress of work in the method that is best for what is being done.

As a project manager, you:

1. Communicate with the project team on the progress of activities.

2. Communicate with the project team on following the quality process for all activities.

3. Assess performance of schedule and costs performance.

4. Communicate with project team members on team acquisitions, development, and performance.

5. Determine whether the risk response strategies are getting implemented.

6. Determine whether procurement vendors performing work per agreements.

7. Determine whether stakeholder engagement management is being handled properly.

	Task Name	Duration	Start	Finish	% Comp	Predecessors	Comments	Resource Names	Add New Column
43	▷ Execute Project	53 days	Tue 2/26/19	Thu 5/9/19	53%	42	Direct and Manage Project Work	project manager	
74	Monitor and Control Project	5 days	Tue 2/26/19	Mon 3/4/19	53%	43SS	were are changes documented. Were all inspections successful or fixed.	project manager	
75	Deploy to production	5 days	Tue 3/5/19	Mon 3/11/19	0%	74	When all objectives have been achieved	system architect	
76	Go-live	5 days	Tue 3/12/19	Mon 3/18/19	0%	75	Work with customer to (	sponsor	
77	Close project	5 days	Tue 3/19/19	Mon 3/25/19	0%	76	Determine criteria for total customer	project manager	

Figure 13. Monitor and control for the IT infrastructure project

Here are the formulas that will be necessary for earned value management exam questions.

Earn Value Management Formulas and Meanings			
Abbr.	Terminology	Formula	Explanation
CV	Cost Variance	EV - AC	
SV	Schedule Variance	EV - PV	
CPI	Cost Performance Index	EV / AC	At what rate is the project spending money?
SPI	Schedule Performance Index	EV / PV	How fast is the project team working?
EAC	Estimate at Completion	AC + (BAC - EV) BAC / CPI AC + [(BAC-EV) / (CPI*SPI)]	Atypical Typical Forecast
ETC	Estimate to Completion	EAC - AC	How long until completion?
VAC	Variance at Completion	BAC - EAC	Forecast to be over or under budget?
TCPI	To Complete Performance Index	(BAC - EV) / (BAC - AC) (BAC - EV) / (EAC - AC)	Cost performance needed to complete work Assumes original budget cannot be met

Process	Inputs	Tools and Techniques	Outputs
13.4 Monitor Stakeholder Engagement	Project management plan » Scope management plan » Schedule management plan » Costs management plan » Quality management plan » Human resources management plan » Risks management plan » Communication management plan » Procurement management plan » Stakeholder management plan » Requirements management plan » Scope baseline » Schedule baseline » Cost baseline Project documents » Assumptions log » Basis of estimates » Cost forecasts » Issues log » Quality report » Lessons learned register » Milestone list » Risk register » Risk report » Schedule forecast Work performance information » Deliverables » Implementation status for change requests » Forecast estimates to complete EEF OPA	Data analysis » Alternative analysis » Cost-benefit analysis » Earned value analysis » Root cause analysis » Trend analysis » Variance analysis Estimate at completion Schedule forecasts Cost forecasts Decision-making Meetings	Work performance reports » Status reports » Progress reports Change requests Project management plan updates » Resource management plan » Communications management plan » Stakeholder engagement plan Project documents updates » Cost forecasts » Issues log » Lessons learned register » Project communications » Risk register » Stakeholder register » Schedule forecasts

Inputs

Any component of the *project management plan* can be used as an input to this process, such as

- » *Scope management plan*
- » *Schedule management plan*
- » *Costs management plan*
- » *Quality management plan*
- » *Human resource management plan*
- » *Risks management plan*
- » *Communication management plan*
- » *Procurement management plan*
- » *Stakeholder management plan*
- » *Requirements management plan*
- » *Scope baseline*
- » *Schedule baseline*
- » *Cost baseline*

Project documents to be read for this process are the *assumptions log*, *basis of estimates*, *cost forecasts*, *issues log*, *quality report*, *lessons learned register*, *milestone list*, *risk register*, *risk report*, and *schedule forecasts*.

Work performance information is work performance data that has been transformed. Examples of work performance information are *deliverables*, *implementation status for change requests*, and *forecast estimates to complete*.

EEF and *OPA* also influence this process, such as industry standards, stakeholder tolerance risk, and project information systems, along with procedures, policies, and practices.

Tools and Techniques

Expert judgments are considerations by those with experience, skills, or specialized knowledge in this process.

Data analysis includes *alternative analysis*, *cost-benefit analysis*, *earned value analysis*, *root cause analysis*, *trend analysis*, and *variance analysis*.

Earned value analysis is used to capture information on schedule forecasts and cost forecasts. Trend analysis is performed to see if the team's performance is improving or deteriorating in the project.

Variance analysis reviews the difference between planned and actual performance. For example, you are a contractor responsible for the refurbishment of a vehicle display area. The estimated refurbishment cost is $500 per square foot. The total display area that needs to be refurbished is 1,000 square feet. Based on your past experience, you know your team can refurbish 100 square feet per week.

After 4 weeks, you have 45% of the job complete, and you have spent $250,000.

Determine the value of each of the terms below by filling in the following chart:

Estimate at completion (EAC) is a forecast of the project's final cost.

Schedule forecasts are the computed time estimates of the earn value management (EVM) compared against schedule baseline:

>> Estimate to completion (ETC)

>> Schedule variance (SV)

>> Schedule performance index (SPI)

Cost forecasts are the computed cost estimates of the earn value management (EVM) compared against cost baseline:

>> Estimate to completion (ETC)

>> Cost variance (CV)

>> Cost performance index (CPI)

>> Estimate at completion (EAC)

>> Budget at completion (BAC)

Forecasts may be used to determine if the project is still within defined tolerance ranges and identify any necessary change requests.

Decision-making techniques such as voting are used; votes can be decided by unanimity, majority, or plurality.

Meetings can be face to face, virtual, formal, or informal.

Outputs

Work performance reports are combined, recorded, and distributed as prescribed in the communications management plan. Examples or work performance reports are *status reports* and *progress reports*.

Change requests may include corrective action, preventive action, or defect repair.

Project management plan updates occur with any changes during the process. These may be made to the *resource management plan*, the *communications management plan*, and the *stakeholder engagement plan*.

Project document updates can occur with any change to the *cost forecasts*, *issues log*, *lessons learned register*, *project communications*, *risk register*, *stakeholder register*, or *schedule forecasts*.

Exam Alert!

1. Which process best exemplifies monitoring and control in project integration?

    a) Direct and manage project work

    b) Monitor and control project work

    c) Manage project knowledge

    d) Perform integrated change control

Answer: *b.* Monitor and control project work. See glossary

2. Harry is a contractor responsible for the refurbishment of an automobile showroom. The estimated refurbishment cost is $500 per square foot. The total showroom area that needs to be refurbished is 1,000 square feet. Based on your past experience, you know your team can refurbish 100 square feet per week. How is the project performing?

    a) On schedule and on budget

    b) Behind schedule and over budget

    c) Ahead of schedule and over budget

    d) Behind schedule and ahead of budget

Answer: *c.* Ahead of schedule and over budget. Review the formula and calculation below

Cost Variance	(EV - AC) = ($25,000.00)
Schedule Variance	(EV - PV) = $25,000.00

3.   Harry is a contractor responsible for the refurbishment of an automobile showroom. The estimated refurbishment cost is $500 per square foot. The total showroom area that needs to be refurbished is 1,000 square feet. Based on your past experience, you know your team can refurbish 100 square feet per week. How is the steady-state value?

   a) 525,000

   b) 375,000

   c) 555,555.56

   d) 475,000

Answer: *c.*

Estimate at Completion *(typical, steady-state, or continuous)*	(BAC / CPI) = $555,555.56

4.   Harry is a contractor responsible for the refurbishment of an automobile showroom. The estimated refurbishment cost is $500 per square foot. The total showroom area that needs to be refurbished is 1,000 square feet. Based on your past experience, you know your team can refurbish 100 square feet per week. How is the forecast estimate at completion?

   a) 525,000

   b) 375,000

   c) 555,555.56

   d) 516,224.19

Answer: *d.*

Estimate at Completion (forecast)	(AC + (BAC-EV)) / (CPI * SPI) = $516,224.19

Complete table solutions below:

Estimated refurbishment cost   500.00 per square feet

Total showroom area   1,000.00 square feet

Refurbishment pace   100.00 square feet per week

Term	Value
Budget at Completion	($500 x 1,000) = $500,000.00
Planned Value	(4 / 10 x BAC) = $200,000.00
Earned Value	(45% x BAC) = $225,000.00
Actual Cost	$250,000.00
Cost Variance	(EV - AC) = $25,000.00
Schedule Variance	(EV - PV) = $25,000.00
Cost Performance Index	(EV / AC) = 0.90
Schedule Performance Index	(EV / PV) = 1.13
Estimate at Completion (atypical)	(AC + (BAC-EV)) = 525,000
Estimate at Completion (forecast)	(AC+ (BAC-EV)) / (CPI * SPI) = 516,224.19
Estimate at Completion (*typical, steady-state or continuous*)	(BAC / CPI) = $555,555.56
Estimate to Complete	(EAC - AC) = $305,555.56
Variance at Completion	(BAC - EAC) = $55,555.56

Total duration (1,000 / 100)   = 10.00 weeks

Duration Elapsed   = 4.00 weeks

Percentage completion   = 45%

4.6 Perform Integrated Change Control

According to PMBOK, the *perform integrated change control* process reviews all change requests, approves changes, and manages changes to deliverables, project documents, and the project management plan and communicating decisions.[79]

What we thought was a perfect plan can sometimes be derailed by an event in any of the knowledge areas. For example:

A part broke.	After an impact assessment was performed, a change request was created and approved, then a fix was performed.
Funds were needed for the unforeseen part.	After an impact assessment was performed, a change request was created and approved, then funds were made available.
A resource was needed, did not work out, or was replaced.	After an impact assessment was performed, a change request was created and approved, then a replacement resource was acquired.
A new stakeholder emerged.	After an impact assessment was completed, a change request was created and approved that changed the scope of the project. The sponsor was notified of the scope change and why.

Process	Inputs	Tools and Techniques	Outputs
4.6 Perform Integrated Change Control	Project management plan » Change management plan » Configuration management plan » Cost baseline » Schedule baseline » Scope baseline Project documents » Basis of estimates » Requirement traceability matrix » Risk report Work performance reports Change requests OPA EEF	Expert judgments Change control tools Data analysis » Alternative analysis » Cost-benefit analysis Decision-making » Voting » Autocratic decision-making » Multicriteria decision analysis Meetings	Approved change requests Project management plan updates Project documents updates

---

79 *PMBOK Guide*, Sixth Edition, 113.

Inputs

The *project management plan* is a how-to guide on how the project will be monitored and controlled and closed. Plans contained in the document are the *change management plan for* how changes will be performed and the *configuration management plan*, which provides guidance on configurable items within the project. Also, the *cost baseline*, *schedule baseline*, and *scope baseline* are used to assess impact to changes in project costs, project schedule, and project and product definition.

Project documents contain the *basis of estimates*, *requirement traceability matrix*, and *risk report*.

Work performance reports detail changes occurring via the perform integrated change control process.

Change requests occur via the perform integrated change control process.

Organizational process assets and *enterprise environmental factors* for procedures, policies, and practices as well as internal and external factors may influence changes.

Tools and Techniques

Expert judgments are considerations provided by those who have specialized knowledge, experience, and skills to perform integrated change control.

Change control tools ensures that all **changes** proposed during the project are **defined**, reviewed as well as approved before they are even implemented. It avoids all unnecessary **changes** that can disrupt the project.[80]

Data analysis includes *alternative analysis* and *cost–benefit analysis*.

Decision-making includes *voting*, *autocratic decision-making*, and *multicriteria decision analysis*.

Meetings can be face to face, virtual, formal, or informal.

Outputs

Approved change requests are an output.

---

80   Project Management Knowledge, https://project-management-knowledge.com/definitions/c/change-control-tools/

Project management plan updates may be made to any component of the plan.

Project documents updates are where all changes are recorded in the change log.

It is extremely important to understand the change control process since it is part of the monitoring and control process group, which accounts for 25% of the questions on the exam.

Change Control Process

It is MANDATORY to know the change control process order for the exam:

1. Prevent changes from occurring.

2. Identify the change.

3. Evaluate the impact of the change.

4. Issue change request.

5. Get change control board (CBB) approval.

6. Update change log and project documents.

7. Communicate change to stakeholder to get buy-in.

8. Implement change.

Exam Alert!

1. Judy is a superb project manager at her firm. Judy is currently working on a project where a fix is necessary. As a project manager, what should Judy do next?

   a) Check the release documents

   b) Notify the sponsor

   c) Evaluate the impact of the change

   d) Implement the risk response plan

Answer: *c*. If you cannot prevent a change then you must evaluate the impact of the change on the project.

2. Judy is a top project manager at her firm. Judy is currently working on a project where a fix *might be* necessary. As a project manager, what should Judy do next?

   a) Prevent changes from occurring

b) Notify the sponsor

c) Evaluate the impact of the change

d) Implement the risk response plan

Answer: *a.* See change control process on the previous page

5.5 Validate Scope

According to PMBOK, the *validate scope* process formalizes acceptance of the completed project deliverables.[81]

Each time all the activities of requirements are completed, the deliverable will be presented for acceptance. This process continues until the last deliverable is completed and presented to the sponsor for acceptance.

For example, the deliverables for the infrastructure project that must be validated as correct are:

Development database	In a cloud environment
QA test database	In a virtual environment
Primary database server—Real Application cluster	3 servers, Linux system, public network connection, 2 interconnects, 100TB, 12 CPUs
Standby database server—Real Application cluster	3 servers, Linux system, public network connection, 2 interconnects, 100TB, 12 CPUs
Firewall	Prod environment
2 load balancers	Prod environment
Application environment	2 instances, business management software

---

81   *PMBOK Guide*, Sixth Edition, 163.

Process	Inputs	Tools and Techniques	Outputs
5.5 Validate Scope	Project management plan » Scope management plan » Requirements management plan Project documents » Lessons learned register » Quality report » Requirements documentation » Requirements traceability matrix » Verified deliverables » Work performance data	Inspection Decision-making » Voting	Acceptable deliverables Work performance information Change requests Project documents updates » Lessons learned register » Requirements documentation » Requirements traceability matrix

Inputs

The *project management plan* is a how-to guide on how the project will be managed. The project management plan has the *scope management plan*, which is a document that explains how the project scope will be defined, developed, and verified. The *requirements management plan* is used to document the information needed to manage project requirements efficiently.

The *project documents* include the *lessons learned register*, *quality report*, *requirements documentation*, *requirements traceability matrix*, *verified deliverables*, and *work performance data*.

Tools and Techniques

Inspection is needed to verify the deliverables are correct.

Also, *decision-making* techniques are used, such as *voting* on whether enough has been done to decide if a deliverable has been validated. For example, upon the completion of one of my projects, the sponsor wanted more comparison of data, and the team voted we had gone beyond what was necessary, so the project was closed.

Outputs

The outputs are *acceptable deliverables* by the sponsor, *work performance information* such as summary reports, and *change requests* if fixes are needed.

Also, *project documents updates* are made to the *lessons learned register* for earlier solved issues, *requirements documentation* for what needed to be done to satisfy deliverables, and *requirements traceability matrix*, which links requirements to the deliverables.

Exam Alert!

1. What is an output to the validate scope process?

   a) Work performance data

   b) Acceptable deliverables

   c) Verified deliverables

   d) Work performance information

Answer: *b*.

5.6 Control Scope

According to PMBOK, *control scope* is the process of monitoring the status of the project and product scope and managing changes to the scope baseline.[82]

Controlling the scope includes monitoring scope creep and gold-plating during the project.

Scope creep occurs when the sponsor or other stakeholder adds requirements or deliverables that were not a part of the original approved project plan or approved scope baseline. Scope creep causes additional cost and time to the project. Any changes to the scope must be approved by the sponsor.

Gold-plating occurs when a project team member adds requirements or deliverables that were not a part of the original approved project plan or approved scope baseline. Gold-plating of items, requirements, or deliverables to the project may cause the sponsor not to accept the project at closing.

---

82   *PMBOK Guide*, Sixth Edition, 167.

Process	Inputs	Tools and Techniques	Outputs
5.6 Control Scope	Project management plan » Scope management plan » Requirements management plan » Change management plan » Configuration management plan » Scope baseline Performance measurement baseline Project documents » Lessons learned register » Requirements documentation » Requirements traceability matrix<(F¦ Work performance data OPA	Data analysis » Variance analysis » Trend analysis	Work performance information Change requests Project management plan updates » Scope management plan » Schedule baseline » Cost baseline » Scope baseline » Performance measurement baseline Project documents » Lessons learned register » Requirements documentation » Requirements traceability matrix

Inputs

The *project management plan* is a how-to guide on how the project will be managed.

» The *scope management plan* is a document that explains how the project scope will be defined, developed, and verified.

» The *requirements management plan* is used to document the necessary information required to efficiently manage project requirements.

» The *change management plan* is how changes will be managed to control scope.

» The *configuration management plan* describes how to identify and account for project artifacts as well has how to report changes under control management.

» The *scope baseline* acts as a reference point for which requirements are included and which are not. It has several components. These include the project scope document, the WBS itself, and the WBS dictionary.

The *performance measurement baseline* is the integration of scope, schedule, and cost baseline, which is used to manage, measure, and control project execution.

Project documents include the *lessons learned register, requirements documentation,* and *requirements traceability matrix.*

Work performance data is raw data that is reported on change requests, such as the number of change requests received and accepted as well as deliverables verified, validated, and completed.

Organizational process assets are the procedures, policies, and practices and how they influence controlling scope.

Tools and Techniques

Data analysis is a technique used when monitoring the control scope process using methods such as *variance analysis* and *trend analysis*.

Variance analysis is used to compare the baseline to the actual results.

Trend analysis is used to determine if there a pattern such as whether the performance is improving or deteriorating over time.

Outputs

The outputs of the scope control process include *work performance information* and *change requests*.

Project management plan updates contains the *scope management plan, schedule baseline, cost baseline, scope baseline*, and *performance measurement baseline*.

Project documents include the *lessons learned register, requirements documentation*, and *requirements traceability matrix*.

Exam Alert!

1. All are inputs to control scope except

    a) Scope management plan

    b) Change management plan

    c) Change requests

    d) Scope baseline

Answer: *c.* Change requests is an output to control scope.

6.6 Control Schedule

According to PMBOK, the *control schedule* process monitors the status of the project to update the project schedule and manage changes to the schedule baseline.[83]

> ## Case Study— IT Infrastructure Project in the Role of Technical Project Manager
>
> In the IT infrastructure project, the schedule for completing each activity was closely planned by the project team, the subject matter expert, and a schedule analysis performed using techniques such as PERT.
>
> As the project manager, you manage with the schedule baseline as the barometer. For example, an activity such as an upgrade of a database completed faster than expected is good, so you should look for a successor activity that you can start early, providing resources are available to perform the work. A migration taking longer than expected to complete is bad. As a project manager, I looked for ways to get back on a schedule, such as performing activities in parallel if possible, provided again that the resource is available to perform the work.
>
> Updates to the appropriate documents must be performed when managing, monitoring, and controlling the schedule for assumptions made, work performed, baseline comparison, and lessons learned.

Process	Inputs	Tools and Techniques	Outputs
6.6 Control Schedule	Project management plan » Schedule management plan » Scope baseline » Schedule baseline » Performance measurement baseline Project documents » Lessons learned register » Project calendars » Project schedule » Resource calendars » Schedule data Work performance data OPA	Data analysis » Earned value analysis » Iteration burndown chart » Performance reviews » Trend analysis » Variance analysis » What-if scenario analysis Project management software Critical path method PMIS Resource optimization Leads and lags Schedule compression	Work performance information Schedule forecasts Change requests Project management plan updates » Schedule management plan » Schedule baseline » Performance measurement baseline » Cost baseline Project documents updates » Assumption log » Basis of estimates » Lessons learned register » Project schedule » Resource calendars » Schedule data

83 *PMBOK Guide*, Sixth Edition, 222.

Inputs

The *project management plan* is a how-to guide on how the project will be monitored.

> » The *schedule management plan* is the document developing, maintaining, and communicating schedules for time and resources.

> » The *scope baseline* acts as a reference point for which requirements are included and which are not. It has several components. These include the project scope document, the WBS itself, and the WBS dictionary.

> » The *schedule baseline* is the approved version of a schedule that can be changed only through formal change control procedures and is used as a basis for comparison to actual results.

> » The *performance measurement baseline* is the integration of scope, schedule, and cost baseline, which is used to manage, measure, and control project execution.

Project documents are the *lessons learned register*, *project calendars*, *project schedule*, *resource calendars*, and *schedule data*.

Further inputs include the *work performance data*, which has the start, end, and duration dates as well as completion percentage of each activity and the project.

Organizational process assets are the policies, practices, and procedures that might influence the control schedule.

Tools and Techniques

Data analysis techniques that can be used are the *earned value analysis*, *iteration burndown chart*, *performance reviews*, *trend analysis*, *variance analysis*, and *what-if scenario analysis*.[84]

---

84 *Wikipedia, The Free Encyclopedia*, s.v. "Project Burn Down Chart," https://en.wikipedia.org/wiki/Burn_down_chart#/media/File:Burn_down_chart.png.

Figure 14 Burn down chart used in Agile environment

What-if scenario analysis is a process of analyzing possible future events by considering alternative possible outcomes (sometimes called "alternative worlds"). Thus, scenario analysis, which is one of the main forms of projection, does not try to show one exact picture of the future. Instead, it presents several alternative future developments.[85]

Other data analysis tools and techniques are *project management software*, *critical path method*, *resource optimization*, *PMIS*, *leads and lags*, and *schedule compression*.

Outputs

The outputs for control schedule include *work performance information*, *schedule forecasts*, and *change requests*.

Project management plan updates include *schedule management plan*, *schedule baseline*, *performance measurement baseline*, and *cost baseline*.

Project documents updates include the *assumption log*, *basis of estimates*, *lessons learned register*, *project schedule*, *resource calendars*, and *schedule data*.

85 *Wikipedia, The Free Encyclopedia*, s.v. "Scenario Analysis," https://en.wikipedia.org/wiki/Scenario_ analysis.

Exam Alert!

1. All of these are tools and techniques used in the control schedule process except

    a) Critical path method

    b) PMIS

    c) Resource optimization

    d) Change requests

Answer: *d.* Change requests is an output.

7.4 Control Costs

According to PMBOK, the *control costs* process monitors project costs to the cost baseline.[86] Control Costs is the process of monitoring the status of the project to update the project costs and managing changes to the cost baseline.

Case Study— IT Infrastructure Project in the Role of Technical Project Manager

What are ways to best control costs?

1. Control costs by preventing scope creep and gold-plating.

2. Control costs by controlling activities' start and end dates.

3. Control costs by determining a realistic budget regardless of funding limits.

4. Control costs by following the quality process and minimizing fixes and rework.

5. Control costs with reasonable costs that fit the budget and no unnecessary extended work.

6. Control costs by colocating as many implementers as possible.

7. Control costs by using resources internal to the organization first before procuring elsewhere.

---

86 *PMBOK Guide*, Sixth Edition, 257.

Process	Inputs	Tools and Techniques	Outputs
6.6 Control costs	Project management plan » Cost management plan » Cost baseline » Performance measurement baseline Project documents » Lessons learned register » Project funding requirements » Work performance data OPA	Expert judgments Data Analysis » Earned value analysis » Variance analysis » Trend analysis » What if scenario analysis » To-complete performance index (TCPI) PMIS	Work performance information Cost forecasts Change requests Project management plan updates » Cost management plan » Cost baseline » Performance measurement baseline Project documents updates » Assumption log » Basis of estimates » Cost estimates » Lessons learned register » Risk register

Inputs

The *project management plan* is a how-to guide on how the project will be designed, managed, monitored and controlled, and closed.

> » The *cost management plan* is the document of planning and controlling the budget of a business.

> » The *cost baseline* is used as an example in which cost performance is measured and monitored to gauge the importance of the project. This cost baseline is created by estimating the costs by the period that the project will be completed.

> » The *performance measurement baseline* is the integration of scope, schedule, and cost baseline, which is used to manage, measure, and control project execution.

Project documents, which include the *lessons learned* and *project funding requirements*, are used to control costs.

Controlling costs includes *work performance data*, such as what costs have been authorized, incurred, invoiced, and paid, plus *organizational process assets,* which can influence control costs.

Tools and Techniques

Expert judgments are considerations by those with experience, skill, and specialized knowledge in controlling costs.

Data analysis techniques include *earned value analysis, variance analysis, trend analysis, what–if scenario analysis,* and *to-complete performance index (TCPI)*.

TCPI is a calculated projection of cost performance that a project must achieve on the value of the remainder of the project work to achieve a specified result.[87] TCPI is measure with the formula

$$TCPI = (BAC - EV) / (BAC - AC)$$

When TCPI turns out to be higher than one (> 1.0), a more standard case for BAC calculations, the value of the remaining project work must be executed at a better cost performance level than the project's completed work.

However, once it becomes clear that the current BAC is not obtainable, the project manager/team, with sponsor approval, should develop a new forecast EAC by completely re-estimating the cost of the remaining work. The new EAC replaces BAC in the TCPI formula denominator, and the TCPI formula becomes

$$TCPI = (BAC - EV) / (EAC - AC)$$

Lastly, *PMIS* is a software tool to help the project manager control costs.

Outputs

Work performance information includes information on how the project is performing. For projects using earned value analysis, CV, CPI, EAC, VAC, and TCPI are documented, summarized, and categorized in work performance reports.

Cost forecasts, using a calculated EAC or a bottom up EAC, are documented for stakeholders.

Change requests are created, which may result in the cost and schedule baselines getting changed in the project baseline.

Project management plan updates are made to the *cost management plan,* which is the document planning and controlling the budget of a business; *the cost baseline;* and the *performance measurement baseline,*

---

87   Project Management Institute, "TCPI," https://www.pmi.org/learning/library/to-complete-performance-index-tcpi-6009.

which is the integration of scope, schedule, and cost baseline and is used to manage, measure, and control project execution.

Project documents updates are made to the *assumptions log*, *basis of estimates*, *cost estimates*, *lessons learned register*, and *risk register*.

Exam Alert!

1.   Which tool/technique is best for controlling cost and schedule?

   a) EVM

   b) PERT

   c) PMIS

   d) Cost forecast

Answer: *c.*

2.   Which tool/technique is best for planning cost and schedule?

   a) EVM

   b) PERT

   c) PMIS

   d) Cost forecast

Answer: *b.*

8.3 Control Quality

According to PMBOK, the *control quality* process monitors and records the results of executing the quality management plan activities to assess performance and ensure project outputs are complete, correct, and meet customer expectations.[88]

There should not be open issues, fixes, or rework when the product, result, or service is delivered. While *manage quality* is when we check that the quality process is being performed correctly, *control quality* assures that the product, result, or service is performing correctly.

---

88 *PMBOK Guide,* Sixth Edition, 337.

Case Study— IT Infrastructure Project in the Role of Technical Project Manager

With the infrastructure project, quality checks included:

1. A computer system, networks, and shared storage are properly installed and tested.

2. The operating systems are installed as recommended, configured, and tested.

3. The database system is installed as recommended, configured, and tested on appropriate systems.

4. The shared storage is configured and verified.

5. The application is installed and configured as recommended.

6. All systems are working together with no issues.

If risk response strategies are implemented, then the fixes should be working properly with no issues.

Process	Inputs	Tools and Techniques	Outputs
8.3 Control Quality	Project management plan » Quality management plan » Project documents » Lessons learned register » Quality metrics » Test and evaluation documents » Approved change requests » Deliverables Work performance data OPA EEF	Data Gathering » Checklists » Check sheets/tally sheets » Statistical gathering » Questionnaires/surveys Data analysis » Performance reviews » Root cause analysis Inspection Testing/product evaluations Data representation » Cause-and-effect diagrams » Flowcharts » Check sheets » Pareto diagrams » Histograms » Control charts » Scatter diagrams Meetings	Quality control measurements Verified deliverables Work performance information Change requests Project Management plan updates » Quality management plan Project documents updates » Issues log » Lessons learned register » Risk register » Test and evaluation documents

Inputs

The *project management plan* is a how-to guide on how the project will be monitored and controlled and closed. The *quality management plan* defines the acceptable level of quality, which is typically determined by the customer, and describes how the project will ensure this level of quality in its deliverables and work processes.

The *project documents* for the inputs are

> » *Lessons learned register* from previous results and quality metrics for the project
>
> » *Test and evaluation documents*, which are used to evaluate achievement of the quality objectives
>
> » *Approved change requests*
>
> » *Deliverables*

Work performance data is used for the observation of quality metrics.

Organizational process assets and *enterprise environmental factors* are used to determine the influence of policies, practices, and procedures on control quality.

Tools and Techniques

Data gathering is one approach to controlling quality using tools and techniques such as *checklists*, *check sheets* or *tally sheets*, *statistical gathering*, and *questionnaires/surveys*.

Another approach to controlling quality is *data analysis*, relying on *performance reviews* and *root cause analysis*.

Inspection is the examination of a work product to see if it conforms to industry, company, or customer standards.

Testing and product evaluations involve verifying that the product, service, or results are free of errors.

Data representation is another approach, using the 7 basic quality tools discussed previously:

1. Cause-and-effect diagrams
2. Flowcharts
3. Check sheets

4. Pareto diagrams

5. Histogram

6. Control charts

7. Scatter diagrams

Lastly, *meetings* are used when controlling quality.

Outputs

Quality control measurements are the documented results of control quality. Quality control measurements should be in the agreed-upon format stated in the quality management plan.

Verified deliverables determine the correctness of the deliverables.

Work performance information contains information on project requirements fulfillments, causes for rejection, rework required, recommendations for corrective action, a list of verified deliverables, and the status of quality metrics.

Change requests may be necessary because of the control quality process.

Project management plan updates that may be necessary because of control quality process to the *quality management plan.*

Project documents updates include updates to the *issues log*, *lessons learned register*, *risk register*, and *test and evaluation documents.*

Exam Alert!

1. Terri is a new project manager at a manufacturing firm. Terri currently has completed the planning stage. Her team has begun implementing the work according to the project plan. One of Terri's team members has noticed a problem with her task but has not yet found a fix. All are tools and techniques used to determine the problem except:

   a) Prototypes

   b) An oscilloscope

   c) Fishbone

   d) Bottom-up estimating

Answer: *b*. An oscilloscope is outside the scope of PMP. Prototypes are used to find problems in a design, bottom-up estimating is used to estimate the time and cost issues of a project, fishbone is used to find root causes.

2.   David is a new project manager for the Razor LLC. David wants to get off to the best start understanding ways to deliver a quality product. David and his team are planning for accuracy in quality. Which of the following tools is one of the seven rules of quality control?

   a) Analysis technique

   b) Cause-and-effect diagram

   c) Data representation

   d) Manage quality

Answer: *b*. Only cause-and-effect diagram is one of the seven rules of quality control.

9.6 Control Resources

According to PMBOK, the *control resources* process ensures the physical resources assigned and allocated to the project are available as planned versus actual utilization of resources and taking corrective actions as necessary.[89]

Case Study— IT Infrastructure Project in the Role of Technical Project Manager

The control of resources comes in two parts: people and equipment.

With equipment, you control use, either leasing or buying options. With people, you control how much time they are allowed to work on activities on a project.

The equipment resources, in this case, are computer, network, and storage systems and their redundant systems. The people resources are hardware and software engineers, storage administrators, network administrators, database administrators, application developers and administrators, and the project manager.

Other resources that need to be controlled are people or equipment that has been procured. Procurement resources must follow the agreed-upon contract.

89   *PMBOK Guide*, Sixth Edition, 352.

Process	Inputs	Tools and Techniques	Outputs
9.6 Control Resources	Project management plan » Resource management plan Project documents » Issues log » Lessons learned register » Physical resource assignments » Project schedule » Resource breakdown structure » Resource requirements » Risk register Work performance data Agreements OPA	Data Analysis » Alternative analysis » Cost-benefit analysis » Performance reviews » Trend analysis » Problem-solving Interpersonal and team skills » Negotiation » Influencing PMIS	Work performance information Change requests PMP updates » Resource management plan » Schedule baseline » Cost baseline Project documents updates » Assumption log » Issues log » Lessons learned register » Physical resource assignments » Resource breakdown structure » Risk register

Inputs

The *project management plan* is a how-to guide on how the project will be monitored and controlled for controlling resources. The *resource management plan* is the efficient and effective development of an organization's resources when they are needed.

Project documents are also used when controlling resources via the *issues log*, *lessons learned register*, *physical resource assignments*, *project schedule*, *resource breakdown structure*, *resource requirements*, and *risk register*.

Other documents utilized when controlling resources are *work performance data*, *agreements*, and *organizational process assets*.

Tools and Techniques

Data analysis techniques include *alternative analysis*, *cost-benefit analysis*, *performance reviews*, *trend analysis*, *and problem-solving*.

Interpersonal and team skills are necessary when controlling resources are *negotiation* and *influencing* techniques.

Lastly, *PMIS* is a tool used when controlling resources.

Outputs

Work performance information will contain information about how resources are performing and how resources are allocated across project activities.

Change requests are issued for corrective or preventive action in case resources need to be added or replaced.

Project management plan updates could be made to the *resource management plan*, *schedule baseline*, and *cost baseline*.

Project documents updates include updates to the *assumption log*, *issues log*, *lessons learned register*, *physical resource assignments*, *resource breakdown structure*, and *risk register*.

Exam Alert!

1. The executive steering committee of your organization is in the process of selecting projects for the next fiscal year. During that meeting you are called in to explain to the committee various approaches to selecting projects. One committee member prefers to use a method that shows the series of the sum of discounted cash flows, given a specific interest rate. Which of the following methods will you use?

    a) Present value

    b) Net present value

    c) Expectancy Theory

    d) Benefit-cost ratio

Answer: *b.* Net present value shows the series of the sum of discounted cash flows offset by project costs. Present value explains what the value of a future cash flow would be in terms of the value of that money today. Benefit cost ratio is derived from a benefit cost analysis, wherein the benefits of the project are divided by the cost to complete the project. Multi-objective programming is a mathematical approach using algorithms, or a specific set of steps to solve a particular problem..

2. What is the correct order of team development?

    a) Performing, storming, norming, forming, and adjourning

    b) Performing, storming, adjourning, forming, and norming

    c) Forming, norming, storming, performing, and adjourning

    d) Forming, storming, norming, performing, and adjourning

Answer: *d.* Only *d* is in the correct order.

10.3 Monitor Communications

According to PMBOK, the *monitor communications* process ensures the information needs of the project and its stakeholders are met.[90]

> ### Case Study— IT Infrastructure Project in the Role of Technical Project Manager
>
> Project information is captured and distributed to the appropriate stakeholders in a format and time agreed upon in the communications management plan.
>
> » Summary information and the categorized information is getting to those who require it, such as senior managers.
>
> » Recaps of meeting are the topics covered then used to inform affected stakeholders.
>
> » The meetings are accomplished via email, presentations, and conferences. The meetings are attended both locally and virtually.
>
> » All meetings are monitored and tracked by the project team in accordance with the communications management plan.

Process	Inputs	Tools and Techniques	Outputs
10.3 Monitor Communications	Project management plan » Resource management plan » Communications management plan » Stakeholder engagement plan Project documents » Issues log » Lessons learned register » Project communications Work performance data OPA EEF	Expert judgments PMIS Data analysis » Stakeholder engagement assessment matrix Interpersonal and team skills » Observation » Conversation skills Meetings	Work performance information Change requests Project management plan updates » Communications management plan » Stakeholder engagement plan Project document updates » Issues log » Lessons learned register

Inputs

90   *PMBOK Guide*, Sixth Edition, 388.

» The *resource management plan* is the efficient and effective development of an organization's resources when they are needed.

» The *communications management plan* contains instructions on how to communicate and how to manage, monitor, and control communications.

» The *stakeholder engagement plan* contains how to engage, manage, and monitor the stakeholders.

Project documents contain the most recent *issues logs*, *lessons learned regis*ter, and *project communications*.

Work performance data contains the quantity of communication that has been distributed.

Organizational process assets are the policies, practices, and procedures; the *enterprise environmental factors* are the internal and external factors the project team has no control over and how they influence the monitor communications process.

Tools and Techniques

Expert judgments are considerations provided by those with experience, skills, and specialized knowledge in the monitor communication process.

PMIS is a tool used in the monitor communication process.

Data analysis for control monitor communication is the *stakeholder engagement assessment matrix*.

Interpersonal and team skills necessary for the monitor communication process are *observation* and *conversation skills*.

Meetings are used to discuss the effectiveness of the monitor communication process.

Outputs

Work performance information has information on the effectiveness of the communication process.

Change requests are issued when adjustments, actions, or interventions on the communications management plan are necessary.

Project management plan updates are performed on the *communications management plan* or the *stakeholder engagement plan*.

Project document updates can be made to the *issues log* or the *lessons learned register.*

Exam Alert!

1. Which answer best describes monitor communications?

   a) The process of developing an appropriate approach and plan for project communication activities based on the information needs of each stakeholder, available organizational assets, and the needs of the project

   b) The document that includes information on staff acquisition and release, resource calendars, recognition and rewards, and compliance and safety

   c) The process to monitor communications and the process of ensuring the information needs of the project and its stakeholders are met

   d) The process of ensuring the information needs of the project and its stakeholders are met

   Answer: *c.* Only answer *c* describes monitor communications accurately.

2. Joseph is a new project manager for MyWay Inc. Joseph's team consists of 6 members, including Tom. Two new members have just been added. What is the number of channels of communication?

   a) 13

   b) 12

   c) 15

   d) 28

   Answer: *d.*

   The communication channel formula is $n(n + 1) / 2$.

   (Where n = the number of people on the project).

   $$6 + 2 = 8$$

   $$8(7) = 56$$

   $$56 / 2 = 28$$

3. Joseph is a new project manager for MyWay Inc. Joseph's team consists of 6 members, including Tom. Two new members have just been added. How many more channels of communication are there now?

    a) 13

    b) 12

    c) 15

    d) 28

Answer: *a.*

The communication channel formula is n x (n - 1)/2.

> (Where n = the number of people on the project).
>
> Previous channels for 6 members.
>
> (8(7) / 2) - (6(5) / 2)
>
> 28 - 15 = 13
>
> 6x(6-1)/2=6x5/2=15.
>
> Add 2 members. Additional channels=8x(8-1)/2=(56/2)=28.
>
> More channels= (Additional channels-Previous channels)=28-15=13

11.7 Monitor Risks

According to PMBOK, the *monitor risks* process monitors the implementation of the agreed-upon risk response plan, tracking identified risks, analyzing new risks, and evaluating the risk process.[91]

---

91 *PMBOK Guide*, Sixth Edition, 453.

Case Study— IT Infrastructure Project in the Role of Technical Project Manager

The risks in the technical infrastructure IT project were planned in the risk management plan, identified, and added to the risk register. The identified risks were also subjected to qualitative and quantitative risk analysis for the likelihood of occurrence and monetary cost to the project.

If the risk did occur, we put together a risk response strategy and implemented the appropriate strategy for the risk that occurred.

So, in this process, we monitored the risk response strategy's effectiveness.

» Did the response strategy work?

» Were there secondary or residual risks that required a new response strategy?

» Is the risk management plan still appropriate?

» Are the project assumptions still valid?

» What is the impact on the contingency reserves?

These are just a few questions to consider when tracking risks.

Process	Inputs	Tools and Techniques	Outputs
11.7 Monitor Risks	Project management plan » Risk management plan Project documents » Issues log » Lessons learned register » Risk register » Risk report Work performance data Work performance reports	Data analysis » Technical performance analysis » Reserve analysis Audits Meetings	Work performance information Change requests Project management updates Project documents updates » Assumptions log » Issues log » Lessons learned register » Risk register » Risk report OPA updates

Inputs

The *project management plan* is a how-to guide on how the project will be monitored and controlled and closed. The *risk management plan* is a document that a project manager prepares to foresee risks, estimate impacts, and define responses to issues.

The *project documents* used to generate a document for monitoring risks are the *issues log*, *lessons learned register*, *risk register*, and *risk report*.

The *work performance data* contains information on the status of risk responses that have been implemented, risks that have occurred, risks that are active, and risks that are closed.

The *work performance reports* provide information on performance measurements such as variance analysis, earned value data, and forecasting data.

Tools and Techniques

Data analysis techniques include *technical performance analysis*, which compares performance achievements to project execution. *Reserve analysis* is an analysis of the budget or schedule contingency reserve because of positive or negative impacts to the project.

Audits, in this case, are reviews of the risk management process and its effectiveness.

Meetings about risks and risk management can be done face to face, virtually, formally, or informally to get the most up-to-date status of the risks.

Outputs

Work performance information compares individual risks with how they have occurred versus how these individual risks would have occurred.

Change requests might occur to the schedule or cost baseline in the process of monitoring risk.

Project management updates might occur to any component of the project management plan.

Project documents updates are made to the *assumptions log*, *issues log*, *lessons learned register*, *risk register*, and *risk report*.

Organizational process assets updates may occur to procedures, policies, or practices because of monitoring risk.

Exam Alert!

1. Which answer best describes the risk management plan?

    a) It contains all the requirements of the project.

    b) It is the process of defining how to conduct risk management activities for a project.

    c) It is not a desirable choice when managing large projects.

    d) It is used for mapping the probability of each risk occurrence and the impact on project objectives if the risk occurs.

Answer: *b*. Option *a* describes requirements documentation, *c* is not the choice because you want a risk management plan, and *d* describes the probability impact matrix.

2. Joe is a project manager and has a sponsor who does not like risk, so Joe must identify the risks and list the probability of occurrence. Which answer best describes the probability and impact matrix?

    a) It contains all the requirements of the project.

    b) It is the process of defining how to conduct risk management activities for a project.

    c) It is not a desirable choice when managing large projects.

    d) It is used for mapping the probability of each risk occurrence and the impact on project objectives if the risk occurs.

Answer: *d*. Answer a describes collect requirements, *b* is the risk management plan, and *c* is never the answer.

12.3 Control Procurements

According to PMBOK, the *control procurements* process manages procurement relationships, monitors contract performance, makes changes and corrections as appropriate, and closes out contracts.[92]

Case Study— IT Infrastructure Project in the Role of Technical Project Manager

As a project manager, whether you are managing physical resources such as renting, leasing or purchasing equipment, or managing people resources with fixed-based or cost-based contracts, you are managing the procurement of the project and the agreed-upon contract.

In the infrastructure project, physical resources were the technical resources such as computers, storage, and network systems. Also, technical software resources were the operating, cluster, database, and application systems that were used.

Process	Inputs	Tools and Techniques	Outputs
12.3 Control Procurements	Project management plan » Requirements management plan » Risk management plan » Procurement management plan » Change management plan » Schedule baseline Project documents » Assumptions log » Issues log » Lessons learned register » Milestone list » Quality report » Requirements documentation » Requirements traceability matrix » Risk register » Stakeholder register Agreements Procurement documentation Approved change requests Work performance data OPA EEF	Expert judgments Claims administration Data analysis » Performance reviews » Earned value analysis » Trend analysis Inspection Audits	Closed procurements Work performance information Procurement documentation updates Change requests Project management plan updates » Risk management plan » Procurement management plan » Schedule baseline » Cost baseline Project documents updates » Lessons learned register » Milestone list » Resource requirements » Requirements traceability matrix » Risk register » Stakeholder register OPA updates

Inputs

The *project management plan* contains the following:

> » The *requirements management plan* is used to document the information required to efficiently manage project requirements.

» The *risk management plan* is a document that a project manager prepares to foresee risks, estimate impacts, and define responses to issues.

» The *procurement management plan* is the creation of relationships with outside vendors and suppliers of goods and services needed to complete a project.

» The *change management plan* is the document that states how the change will be managed.

» The *schedule baseline* is the approved version of a schedule that can be changed only through formal change control procedures and is used as a basis for comparison to actual results.

Project documents that are used as inputs are the *assumptions log, issues log, lessons learned register, milestone list, quality report, requirements documentation, requirements traceability matrix, risk register,* and *stakeholder register.*

Agreements are the understanding between parties stating terms and conditions of the procurement contracts.

Procurement documentation contains a statement of work, payment information, contractor work, performance information, plans, drawings, and more.

Approved change requests, in this case, are the changes in the terms and conditions of the contract, which include the procurement statement of work, pricing, services, or results descriptions.

Work performance data comprises seller data on project status (e.g., technical performance), the status of activities, and the costs that have been incurred.

Organizational process assets include policies, practices, and procedures.

Enterprise environmental factors are factors outside the project team's control.

Tools and Techniques

Expert judgments are considerations provided by those with experience, skills, and specialized knowledge in controlling procurements.

Claims administration handles contested changes or compensation in situations in which the buyer and seller cannot reach an agreement. These claims are documented, processed, monitored, and managed throughout the contract life cycle per the terms of the contract.

Data analysis techniques used for controlling and monitoring procurements are *performance reviews*, *earned value analysis*, and *trend analysis*.

Inspection is when the contractor performs the structural review of the work—either a review of the deliverables or a physical review.

Audits are the review of the procurement process. While inspection checks whether the outcome of a product, deliverable or result is correct, auditing checks whether the process was performed responsibly for the end product, deliverable, or result. The product, deliverable, or result can be defective, but if the process passes the audit, then only the product, deliverable, or result needs to be fixed. However, if the product, deliverable, or result is correct, but the process fails the audit, then the process or the way things are done and the product, deliverable, or result need to be retested.

Inspections will occur in the monitoring and control process. Audits are performed in the execute process group.

Outputs

With *closed procurements*, the buyer, through formal notice issued by the authorized procurement administrator, notifies the seller that the contract has been completed. The authorized procurement administrator works in the buyer's procurement department. The authorized procurement administrator is assigned once it is established that procurement resources are necessary or wanted.

Work performance information includes information on how a seller is performing by comparing the deliverable received to the technical performance achieved and the cost incurred.

Procurement documentation updates may include all approved change requests, requested but unapproved contract changes, and supporting schedules.

Change requests may result from the control procurement process.

Project management plan updates may occur to the *risk management plan*, *procurement management plan*, *schedule baseline*, and *cost baseline* because of the control procurement process.

Project documents updates are made to the *lessons learned register*, *milestone list*, *resource requirements*, *requirements traceability matrix*, *risk register*, and *stakeholder register*.

Organizational process assets updates to policies, practices, and procedures may occur due to the control procurement process.

Exam Alert!

1. Janine is a longtime project manager at Aspire LLC. Janine needs to work with the procurement department to secure people with sufficient skills. Which answer best describes the control procurements process?

    a) The process of documenting project decisions, specifying the approach, and identifying potential sellers

    b) The process of creating templates for the risk management plan, risk register, and risk report

    c) The process of managing procurement relationships, monitoring contract performance, making changes and corrections as appropriate, and closing out contracts

    d) The process of obtaining seller responses, selecting a seller, and awarding a contract

Answer: *c.* The process of managing procurement relationships, monitoring contract performance, making changes and corrections as appropriate, and closing out contracts

2. Which is a tool or technique of the control procurements process?

    a) Project management plan

    b) Communication management plan

    c) Change requests

    d) Claims administration

Answer: d. The project management plan and communication management plan are documents, a change request is an output.

13.4 Monitor Stakeholder Engagement

According to PMBOK, the *monitor stakeholder engagement* process monitors project stakeholder relationships and tailors strategies for engaging stakeholders through modification of engagement strategies and plans.[93]

---

93 *PMBOK Guide*, Sixth Edition, 530.

Case Study— IT Infrastructure Project in the Role of Technical Project Manager

The primary stakeholder is the person who is responsible for the project and its funding; however, there are other stakeholders.

1. The project manager and the project team that perform the planning, execution, monitoring, and eventual closing of the project are stakeholders.

2. Other systems that are affected by your project become stakeholders.

3. If you are using a resource from a function manager, the function manager becomes a stakeholder.

4. Anyone who is positively or negatively affected by your project becomes a stakeholder.

Stakeholders can be internal or external to the organization. All stakeholders must be engaged as established by the stakeholder engagement plan.

Inputs

The *project management plan* is a how-to guide on how the project will be monitored and controlled.

> » The *resource management plan* is the efficient and effective development of an organization's resources when they are needed.

> » The *communications management plan* states how communication will be planned, managed, distributed, and eventually disposed of.

> » The *stakeholder engagement plan* provides a method for documenting the stakeholders' needs and expectations.

The *project documents* include the *issues log*, *lessons learned register*, *project communications*, *risk register*, and *stakeholder register*.

Work performance data contains data such as which stakeholder is supportive of the project.

Organizational process assets contain the policies, practices, and procedures.

Enterprise environmental factors are both internal and external factors that may influence stakeholder engagement.

Tools and Techniques

One of the tools and techniques that is used in stakeholder engagement is *data analysis*, which includes *alternative analysis*, *root cause analysis*, and *stakeholder analysis*, as well as *decision-making*, which includes *multicriteria decisions analysis*.

Data representation at this stage includes the *stakeholder engagement assessment matrix*.

Furthermore, there are *communication skills*, which include *feedback* and *presentation skills*, that a project manager must have to engage stakeholders.

Then there are the *interpersonal and team skills*, such as *active listening*, *cultural awareness*, *leadership*, *networking*, and *political awareness*.

Lastly, *meetings* can be done face to face, virtually, formally, or informally to engage stakeholders.

Outputs

Work performance information documents the status of the stakeholder engagement level compared to desired levels.

Change requests can occur because of monitoring stakeholder engagement.

Project management plan updates include the *resource management plan*, *communications management plan*, and *stakeholder engagement plan*.

Project documents updates are made to the *issues log*, *lessons learned register*, *project communications*, *risk register*, and *stakeholder register*.

Exam Alert!

1. Kazem is a project manager with many years of experience. Kazem knows how important customer communication and satisfaction are to project management. What is the best definition of the monitor stakeholder engagement process?

    a) The process of identifying project stakeholders regularly and analyzing and documenting relevant information regarding their interests, involvement, interdependencies, influence, and impact on project success

    b) The process of communicating and working with stakeholders to meet their needs and expectations, address issues, and foster appropriate stakeholder engagement

    c) The process of providing an overview of the project stakeholder management process

    d) The process of monitoring project stakeholder relationships and tailoring strategies for engaging stakeholders through the modification of engagement strategies and plans

    Answer: *d*. Option *a* is identifying stakeholders, *b* is manage stakeholder engagement, and *c* does not exist.

2. The following describe monitor stakeholder engagement except

    a) Managing stakeholder relationships

    b) Ignoring the stakeholders until they go away

    c) Engaging with the stakeholders

    d) Formulating strategies with the stakeholders

    Answer: *b*. You would think answer b would be common sense, but it is surprising how many testers will miss a question like this on the exam. You never ignore stakeholders because communication, collaboration and compromise are primary tools as a project manager.

Section 6: Closing Group Processes

Close Project or Phase
4.7 Close Project or Phase

4.7 Close Project or Phase

According to PMBOK, the *close project or phase* process finalizes all activities for the project, phase, or contract.[94]

It is paramount to understand the order of the closing process for the PMP exam but also in project management in real life.

The order of the closing process:

Obtain acceptance from the customer or sponsor.	Though the project is completed, the project is not successfully closed until the sponsor accepts and signs off on all deliverables.
Conduct post-project or phase-end review.	Hold meetings with the project team to conduct exit interviews on the project.
Record impacts of tailoring any process.	This information will be in the change log, assumptions log, and issues log.
Document lessons learned.	Deliver the lessons learned register to the PMO for future projects.
Apply appropriate updates to the OPA.	Procedures, policies, practices, and templates could change because of this project.
Archive all relevant project documents.	These documents can be archived in the project management information system (PMIS) to be used as historical data.
Close out all procurement activities.	Ensure termination of all relevant agreements.
Perform team member assessments.	Release project resources.

---

94 *PMBOK Guide,* Sixth Edition, 121.

Process	Inputs	Tools and Techniques	Outputs
4.7 Close Project or Phase	Project charter Project management plan » All components Project documents » Assumptions log » Basis of estimates » Change log » Issues log » Lessons learned register » Milestone list » Project communications » Quality control measurements » Quality report » Requirements documentation » Risk register » Risk report » Accepted deliverables » Business documents » Business case » Benefits management plan Agreements Procurement documents OPA	Expert judgments Data analysis » Document analysis » Regression analysis » Trend analysis » Variance analysis Meetings	Final product documents Final product, service, or result Final report OPA updates

Inputs

The *project charter* contains the deliverables that must be met for a project to be considered closed successfully. The project can be closed once all deliverables have been successfully completed to the customer's satisfaction.

The *project management plan* is a how-to guide on how the project will be designed, managed, monitored and controlled, and closed. All components are used when closing the project.

Project documents used when closing the project include the *assumptions log, basis of estimates, change log, issues log, lessons learned register, milestone list, project communications, quality control measurements, quality report, requirements documentation, risk register, risk report, accepted deliverables, business documents, business case*, and *benefits management plan*.

Agreements such as contracts as well as all *procurement documents* must be completed and closed.

Organizational process assets and *enterprise environmental factors* can also influence closing process via processes, policies, and procedures.

Tools and Techniques

Expert judgments are considerations provided by those with experience and expertise such as PMOs, consultants, and other project managers in management control, audit, legal, procurement, and legislation.

Management control is getting customer acceptance and collecting all project documents.

Audit is analysis of the processes that produce the deliverables.

Also necessary are those with experience in the procurement process and those with knowledge of and experience in the law.

Data analysis techniques used are *document analysis*, *regression analysis*, *trend analysis*, and *variance analysis*.

Meetings are used to confirm deliverables have been accepted.

Outputs

The outputs of the *close project or phase* process are the *final product documents*; *the final product, service, or result*; *the final report*; and *organizational process assets updates*.

Exam Alert!

1. Susan is a first-time project manager; however, she is excited to make a good impression. Halfway through her project, Susan gets an email from the client that the project will be canceled because of a funding issue. What should Susan do next?

    a) Try to negotiate with the client and suggest where to find additional funding.

    b) Prepare the final project report.

    c) Tell the team this is only a temporary setback. It has happened before on a similar project, but the problem was cleared shortly.

    d) Ask senior management to talk to the client.

Answer: *b.* Susan should immediately begin the closing process. Prepare final report is the only answer that is part of the closing process.

2. Which is a tool and technique of the close project or phase process?

    a) Regression analysis

    b) OPA

    c) EEF

    d) Deliverables

Answer: *a.* *b* and *c* are inputs to other processes. Deliverables is an output to direct and manage project work.

PART IV:

Ethics: Professional and Social Responsibility

If it does not seem right or seems dishonest, then it is not right and dishonest, so you should not do it.

The PMI Code of Ethics and Professional Conduct was written to help the project management professional make wise decisions.[95]

The PMI Code of Ethics and Professional Conduct applies to all:

- » PMI members
- » PMI non-members who hold a PMI certification
- » PMI non-members who apply to PMI to initiate the PMI certification process
- » PMI non-members who serve PMI in a voluntary capacity

There are four basic tenets to the code, each with aspirational and mandatory standards:

1. Responsibility
2. Respect
3. Fairness
4. Honesty

---

95 PMI, "Code of Ethics & Professional Conduct," https://www.pmi.org/about/ethics/code.

Responsibility

A duty to satisfactorily perform or complete a task that you promise to do, that you must fulfill, and that has a consequent penalty for failure.

Respect

Treating people in a positive manner that acknowledges them for who they are and what they are doing.

Fairness

The quality of making judgments that are free from discrimination.

Honesty

A facet of moral character that connotes positive and virtuous attributes such as integrity, truthfulness, and straightforwardness, along with the absence of lying, cheating, theft, et cetera.

Summary

The success and failure of a project starts with whether the project is feasible. Are the constraints too limited—is there not enough time or not enough funding? Is the technology either nonexistent or not mature enough to make the project possible? The feasibility of the project is determined upon the completion of the project plan. Once the project plan is approved, the project is executed and monitored according to the plan. The project team can complete the deliverables, but the sponsor is responsible for accepting the deliverables. Acceptance of deliverables is immediately followed by the closure of the project, fulfillment of contracts, archiving of documents, and releasing of resources.

As a project manager, especially in IT infrastructure project management, you can expect to manage multiple projects simultaneously. Passing the PMP exam demonstrates to everyone that you are a master of the language of project management and are more than capable of leading and managing the project. This book is your guide to successfully passing the PMP exam as well as leading and managing IT infrastructure projects as a technical project manager.

Mock Exam—Concentration

1. Ali is a new project manager for the Razor LLC. Ali wants to get off to the best start understanding the project, people, and environment. Interpersonal and team skills is a tool and technique of which process?

   a) Meetings

   b) Develop project charter

   c) OPA

   d) Planning

2. All the following are inputs to develop project charter except

   a) SOW

   b) assumptions and constraints

   c) OPA

   d) Data analysis

3. The outputs to develop project charter are

   a) Project management plan and requirements plan

   b) Project charter and assumptions log

   c) Quality management plan and change management plan

   d) Stakeholder management plan

4. All are inputs to identify stakeholder group except

   a) Project charter

   b) EEF

   c) Expert judgment

   d) OPA

5. All describe a project charter except

   a) Formally authorizes the existence of a project

   b) Provides project manager the authority to apply organizational resources to the project

c) States the high-level constraints and assumptions of the project

d) States the details of project deliverables

6. Which best describes the process develop project charter?

   a) The process of developing a document that formally authorizes the existence of a project and provides the project manager with authority to apply organizational resources to project activities.

   b) The process of documenting how the project and product scope will be defined, validated, and controlled throughout the project.

   c) The process of developing detailed descriptions of the project and products. This is what the project includes and excludes.

   d) The process of estimating the number of work periods needed to complete activities with the estimated resources.

7. Which tool and technique would a project manager use to collect information about a potential project during the project integration management?

   a) Data analysis

   b) Data representation

   c) Manage quality

   d) Data gathering

8. All are tools and techniques in identify stakeholders process except

   a) Brainstorming

   b) Data analysis

   c) Change requests

   d) Data representation

9. What is the output of the identify stakeholder process?

   a) Project management plan

   b) Stakeholder register

   c) Quality management plan

   d) Requirements management plan

10. The output of the develop project management plan is

   a) Change management plan

   b) Configuration management plan

   c) Project management plan

   d) Stakeholder baseline

11. Which is the correct definition of the develop project management plan?

   a) The process of developing a document that formally authorizes the existence of a project and provides the project manager with authority to apply organizational resources to project activities.

   b) The process of documenting how the project and product scope will be defined, validated, and controlled throughout the project.

   c) The process of developing detailed descriptions of the project and products. This is what the project includes and excludes.

   d) The process of what needs to be done to define, prepare, and coordinate all subsidiary activities to produce a document that defines the project.

12. All are part of develop project management plan except

   a) Define all subsidiary activities

   b) State high-level requirements

   c) Prepare all subsidiary activities

   d) Coordinate all subsidiary activities

13. All are part of a project management plan except

   a) How work will be executed

   b) How work will be monitored

   c) Implementing project work

   d) How work will be closed

14. Which is the best definition of the project management plan?

   a) The process of developing a document that formally authorizes the existence of a project and provides the project manager with authority to apply organizational resources to project activities.

b) The document that describes how work will be executed, monitored and controlled, and closed.

c) The process of developing detailed descriptions of the project and products. This is what the project includes and excludes.

d) The process of what needs to be done to define, prepare, and coordinate all subsidiary activities to produce a document that defines the project.

15. All are contained in plan scope management except

a) How the project and product scope will be defined

b) Implementing change requests

c) How the project and product scope will be validated

d) How the project and product scope will be controlled throughout the project

16. Which best describes the process plan scope management?

a) The process of developing a document that formally authorizes the existence of a project and provides the project manager with authority to apply organizational resources to project activities.

b) The process of documenting how the project and product scope will be defined, validated, and controlled throughout the project.

c) The process of developing detailed descriptions of the project and products. This is what the project includes and excludes.

d) The process of estimating the number of work periods needed to complete activities with the estimated resources.

17. All are contained in the define scope process except

a) What the project includes and excludes.

b) Output is the project scope statement.

c) Detailed description of the project and products.

d) How the project and product scope will be validated.

18. Which best describes the process define scope?

a) The process of developing a document that formally authorizes the existence of a project and provides the project manager with authority to apply organizational resources to project activities.

b) The process of documenting how the project and product scope will be defined, validated, and controlled throughout the project.

c) The process of developing detailed descriptions of the project and products. This is what the project includes and excludes.

d) The process of estimating the number of work periods needed to complete activities with the estimated resources.

19. All the following describe estimate activity durations except

a) Determine risks

b) The process of estimating work periods

c) The work periods to complete activities

d) Estimated resources to complete activities

20. Which best describes the process estimate activity durations?

a) The process of developing a document that formally authorizes the existence of a project and provides the project manager with authority to apply organizational resources to project activities.

b) The process of documenting how the project and product scope will be defined, validated, and controlled throughout the project.

c) The process of developing detailed descriptions of the project and products. This is what the project includes and excludes.

d) The process of estimating the number of work periods needed to complete activities with the estimated resources.

21. The output to develop project management plan is

a) Project charter

b) EEF

c) Project management plan

d) OPA

22. The outputs of plan scope management are

a) Scope management plan and requirements management plan

b) Quality management plan and process improvement plan

c) Resource management plan and resource breakdown structure

d) Risk management plan and risk improvement plan

23. The _____ are influences out of the project manager's control.

a) Enterprise environmental factors

b) OPA

c) Evolution environmental factors

d) Extreme environmental factors

24. _____ are factors internal to the organization that affect the project.

a) Optimal process assets

b) Omni process assets

c) Organization process assets

d) Optical process assets

25. Ahmal is a project manager with many years of experience. Ahmal's current project is especially difficult because of problems with the timeline getting extended many times. This could be because the scope may not be well defined, causing increases in cost because of increased hours of work on the project for fixes. All may be found in the project charter except

a) Project purpose

b) High-level requirements

c) Detail requirements

d) Key stakeholder list

26. Susan is a project manager with many years of experience. Susan's current project is especially difficult because of problems with the timeline getting extended many times. This could be because the scope may not be well defined, causing increases in cost because of increased hours of work on the project for fixes. What best describes the process collect requirements?

a) Project purpose.

b) The process to determine, document, and manage stakeholder needs and requirements to meet project objectives.

c) Detail requirements.

d) Key stakeholder list.

27. Susan is a project manager with many years of experience. Susan's current project is especially difficult because of problems with the timeline getting extended many times. This could be because the scope may not be well defined, causing increases in cost because of increased hours of work on the project for fixes. Which tool and technique links product requirements from their origins to the deliverables that satisfy them?

    a) Project purpose

    b) Requirements traceability matrix

    c) Detail requirements

    d) Key stakeholder list

28. The output of define scope is

    a) Project documents

    b) Data analysis

    c) Project scope statement

    d) Risk management plan

29. David is a project manager with many years of experience. David's current project is especially difficult because of problems with the timeline getting extended many times. This could be because the scope may not be well defined, causing increases in cost because of increased hours of work on the project for fixes. What best describes the process define scope?

    a) Project purpose.

    b) The process to determine, document, and manage stakeholder needs and requirements to meet project objectives.

    c) Detail requirements.

    d) The process of developing detailed descriptions of the project and products. This is what the project includes and excludes.

30. Susan is a project manager with many years of experience. Susan's current project is especially difficult because of problems with the timeline getting extended many times. This could be because the scope may not be well defined, causing increases in cost because of increased hours of work on the project for fixes. What is the output of define scope?

    a) Project scope statement and project documents updates.

b) The process of determining, documenting, and managing stakeholder needs and requirements to meet project objectives.

c) Detail requirements.

d) The process of developing detailed descriptions of the project and products. This is what the project includes and excludes.

31. Which best describes the process define scope?

a) The process of developing a detailed description of the project and product

b) The process of creating a scope management plan that documents how the project and product scope will be defined, validated, and controlled

c) The process of subdividing project deliverables and project work into smaller, more manageable components

d) The process of monitoring the status of the project and product scope and managing changes in the scope baseline

32. The output of create WBS is

a) Decomposition

b) Scope baseline

c) Project management plan

d) Product scope statement

33. Which process best describes create WBS?

a) The process of developing a detailed description of the project and product

b) The process of creating a scope management plan that documents how the project and product scope will be defined, validated, and controlled

c) The process of subdividing project deliverables and project work into smaller, more manageable components

d) The process of monitoring the status of the project and product scope and managing changes in the scope baseline

34. Which are number systems in the WBS dictionary and WBS, respectively?

a) Code of account identifier and (1.0, 1.1, 1.1.1)

b) Chart of accounts and (a, ab, abc)

c) Control chart and (1,2,3)

d) All of the above

35. The scope baseline consists of

a) The process of developing a detailed description of the project and product

b) The project scope statement, WBS, WBS dictionary, and planning package

c) The process of subdividing project deliverables and project work into smaller, more manageable components

d) The process of monitoring the status of the project and product scope and managing changes in the scope baseline

36. The output of plan schedule management is

a) Cost baseline

b) Scope baseline

c) Schedule baseline

d) Schedule management plan

37. All describe the project schedule management except

a) Define activities

b) Sequence activities

c) Change requests

d) Estimate activity durations

38. As a project manager, James planning the activities in the project schedule management for the project. Which of the following depicts the order of activities in schedule management?

a) Collect requirements, define scope, create WBS

b) Identify risks, perform qualitative risk analysis, perform quantitative risk analysis, and plan risk responses

c) Plan schedule management, define activities, sequence activities, estimate activity durations, and develop schedule

d) Estimate costs and determine budget

39. Jason is a new project manager currently in the planning phase of a project. Jason has defined the

activities. As a project manager, what should Jason do next?

a) Sequence activities

b) Estimate costs

c) Plan schedule management

d) Identify risks

40. Peter is a new project manager currently in the planning phase of a project. Peter has defined the activities. As a project manager, what did Peter do prior to defining activities?

a) Sequence activities

b) Estimate costs

c) Plan schedule management

d) Identify risks

41. As a senior project manager, you are planning the activities in the project schedule for the project. What is the output of plan schedule management?

a) Collect requirements, define scope, create WBS

b) Identify risks, perform qualitative risk analysis, perform quantitative risk analysis, plan risk responses

c) Schedule management plan

d) Estimate costs, determine budget

42. The output of define activities is

a) Activity list, milestone list, activity attributes and change requests

b) Identify risks, perform qualitative risk analysis, perform quantitative risk analysis, and plan risk responses

c) Plan schedule management, define activities, sequence activities, estimate activity resources, estimate activity costs, and develop schedule

d) Estimate costs and determine budget

43. As a junior project manager, you are planning the activities in the project schedule. Which of the following depicts the order of activities in schedule management?

a) Collect requirements, define scope, and create WBS

b) Identify risks, perform qualitative risk analysis, perform quantitative risk analysis, and plan risk responses

c) Plan schedule management, define activities, sequence activities, estimate activity durations, and develop schedule

d) Estimate costs and determine budget

44. utput to define activity consists of all except

a) Activity list

b) Milestone list

c) Rolling wave

d) Activity attributes

45. The output of sequence activities is

a) Change request

b) Project management plan

c) Project schedule network diagram

d) Data analysis

46. Jason is a new project manager currently in the planning phase of a project. Jason has defined the activities. As a project manager, what should Jason do next?

a) Sequence activities

b) Estimate costs

c) Collect requirements

d) Identify risks

47. John is one of the top project managers in the company. John is concerned about the order of some of the sequenced activities. Of the four types of PDM relationships, which is used most often?

a) Finish to start (FS)

b) Finish to finish (FF)

c) Start to finish (SF)

d) Start to start (SS)

48. Robert is a junior project manager at a consulting firm. Robert has been signed to a high-profile project and needs to be sure the sequence of activities is accurate. Of the four types of PDM relationships, which is used least often?

a) Finish to start (FS)

b) Finish to finish (FF)

c) Start to finish (SF)

d) Start to start (SS)

49. Which is one of the tools and techniques for estimating activity duration?

a) Parametric analogous

b) Schedule compression

c) Critical path method

d) EEF

50. The best description of estimate activity duration is

a) The process of estimating the number of work periods needed to complete activities with the estimated resources

b) The process of defining how the project cost will be estimated, budgeted, managed, and monitored and controlled

c) The process of identifying quality requirements and standards for the project and its deliverables and documenting how the project will demonstrate compliance with quality requirements

d) The process of estimating team resources and quantity of materials, equipment, and supplies necessary to perform project work

51. What is the output to estimate activity duration?

a) Duration estimates

b) Change requests

c) Project management plan

d) Data analysis

52. Which process best describes develop schedule?

    a) The process of analyzing sequences, durations, resource requirements, and schedule constraints to create a project model for project executions, monitoring and controlling

    b) Critical path method

    c) Project documents

    d) Schedule baseline

53. All are tools and techniques for develop schedule except

    a) Critical path

    b) Resource optimization

    c) Schedule data

    d) Schedule compression

54. What is the critical path in days of a project in which the following activities are defined as: activity A has a duration of 5 days and starts the project; activities B and C are duration 3 and 4 days, respectively, and follow A; activity E has a duration of 2 days and follows activity B; activity F has a duration of 2 days and follows activity E; activity D has a duration of 2 days and follows activity C; activity G has a duration of 5 days and follows F and D.

    a) 17 days

    b) 16 days

    c) 18 days

    d) 14 days

55. Now what is the critical path of a project in which the following activities are defined as: activity A has a duration of 5 days and starts the project; activities B and C are duration 3 and 4 days, respectively, and follow A; activity E has a duration of 2 days and follows activity B; activity F has a duration of 2 days and follows activity E; activity D has a duration of 2 days and follows activity C; activity G has a duration of 5 days and follows F and D.

    a) ABEFG

    b) ACDG

    c) There is no critical path.

    d) Critical path can be reduced or changed.

56. What is the float in days of project activities E and C, respectively, where activities are defined as: activity A has a duration of 5 days and starts the project; activities B and C are duration 3 and 4 days, respectively, and follow A; activity E has a duration of 2 days and follows activity B; activity F has a duration of 2 days and follows activity E; activity D has a duration of 2 days and follows activity C; activity G has a duration of 5 days and follows F and D.

   a) 0,1

   b) 1,0

   c) Float is negative, so project is ahead of schedule.

   d) Float is negative, so activity is ahead of schedule.

57. The best description of plan cost management is

   a) The process of defining how the project cost will be estimated, budgeted, managed, and monitored and controlled

   b) The process of defining how to estimate, acquire, manage, and utilize physical and team resources

   c) The process of defining how to conduct risk management activities

   d) The process of identifying the relationships among project activities

58. The output of plan cost management is

   a) Risk management plan

   b) Cost baseline

   c) Cost management plan

   d) Schedule baseline

59. Which is not a tool and technique used in estimate activity duration?

   a) Analogous estimating

   b) Bottom-up estimating

   c) Three-point estimating (PERT)

   d) Duration estimates

60. The best description of estimate costs is

   a) The process of analyzing sequences, durations, resource requirements, and schedule constraints to create a project model for project executions, monitoring, and controlling

b) The process of developing an approximation of the monetary resources needed to complete the work

c) The process of developing an approach and plan for project communications activities based on information needs of each stakeholder and the project

d) The process of defining how to estimate, acquire, manage, and utilize physical and team resources

61. The best description of determine budget process is

a) The process of aggregating the estimated costs of individual activities or work packages to establish an authorized cost baseline

b) The process of developing an approximation of the monetary resources needed to complete the work

c) The process of developing options, selecting strategies, and agreeing on actions to address project risk exposure

d) The process of documenting project decisions, specifying the approach, and identifying potential sellers

62. All are outputs of determine budget except

a) Cost baseline

b) Project funding

c) Data analysis

d) Cost estimates

63. As a project manager III, Michael is planning the activities in the project schedule. Which of the following depicts the order of activities in plan cost management?

a) Collect requirements, define scope, and create WBS

b) Identify risks, perform qualitative risk analysis, perform quantitative risk analysis, and plan risk responses

c) Plan schedule management, define activities, sequence activities, estimate activity resources, estimate activity costs, and develop schedule

d) Estimate costs and determine budget

64. Which best describes plan quality management?

   a) The process of identifying quality requirements and standards for the project and its deliverables and documenting how the project will demonstrate compliance with quality requirements and/or standards

   b) The process of monitoring and recording the results of executing the quality management activities to assess performance and ensure the project outputs are complete, correct, and meet customer requirements

   c) The process of translating the quality management plan into executable quality activities that incorporate the organization's quality policies into the project

   d) None of the above

65. There has been a concern of too many issues after each completed activity in the project. Willian is a project manager and what to fix this problem. Which is a part of cost of conformance?

   a) Rework

   b) Testing

   c) Internal failure costs

   d) Liabilities

66. David is a project manager for a top five IT consulting firm. David believes issues of activities failing can be averted. Which is a part of cost of nonconformance?

   a) Training

   b) Destructive testing loss

   c) Inspections

   d) Lost business

67. Richard is excited about his first full-time project manager role. Richard has multiple project for which is assigned. Nonconformance issues continue to be a problem on one of Richard's projects. All are a part of preventive costs except

   a) Time to do it right

   b) Training

   c) Inspections

   d) Document processes

68. As a project manager it is a good practice to have as many tools as possible to track whether quality is occurring as high level on a project. Which of the following is not one of the seven basic quality tools?

a) Flowcharts

b) Control charts

c) Risk management

d) Check sheets

69. Joseph has been a project manager for twelve years. The process of defining how to estimate, acquire, manage, and utilize physical and team resources fits which process?

a) Develop team

b) Plan resource management

c) Organizational theory

d) Team charter

70. Which tool and technique of plan resource management identify responsible, accountable, consult, and inform parties of tasks/activities?

a) RBS

b) RACI charts

c) Responsibility assignment matrix

d) Organizational theory

71. The following resources necessary to perform work could be represented in estimate activity resource except

a) Team resources and quantity of materials

b) Equipment

c) Supplies necessary

d) Analogous estimating

72. Which answer represents the best definition of estimate activity resource?

a) The process of developing approaches to involve project stakeholders based on their needs, expectations, interests, and potential impact on the project

b) The process of estimating team resources and the quantity of materials, equipment, and supplies necessary to perform project work

c) The process of translating the quality management plan into executable project activities that incorporate the organization's quality policies

d) The process of numerically analyzing the combined effect of identified individual project risks

73. Thomas is a new project manager with minimal experience in acquiring proper resources to do the necessary work. The following tools and techniques can assist Thomas in estimating resources except

a) Bottom-up estimating

b) Analogous estimating

c) Parametric estimating

d) Resource breakdown structure (RBS)

74. Which process best describes estimate activity resource?

a) The process of estimating team resources and the quantity of materials, equipment, and supplies necessary to perform project work

b) The process of defining how to estimate, acquire, manage, and utilize physical and team resources

c) The process of identifying quality requirements and standards for the project and its deliverables and documenting how the project will demonstrate compliance with quality requirements

d) The process of defining how to conduct risk management activities

75. Charles is a seasoned project manager and is wizard at communication management. Which answer below best fits the tools and technique of plan communication management?

a) Change log

b) Project management plan

c) Manage quality

d) Interpersonal and team skills

76. Patricia is starting a new project that involves infrastructure and database migration. Patricia needs to create documents for the best plan of communication for the team. Which answer best describes a communications management plan?

a) The process of developing an appropriate approach and plan for project communication activities based on the information needs of each stakeholder, available organizational assets, and the needs of the project

b) The document that includes information on staff acquisition and release, resource calendars, recognition and rewards, compliance, and safety

c) The process of ensuring timely and appropriate collection, creation, distribution, storage, retrieval, management, monitoring, and ultimate disposition of project information

d) The process of ensuring the information needs of the project and its stakeholders

77. What is the output of plan communications management?

a) Project management plan

b) Project documents

c) Communications management plan

d) Communication baseline

78. Jennifer is an IT project manager at an airline's electronics company. The project is behind schedule and additional people will need to be brought onto the project to get the project back on schedule. What tools and techniques can the project manager use to determine the number of communication channels?

a) Ev - Ac

b) PERT

c) AC + (BAC - EV)

d) N(n+1) / 2

79. As a project manager, you are planning the activities in the project schedule. Which of the following depicts the order of activities in risk management?

a) Collect requirements, define scope, and create WBS

b) Identify risks, perform qualitative risk analysis, perform quantitative risk analysis, and plan risk responses

c) Plan schedule management, define activities, sequence activities, estimate activity resources, estimate activity costs, and develop schedule

d) Estimate costs and determine budget

80. Linda is a new project manager with some experience in risk analysis to do the necessary work. What is the output of plan risk management?

   a) Communication management plan

   b) Configuration management plan

   c) Home improvement plan

   d) Risk management plan

81. Elizabeth is starting a new project that involves infrastructure and database upgrades. What description best identifies with plan risk management?

   a) The process of defining how to conduct risk management activities

   b) The process of using existing knowledge and creating new knowledge to achieve the project's objectives and contribute to organizational learning

   c) The process of translating the quality management plan into executable project activities that incorporate the organization's quality policies

   d) Risk baseline

82. Which process best describes plan communications management?

   a) The process of numerically analyzing the combined effect of identified individual project risks

   b) The process of developing an approach and plan for project communications activities based on the information needs of each stakeholder and the project

   c) Plan-Do-Check-Act

   d) The process of prioritizing individual project risks for further analysis by assessing their probability of occurrence and impact

83. Which process best describes project risk management?

   a) The process of prioritizing individual project risks for further analysis by assessing their probability of occurrence and impact

   b) The process of defining how to estimate, acquire, manage, and utilize physical and team resources

   c) The process of defining how to conduct risk management activities

   d) The process of identifying individual risks as well as sources of overall project risks and documenting their characteristics

84. The output of plan risk management is

    a) Cost management plan

    b) Risk management plan

    c) Scope baseline

    d) Risk baseline

85. Which process best describes identify risk?

    a) The process of identifying individuals risks as well as sources of overall project risks and documenting their characteristics

    b) Data analysis and interpersonal skills

    c) Project management plan

    d) The process of defining how to estimate, acquire, manage, and utilize physical and team resources

86. Barbara is starting a new project that involves application and database migration. A tool and technique that can be used in assessing risk impact is

    a) Project management plan

    b) Project document updates

    c) Risk probability and impact assessment

    d) Risk register

87. Kenneth is a new project manager with minimal experience in acquiring proper resources to do the necessary work. Which description best describes perform qualitative risk analysis?

    a) The process of prioritizing individual project risks for further analysis by assessing their probability of occurrence and impact

    b) The process of numerically analyzing the effect of identified risks on overall project objects

    c) Identify risks, perform qualitative risk analysis, perform quantitative risk analysis, and plan risk responses

    d) Plan schedule management, define activities, sequence activities, estimate activity resources, estimate activity costs, and develop schedule

88. Which answer is the best description of perform quantitative risk analysis?

    a) The process of numerically analyzing the effect of identified risks on overall project objects

b) Identify risks, perform qualitative risk analysis, perform quantitative risk analysis, and plan risk responses

c) Plan schedule management, define activities, sequence activities, estimate activity resources, estimate activity costs, and develop schedule

d) Estimate costs and determine budget

89. The following are tools and techniques to perform quantitative risk analysis except

a) Simulations

b) EEF

c) Tornado diagram

d) Facilitation

90. Sandra is a senior project manager at a solar auto electronics company. This new role brings many new challenges she rarely faced before. The following are strategies for negative risks/threats except

a) Avoid

b) Mitigate

c) Share

d) Transfer

91. The following are strategies for positive risks/threats except

a) Exploit

b) Mitigate

c) Share

d) Enhance

92. Dorothy is a project manager at a local marketing firm. Dorothy needs to perform risk analysis which includes quantitative and qualitative risk analysis. All are tools and techniques to plan risk responses except

a) Expert judgment

b) Interpersonal and team skills

c) Contingency response strategy

d) Change requests

93. Which description best describes the process plan procurement management?

    a) The process of documenting project decisions, specifying the approach, and identifying potential sellers

    b) The process of using existing knowledge and creating new knowledge to achieve the project's objectives and contribute to organizational learning

    c) The process of obtaining team members, facilities, equipment, materials, supplies, and other resources necessary to complete the project work

    d) The process of developing an approach and plan for project communications activities based on information needs of each stakeholder and the project

94. Andrew is a seasoned project manager and is a wizard at an electric automobile company. The process of documenting project procurement decisions, specifying the approach, and identifying potential sellers best describes which process?

    a) Data analysis

    b) Procurement management plan

    c) OPA

    d) Plan procurement management

95. The following are contract types in plan procurement management except

    a) Fixed-priced contracts

    b) Time and material contracts

    c) Standard contracts

    d) Cost-reimbursable contracts

96. Which answer best describes plan stakeholder engagement?

    a) The process of developing approaches to involve project stakeholders based on their needs and expectations, addressing issues, and fostering appropriate stakeholder engagement

    b) The process of monitoring project stakeholder relationships and tailoring strategies for engaging stakeholders through the modification of engagement strategies and plans

    c) The process of communicating and working with stakeholders to meet their needs and expectations

d) The process of not communicating and working with stakeholders to meet their needs and expectations

97. What is the output of plan stakeholder management?

   a) Stakeholder management plan

   b) Stakeholder baseline

   c) Risk register

   d) RBS

98. Bill is an experienced project manager who wants to be sure his team collects all the necessary requirements. Which best describes plan scope management?

   a) The process of developing a detailed description of the project and product

   b) The process of creating a scope management plan that documents how the project and product scope will be defined, validated, and controlled

   c) The process of subdividing project deliverables and project work into smaller, more manageable components

   d) The process of monitoring the status of the project and product scope and managing changes in the scope baseline

99. The output of plan scope management process is

   a) Scope baseline

   b) Requirements plan

   c) Scope management plan

   d) EEF

100. Bill is an experienced project manager who wants to be sure his team collects all the necessary requirements. Which best describes WBS?

   a) The process of developing a detailed description of the project and product

   b) The process of creating a scope management plan that documents how the project and product scope will be defined, validated, and controlled

   c) The process of subdividing project deliverables and project work into smaller, more manageable components

   d) The process of monitoring the status of the project and product scope and managing changes in the scope baseline

101. Bill is an experienced project manager who wants to be sure his team collects all the necessary requirements. Which best describes controlling scope?

a) The process of developing a detailed description of the project and product

b) The process of creating a scope management plan that documents how the project and product scope will be defined, validated, and controlled

c) The process of subdividing project deliverables and project work into smaller, more manageable components

d) The process of monitoring the status of the project and product scope and managing changes in the scope baseline

102. Bill is an experienced project manager who wants to be sure his team collects all the necessary requirements. What are the outputs to plan scope management?

a) Accepted deliverables and change requests

b) Requirements documentation and requirements traceability matrix

c) The process of subdividing project deliverables and project work into smaller, more manageable components

d) Scope management plan and requirements management plan

103. What are tools and techniques to collect requirements?

a) Prototypes

b) Project documents

c) Requirements documentations

d) Project management plan

104. The output of the collect requirements process is

a) OPA

b) Data analysis

c) Requirements documentation

d) Subject matter expert

105. Bill is an experienced project manager who wants to be sure his team collects all the necessary requirements. All are ways to collect requirements during project planning except

a) Prototypes

b) Data analysis

c) Project documents

d) Expert judgments

106. What is the description that best defines collect requirements?

a) The process to determine, document, and manage stakeholder needs and requirements to meet project objectives

b) Requirements baseline

c) The process of identifying the relationships among project activities

d) Decompose into lower-level components

107. Steven is a new project manager with minimal experience in project management to do the necessary work. Which best describes the process define scope?

a) The process of developing a detailed description of the project and product

b) The process of creating a scope management plan that documents how the project and product scope will be defined, validated, and controlled

c) The process of subdividing project deliverables and project work into smaller, more manageable components

d) The process of monitoring the status of the project and product scope and managing changes in the scope baseline

108. Kimberly is a project manager responsible for the delivery of building a new structure onto a building. Which process best describes create WBS?

a) The process of developing a detailed description of the project and product

b) The process of creating a scope management plan that documents how the project and product scope will be defined, validated, and controlled.

c) The process of subdividing project deliverables and project work into smaller, more manageable components

d) The process of monitoring the status of the project and product scope and managing changes in the scope baseline

109. Senior management called the project manager, Emily, into a meeting to talk about cost concerns. Senior management wants Emily to take as much time as needed. However, they do want the most accurate estimate of the current cost. Which cost management tool and technique will provide the most accurate cost estimates?

a) Bottom-up estimating

b) Analogous estimating

c) Parametric estimating

d) EVM

110. Amanda is a new project manager at a manufacturing firm. Senior management wants the most accurate information from Amanda to determine what the project will cost and how long the project will take. Amanda has been instructed to take as long as she needs. What tool and technique would Amanda use to satisfy this requirement from senior management?

a) Prototypes

b) An oscilloscope

c) Fishbone

d) Bottom-up estimating

111. Raymond is a top-level project manager at a construction company. During the implementation phase of a project, there was an atypical issue that caused a minor setback for Raymond and his team. Then BAC = 120, EV = 10, PV = 12, AC = 11. What is the EAC of the project?

a) 132

b) 120

c) 121

d) 156.2

112. Joyce is a top-level project manager at aa construction company. During the implementation phase of a project, there was a typical issue that caused a minor setback for Joyce and her team. Then BAC = 120, EV = 10, PV = 12, AC = 11. What is the EAC of the project?

a) 132

b) 120

c) 121

d) 156.2

113. Nathan is a top-level project manager as construction company. Then BAC = 120, EV = 10, PV = 12, AC = 11. What is the EAC forecast earning of the project?

a) 132

b) 120

c) 121

d) 156.2

114. Lauren is a seasoned project manager and is very good at solving project that are not in conformance. Which is a part of cost of conformance?

a) Rework

b) Testing

c) Internal failure costs

d) Liabilities

115. Douglas is a project manager with some experience in quality project management to do the necessary work. Which is a part of cost of nonconformance?

a) Training

b) Destructive testing loss

c) Inspections

d) Lost business

116. Jeremy is a project manager at a local marketing firm. Jeremy needs to perform quality audit. All are a part of preventive costs except

a) Time to do it right

b) Training

c) Inspections

d) Document processes

117. Gerald is a project manager responsible for the delivery of building a new structure onto a building. The process of defining how to estimate, acquire, manage, and utilize physical and team resources fits which process?

a) Develop team

b) Plan resource management

c) Organizational theory

d) Team charter

118. Which answer below best fits the tools and techniques of manage communications?

a) Change log

b) Project management plan

c) Manage quality

d) Interpersonal and team skills

119. As a project manager, Jacob is planning the activities in the risk management. Which of the following depicts the order of activities in risk management?

a) Collect requirements, define scope, and create WBS

b) Identify risks, perform qualitative risk analysis, perform quantitative risk analysis, and plan risk responses

c) Plan schedule management, define activities, sequence activities, estimate activity resources, estimate activity costs, and develop schedule

d) Estimate costs and determine budget

120. The process of documenting project procurement decisions, specifying the approach, and identifying potential sells best describes which process?

a) Data analysis

b) Procurement management plan

c) OPA

d) Plan procurement management

121. Janine is a longtime project manager in the Aspire LLC company. Janine needs to work with the procurement department to secure people with sufficient skills. Which answer best describes plan stakeholder engagement?

    a) The process of developing approaches to involve project stakeholders based on their needs and expectations, address issues, and foster appropriate stakeholder engagement

    b) Templates for the risk management plan, risk register, and risk report

    c) The process of managing procurement relationships, monitoring contract performance, making changes and corrections as appropriate, and closing out contracts

    d) The process of obtaining seller responses, selecting a seller, and awarding a contract

122. Frances is starting a new project that involves infrastructure and database migration. Frances needs to create documents for the best plan of communication for the team. Deliverables is an output of which process group?

    a) OPA

    b) EEF

    c) Final report

    d) Direct and manage project work

123. Samuel is a new project manager with good experience in change management to do the necessary work. The following are inputs to process direct and manage project work except

    a) Approved changes

    b) Project management plan

    c) Deliverables

    d) OPA

124. Which description best describes the process direct and manage project work?

    a) The process of leading and performing the work defined in the project plan and implementing the approved changes to achieve the project objectives

    b) The process of improving competencies of team members and the overall team environment to enhance project performance

    c) The process of obtaining seller responses, selecting sellers, and awarding a contract

d) The process of documenting project decisions, specifying the approach, and identifying potential sellers

125. Jose is a project manager with great people skills. Interpersonal and team skills involve all of the following except

a) Active listening

b) Expert judgment

c) Networking

d) Political awareness

126. The following are a part of tools and techniques in manage project knowledge except

a) Knowledge management

b) Information management

c) Interpersonal and team skills

d) Lessons learned register

127. Which process best describes manage project knowledge?

a) The process of using existing knowledge and creating new knowledge to achieve the project's objectives and contribute to organizational learning

b) The process of communicating and working with stakeholders to meet their needs, expectations, interests, and potential impact on the project

c) The process of developing a document that formally authorized the existence of a project and provides the project manager with authority to apply organizational resources to project activities

d) The process of what needs to be done to define, prepare, and coordinate all subsidiary activities to produce a document that defines the project

128. All are tools and techniques to manage project knowledge except

a) Information management

b) Active listening

c) Deliverables

d) Knowledge management

129. The following are inputs of the manage quality process except

    a) Project documents

    b) Project management plan

    c) EEF

    d) OPA

130. Which of the following is an input to the manage quality process?

    a) Quality reports

    b) Quality metrics

    c) Data gathering

    d) EEF

131. Which description best identifies the process manage quality?

    a) The process of obtaining seller responses, selecting sellers, and awarding a contract

    b) The process of translating the quality management plan into executable project activities that incorporate the organization's quality policies

    c) The process of communicating and working with stakeholders to meet their needs, expectations, interests, and potential impact on the project

    d) The process of leading and performing the work defined in the project plan and implementing the approved changes to achieve the project objectives

132. All are quality management styles except

    a) Philip Crosby

    b) Kaizen

    c) Deming

    d) Maslow

133. Pepper is a new project manager for TF Banking Services. Pepper is in the process of acquiring resources. All are tools and techniques Pepper can use to aid in her search except

    a) Virtual teams

    b) Multicriteria analysis

    c) Resource management plan

    d) Negotiation

134. Which process best describes acquire resources?

    a) The process of improving competencies of team members and the overall team environment to enhance project performance

    b) The process of obtaining team members, facilities, equipment, materials, supplies, and other resources necessary to complete the project work

    c) The process of tracking team member performance, providing feedback, resolving issues, and managing team changes to optimize project performance

    d) The process of defining how to estimate, acquire, manage, and utilize physical and team resources

135. You are the project manager of a project that is budgeted to cost one million at completion. The project's duration is ten months, and its budget is spread evenly across each month. It is currently 50% complete and has so far cost $750k, however only produced a value of $500k. What is the schedule variance (SV) of the project?

    a) $0

    b) $200k

    c) $500k

    d) $750k

136. When developing teams, what is the most desired location of team members?

    a) Virtual teams

    b) Colocation

    c) Meetings

    d) Team performance assessments

137. When developing teams, what is the most desired location of team members?

    a) Virtual teams

    b) Colocation

    c) Meetings

    d) Team performance assessments

138. All the following are inputs to manage team except

    a) PMP

    b) Project documents updates

c) Work performance reports

d) Team performance

139. Which description best defines develop team?

a) The process of tracking team member performance, providing feedback, resolving issues, and managing team changes to optimize project performance

b) The process of ensuring timely and appropriate collection, creation, distribution, storage, retrieval, management, monitoring, and ultimate disposition of project information

c) The process of leading and performing the work defined in the project plan and implementing the approved changes to achieve the project objectives

d) The process of improving competencies of team members and the overall team environment to enhance project performance

140. Of the four types of conflict management, which is considered the best outcome?

a) Avoid

b) Force

c) Compromise

d) Collaborate

141. Which best describes the process manage resources?

a) The process of reviewing all change requests; approving changes; managing changes to deliverables, project documents, and the project management plan; and communicating decisions

b) The process of tracking team member performance, providing feedback, resolving issues, and managing team changes to optimize project performance

c) The process of obtaining team members, facilities, equipment, materials, supplies, and other resources necessary to complete the project work

d) The process of translating the quality management plan into executable project activities that incorporate the organization's quality policies

142. Of the four types of conflict management, which is considered the worst outcome?

   a) Avoid

   b) Force

   c) Compromise

   d) Collaborate

143. Manage communications is a process of which knowledge area?

   a) Plan communications management

   b) Project quality management

   c) Manage communications is not a process

   d) Project communications management

144. Which best describes the process manage communications?

   a) PMP

   b) The process of ensuring timely and appropriate collection, creation, distribution, storage, retrieval, management, monitoring, and the ultimate disposition of project information

   c) Work performance reports

   d) Team performance

145. All are traits of interpersonal and team skills except

   a) Active listening

   b) Conflict management

   c) Political awareness

   d) Change requests

146. Frank is a project manager with Carmon Lip Balm LLC. Frank and his project team meticulously put together a project plan which captured and strategized for many risks. One of them has just materialized. As a project manager, what should Frank do next?

   a) Plan risk management

   b) Monitor risks

c) Use his interpersonal skills and team management

d) Implement risk responses

147. Which definition correctly defines implement risk responses?

a) The process of implementing the agreed-upon risk response

b) The process of obtaining seller responses, selecting sellers, and awarding a contract

c) The process of monitoring the status of the project and product scope and managing changes to the scope baseline

d) The process of improving competencies of team members and the overall team environment to enhance project performance

148. Which of the following is an output of implement risk response?

a) Expert judgment

b) Risk management plan

c) Interpersonal skills

d) Change requests

149. The process of obtaining seller responses, selecting a seller, and awarding a contract describes which process?

a) Plan procurement management

b) Conduct procurements

c) Control procurements

d) Project procurement management

150. All are tools and techniques to select a seller except

a) Advertising

b) Bidder conference

c) Proposal evaluation

d) Asking your best friend

151. Which definition accurately describes the conduct procurements process?

a) The process of obtaining seller responses, selecting sellers, and awarding a contract

b) The process of formalizing acceptance of the completed project deliverables

c) The process of performing integrated change control

d) The process of monitoring and recording the results of executing the quality management plan activities to assess performance and ensure project outputs are complete, correct, and meet customer expectations

152. The process of communicating and working with stakeholders to meet their needs and expectations, address issues, and foster appropriate involvement describes which process?

a) Manage stakeholder engagement

b) Monitor communications

c) Manage communications

d) Monitor stakeholder engagement

153. All are tools and techniques of manage stakeholder engagement except

a) Feedback

b) Negotiation

c) Ground rules

d) Change request

154. The output of manage stakeholder engagement is

a) EEF

b) Expert judgment

c) Change request

d) Change log

155. Which process best exemplifies monitoring and control in project integration?

a) Direct and manage project work

b) Monitor and control project work

c) Manage project knowledge

d) Perform integrated change control

156. What is the best definition of monitoring and control?

a) The process of tracking, reviewing, and reporting the overall progress to meet performance objectives defined in the project management plan

b) The process of reviewing all change requests; approving changes; managing changes to deliverables, project documents and the project management plan; and communicating decisions

c) The process of formalizing acceptance of the completed project deliverables

d) The process of monitoring the status of the project and product scope and managing changes to the scope baseline

157. Judy is a top project manager at her firm. Judy is currently working on a project in which a fix is necessary. As a project manager, what should Judy do next?

a) Check the release documents

b) Notify the sponsor

c) Evaluate the impact of the change

d) Implement the risk response plan

158. What is the best definition of perform integrated change control?

a) The process of tracking, reviewing, and reporting the overall progress to meet performance objectives defined in the project management plan

b) The process of reviewing all change requests; approving changes; managing changes to deliverables, project documents, and the project management plan; and communicating decisions

c) The process of formalizing acceptance of the completed project deliverables

d) The process of monitoring the status of the project and product scope and managing changes to the scope baseline

159. All are tools and techniques of the process perform integrated change control except

a) Meetings

b) Expert judgment

c) Project management updates

d) Multicriteria decision analysis

160. What is the best definition of validate scope?

a) The process of tracking, reviewing, and reporting the overall progress to meet performance objectives defined in the project management plan

b) The process of reviewing all change requests; approving changes; managing changes to deliverables, project documents, and the project management plan; and communicating decisions

c) The process of formalizing acceptance of the completed project deliverables

d) The process of monitoring the status of the project and product scope and managing changes to the scope baseline

161. Which is the output to validate scope?

a) Work performance data

b) Acceptable deliverables

c) Verified deliverables

d) Work performance information

162. Which is an input to validate scope?

a) Verified deliverables

b) Acceptable deliverables

c) Inspection

d) Scope baseline

163. What is the best definition of perform integrated change control?

a) The process of tracking, reviewing, and reporting the overall progress to meet performance objectives defined in the project management plan

b) The process of reviewing all change requests; approving changes; managing changes to deliverables, project documents and the project management plan; and communicating decisions

c) The process of formalizing acceptance of the completed project deliverables

d) The process of monitoring the status of the project and product scope and managing changes to the scope baseline

164. All are inputs to control scope except

a) Scope management plan

b) Change management plan

c) Change requests

d) Scope baseline

165. Which is a tool and technique for control scope?

    a) Trend analysis

    b) EEF

    c) Work performance information

    d) Project document updates

166. What is the best definition of control schedule?

    a) The process of monitoring the status of the project and product scope and managing changes to the scope baseline

    b) The process of monitoring project costs to the cost baseline

    c) The process of monitoring and recording the results of executing the quality management plan activities to assess performance and ensure project outputs are complete, correct, and meet customer expectations

    d) The process of ensuring the physical resources assigned and allocated to the project are available as planned versus actual utilization of resources and taking corrective actions as necessary

167. The following are tools and technique used in control schedule except

    a) Critical path method

    b) PMIS

    c) Resource optimization

    d) Change requests

168. All are outputs for the control schedule process except

    a) Schedule forecasts

    b) Change requests

    c) Work performance information

    d) PMIS

169. What is the best definition of control costs?

    a) The process of monitoring the status of the project and product scope and managing changes

to the scope baseline

b) The process of monitoring project costs to the cost baseline

c) The process of monitoring and recording the results of executing the quality management plan activities to assess performance and ensure project outputs are complete, correct, and meet customer expectations

d) The process of ensuring the physical resources assigned and allocated to the project are available as planned versus actual utilization of resources and taking corrective actions as necessary

170. All are tools and techniques of control costs except

a) Earned value analysis

b) Trend analysis

c) TCPI

d) PERT

171. Which of the following is an output to control costs?

a) Cost forecasts

b) PMIS

c) Cost management plan

d) OPA

172. What is the best definition of control quality?

a) The process of monitoring the status of the project and product scope and managing changes to the scope baseline

b) The process of monitoring the status of the project to update the project schedule and manage changes to the schedule baseline

c) The process of monitoring and recording the results of executing the quality management plan activities to assess performance and ensure project outputs are complete, correct, and meet customer expectations

d) The process of ensuring the physical resources assigned and allocated to the project are available as planned versus actual utilization of resources and taking corrective actions as necessary

173. Which description best describes control quality?

    a) The process of monitoring and recording the results of executing the quality management plan activities to assess performance and ensure project outputs are complete, correct, and meet customer expectations

    b) EVM

    c) PERT

    d) The process of finalizing all activities for the project, phase, or contract

174. Terri is a new project manager at a manufacturing firm. Terri has currently completed the planning stage. Her team has begun implementing the work according to the project plan. One of Terri's team members has noticed a problem with her task but has not yet found a fix. What tools can be used to determine the cause of the problem?

    a) Prototypes

    b) An oscilloscope

    c) Fishbone

    d) Bottom-up estimating

175. David is a new project manager for Razor LLC. David wants to get off to the best start understanding ways to deliver a quality product. David and his team are planning for accuracy in quality. Which of the following tools is one of the seven rules of quality control?

    a) Analysis technique

    b) Cause-and-effect diagram

    c) Data representation

    d) Quality audit

176. Susan is a new project manager for Bikes Incorporated. Susan wants to get off to the best start understanding ways to deliver a quality product. Susan and her team are planning for accuracy in quality. Susan can check for quality using each of these rules of quality control except

    a) Control chart

    b) Quality audit

    c) Pareto chart

    d) Scatter diagram

177. Aaron is the project manager at a communication company that builds precision devices. Aaron's team has produced a device that is consistently measured with the same output value with little scatter, but the output is not close to the true value. This is an example of what?

a) Accuracy

b) Cost of quality

c) Prevention over inspection

d) Precision

178. What is the best definition of control resources?

a) The process of monitoring the status of the project and product scope and managing changes to the scope baseline

b) The process of monitoring project costs to the cost baseline

c) The process of monitoring and recording the results of executing the quality management plan activities to assess performance and ensure project outputs are complete, correct, and meet customer expectations

d) The process of ensuring the physical resources assigned and allocated to the project are available as planned versus actual utilization of resources and taking corrective actions as necessary

179. Your company is a nationally recognized organization for getting projects done on time, on scope, and on budget. Your project is approximately 85% complete and you just finished the monthly status meeting with the customer. In that meeting the customer informed you that they have run out of money to pay for the rest of the project. What is the first thing you should do?

a) Release project team

b) Begin closing the project

c) Stop all project work

d) Adjust the schedule by shifting work to later in the project to allow the customer to get the funds

180. What is the correct order of team development?

a) Performing, storming, norming, forming, and adjourning

b) Performing, storming, adjourning, forming, and norming

c) Forming, norming, storming, performing, and adjourning

d) Forming, storming, norming, performing, and adjourning

181. What are the least and most desired methods of conflict resolution?

a) Avoid and collaboration

b) Compromise and smoothing

c) Force and avoid

d) Compromise and collaboration

182. The document that includes information on staff acquisition and release, resource calendars, recognition and rewards, compliance, and safety is

a) Resource plan

b) Project management plan

c) Staffing management plan

d) Project resource plan

183. Which answer best describes the process manage communications?

a) The process of developing an appropriate approach and plan for project communication activities based on the information needs of each stakeholder, the available organizational assets, and the needs of the project

b) The document that includes information on staff acquisition and release, resource calendars, recognition and rewards, compliance, and safety

c) The process of ensuring timely and appropriate collection, creation, distribution, storage, retrieval, management, monitoring, and the ultimate disposition of project information

d) The process of ensuring the information needs of the project and its stakeholders

184. Which answer best describes monitor communications?

a) The process of developing an appropriate approach and plan for project communication activities based on the information needs of each stakeholder, the available organizational assets, and the needs of the project

b) The document that includes information on staff acquisition and release, resource calendars, recognition and rewards, compliance, and safety

c) The process of ensuring timely and appropriate collection, creation, distribution, storage, retrieval, management, monitoring, and the ultimate disposition of project information

d) The process of ensuring the information needs of the project and its stakeholders are met

185. Emily is a new project manager for FierceGrlz llc. Emily's team consists of 6 members including Tom. Two new members have just been added. What is the number of channels of communication?

a) 13

b) 12

c) 15

d) 28

186. Emily is a new project manager for FierceGrlz llc. Emily's team consists of 6 members including Tom. Two new members have just been added. How many more channels of communication are there now?

a) 13

b) 12

c) 15

d) 28

187. What process best identifies the monitor risks process?

a) The process of monitoring the implementation of the agreed-on risk response plan, tracking identified risks, analyzing new risks, and evaluating the risk process

b) The process of formalizing acceptance of the completed project deliverables

c) The process of tracking, reviewing, and reporting the overall progress to meet performance objectives defined in the project management plan

d) Data analysis

188. Joe is a project manager who has a sponsor who does not like risk, so Joe must identify the risks and list the probability of occurrence. What answer best describes the risk management plan?

a) It is all the requirements of the project.

b) It is the process of defining how to conduct risk management activities for a project.

c) It is not a desirable choice when managing large projects.

d) It is a grid for mapping the probability of each risk occurrence and the impact on project objectives if the risk occurs.

189. Joe is a project manager who has a sponsor who does not like risk, so Joe must identify the risks and list the probability of occurrence. What answer best describes the probability impact matrix?

   a) It is all the requirements of the project.

   b) It is the process of defining how to conduct risk management activities for a project.

   c) It is not a desirable choice when managing large projects.

   d) It is a grid for mapping the probability of each risk occurrence and the impact on project objectives if the risk occurs.

190. Janine is a longtime project manager in the Aspire LLC company. Janine needs to work with the procurement department to secure people with sufficient skills. What answer best describes control procurements management?

   a) The process of documenting project decisions, specifying the approach, and identifying potential sellers

   b) Templates for the risk management plan, risk register, and risk report

   c) The process of managing procurement relationships, monitoring contract performance, making changes and corrections as appropriate, and closing out contracts

   d) The process of obtaining seller responses, selecting a seller, and awarding a contract

191. What process best describes conduct procurements

   a) The process of documenting project decisions, specifying the approach, and identifying potential sellers

   b) The process of communicating and working with stakeholders to meet their needs and expectations, address issues, and foster appropriate stakeholder engagement

   c) The process of obtaining seller responses, selecting sellers, and awarding a contract

   d) Templates for the risk management plan, risk register, and risk report

192. Which statement best describes the process control procurements?

   a) The process of documenting project decisions, specifying the approach, and identifying potential sellers

   b) Templates for the risk management plan, risk register, and risk report

   c) The process of managing procurement relationships, monitoring contract performance, making changes and corrections as appropriate, and closing out contracts

d) The process of communicating and working with stakeholders to meet their needs and expectations, address issues, and foster appropriate stakeholder engagement

193. Kazem is a project manager with many years of experience. Kazem knows how important customer communication and satisfaction are to how a project is managed. What is the best definition of monitor stakeholder engagement?

   a) The process of identifying project stakeholders regularly and analyzing and documenting relevant information regarding their interests, involvement, interdependencies, influence, and impact on project success

   b) The process of communicating and working with stakeholders to meet their needs and expectations, address issues, and foster appropriate stakeholder engagement

   c) The process of providing an overview of the project stakeholder management process

   d) The process of monitoring project stakeholder relationships and tailoring strategies for engaging stakeholders through the modification of engagement strategies and plans

194. The following describe monitor stakeholder engagement except

   a) Managing stakeholder relationships

   b) Ignoring the stakeholders until they go away.

   c) Engaging with the stakeholders

   d) Formulating strategies with the stakeholders

195. The sponsor is not very happy with the progress of the project. The sponsor says to stop all efforts on the project immediately. As a project manager, what would you do next?

   a) Start the closing process

   b) Gain formal acceptance

   c) Release the team

   d) Close the project

196. What is the best definition of close process?

   a) The process of finalizing all activities for the project, phase, or contract

   b) The process of monitoring project costs to the cost baseline

   c) The process of monitoring the status of the project and product scope and managing changes

to the scope baseline

d) The process of ensuring the information needs of the project and its stakeholders are met

197. The sponsor has accepted all deliverables of the project. As a project manager, what would you do next?

a) Release the team

b) Gain formal acceptance

c) Document lessons learned

d) Close the project

198. The following are part of the closing process except

a) Obtain stakeholder satisfaction

b) Release the team

c) EEF

d) Prepare final project report

199. The sponsor has accepted all deliverables of the project. As a project manager, what would you do next?

a) Release the team

b) Gain formal acceptance

c) Document lessons learned

d) Close the project

200. The following are part of the closing process except

a) Obtain stakeholder satisfaction

b) Release the team

c) EEF updates

d) Prepare final project report

Mock Exam—Concentration Solutions

1. b	2. d	3. b	4. c
5. d	6. a	7. d	8. c
9. b	10. c	11. a	12. b
13. c	14. a	15. b	16. b
17. d	18. c	19. a	20. d
21. c	22. a	23. a	24. c
25. c	26. b	27. b	28. c
29. d	30. a	31. a	32. b
33. c	34. a	35. b	36. d
37. c	38. c	39. a	40. c
41. c	42. a	43. c	44. c
45. c	46. a	47. a	48. c
49. a	50. a	51. a	52. a
53. a	54. a	55. a	56. a
57. a	58. c	59. d	60. b
61. a	62. c	63. d	64. a
65. b	66. d	67. c	68. c
69. b	70. b	71. d	72. b
73. d	74. a	75. d	76. a
77. c	78. d	79. b	80. d
81. b	82. b	83. c	84. b
85. a	86. c	87. b	88. a
89. b	90. c	91. b	92. d
93. a	94. d	95. c	96. a

97. a	98. b	99. c	100. c
101. d	102. d	103. a	104. c
105. c	106. a	107. a	108. c
109. a	110. d	111. c	112. a
113. d	114. b	115. d	116. c
117. b	118. d	119. b	120. d
121. a	122. d	123. c	124. a
125. b	126. d	127. a	128. c
129. c	130. b	131. b	132. d
133. c	134. b	135. a	136. b
137. b	138. b	139. d	140. d
141. b	142. a	143. d	144. b
145. d	146. d	147. a	148. d
149. b	150. d	151. a	152. a
153. d	154. c	155. b	156. a
157. c	158. b	159. c	160. c
161. b	162. a	163. b	164. c
165. a	166. a	167. d	168. d
169. b	170. d	171. a	172. c
173. a	174. c	175. b	176. b
177. d	178. d	179. b	180. d
181. a	182. c	183. c	184. d
185. d	186. a	187. a	188. b
189. d	190. c	191. c	192. c
193. d	194. b	195. a	196. a
197. c	198. c	199. c	200. a

Mock Exam 200 Questions–4 Hours

1. Assume a project costs $10,000 today and will return $2,500 per year for five years. Your required return on investments is 10%. As a project manager should you do the project?

    a) No, because the project will make a great profit.

    b) No, because payback period is four years.

    c) No, because "the required return on investments is 10%."

    d) Yes, because project meets organization's strategic goals.

2. Lauren is a contractor responsible for refurbishment of an automobile showroom. The estimated refurbishment cost is $500 per square foot. The total showroom area that needs to be refurbished is 1,000 square feet. Based on Lauren's past experience, she knows the project team can refurbish 100 square feet per week. What is the steady-state value?

    a) 525,000

    b) 375,000

    c) 555,555.56

    d) 475,000

3. Walter is a new project manager for Razor LLC. David wants to get off to the best start in understanding the project, people, and environment. Interpersonal and team skills is a tool and technique of which process?

    a) Meetings

    b) Develop project charter

    c) Organizational process assets

    d) Planning

4. Megan is a new project manager for an existing project with issues. What document do you need to determine the project goals, high-level risks, and high-level constraints?

    a) Communication plan

    b) Project management plan

    c) SOW

d) Project charter

5. If a stakeholder has high interest but low power, what is the best way to manage the stakeholder?

   a) Keep satisfied

   b) Manage closely

   c) Keep informed

   d) Monitor

6. The output of the develop project management plan process is

   a) Project charter

   b) Enterprise environmental factors

   c) Project management plan

   d) Organizational process assets

7. The following are tools and techniques for the develop project management plan process except

   a) Meetings

   b) Project management plan

   c) Interpersonal and team skills

   d) Expert judgments

8. Which of the following is an input to develop the project management plan?

   a) Data gathering

   b) Project management plan

   c) Inspection

   d) Project charter

9. The _____ are influences out of the project manager's control.

   a) Enterprise environmental factors

   b) Organizational process assets

   c) Evolution environmental factors

   d) Extreme environmental factors

10. Susan is a project manager with many years of experience. Susan's current project is especially

difficult because of problems with the timeline getting extended many times. This could be because the scope may not be well defined, and the delays are causing increases in cost because of increased hours of work on the project for fixes. All are found in the project charter except

a) Project purpose

b) High-level requirements

c) Detailed requirements

d) Key stakeholder list

11. Which of the following are outputs to the plan scope management process?

a) Scope management plan and requirements management plan

b) Project charter and project management plan

c) Quality management plan and process improvement plan

d) Risk management plan and risk response plan

12. Which document would the project manager use to achieve the plan benefits of timeline, tools, and resources to ensure benefits are fully realized?

a) Project management plan

b) Benefits management plan

c) Projects documents

d) OPA

13. Which of the following is an output of the collect requirements process?

a) OPA

b) Requirements traceability matrix

c) Project management plan

d) Data analysis

14. Which best describes the define scope process?

a) The process of developing a detailed description of the project and product

b) The process of creating a scope management plan that documents how the project and product scope will be defined, validated, and controlled

c) The process of subdividing project deliverables and project work into smaller, more manageable components

d) The process of monitoring the status of the project and product scope and managing changes in the scope baseline

15. Work that is performed that is outside the scope of the project but is demanded by a sponsor, senior management, or stakeholders other than the project team is called _____.

   a) Gold-plating

   b) Work that is necessary

   c) Work that is unnecessary

   d) Scope creep

16. Which are number systems in the WBS dictionary and WBS, respectively?

   a) Code of account identifier and $(1.0, 1.1, 1.1.1)$

   b) Chart of accounts and (a, ab, abc)

   c) Control chart and $(1, 2, 3)$

   d) All of the above

17. The following are tools and techniques used to collect requirements except

   a) Data analysis

   b) Decision-making

   c) Organizational process assets

   d) Interpersonal skills and team skills

18. The scope baseline consists of

   a) The process of developing a detailed description of the project and product

   b) The project scope statement, WBS, WBS dictionary, and planning package

   c) The process of subdividing project deliverables and project work into smaller, more manageable components

   d) The process of monitoring the status of the project and product scope and managing changes in the scope baseline

19. As a project manager, you are planning the activities in the project schedule. What is the output of plan schedule management?

    a) Collect requirements, define scope, and create WBS

    b) Identify risks, perform qualitative risk analysis, perform quantitative risk analysis, and plan risk responses

    c) Create the schedule management plan

    d) Estimate costs and determine the budget

20. The inputs to the plan schedule management process are

    a) Project charter, project management plan, scope management plan, development approach, EEF, and OPA

    b) Perform qualitative risk analysis, perform quantitative risk analysis, and plan risk responses

    c) Project management plan, project documents, approved change requests, EEF, and OPA

    d) Project charter, project management plan, quality management plan, project life cycle, development, EEF, and OPA

21. Susan is a first-time project manager; however, she is excited to make a good impression. Halfway through her project, Susan gets an email from the client that the project will be canceled because of a funding issue. What should Susan do next?

    a) Try to negotiate with the client and suggest where to find additional funding.

    b) Prepare the final project report.

    c) Tell the team this is only a temporary setback. It has happened before on a similar project, but the problem was cleared shortly.

    d) Ask senior management to talk to the client.

22. Which of the following depicts the order of activities in schedule management?

    a) Collect requirements, define scope, and create the WBS

    b) Identify risks, perform qualitative risk analysis, perform quantitative risk analysis, and plan risk responses

    c) Plan schedule management, define activities, sequence activities, estimate activity durations, and develop schedules

d) Estimate costs and determine budget

23. In the define activities process, work is decomposed into which of the following?

a) Work packages

b) WBS

c) Activities

d) WBS and activities

24. Carl is a new project manager who is currently in the planning phase of a project. Jason has defined the activities—what should he do next?

a) Sequence activities

b) Estimate costs

c) Collect requirements

d) Identify risks

25. The work performed outside of scope and suggested by the project team is called _____

a) Gold-plating

b) Work that is necessary

c) Work that is unnecessary

d) Scope creep

26. The following are inputs to collect requirements except

a) Project management plan

b) Communication management plan

c) Project documents

d) EEF

27. Jesse is a new project manager who is currently in the planning phase of a project. Jesse has defined the activities. As a project manager, what did Jesse do before defining the activities?

a) Sequence activities

b) Estimate costs

c) Plan schedule management

d) Identify risks

28. Madison is a project manager responsible for the delivery of building a new structure onto a building. Of the four types of PDM relationships, which is used most often?

a) Finish to start (FS)

b) Finish to finish (FF)

c) Start to finish (SF)

d) Start to start (SS)

29. Jacqueline is a project manager at a local marketing firm. Jacqueline needs to perform a sequence of the activities. Which of the following depicts the order of activities in schedule management?

a) Collect requirements, define scope, and create WBS

b) Identify risks, perform qualitative risk analysis, perform quantitative risk analysis, and plan risk responses

c) Plan schedule management, define activities, sequence activities, estimate activity durations, and develop schedule

d) Estimate costs and determine budget

30. Which answer best represents the order of plan scope management?

a) Identify risks, perform qualitative risk analysis, perform quantitative risk analysis, and plan risk responses

b) Collect requirements, define scope, and create WBS

c) Plan schedule management define activities, sequence activities, estimate activity durations, and develop schedule

d) Estimate costs and determine budget

31. The following are tools and techniques of the develop schedule process except

a) Schedule compression

b) Data analysis

c) Project documents

d) Critical path method

32. Which is a tool and technique of the plan cost management process?

   a) Alternative analysis

   b) Project documents

   c) Project plan updates

   d) Rolling wave technique

33. Mary is a new project manager. How much will it cost for Mary to complete the project if most likely = $2,000, optimistic = $1,000, and pessimistic = $3,000, using three-point estimation?

   a) 44

   b) 2,000

   c) 2,167

   d) 32

34. The following are tools and techniques that can be used to determine budget except

   a) Expert judgments

   b) Historical information review

   c) Funding limit reconciliation

   d) Business documents

35. Which is an output of the determine budget process?

   a) Cost baseline

   b) Alternative analysis

   c) Project management plan

   d) Voting

36. What is the output of the plan quality management process?

   a) Project management plan

   b) Project documents

   c) Risk management plan

   d) Quality management plan

37. Which best describes the plan quality management process?

   a) The process of identifying quality requirements and standards for the project and its deliverables and documenting how the project will demonstrate compliance with quality requirements and standards

   b) The process of monitoring and recording the results of executing the quality management activities to assess performance and ensure the project outputs are complete, correct, and meet customer requirements

   c) The process of translating the quality management plan into executable quality activities that incorporate the organization's quality policies into the project

   d) None of the above

38. Terry is a new project manager at a telecommunication company. Terry has a lot of experience in project management to do the necessary work. The process of defining how to estimate, acquire, manage, and utilize physical and team resources fits which process?

   a) Develop team

   b) Plan resource management

   c) Organizational theory

   d) Team charter

39. Theodore is a new project manager with minimal experience in acquiring proper resources to do the necessary work. The following tools and techniques can assist Theodore to estimate resources except

   a) Bottom-up estimating

   b) Analogous estimating

   c) Parametric estimating

   d) Resource breakdown structure (RBS)

40. Christian is a project manager at a local marketing firm. Christian needs to manage the project team to prevent scope creep and gold-plating. All the following are inputs to manage a team except

   a) Project management plan

   b) Project documents updates

   c) Work performance reports

   d) Team performance

41. Which is a tool and technique of plan communications management?

    a) Change log

    b) Project management plan

    c) Manage quality

    d) Interpersonal and team skills

42. Which answer below best fits the tools and technique of plan communication management?

    a) Change log

    b) Project management plan

    c) Manage quality

    d) Communication technology

43. Conversations and meetings are part of which tool and technique?

    a) Communications analysis

    b) Communications technology

    c) Communications model

    d) Communications method

44. Of the four types of PDM relationships, which is used least often?

    a) Finish to start (FS)

    b) Finish to finish (FF)

    c) Start to finish (SF)

    d) Start to start (SS)

45. Which of the following depicts the order of activities in estimate costs?

    a) Collect requirements, define scope, and create WBS

    b) Identify risks, perform qualitative risk analysis, perform quantitative risk analysis, and plan risk responses

    c) Plan schedule management, define activities, sequence activities, estimate activity durations, and develop schedule

    d) Estimate costs and determine budget

46. Which of the following depicts the order of activities in plan risk management?

 a) Collect requirements, define scope, and create WBS

 b) Identify risks, perform qualitative risk analysis, perform quantitative risk analysis, and plan risk responses

 c) Plan schedule management, define activities, sequence activities, estimate activity resources, estimate activity costs, and develop schedule

 d) Estimate costs and determine budget

47. Which is a tool and technique of plan risk management?

 a) Stakeholder analysis

 b) Project documents

 c) Decomposition

 d) Project management plan updates

48. The output to identify risk is

 a) Project management plan

 b) Procurement plan

 c) Project documents

 d) Risk register

49. Which is an output of the plan risk management process?

 a) Project management plan

 b) Communications management plan

 c) Data analysis

 d) Risk management plan

50. A tool and technique that can be used in assessing risk impact is

 a) Project management plan

 b) Project document updates

 c) Risk probability and impact assessment

 d) Risk register

51. Which is an input to the process perform qualitative risk analysis?

    a) Project management plan

    b) Alternative analysis

    c) OPA updates

    d) EEF updates

52. Which answer is the best description of perform quantitative risk analysis?

    a) It is the process of numerically analyzing the effect of identified risks on overall project objects.

    b) It is the process by which we identify risks, perform qualitative risk analysis, perform quantitative risk analysis, and plan risk responses.

    c) It is the process by which we plan schedule management, define activities, sequence activities, estimate activity resources, estimate activity costs, and develop schedules.

    d) It involves estimating costs and determining budget.

53. Which is both an input and output of the process perform quantitative risk analysis?

    a) Risk report

    b) Analysis report

    c) Rolling wave

    d) Decomposition

54. All are tools and techniques of the plan risk responses process except

    a) Expert judgments

    b) Interpersonal and team skills

    c) Contingency response strategy

    d) Change requests

55. Which is a tool or technique of the plan risk response process?

    a) Interpersonal and team skills

    b) Process improvement plan

    c) Project management plan

    d) Quality management plan

56. The process of documenting project procurement decisions, specifying the approach, and identifying potential sellers best describes which process?

    a) Data analysis

    b) Procurement management plan

    c) Organizational process assets

    d) Plan procurement management

57. The output to the plan procurement management process is

    a) Procurement management plan

    b) Project management plan

    c) Conduct procurement

    d) Control procurement

58. Which answer best describes the plan stakeholder engagement plan?

    a) The process of developing approaches to involve project stakeholders based on their needs and expectations, addressing issues, and fostering appropriate stakeholder involvement

    b) The process of monitoring project stakeholder relationships and tailoring strategies for engaging stakeholders through the modification of engagement strategies and plans

    c) The process of communicating and working with stakeholders to meet their needs and expectations

    d) The process of not communicating and working with stakeholders to meet their needs and expectations

59. The output to plan stakeholder engagement is

    a) Assumption and constraint analysis

b) Stakeholder engagement plan

c) Project management plan

d) Process improvement plan

60. Deliverables is an output of which process group?

a) Organizational process assets

b) Enterprise environmental factors

c) Final report

d) Direct and manage project work

61. The following are components of tools and techniques in the manage project knowledge process except

a) Knowledge management

b) Information management

c) Interpersonal and team skills

d) Lessons learned register

62. Which of the following is an input of the manage project knowledge process?

a) Alternative analysis

b) Deliverables

c) OPA updates

d) Project management plan updates

63. Which of the following is an input to the manage quality process?

a) Quality reports

b) Quality metrics

c) Data gathering

d) Enterprise environmental factors

64. Pepper is a new project manager for TF Banking Services. Pepper is in the process of acquiring resources. All are tools and techniques Pepper can use to aid in her search except

a) Virtual teams

b) Multicriteria analysis

c) Resource management plan

d) Negotiation

65. You must select one and only one project to take on for your company. The net present value (NPV) for each project is as follows: Project A's NPV is $10K, Project B's NPV is $20K, and Project C's NPV is $30K.

a) Project C

b) Project A

c) This problem cannot be solved without knowing the interest rate for each project.

d) Project B

66. All of the following are inputs to manage a team except

a) Project management plan

b) Project documents updates

c) Work performance reports

d) Team performance

67. Which best describes the process to manage communications?

a) Project management plan

b) The process of ensuring timely and appropriate collection, creation, distribution, storage, retrieval, management, monitoring, and the ultimate disposition of project information

c) Work performance reports

d) Team performance

68. Frank is a project manager with Carmon Lip Balm LLC. Frank and his project team meticulously put together a project plan which captured and strategized for many risks. One of the risks has just materialized. As a project manager, what should Frank do next?

a) Plan risk management

b) Monitor risks

c) Use his interpersonal and team management skills

d) Implement risk responses

69. Debbie is a project manager at Cool Socks, Inc. Debbie is in the planning process for a new project and has completed the sequence activities process. The kickoff of the project occurred 3 months ago. The project team is currently managing the project. As a project manager, what would you do next?

a) Estimate activity durations

b) Close the project

c) Control schedule

d) Identify stakeholders

70. Which of the following is an output of the process implement risk response plan?

a) Change requests

b) Data analysis

c) Approved changes

d) OPA

71. The process of obtaining seller responses, selecting a seller, and awarding a contract describes which process?

a) Plan procurement management

b) Conduct procurements

c) Control procurements

d) Project procurement management

72. All are tools and techniques to select a seller except

a) Advertising

b) Bidder conference

c) Proposal evaluation

d) Asking your best friend

73. The process of communicating and working with stakeholders to meet their needs and expectations, address issues, and foster appropriate involvement describes which process?

    a) Manage stakeholder engagement

    b) Monitor communications

    c) Manage communications

    d) Monitor stakeholder engagement

74. Which process best exemplifies monitoring and control in project integration?

    a) Direct and manage project work

    b) Monitor and control project work

    c) Manage project knowledge

    d) Perform integrated change control

75. Harry is a contractor responsible for refurbishment of an automobile showroom. The estimated refurbishment cost is $500 per square foot. The total showroom area that needs to be refurbished is 1,000 square feet. Based on your past experience, you know your team can refurbish 100 square feet per week. How is the project performing?

    a) On schedule and on budget

    b) Behind schedule and over budget

    c) Ahead of schedule and over budget

    d) Behind schedule and ahead of budget

76. Which of the following is a tool and technique of direct and manage project work?

    a) Change requests

    b) PMIS

    c) Project management plan

    d) OPA updates

77. Judy is a superb project manager at her firm. Judy is currently working on a project in which a fix is necessary. As a project manager, what should Judy do next?

    a) Check the release documents

    b) Notify the sponsor

c) Evaluate the impact of the change

d) Implement the risk response plan

78. Judy is a top project manager at her firm. Judy is currently working on a project in which a fix *might be* necessary. As a project manager, what should Judy do next?

a) Prevent changes from occurring

b) Notify the sponsor

c) Evaluate the impact of the change

d) Implement the risk response plan

79. What is an output to the validate scope process?

a) Work performance data

b) Acceptable deliverables

c) Verified deliverables

d) Work performance information

80. All are inputs to control scope except

a) Scope management plan

b) Change management plan

c) Change requests

d) Scope baseline

81. All these are tools and techniques used in the control schedule process except

a) Critical path method

b) PMIS

c) Resource optimization

d) Change requests

82. Which tool/technique is best for controlling cost and schedule?

a) EVM

b) PERT

c) PMIS

d) Cost forecast

83. Which tool/technique is best for planning cost and schedule?

a) EVM

b) PERT

c) PMIS

d) Cost forecast

84. Terri is a new project manager at a manufacturing firm. Terri currently has completed the planning stage. Her team has begun implementing the work according to the project plan. One of Terri's team members has noticed a problem with her task but has not yet found a fix. What tools can be used to determine the cause of the problem?

a) Prototypes

b) An oscilloscope

c) Fishbone

d) Bottom-up estimating

85. David is a new project manager for Razor LLC. David wants to get off to the best start understanding ways to deliver a quality product. David and his team are planning for accuracy in quality. Which of the following tools is one of the seven rules of quality control?

a) Analysis technique

b) Cause-and-effect diagram

c) Data representation

d) Quality audit

86. Robert is a new project manager at Use or Lose It! Inc. Robert does not trust his employees to do their jobs, so he must monitor their every action to make sure he gets the results he wants. Robert is practicing

a) RAM

b) McGregor's Theory X

c) Expectancy Theory

d) McGregor's Theory Y

87. What is the correct order of team development?

   a) Performing, storming, norming, forming, and adjourning

   b) Performing, storming, adjourning, forming, and norming

   c) Forming, norming, storming, performing, and adjourning

   d) Forming, storming, norming, performing, and adjourning

88. Which answer best describes monitor communications?

   a) The process of developing an appropriate approach and plan for project communication activities based on the information needs of each stakeholder, the available organizational assets, and the needs of the project

   b) The document that includes information on staff acquisition and release, resource calendars, recognition and rewards, and compliance and safety

   c) The process to monitor communications and the process of ensuring the information needs of the project and its stakeholders are met

   d) The process of ensuring the information needs of the project and its stakeholders are met

89. Jackson is a new project manager for Destiny One, Corp. Jackson's team consists of 6 members including Tom. Two new members have just been added. What is the number of channels of communication?

   a) 13

   b) 12

   c) 15

   d) 28

90. Jackson is a new project manager for Destiny One, Corp. Jackson's team consists of 6 members including Tom. Two new members have just been added. How many more channels of communication are there now?

   a) 13

   b) 12

   c) 15

   d) 28

91. Which answer best describes the risk management plan?

    a) It contains all the requirements of the project.

    b) It is the process of defining how to conduct risk management activities for a project.

    c) It is not a desirable choice when managing large projects.

    d) It is used for mapping the probability of each risk occurrence and the impact on project objectives if the risk occurs.

92. Joe is a project manager and has a sponsor who does not like risk, so Joe must identify the risks and list the probability of occurrence. Which answer best describes the probability and impact matrix?

    a) It contains all the requirements of the project.

    b) It is the process of defining how to conduct risk management activities for a project.

    c) It is not a desirable choice when managing large projects.

    d) It is used for mapping the probability of each risk occurrence and the impact on project objectives if the risk occurs.

93. Janine is a longtime project manager at Aspire LLC. Janine needs to work with the procurement department to secure people with sufficient skills. Which answer best describes the control procurements process?

    a) The process of documenting project decisions, specifying the approach, and identifying potential sellers

    b) The process of creating templates for the risk management plan, risk register, and risk report

    c) The process of managing procurement relationships, monitoring contract performance, making changes and corrections as appropriate, and closing out contracts

    d) The process of obtaining seller responses, selecting a seller, and awarding a contract

94. Which is a tool or technique of the control procurements process?

    a) Project management plan

    b) Communication management plan

    c) Change requests

    d) Claims administration

95. Kazem is a project manager with many years of experience. Kazem knows how important customer communication and satisfaction are to how a project is managed. What is the best definition of the monitor stakeholder engagement process?

a) The process of identifying project stakeholders regularly and analyzing and documenting relevant information regarding their interests, involvement, interdependencies, influence, and impact on project success

b) The process of communicating and working with stakeholders to meet their needs and expectations, address issues, and foster appropriate stakeholder engagement

c) The process of providing an overview of the project stakeholder management process

d) The process of monitoring project stakeholder relationships and tailoring strategies for engaging stakeholders through the modification of engagement strategies and plans

96. The following describe monitor stakeholder engagement except

a) Managing stakeholder relationships

b) Ignoring the stakeholders until they go away

c) Engaging with the stakeholders

d) Formulating strategies with the stakeholders

97. Susan is a first-time project manager; however, she is excited to make a good impression. Halfway through her project, Susan gets an email from the client that the project will be canceled because of a funding issue. What should Susan do next?

a) Try to negotiate with the client and suggest where to find additional funding.

b) Prepare the final project report.

c) Tell the team this is only a temporary setback. It has happened before on a similar project, but the problem was cleared shortly.

d) Ask senior management to talk to the client.

98. Which is a tool and technique of the close project or phase process?

a) Regression analysis

b) OPA

c) EEF

d) Deliverables

99. Judy is a superb project manager at her firm. Judy is currently working on a project in which a fix is necessary. As a project manager, what should Judy do next?

    a) Check the release documents

    b) Notify the sponsor

    c) Evaluate the impact of the change

    d) Implement the risk response plan

100. Judy is a top project manager at her firm. Judy is currently working on a project in which a fix *might be* necessary. As a project manager, what should Judy do next?

    a) Prevent changes from occurring

    b) Notify the sponsor

    c) Evaluate the impact of the change

    d) Implement the risk response plan

101. What is an output to the validate scope process?

    a) Work performance data

    b) Acceptable deliverables

    c) Verified deliverables

    d) Work performance information

102. All are inputs to control scope except

    a) Scope management plan

    b) Change management plan

    c) Change requests

    d) Scope baseline

103. All these are tools and techniques used in the control schedule process except

    a) Critical path method

    b) PMIS

    c) Resource optimization

    d) change requests

104. Which tool/technique is best for controlling cost and schedule?

    a) EVM

    b) PERT

    c) PMIS

    d) Cost forecast

105. Which tool/technique is best for planning cost and schedule?

    a) EVM

    b) PERT

    c) PMIS

    d) Cost forecast

106. Terri is a new project manager at a manufacturing firm. Terri currently has completed the planning stage. Her team has begun implementing the work according to the project plan. One of Terri's team members has noticed a problem with her task but has not yet found a fix. What tools can be used to determine the cause of the problem?

    a) Prototypes

    b) An oscilloscope

    c) Fishbone

    d) Bottom-up estimating

107. David is a new project manager for Razor LLC. David wants to get off to the best start understanding ways to deliver a quality product. David and his team are planning for accuracy in quality. Which of the following tools is one of the seven rules of quality control?

    a) Analysis technique

    b) Cause-and-effect diagram

    c) Data representation

    d) Quality audit

108. You've led your team through the procurement planning process. Several procurement specialists on your team were integral in completing the procurement management plan. You are reviewing a list that you will use to score the bids and award a contract to the best qualified vendor. You want to ensure that you complete this process thoroughly and use all available information to you. Which of the following documents would not be included as part of the evaluation?

 a) Invitation for bid (IFB)

 b) Request for contract (RFC)

 c) Request for proposal (RFP)

 d) Request for quote (RFQ)

109. What is the correct order of team development?

 a) Performing, storming, norming, forming, and adjourning

 b) Performing, storming, adjourning, forming, and norming

 c) Forming, norming, storming, performing, and adjourning

 d) Forming, storming, norming, performing, and adjourning

110. Which answer best describes monitor communications?

 a) The process of developing an appropriate approach and plan for project communication activities based on the information needs of each stakeholder, the available organizational assets, and the needs of the project

 b) The document that includes information on staff acquisition and release, resource calendars, recognition and rewards, and compliance and safety

 c) The process to monitor communications and the process of ensuring the information needs of the project and its stakeholders are met

 d) The process of ensuring the information needs of the project and its stakeholders are met

111. William is a new project manager for Namechangers Co. William's team consists of 6 members including Tom. Two new members have just been added. What is the number of channels of communications now?

 a) 13

 b) 12

 c) 15

 d) 28

112. William is a new project manager for Namechangers Co. William's team consists of 6 members including Tom. Two new members have just been added. How many more channels of communication are there now?

    a) 13

    b) 12

    c) 15

    d) 28

113. Which of the following depicts the order of activities in cost management?

    a) Collect requirements, define scope, and create WBS

    b) Identify risks, perform qualitative risk analysis, perform quantitative risk analysis, and plan risk responses

    c) Plan schedule management, define activities, sequence activities, estimate activity resources, estimate activity costs, and develop schedule

    d) Estimate costs and determine budget

114. Joe is a project manager and has a sponsor who does not like risk, so Joe must identify the risks and list the probability of occurrence. Which answer best describes the probability and impact matrix?

    a) It contains all the requirements of the project.

    b) It is the process of defining how to conduct risk management activities for a project.

    c) It is not a desirable choice when managing large projects.

    d) It is used for mapping the probability of each risk occurrence and the impact on project objectives if the risk occurs.

115. Janine is a longtime project manager at Aspire LLC. Janine needs to work with the procurement department to secure people with sufficient skills. Which answer best describes the control procurements process?

    a) The process of documenting project decisions, specifying the approach, and identifying potential sellers

    b) The process of creating templates for the risk management plan, risk register, and risk report

    c) The process of managing procurement relationships, monitoring contract performance, making changes and corrections as appropriate, and closing out contracts

d) The process of obtaining seller responses, selecting a seller, and awarding a contract

116. The project management plan plans the overall activities of the project and contains detailed requirements of the project. The SOW is the statement of work, which contains the objects of the project. The project charter contains the high-level requirements of the project. All are inputs to the identify stakeholders process except

a) Project charter

b) EEF

c) Expert judgments

d) Organizational process assets

117. Which is a tool or technique of the control procurements process?

a) Project management plan

b) Communication management plan

c) Change requests

d) Claims administration

118. Kazem is a project manager with many years of experience. Kazem knows how important customer communication and satisfaction are to how a project is managed. What is the best definition of the monitor stakeholder engagement process?

a) The process of identifying project stakeholders regularly and analyzing and documenting relevant information regarding their interests, involvement, interdependencies, influence, and impact on project success

b) The process of communicating and working with stakeholders to meet their needs and expectations, address issues, and foster appropriate stakeholder engagement

c) The process of providing an overview of the project stakeholder management process

d) The process of monitoring project stakeholder relationships and tailoring strategies for engaging stakeholders through the modification of engagement strategies and plans

119. The following describe monitor stakeholder engagement except

a) Managing stakeholder relationships

b) Ignoring the stakeholder until they go away

c) Engaging with the stakeholders

d) Formulating strategies with the stakeholders

120. Which is a tool and technique of the close project or phase process?

a) Regression analysis

b) OPA

c) EEF

d) Deliverables

121. Senior management is attempting to decide in which project to invest. Which one would you recommend?

a) Has a present value of $1,157.00

b) Payback period is four years

c) Net present value will be -$523.03

d) IRR will be 7.93%

122. All the following are inputs to the develop project charter process except

a) SOW

b) Enterprise environmental factors

c) Organizational process assets

d) Data gathering

123. The following are part of the closing process except

a) Obtain stakeholder satisfaction

b) Release the team

c) EEF

d) Prepare final project report.

124. The sponsor has accepted all deliverables of the project. As a project manager, what would you do next?

a) Release the team

b) Gain formal acceptance

c) Document lessons learned

d) Close the project

125. The following are part of the closing process except

a) Obtain stakeholder satisfaction

b) Release the team

c) EEF updates

d) Prepare final project report

126. The outputs to develop project charter are

a) Project management plan and requirements plan

b) Project charter and assumptions log

c) Quality management plan and change management plan

d) Stakeholder management plan

127. All are inputs to identify stakeholder group except

a) Project charter

b) EEF

c) Expert judgment

d) OPA

128. All describe a project charter except

a) Formally authorizes the existence of a project

b) Provides project manager the authority to apply organizational resources to the project

c) States the deliverables of the project

d) States the details of project deliverables

129. What process best identifies the monitor risks process?

a) The process of monitoring the implementation of agreed-on risk response plan, tracking identified risks, analyzing new risks, and evaluating the risk process

b) The process of formalizing acceptance of the completed project deliverables

c) The process of tracking, reviewing, and reporting the overall progress to meet performance objectives defined in the project management plan

d) Data analysis

130. Joe is a project manager who has a sponsor who does not like risk, so Joe must identity the risk and list the probability of occurrence. What answer best describes the risk management plan?

a) It is all the requirements of the project.

b) It is the process of defining how to conduct risk management activities for a project.

c) It is not a desirable choice when managing large projects.

d) It is a grid for mapping the probability of each risk occurrence and the impact on project objectives if the risk occurs

131. Which best describes the process plan scope management?

a) The process of developing a document that formally authorizes the existence of a project and provides the project manager with authority to apply organizational resources to project activities.

b) The process of how the project and product scope will be defined, validated, and controlled throughout the project.

c) The process of developing detailed descriptions of the project and products. This is what the project includes and excludes.

d) The process of estimating the number of work periods needed to complete activities with the estimated resources.

132. All are contained in the define scope process except

a) What the project includes and excludes

b) Output is the project scope statement

c) Detailed description of the project and products

d) How the project and product scope will be validated

133. Joe is a project manager who has a sponsor who does not like risk, so Joe must identity the risk and list the probability of occurrence. What answer best describes the probability impact matrix?

a) It is all the requirements of the project.

b) It is the process of defining how to conduct risk management activities for a project.

c) It is not a desirable choice when managing large projects.

d) It is a grid for mapping the probability of each risk occurrence and the impact on project objectives if the risk occurs.

134. Which best describes the process define scope?

a) The process of developing a document that formally authorized the existence of a project and provides the project manager with authority to apply organizational resources to project activities.

b) The process of how the project and product scope will be defined, validated, and controlled throughout the project.

c) The process of developing detailed descriptions of the project and products. This is what the project includes and excludes.

d) The process of estimating the number of work periods needed to complete activities with the estimated resources.

135. All the following describe estimate activity durations except

a) Determine risks

b) The process of estimating work periods

c) The work periods to complete activities

d) Estimated resources to complete activities

136. Which answer best describes the process manage communications?

a) The process of developing an appropriate approach and plan for project communication activities based on the information needs of each stakeholder, the available organizational assets, and the needs of the project

b) The document that includes information on staff acquisition and release, resource calendars, recognition and rewards, compliance, and safety

c) The process of ensuring timely and appropriate collection, creation, distribution, storage, retrieval, management, monitoring, and the ultimate disposition of project information

d) The process of ensuring the information needs of the project and its stakeholders

137. Which answer best describes monitor communications?

   a) The process of developing an appropriate approach and plan for project communication activities based on the information needs of each stakeholder, the available organizational assets, and the needs of the project

   b) The document that includes information on staff acquisition and release, resource calendars, recognition and rewards, compliance, and safety

   c) The process of ensuring timely and appropriate collection, creation, distribution, storage, retrieval, management, monitoring, and the ultimate disposition of project information

   d) The process of ensuring the information needs of the project and its stakeholders are met

138. Clark is a new project manager for Illusions, Co. Clark's team consists of 6 members including Tom. Two new members have just been added. What is the number of channels of communication?

   a) 13

   b) 12

   c) 15

   d) 28

139. Clark is a new project manager for Illusions, Co. Clark's team consists of 6 members including Tom. Two new members have just been added. How many more channels of communication are there now?

   a) 13

   b) 12

   c) 15

   d) 28

140. Which best describes the process estimate activity durations?

   a) The process of developing a document that formally authorized the existence of a project and provides the project manager with authority to apply organizational resources to project activities.

   b) The process of how the project and product scope will be defined, validated, and controlled throughout the project.

c) The process of developing detailed descriptions of the project and products. This is what the project includes and excludes.

d) The process of estimating the number of work periods needed to complete activities with the estimated resources.

141. The output to develop project management plan is

   a) Project charter

   b) EEF

   c) Project management plan

   d) OPA

142. The outputs of plan scope management are

   a) Scope management plan and requirements management plan

   b) Quality management plan and process improvement plan

   c) Resource management plan and resource breakdown structure

   d) Risk management plan and risk improvement plan

143. The _____ are influences out of the project manager's control.

   a) Enterprise environmental factors

   b) OPA

   c) Evolution environmental factors

   d) Extreme environmental factors

144. _____ are factors internal to the organization that affect the project.

   a) Optimal process assets

   b) Omni process assets

   c) Organization process assets

   d) Optical process assets

145. Susan is a new project manager for Bikes Incorporated. Susan wants to get off to the best start understanding ways to deliver a quality product. Susan and her team are planning for accuracy in quality. Susan can check for quality using each of these rules of quality control except

   a) Control chart

b) Quality audit

c) Pareto chart

d) Scatter diagram

146. Aaron is the project manager at a communication company that builds precision devices. Aaron's team has produced a device that is consistently measured with same output value with little scatter, but the output is not close to the true value. This is an example of what?

a) Accuracy

b) Cost of quality

c) Prevention over inspection

d) Precision

147. What is the best definition of control resources?

a) The process of monitoring the status of the project and product scope and managing changes to the scope baseline

b) The process of monitoring project costs to the cost baseline

c) The process of monitoring and recording the results of executing the quality management plan activities to assess performance and ensure project outputs are complete, correct, and meet customer expectations

d) The process of ensuring the physical resources assigned and allocated to the project are available as planned versus actual utilization of resources and taking corrective actions as necessary

148. The earned value on your project is $150,000, the planned value is $200,000. You've actually spent $180,000 to date. What is the efficiency rate of your schedule?

a) 0.83

b) 0.75

c) $30,000

d) -$30,000

149. What is the correct order of team development?

a) Performing, storming, norming, forming, and adjourning

b) Performing, storming, adjourning, forming, and norming

c) Forming, norming, storming, performing, and adjourning

d) Forming, storming, norming, performing, and adjourning

150. What are the least and most desired methods of conflict resolution?

a) Avoid and collaboration

b) Compromise and smoothing

c) Force and avoid

d) Compromise and collaboration

151. The document that includes information on staff acquisition and release, resource calendars, recognition and rewards, compliance, and safety is

a) Resource plan

b) Project management plan

c) Staffing management plan

d) Project resource plan

152. Deliverables is an output of which process group?

a) OPA

b) EEF

c) Final report

d) Direct and manage project work

153. The following are inputs to process direct and manage project work except

a) Approved changes

b) Project management plan

c) Deliverables

d) OPA

154. Which description best describes the process direct and manage project work?

a) The process of leading and performing the work defined in the project plan and implementing the approved changes to achieve the project objectives

b) The process of improving competencies of team members and the overall team environment to enhance project performance

c) The process of obtaining seller responses, selecting sellers, and awarding a contract

d) The process of documenting project decisions, specifying the approach, and identifying potential sellers

155. Interpersonal and team skills involve all except

a) Active listening

b) Expert judgment

c) Networking

d) Political awareness

156. The following are a part of tools and techniques in manage project knowledge except

a) Knowledge management

b) Information management

c) Interpersonal and team skills

d) Lessons learned register

157. Which process best exemplifies monitoring and control in project integration?

a) Direct and manage project work

b) Monitor and control project work

c) Manage project knowledge

d) Perform integrated change control

158. What is the best definition of monitoring and control?

a) The process of tracking, reviewing, and reporting the overall progress to meet performance objectives defined in the project management plan

b) The process of reviewing all change requests; approving changes; managing changes to deliverables, project documents and the project management plan; and communicating decisions

c) The process of formalizing acceptance of the completed project deliverables

d) The process of monitoring the status of the project and product scope and managing changes to the scope baseline

159. Judy is a top project manager at her firm. Judy is currently working on a project in which a fix is necessary. As a project manager, what should Judy do next?

a) Check the release documents

b) Notify the sponsor

c) Evaluate impact of the change

d) Implement the risk response plan

160. What is the best definition of perform integrated change control?

a) The process of tracking, reviewing, and reporting the overall progress to meet performance objectives defined in the project management plan

b) The process of reviewing all change requests; approving changes; managing changes to deliverables, project documents, and the project management plan; and communicating decisions

c) The process of formalizing acceptance of the completed project deliverables

d) The process of monitoring the status of the project and product scope and managing changes to the scope baseline

161. All are tools and techniques of the process perform integrated change control except

a) Meetings

b) Expert judgment

c) Project management updates

d) Multicriteria decision analysis

162. Of the four types of conflict management, which is considered the worst outcome?

a) Avoid

b) Force

c) Compromise

d) Collaborate

163. Manage communications is a process of which knowledge area?

   a) Plan communications management

   b) Project quality management

   c) Manage communications is not a process.

   d) Project communications management

164. Which best describes the process manage communications?

   a) PMP

   b) The process of ensuring timely and appropriate collection, creation, distribution, storage, retrieval, management, monitoring, and the ultimate disposition of project information

   c) Work performance reports

   d) Team performance

165. All are traits of interpersonal and team skills except

   a) Active listening

   b) Conflict management

   c) Political awareness

   d) Change requests

166. Frank is a project manager with Carmon Lip Balm LLC. Frank and his project team meticulously put together a project plan that captured and strategized for many risks. One of the has just materialized. As a project manager, what should Frank do next?

   a) Plan risk management

   b) Monitor risks

   c) Use his interpersonal skills and team management

   d) Implement risk responses

167. Which definition correctly defines implement risk responses?

   a) The process of implementing the agreed-upon risk response

   b) The process of obtaining seller responses, selecting sellers, and awarding a contract

   c) The process of monitoring the status of the project and product scope and managing changes

to the scope baseline

d) The process of improving competencies of team members and the overall team environment to enhance project performance

168. Which of the following is an output of implement risk response?

a) Expert judgment

b) Risk management plan

c) Interpersonal skills

d) Change requests

169. Which process best describes project risk management?

a) The process of prioritizing individual project risks for further analysis by assessing their probability of occurrence and impact

b) The process of defining how to estimate, acquire, manage, and utilize physical and team resources

c) The process of defining how to conduct risk management activities

d) The process of identifying individual risks as well as sources of overall project risks and documenting their characteristics

170. The output of plan risk management is

a) Cost management plan

b) Risk management plan

c) Scope baseline

d) Risk baseline

171. Which process best describes identify risk?

a) The process of identifying individual risks as well as sources of overall project risks and documenting their characteristics

b) Data analysis and interpersonal skills

c) Project management plan

d) The process of defining how to estimate, acquire, manage, and utilize physical and team resources

172. A tool and technique that can be used in assessing risk impact is

   a) Project management plan

   b) Project document updates

   c) Risk probability and impact assessment

   d) Risk register

173. Which description best describes perform qualitative risk analysis?

   a) The process of prioritizing individual project risks for further analysis by assessing their probability of occurrence and impact

   b) The process of numerically analyzing the effect of identified risks on overall project objects

   c) Identify risks, perform qualitative risk analysis, perform quantitative risk analysis, and plan risk responses

   d) Plan schedule management, define activities, sequence activities, estimate activity resources, estimate activity costs, and develop schedule

174. Which answer is the best description of perform quantitative risk analysis?

   a) The process of numerically analyzing the effect of identified risks on overall project objects

   b) Identify risks, perform qualitative risk analysis, perform quantitative risk analysis, and plan risk responses

   c) Plan schedule management, define activities, sequence activities, estimate activity resources, estimate activity costs, and develop schedule

   d) Estimate costs and determine budget

175. The following are tools and techniques to perform quantitative risk analysis except

   a) Simulations

   b) EEF

   c) Tornado diagram

   d) Facilitation

176. The following are strategies for negative risks/threats except

   a) Avoid

   b) Mitigate

c) Share

d) Transfer

177. The following are strategies for positive risks/threats except

a) Exploit

b) Mitigate

c) Share

d) Enhance

178. All are tools and techniques to plan risk responses except

a) Expert judgment

b) Interpersonal and team skills

c) Contingency response strategy

d) Change requests

179. Senior management called the project manager into a meeting to talk about cost concerns. Senior management wants the project manager to take as much time as needed. However, they do want the most accurate estimate of the current cost. Which cost management tool and technique will provide the most accurate cost estimates?

a) Bottom-up estimating

b) Analogous estimating

c) Parametric estimating

d) EVM

180. Terri is a new project manager at a manufacturing firm. Senior management wants Terri to determine the most accurate costs and time the project will take. Terri has been instructed to take as long as she needs. What tool and technique would Terri use to satisfy this requirement from senior management?

a) Prototypes

b) An oscilloscope

c) Fishbone

d) Bottom-up estimating

181. Jim is a top-level project manager at a construction company. During the implementation phase of a project, there was an atypical issue that caused a minor setback for Jim and his team. Then BAC = 120, EV =10, PV = 12, AC = 11. What is the EAC of the project?

    a) 132

    b) 120

    c) 121

    d) 156.2

182. Richard is a Junior project manager at a construction company. During the implementation phase of a project, there was an atypical issue that caused a minor setback for Richard and his team. Then BAC = 120, EV =10, PV = 12, AC = 11. What is the EAC of the project?

    a) 132

    b) 120

    c) 121

    d) 156.2

183. Kimberly is a top-level project manager at a construction company. Then BAC = 120, EV = 10, PV = 12, AC = 11. What is the EAC forecast earning of the project?

    a) 132

    b) 120

    c) 121

    d) 156.2

184. Which is a part of cost of conformance?

    a) Rework

    b) Testing

    c) Internal failure costs

    d) Liabilities

185. Which is a part of cost of nonconformance?

   a) Training

   b) Destructive testing loss

   c) Inspections

   d) Lost business

186. All are a part of preventive costs except

   a) Time to do it right

   b) Training

   c) Inspections

   d) Document processes

187. Which is a part of cost of conformance?

   a) Rework

   b) Testing

   c) Internal failure costs

   d) Liabilities

188. Which is a part of cost of nonconformance?

   a) Training

   b) Destructive testing loss

   c) Inspections

   d) Lost business

189. All are a part of preventive costs except

   a) Time to do it right

   b) Training

   c) Inspections

   d) Document processes

190. Which of the following is not one of the seven basic quality tools?

   a) Flowcharts

   b) Control charts

   c) Risk management

   d) Check sheets

191. Which answer best describes a communications plan?

   a) The process of developing an appropriate approach and plan for project communication activities based on the information needs of each stakeholder, the available organizational assets, and the needs of the project

   b) The document that includes information on staff acquisition and release, resource calendars, recognition and rewards, compliance, and safety

   c) The process of ensuring timely and appropriate collection, creation, distribution, storage, retrieval, management, monitoring, and the ultimate disposition of project information

   d) The process of ensuring the information needs of the project and its stakeholders

192. What is the output of plan communications management?

   a) Project management plan

   b) Project documents

   c) Communications management plan

   d) Communication baseline

193. What tool and technique can the project manager use to determine the number of communication channels?

   a) Ev - Ac

   b) PERT

   c) AC + (BAC - EV)

   d) $n(n + 1) / 2$

194. As a project manager, you are planning the activities in the project schedule. Which of the following depicts the order of activities in risk management?

   a) Collect requirements, define scope, and create WBS

b) Identify risks, perform qualitative risk analysis, perform quantitative risk analysis, and plan risk responses

c) Plan schedule management, define activities, sequence activities, estimate activity resources, estimate activity costs, and develop schedule

d) Estimate costs and determine budget

195. What is the output of plan risk management?

a) Communication management plan

b) Configuration management plan

c) Home improvement plan

d) Risk management plan

196. What description best identifies with plan risk management?

a) The process of defining how to conduct risk management activities

b) The process of using existing knowledge and creating new knowledge to achieve the project's objectives and contribute to organizational learning

c) The process of translating the quality management plan into executable project activities that incorporate the organization's quality policies

d) Risk baseline

197. Which process best describes plan communications management?

a) The process of numerically analyzing the combined effect of identified individual project risks

b) The process of developing an approach and plan for project communications activities based on the information needs of each stakeholder and the project

c) Plan-Do-Check-Act

d) The process of prioritizing individual project risks for further analysis by assessing their probability of occurrence and impact

198. Rajish is a new project manager for Opensystem LLC. Rajish wants to get off to the best start understanding the project, people, and environment. Interpersonal and team skills is a tool and technique of which process?

a) Meetings

b) Develop project charter

c) OPA

d) Planning

199. All the following are inputs to develop project charter except

a) SOW

b) EEF

c) OPA

d) Data analysis

200. Henry is a project manager with many years of experience. Henry wants to understand the objectives of the sponsor of this project. The outputs to develop project charter are

a) Project management plan and requirements plan

b) Project charter and assumptions log

c) Quality management plan and change management plan

d) Stakeholder management plan

Mock Exam 200 Questions–4 Hours Solutions

1.   Answer: *c*. No, because "the required return on investments is 10%."

2.   Answer: *c*.

Estimate at Completion (typical, steady-state or continuous)	(BAC / CPI) = 555,555.56 dollars

3.   Answer: *b*. Develop project charter is the only process in this list. Meetings is a tool and technique for many processes. Organizational process assets is input to many processes, and planning is a process group.

4.   Answer: *d*. The communication plan is a document for planning the communication of the project.

5.   Answer: *c*. Keep informed.

6.   Answer: *c*. Project charter, EEF, and OPA are all inputs to the process.

7.   Answer: *b*. The project management plan is the output of the process, not a tool and technique.

8.   Answer: *d*. The project charter contains the objectives and other information needed to create the PMP. Data gathering and inspection are tools and techniques. The project management plan is the output of the process.

9.   Answer: *a*. Enterprise environmental factors are influences out of the project manager's control. Organizational process assets are factors within the organization's and project team's control. And *c* and *d* are not part of the project management plan.

10. Answer: *c*. The project charter does not contain detailed information of any type. Detailed information is found in the project management plan.

   Note: This is a typical PMP exam question. The problem has nothing to do with the answer. Focus on the "ask" which is "All are found in the project charter except."

11. Answer: *a*. Scope management plan and requirements management plan are outputs to the plan scope management process. The project charter and project management plan are outputs of earlier stages. Answers *c* and *d* are plan quality management and plan risk management, respectively.

12. Answer: *b*. The benefits management plan is a document outlining the activities necessary for achieving the planned **benefits**. It shows a timeline and the tools and resources necessary to

ensure the **benefits** are fully realized over time.

13. Answer: *b*. The OPA and project management plan are inputs. Data analysis is a tool and technique.

14. Answer: *a*. Answer *b* describes the plan scope management process, *c* describes the create WBS process, and *d* best describes monitoring and controlling a process.

15. Answer: *d*. Gold-plating is work outside the scope of the project deemed necessary by the project team. Answers *b* and *c* are general concepts that help narrow down the scope of the project.

16. Answer: *a*.

17. Answer: *c*. Organizational process assets is an input. But *a*, *b*, and *d* are all tools and techniques.

18. Answer: *b*. Answer *a* describes project management plan, and *c* is create WBS.

19. Answer: *c*. Option *a* describes scope management, *b* describes defining risk management, and *d* is cost management.

20. Answer: *a*. Choice *b* describes plan risk management, and *c* is direct and manage projects. As stated earlier, knowing the sequences of the planning group in all knowledge areas is crucial to passing the PMP exam.

21. Answer: *b*. Susan should immediately begin the closing process. Prepare final report is the only answer that is part of the closing process.

22. Answer: *c*. Option *a* describes scope management, *b* defines risk management, and *d* is cost management.

23. Answer: *c*. Decomposition into activities occurs in the define activities process. Decomposition into work packages occurs in the create WBS process. Answer *d* is a typical PMP exam trick to trip you up because it is combining processes like WBS and activities.

24. Answer: *a*. The question clearly states that Jason is still in the planning process, so what process comes after sequence that is in the list of choices and part on the planning process group. Define activities, sequence activities, estimate activity duration, et cetera. Knowing the order of processes in the planning process group is crucial to passing the exam. Memorize the order of processes in the planning process group!

25. Answer: *a*.

26. Answer: *b*. The communication management plan is not an input to collect requirements. The communication management plan is a guide on how the project team will send, receive, distribute, store, and dispose of communication material.

27. Answer: *c*. See the order of processes in the planning process group.

28. Answer: *a*. Finish to start (FS) is the most commonly used.

29. Answer: *c*.

30. Answer: *c*.

31. Answer: *c*. Project documents are inputs.

32. Answer: *a*. Project documents is an input, project plan updates is an output, and rolling wave is a technique in another process.

33. Answer: b). 1000+2000(4) + 3000 / 6=12000

    12000 / 6=2000

34. Answer: *d*. Expert judgments, historical information review, and funding limit reconciliation are all tools and techniques that can be used to determine spending budget.

35. Answer: *a*. Choices *b*, *c*, and *d* are not outputs.

36. Answer: *d*. Choice *a* is an output for develop project plan, *c* is an output for plan risk management, and *b* is not the output for the plan quality management process.

37. Answer: *a*. Choice *b* is monitoring quality, *c* is manage quality, and *d* is not the answer.

38. Answer: *d*.

39. Answer: *b*. Project documents updates is an output.

40. Answer: *b*.

41. Answer: *d*. Choice *b* is an input, *c* is process, and *a* is an output.

42. Answer: *d*.

43. Answer: *b*.

44. Answer: *c*. Start to finish (SF) is very rarely used.

45. Answer: *d*.

46. Answer: *b*.

47. Answer: *a*. Project documents is an input, decomposition is a tool and technique of create WBS, and define activities and project management plan updates is an output of other processes.

48. Answer: d). a, b, and c are inputs to other processes.

49. Answer: *d*. Answers *a* and *b* are outputs to develop project plan and plan communication

management, respectively; *c* is a tool and technique to other processes.

50. Answer: *c*.

51. Answer: *a*.

52. Answer: *a*.

53. Answer: *a*.

54. Answer: *d*.

55. Answer: *a*.

56. Answer: *b*.

57. Answer: *a*.

58. Answer: *a*.

59. Answer: *b*.

60. Answer: *d*. Organizational process assets and enterprise environmental factors are inputs to many process groups. Final report is an output of the close project or phase process group.

61. Answer: *d*. The lessons learned register is an input.

62. Answer *b*. Choice *a* is a tool and technique of another process; *c* and *d* are outputs to other processes.

63. Answer: *b*. Quality reports is an output; enterprise environmental factors is not an input in this process, and data gathering is a tool and technique.

64. Answer: *c*.

65. Answer: *a*.

66. Answer: *b*. Project documents updates is an output.

67. Answer: *b*.

68. Answer: *d*.

69. Answer: *c*. We are clearly in the execute phase of the project. We have already estimated durations because we have entered the execute phase. There is no mention of project close or cancellation. Identifying stakeholders is going on throughout the life cycle. The best answer is control schedule.

70. Answer: *a*. Data analysis is a tool and technique of most processes. Approved changes is an output to performed integrated change control and an input to direct and manage project work. OPA is an input to most processes.

71. Answer: *b.*

72. Answer: *d.*

73. Answer: *a.*

74. Answer: *b.*

75. Answer: *c.*

Cost Variance	(EV - AC) = (25,000.00) dollars
Schedule Variance	(EV - PV) = 25,000.00 dollars

76. Answer: *b.*

77. Answer: *c.*

78. Answer: *a.*

79. Answer: *b.*

80. Answer: *c.* Change requests is an output to control scope.

81. Answer: *d.* Change requests is an output.

82. Answer: *c.*

83. Answer: *b.*

84. Answer: *c.*

85. Answer: *b.*

86. Answer: *b.* McGregor's Theory X assumes that the typical worker has little ambition, avoids responsibility, and is individual-goal oriented. McGregor's Theory Y assumes employees are internally motivated, enjoy their job, and work to better themselves without a direct reward in return.

87. Answer: *d.*

88. Answer: *c.*

89. Answer: *d.* The communication channel formula is n (n + 1) / 2. (Where n = the number of people on the project). 6 + 2 = 8. 8(7) = 56. 56 / 2 = 28

90. Answer: *a.* The communication channel formula is n x (n - 1)/2. (Where n = the number of people on the project). Previous channels for 6 members. 6x (6-1)/2=6x5/2=15. Add 2 members. Additional channels=8x(8-1)/2=(56/2)=28. More channels=(Additional channels - Previous channels)=28-15=13

91. Answer: *b*. Option *a* describes requirements documentation; *c* is not the choice because you want a risk management plan, and *d* describes the probability impact matrix.

92. Answer: *d*.

93. Answer: *c*.

94. Answer: *d*.

95. Answer: *d*. Choice *a* is identifying stakeholders, *b* is manage stakeholder engagement, and *c* does not exist.

96. Answer: *b*.

97. Answer: *b*. Susan should immediately begin the closing process. Prepare final report is the only answer that is part of the closing process.

98. Answer: *a*.

99. Answer: *c*.

100. Answer: *a*.

101. Answer: *b*.

102. Answer: *c*. Change requests is an output to control scope.

103. Answer: *d*. Change requests is an output.

104. Answer: *c*.

105. Answer: *b*.

106. Answer: *c*.

107. Answer: *b*.

108. Answer: *b*. McGregor's Theory X assumes that the typical worker has little ambition, avoids responsibility, and is individual-goal oriented. McGregor's Theory Y assumes employees are internally motivated, enjoy their job, and work to better themselves without a direct reward in return.

109. Answer: *d*.

110. Answer: *c*.

111. Answer: *d*. The communication channel formula is n (n + 1) / 2. (Where n = the number of people on the project). 6 + 2 = 8. 8(7) = 56. 56 / 2 = 28

112. Answer: *a*. The communication channel formula is n x (n - 1)/2. (Where n = the number of people on the project). Previous channels for 6 members. 6x(6-1)/2=6x5/2=15. Add 2 members.

Additional channels=8x(8-1)/2=(56/2)=28. More channels=(Additional channels-Previous channels)=28-15=13

113. Answer: *d*. Option *a* describes scope management, *b* defines risk management, and *c* is schedule management.

114. Answer: *d*.

115. Answer: *c*.

116. Answer: *c*. Expert judgments is a tool and technique.

117. Answer: *d*.

118. Answer: *d*. Choice *a* is identifying stakeholders, *b* is manage stakeholder engagement, and *c* does not exist.

119. Answer: *b*.

120. Answer: *a*.

121. Answer: *d*. IRR will be 7.93%. On the PMP exam, you should always choose the project with the highest return. In this example, answer *a* only gives a dollar value. Answer *b* is just a payback period, which yields no return. And answer *c* is in the negative range.

122. Answer: *d*. Data analysis is a tool and technique, not an input.

123. Answer: *c*.

124. Answer: *c*.

125. Answer: *b*. Obtain customer satisfaction is not a closing process list. Obtain customer **acceptance** is in the closing process list.

126. Answer: *b*.

127. Answer: *c*.

128. Answer: *d*.

129. Answer: *a*.

130. Answer: *b*.

131. Answer: *b*.

132. Answer: *d*.

133. Answer: *d*.

134. Answer: *c.*

135. Answer: *a.*

136. Answer: *c.*

137. Answer: *d.*

138. Answer d: The communication channel formula is n (n + 1) / 2. (Where n = the number of people on the project). 6 + 2 = 8. 8(7) = 56. 56 / 2 = 28

139. Answer: *a.* The communication channel formula is n x (n - 1)/2. (Where n = the number of people on the project). Previous channels for 6 members. 6x(6-1)/2 = 6x5/2 = 15. Add 2 members. Additional channels=8x(8-1)/2 = (56/2) = 28. More channels = (Additional channels - Previous channels) = 28-15 = 13

140. Answer: *d.*

141. Answer: *c.*

142. Answer: *a.*

143. Answer: a. Enterprise environmental factors are influences out of the project manager's control.

144. Answer: c. Only organization process assets is a valid PMP lexicon and is internal to the organization that affects the project.

145. Answer: *a.*

146. Answer: *d.*

147. Answer: *d.*

148. Answer: *b.*

149. Answer: *d.*

150. Answer: *a.*

151. Answer: *c.*

152. Answer: *d.* OPA and EEF are inputs to many process groups. Final report is an output to the close project or phase process group.

153. Answer: *c.*

154. Answer: *a.*

155. Answer: *a.*

156. Answer: *d.*

157. Answer: *b.*

158. Answer *a.* Answer *d* looks tempting, but the key word was *best*.

159. Answer: *c.*

160. Answer: *b.*

161. Answer: *c.* Project management plan updates could be an output.

162. Answer: *a.*

163. Answer: *d.*

164. Answer: *b.*

165. Answer: *d.*

166. Answer: *d.*

167. Answer: *a.*

168. Answer *d*

169. Answer *d.*

170. Answer *b.*

171. Answer *a.*

172. Answer: *c.*

173. Answer: *a.*

174. Answer: *a.*

175. Answer: *b.* EEF is an input to most processes.

176. Answer: *c.*

177. Answer: *b.*

178. Answer: *d.* Change requests is an output to monitor and control processes.

179. Answer: *a.*

180. Answer: *d.*

181. Answer: *c.*

182. Answer: *c.* Atypical: EAC = AC + (BAC - EV)

183. Answer: *d*.

184. Answer: *b*.

185. Answer: *d*.

186. Answer: *c*.

187. Answer: *b*.

188. Answer: *d*.

189. Answer: *c*.

190. Answer: *c*.

191. Answer: *a*.

192. Answer: *c*.

193. Answer: *d*.

194. Answer: *b*.

195. Answer: *d*.

196. Answer: *a*.

197. Answer: *b*.

198. Answer: *b*. Develop project charter is the only process on this list. Meetings is a tool and technique of many processes. OPA is an input to many processes, and planning is a process group.

199. Answer: *d*.

200. Answer: *b*.

Appendix A:

IT Infrastructure Project Architecture

When you know what the end product is supposed to look like in reference to what a customer is requesting in the statement of work in the project charter, then gathering requirements is more straightforward, less complicated, and faster, thus improving the quality of the deliverables.

The end product of the IT infrastructure project could look like this:

Hosting server

A hosting server is a server dedicated to hosting a service or services for users. Hosting servers are most often used for hosting websites but can also be used for organizing files, images, games, and similar content.

Application server

An application server is a component-based product that resides in the middle tier of a server-centric architecture. It provides middleware services for security and state maintenance, along with data access and persistence.

Database server

The term *database server* refers to the back-end system of a **database** application using client/**server** architecture.

Public network

The public network is a type of network to which anyone has access and can use to connect to other networks or the internet.

Interconnect

The private interconnect is a separate network that you configure between cluster nodes.

Interconnects are commonly used in the Oracle Real Application Cluster environments.

Primary cluster database

Storage Area Network (SAN)

A SAN is a secure, high-speed data-transfer network that provides access to consolidated block-level storage. A SAN makes a network of storage devices accessible to multiple servers. SAN devices appear to servers as attached drives, eliminating traditional network bottlenecks.

Shared Storage

Oracle Real Application Cluster® (RAC)

RAC is a component of the Oracle 12c database product that allows a database to be installed across multiple servers.

Oracle Data Guard®

The Oracle Data Guard ensures high availability, data protection, and disaster recovery for enterprise data. Data Guard provides a comprehensive set of services that create, maintain, manage, and monitor one or more standby databases to enable production Oracle databases to survive disasters and data corruptions.

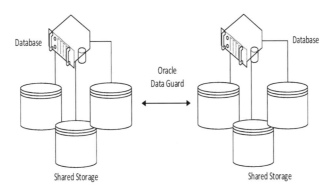

Firewall

A **firewall** is a network security device that monitors incoming and outgoing network traffic and decides whether to allow or block specific traffic based on a **defined** set of security rules.

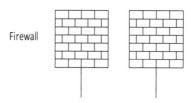

Load balancer

A load balancer is a piece of hardware (or virtual hardware) that acts like a reverse proxy to distribute network and/or application traffic across different servers. A load balancer is used to improve the concurrent user capacity and overall reliability of applications.

DMZ

In computer security, a **DMZ** or demilitarized zone (sometimes referred to as a perimeter network) is a physical or logical subnetwork that contains and exposes an organization's external-facing services to an untrusted network, usually a more extensive network such as the internet.

Cloud server

A cloud server is a logical server that is built, hosted, and delivered through a cloud computing platform over the internet. Cloud servers possess and exhibit similar capabilities and functionality to a typical server but are accessed remotely from a cloud service provider. Typical uses of a cloud are Internet as a Service (IAAS), Service as a Service (SAAS), Database as a Service (DAAS), and Platform as a Service (PAAS). We used cloud servers in development environments to solve computer, software, database, and application-related issues. The cloud was used temporarily in development because long term, the cloud server was too expensive for production.

Virtual server

A virtual server is a server that shares hardware and software resources with other operating systems (OS) as opposed to dedicated servers. Because they are cost effective and provide faster resource control, virtual servers are accessible in web hosting environments

Virtual servers can be used for development, QA, or production environments. Using virtual servers for production saves on the cost, though you lose in performance. Nevertheless, many companies are switching to have their production run on virtual servers.

You can alter this to use the appropriate storage, database, application, hardware, load balancer, firewall, and network methodology and vendor. By looking at this architecture and discussing it with the system architect or system engineer, you can gather most of the physical requirements and have a good idea of who can do the work.

Appendix B:

Common Confusions

1. Project statement of work versus project scope statement

    a. Project statement of work (SOW) is an input to the project charter. Project statement of work contains three things: business need, high-level scope description, and the organization's broad strategic plan. It is important to remember that the SOW contains *high-level description and lacks any detail.*

    b. Project scope statement provides a *detailed description of the deliverables* being created and identifies all work required to create those deliverables. Project scope statement tells you "what's in and what's out."

2. Business case versus business need

    a. Business case is the generic *reason for the project*, such as market demand, strategic opportunity, customer request, technological advance, legal requirement, ecological impact, or social need.

    b. Business need describes what the organization *needs to accomplish* and how that fits in with the overall organizational strategy.

3. Sign-off on the charter versus sign-off on the project plan

    a. Sign-off on the charter should be sign-off by the sponsor.

    b. The entire project team and key stakeholders sign off on the charter.

4. Project scope versus product scope

    a. Project scope describes ways in which the deliverables will be created. It sets forth things like scheduling, budgeting, quality, resources, et cetera.

b. Product scope refers to the deliverable being created and *outlines design specifications and features.*

5. Work performance data versus work performance information

    a. Work performance data, which is an output of direct and manage work is raw data showing the status of a particular project area.

    b. Work performance information is a broader and more descriptive indicator of project status, provides project performance results such as actual versus planned values in the earned value management formulas.

6. Work package versus activity list

    a. Work package is the lowest level of project work decomposed in WBS. Work packages can be further decomposed in the process define activities.

    b. Activities lists are discrete activities necessary to complete the project. The project team can the estimate the resources and duration needed to complete the project.

7. Analogous estimating versus parametric estimating

    a. With analogous estimating, we are looking to a past project that is similar to that being estimated and simply plugging that number into our current estimate while adjusting for any known differences. For example, if we know it took 3 months to deploy software to 500 users during a prior software upgrade, we can use that 3-month time frame as an estimate to deploy new software.

    b. Parametric estimating requires us to scale the figures we take from our historical information. For example, if we know it previously took 6 months to construct a 6,000 square foot building, but in this case, we are constructing a 10,000 square foot building that is similar, we could use parametric estimating to determine that it will take 10 months to construct the new building.

8. Critical chain method versus critical path method

    a. Critical path method reveals the long chain of activities throughout your schedule network diagram which adds up to the longest total duration.

    b. Critical chain method uses "buffers" in the project to protect against schedule delay from resource constraints such as a team member being away or unavailable for a critical time in the project.

9. Baselines (cost baseline, scope baseline, schedule baseline). When baseline is used in PMBOK language, it means it has been approved

a. Cost baseline is the approved budget for the project.

b. Scope baseline are the approved requirements necessary to complete the project.

c. Schedule baseline is the approved timeline it will take to complete the project.

10. Cost of Quality

Cost of Conformance	Cost of Nonconformance
Preventive costs	**Internal Failure Costs**
Training	Rework
Document processes	Scrap
Equipment	
Time to do it right	**External Failure Costs**
Appraisal cost	Liabilities
Testing	Warranty work
Destructive testing loss	Lost business
Inspections	

11. Contingency reserve versus management reserve

a. Contingency reserves are buffers that project managers add to the project cost estimates to account for uncertain events that we know might happen (also called known-unknowns). These costs are included in the cost baseline.

b. Management reserves are not set by the project manager but instead established by senior management reserves and are called (unknowns-unknowns). These costs are not part of the cost baseline.

12. Control quality versus manage quality

a. Control quality is concerned with ensuring correctness of the deliverables. Do the deliverables meet the requirements? Did the deliverables came out as planned? For example, on a car, we would test for brakes stopping as designed or crashworthiness.

b. Manage quality looks to the process and methods of how the quality check was done, such as using proper metrics when we perform the testing. Manage quality is an audit of the quality process.

13. Communication method versus communication technology

    a. Communication method—interactive, push and pull

    b. Communication technology—email, fax, telephone

14. Risk management plan versus risk register

    a. Risk management plan is a document that describes how risk will be managed, controlled, and monitored.

    b. Risk register is a list of specific risks facing the project.

15. Qualitative risk analysis versus quantitative analysis

    a. Qualitative risk analysis uses tools such as probability and impact matrix analysis and risk urgency assessment. Looks to rank the risk.

    b. Quantitative risk analysis looks to quantify the impact of the potential risk events on our project objectives. Provides a numerical assessment of the risk.

16. Corrective actions versus preventive actions

    a. Corrective actions are where a failure has already occurred, so we want to fix the problem and ensure it does not happen again.

    b. Preventive actions are where a failure has not yet occurred, so we want to prevent failures from occurring in the first place.

17. Team performance assessments versus project performance appraisals

    a. Team performance assessments are assessments of the team performance, such as schedule performance or staff turnover. Team performance assessment is an output of the develop team process.

    b. Project performance appraisals are a tool and technique and are individual assessments, such as an annual review at work.

18. Requirements versus constraints

    a. Requirements are features and functionality that a deliverable must include.

    b. Constraints are anything that limits the project team's options, such as a date deadline.

19. The EAC formula and when to use it:

    a. Atypical: $EAC = AC + (BAC - EV)$

b. Typical: EAC = BAC / CPI

c. Forecast: EAC = AC + (BAC - EV) / (CPI*SPI)

20. EAC versus BAC

   a. EAC is a forecast. This is what our project will end up costing

   b. BAC is the current cost of the project. This is the cost performance baseline. We want BAC to be lower than EAC.

21. Verified deliverables versus accepted deliverables

   a. Verified deliverables have gone through the control quality process and are deemed to be correct.

   b. Accepted deliverables have gone through the validate scope process and have been accepted by the sponsor.

22. Procurement performance reviews versus procurement audits

   a. Procurement performance reviews are a tool and technique of control procurement and used to assess the seller's performance in regard to scope, quality, cost, schedule, et cetera.

   b. Procurement audits focus on the entire procurement process. Procurement audits the successes and failures from plan procurement onward throughout the project. Procurement audit is a tool and technique of the close process.

PMP Exam Prep:

Questions, Answers and Explanations

Note: This is a typical PMP exam question. The problem has nothing to do with the answer. Focus on the "ask": for example, "All are found in the project charter except" or "As a project manager, what do you do next?"

"As a Project Manager, What Would You Do Next?" Questions

When I took the PMP exam, it seemed this wording was coming up in every question. This made the questions difficult to answer because I found no book teaching them this way, and no instructors were teaching this format. This was a question asked 80–85% of the time on the PMP exam. If you don't understand how to win this question, the exam will be more difficult to pass.

The key to answering this type of question correctly is as follows:

- Sometimes, answering an "As a project manager, what would you do next?" questions is a matter of knowing where a process comes in the five process groups and 49 processes.

- Once you know the process group you are in, the question becomes more answerable.

    a) Initiating group—For example, if a question suggests high-level requirements, high-level risks, or initial stakeholders, you are in the initial group. If the project charter has not been accepted, then the answer will be in the develop project charter or identify stakeholders' process. If the project charter has been accepted, then you will need to narrow the answer from planning, executing, monitoring, and controlling and closing process groups.

    b) Planning group—all processes in the planning group are in order from develop project management plan to plan stakeholder engagement. If the question asks what comes next for define scope, the answer choices are from create WBS to plan stakeholder engagement. For example, If the question asks what comes before define scope, then the answer choices are from collect requirements to develop project management plan.

    c) Executing group—when a question is clearly in the execute group, then horizontal first, then vertical. For example, if the question asks what is next after direct and manage project work, then the answer is under monitoring and controlling, such as monitor and control project work or control costs. If there is no answer in monitoring and controlling, then the answer is vertical, such as manage project knowledge.

    d) Monitoring and controlling costs—this will depend on the question as well. If the question asks what is next, the answer could be vertical, with a process under monitoring and controlling, or horizontal, in which the project moves to closing. It depends on whether the question asks about the status of the project or suggests the project is accepting all deliverables, or the project is cancelling. Checking the status of the project is vertical from monitoring and control project work to monitor stakeholder engagement. Accepting all deliverables or cancelling immediately moves to closing the project.

e) Closing process group—if the process has all deliverables accepted or canceled, then you are in the closing process group and need to know the order of the closing process

1. Obtain acceptance of deliverables

2. Conduct post-project or phase-end review

3. Record impact of tailoring any process

4. Document lessons learned

5. Apply appropriate updates to organizational process assets (OPA)

6. Archive all relevant project documents

7. Close out all procurement activities

8. Perform team member assessments

- The PMP exam tests whether you know the difference between process groups, knowledge areas, processes, inputs, outputs, and tools and techniques.

- Other times, the PMP exam wants to know the best answer out of the choices provided.

The PMP exam is not testing if you are a project manager or if you will make a good or great project manager. The PMP exam is testing whether you can speak and understand the language of project management at this level.

Exercise to Conquer the "As a Project Manager, What Would You Do Next?" Questions

Project Management Process	Knowledge Area	Process Group	Describe the Process	What Was the Process That Came Before?	What Is the Process That Comes After?
Define Scope					
Develop Project Plan					
Sequence Activities					
Determine Budget					
Plan Procurement Management					
Direct and Manage Project Work					
Develop Team					
Implement Risk Responses					
Perform Integrated Change Control					
Control Costs					
Monitor Communications					
Close Project or Phase					
Collect Requirements					
Estimate Costs					
Perform Quantitative Risk Analysis					
Manage Quality					

Answers to "As a Project Manager, What Would You Do Next?" Questions

Project Management Process	Knowledge Area	Process Group	Describe the Process	What Was the Process That Came Before?	What Is the Process That Comes After?
Define Scope	Scope Management	Planning	What needs to be done to create the scope statement	Collect Requirements	Create WBS
Develop Project Plan	Integration Management	Planning	What needs to be done to create the project management plan	Develop Project Charter	Plan Scope Management
Sequence Activities	Schedule Management	Planning	What needs to be done to order activities	Define Activities	Estimate Activity Durations
Determine Budget	Cost Management	Planning	What needs to be done to determine the planned cost of the project	Estimate Costs	Plan Quality Management
Plan Procurement Management	Procurement Management	Planning	What needs to be done to external resources	Plan Risk Responses	Plan Stakeholder Management
Direct and Manage Project Work	Integration Management	Executing	What needs to be done to manage the project	Develop Project Management Plan	Monitor and Control Project Work
Develop Team	Resource Management	Planning	What needs to be done to train the team	Acquire Resources	Manage Team
Implement Risk Responses	Risk Management	Planning	What needs to be done to apply the risk response plan	Plan Risk Responses	Monitor Risks
Perform Integrated Change Control	Integration Management	Monitoring and Controlling	What needs to be done to manage approved project changes	Monitor and Control Project Work	Close Project and Phase
Control Costs	Cost Management	Monitoring and Controlling	What needs to be done to manage approved cost changes	Determine Budget	Direct and Manage Project Work
Monitor Communications	Communications Management	Executing	What needs to be done to track communication	Manage Communications	Close project or phase
Close Project or Phase	Integration Management	Closing	What needs to be done to end the project	Validate Scope	None
Collect Requirements	Scope Management	Planning	What needs to be done to capture requirements for the project	Plan Scope Management	Define Scope
Estimate Costs	Cost Management	Planning	What needs to be done to capture all costs related to the project	Plan Cost Management	Determine Budget
Perform Quantitative Risk Analysis	Risks Management	Planning	What needs to be done to manage and track approved changes	Perform Qualitative Risk Analysis	Plan Risk Responses
Manage Quality	Quality Management	Executing	What needs to be done to produce products within agreed-upon parameters	Plan Quality Management	Control Quality

Practice Exams

84 Questions on People

1. Abraham is a project manager on an existing project at the Best Acting Company Inc., which sells dreams. After the project kickoff, Abraham and his project team are managing the team resources process. The project plan has been approved. As a project manager, what will Abraham do next?

    a) Create WBS

    b) Control resources

    c) Perform team development

    d) Monitor stakeholder engagement

Answer: c. Performing team development is the next step for the project manager. After the project kickoff the project is in the Execute phase. Create WBS is in the planning phase. Control resources and stakeholder engagement are in the monitoring and control phase.

2. Jonathan is a project manager at a solar car company. Jonathan wants to develop a document that will give him the best chance of managing the project from start to completion. Which document does the project manager need to create next?

    a) Project management plan

    b) Project documents updates

    c) Work performance reports

    d) Team performance

Answer: a. Jonathan needs to create a project management plan which is used by the project manager to manage the project from start to completion. Project documents is not used to track project from start to completion. Work performance reports is a document that shows how well project is performing.

3. As the project manager for the development of a new payroll system, you have many subject matter experts from many different industries working in your project. The chief operating officer (COO) and chief financial officer (CFO) are co-sponsors. The CFO delivers a change request form with a note stating the change will probably result in an additional cost of $50,000 and an additional three weeks to the schedule. The change control board (CCB) will be meeting next week. What is the first thing you should do?

   a) Send the form to the change control board

   b) Get buy-in from the team for the change, since you know it will be approved

   c) Evaluate the impact of the change

   d) Implement the change since the CFO and COO are on the CCB

Answer: c. Once a change has been identified and documented the next step is to evaluate the change for impacts to the rest of the project. The questions states that the CFO believes that will cost an additional $50,000 and add an additional three weeks to the project schedule, but this does not mean that this will be the actual impact. Once the team has an opportunity to review the change, the project manager is responsible for calculating the impact to time, cost and scope. However, these are not the only impacts that need to be evaluated. Technical impacts must also be evaluated by the team.

4. Quasar is a project manager who wants to run an efficient project that completes on time and under budget to the client's satisfaction. When performing the develop project plan process, what will be the output document the project manager will want the most?

   a) Project management plan

   b) Project documents updates

   c) Work performance reports

   d) Team performance

Answer: a. The project management plan is the document the project manager will want most.

5. You are a new project manager that is replacing a previous project manager. You want to know more about the scope baseline of the project. Which three documents will be most useful to you?

   a) Project scope statement, WBS, WBS Dictionary

   b) Scope Management Plan, WBS, WBS Dictionary

   c) Project Management Plan, Scope Management Plan, WBS

d) Project scope statement, Scope Management Plan, WBS

Answer: a. Project scope statement, WBS, WBS Dictionary. – This question tests your knowledge about baselines. If you don't know the definitions for all of the baselines in a project, put them on your brain dump or study them until you do.

6. You are approximately 50% physically complete with your project. The project sponsor has just asked you, the project manager, for a listing of when and how each of your staff is going to be released from the project. Which of the following documents will you present to the project sponsor to answer their question?

    a) Project Management Plan

    b) Resource Management Plan

    c) Staff release plan

    d) Staffing management plan

Answer: b. The resource management plan is a component of the project management plan; therefore, it is a more accurate answer. Answers C and D are distractor answers.

7. You as the project manager want to elicit opinions from experts anonymously and then group them to choose the best option, after several iterations. What are you doing?

    a) Using the Delphi Technique

    b) Employing the Ishikawa Method

    c) Implementing Six Sigma

    d) Gathering Expert Judgment

Answer: a. Using the Delphi Technique. Weirdly enough, the Delphi technique comes up a lot when studying for the PMP exam.

8. David is a new project manager for New Brand Cola LLC. David wants to get off to the best start in understanding the project, people, and environment. As a project manager, David has discovered interpersonal and team skills as a tool and technique of which process?

    a) Meetings

    b) Develop project charter

    c) Organizational process assets

    d) Planning

Answer: b. Develop project charter is the only process on this list. Meetings is a tool and technique for many processes. Organizational process assets are input to many processes, and planning is a process group.

9. Lucia is a new project manager for Razor LLC. Lucia wants to get off to the best start in understanding the project, people, and environment. Meetings are a tool and technique of which process?

   a) Meetings

   b) Develop project charter

   c) Organizational process assets

   d) Planning

Answer: b. Develop project charter is the only process on this list. Meetings is a tool and technique for many processes. Organizational process assets are input to many processes, and planning is a process group.

10. Barron is a new project manager for Best Cereal Products LLC. Barron wants to get off to the best start in understanding the project, people, and environment. All the following are inputs to the develop project charter process except

    a) SOW

    b) Enterprise environmental factors

    c) Organizational process assets

    d) Data gathering

Answer: d. Data gathering is a tool and technique, not an input.

11. Candy is a seasoned project manager at a pickle factory. The project manager needs which tool and technique to collect information?

    a) SOW

    b) Enterprise environmental factors

    c) Organizational process assets

    d) Data gathering

Answer: d. Data gathering is a tool and technique. SOW, enterprise environmental factors, and organizational process assets are inputs for develop project charter.

12. You are a new project manager for an existing project with issues. What document does the project manager need to determine the project goals, high-level risks, and high-level constraints?

    a) Communication plan

    b) Project management plan

    c) SOW

    d) Project charter

Answer: d. The communication plan is a document for planning communication of the project. The project management plan plans the overall activities of the project and contains detailed requirements of the project. The SOW is the statement of work, which includes the objectives of the project. The project charter contains the high-level requirements of the project.

13. You are a new project manager for an existing project with issues. As the project manager, what document do you need to determine how, when, and the level of authority the stakeholders communicate?

    a) Communication management plan

    b) Project management plan

    c) SOW

    d) Project charter

Answer: a. The communication management plan is a document for planning communication of the project. The project management plan plans the overall activities of the project and contains detailed requirements of the project. The SOW is the statement of work, which includes the objectives of the project. The project charter contains the high-level requirements of the project.

14. Priscilla is a project manager who transferred from another department. One of the documents Priscilla must create is vital to the success of the project in meeting its deliverables. Which document is created from the output of the develop project management plan process?

    a) Project charter

    b) Enterprise environmental factors

    c) Project management plan

d) Organizational process assets

Answer: c. Project charter, EEF, and OPA are all inputs to the process.

15. Jonathan is the senior project manager for a High-energy company. In the beginning stages of the project, Jonathan spends much of his time conversing with the sponsor and senior management to develop a document that gives the project manager authority to commit resources to the project. What is the output of the develop project charter process?

    a) Project charter

    b) Enterprise environmental factors

    c) Project management plan

    d) Organizational process assets

Answer: a. The project management plan is the output of the process to develop the project management plan. EEF and OPA are inputs of other processes.

16. The following are tools and techniques for the develop project management plan process except

    a) Meetings

    b) Project management plan

    c) Interpersonal and team skills

    d) Expert judgments

Answer: b. The project management plan is the output of the process, not a tool and technique.

17. Ulysses is a new project manager on an existing project. The project has been in its planning stage. The process that has just been completed is collect requirements. As a project manager, what would you do next?

    a) Define scope

    b) Project management plan

    c) Plan scope management

    d) Expert judgments

Answer: a. Define scope is the planning process that would be performed next. The project management plan is an output of develop project management plan. Plan scope management would have been done previously to collect requirements. Expert judgments is a tool and technique.

18. David has been a project manager for many years. David has been communicating with the sponsor and senior management, combining SOW, assumptions, initial stakeholders, and high-level risk into one document. As the project manager, which of the following documents is he creating?

    a) Data gathering

    b) Project management plan

    c) Inspection

    d) Project charter

Answer: d. The project charter contains the objectives and other information needed to create the PMP. Data gathering and inspection are tools and techniques. The project management plan is the output of the process.

19. Danny is a new project manager on an existing project. The project has been in its planning stage. The process that has just been completed is collect requirements. As a project manager, what would you do next?

    a) Project management plan

    b) Define activities

    c) Plan scope management

    d) Expert judgments

Answer: b. Define activities is the planning process that would be performed next. The project management plan is an output of develop project management plan. Plan scope management would have been done previously to collect requirements. Expert judgments are a tool and technique.

20. Deliverables are an output of which process group?

    a) Organizational process assets

    b) Enterprise environmental factors

    c) Final report

d) Direct and manage project work

Answer: d. Organizational process assets and enterprise environmental factors are inputs to many process groups. The final report is an output of the close project or phase process group.

21. Luke is a new project manager on an existing project. The project has been in its planning stage. The process that has just completed is define activities. As a project manager, what process did you determine was done previously to define activities?

 a) Define scope

 b) Project management plan

 c) Plan schedule management

 d) Expert judgments

Answer: c. Plan schedule management is the planning process that would have been performed prior to define activities. The project management plan is an output of develop project management plan. Plan scope management would have been done previously to collect requirements. Expert judgments is a tool and technique.

22. Which of the following is a tool and technique of direct and manage project work?

 a) Change requests

 b) PMIS

 c) Project management plan

 d) OPA updates

Answer: b. Change requests are an output of perform integrated change control process, the project management plan is an output of develop project plan process, and OPA updates are outputs of other processes. Only b is a tool and technique.

23. Shaq is a new project manager on an existing project. The project has been in its planning stage. The process that has just been completed is define activities. As a project manager, what process did he determine was done prior to define activities?

 a) Define scope

 b) Project management plan

c) Data gathering

d) Create WBS

Answer: d. Create WBS is the planning process that would have been performed prior to define activities. The project management plan is an output of develop project management plan. Plan scope management would have been done prior to collect requirements. Data gathering is a tool and technique.

24. Which process best exemplifies monitoring and control in project integration?

    a) Direct and manage project work

    b) Monitor and control project work

    c) Manage project knowledge

    d) Perform integrated change control

Answer: b. Choices a, c, and d are not the best exemplification of monitoring and control in project integration.

25. Glover is a new project manager on an existing project. The project has been in its execute stage. The process that has just been completed is define activities. As a project manager, which process will he do next?

    a) Define scope

    b) Validate scope

    c) Data gathering

    d) Create WBS

Answer: b. Validate scope is the process that would be performed next because the project is in the execute phase. When execute starts, then the monitor control process starts. Project management and plan scope management are planning processes. Data gathering is a tool and technique.

26. Harry is a contractor responsible for the refurbishment of an automobile showroom. The estimated refurbishment cost is $500 per square foot. The total showroom area that needs to be refurbished is 1,000 square feet. Based on Harry's experience, he knows his team can refurbish 100 square feet per week. As a project manager, how should Harry report how the project is performing?

    a) On schedule and on budget

b) Behind schedule and over budget

c) Ahead of schedule and over budget

d) Behind schedule and ahead of budget

Answer: c. Harry will report the project ahead of schedule and over budget.

Cost Variance	(EV - AC) = ($25,000.00)
Schedule Variance	(EV - PV) = $25,000.00

27. Sophia is a contractor responsible for the refurbishment of an automobile showroom. The estimated refurbishment cost is $500 per square foot. The total showroom area that needs to be refurbished is 1,000 square feet. Based on Sophia's past experience, she knows her team can refurbish 100 square feet per week. As the project manager, how should Sophia report the steady-state progress of the project?

a) $525,000

b) $375,000

c) $555,555.56

d) $475,000

Answer: c. Sophia will report the steady-state as $555,555.56.

Estimate at Completion (typical, steady-state, or continuous)	(BAC / CPI) = $555,555.56

28. Jeffrey is a contractor responsible for the refurbishment of an automobile showroom. The estimated refurbishment cost is $500 per square foot. The total showroom area that needs to be refurbished is 1,000 square feet. Based on Jeffrey's experience, he knows his team can refurbish 100 square feet per week. As a project manager, how should Jeffrey report the forecast estimate at completion to senior management?

a) $525,000

b) $375,000

c) $555,555.56

d) $516,224.19

Answer: d. Jeffrey should report the estimate at completion as $516,224.19.

29.   The process of defining how to estimate, acquire, manage, and utilize physical and team resources is

  a) Develop team

  b) Plan resource management

  c) Organizational theory

  d) Team charter

Answer: b. The keyword here is "how," which describes the plan—in this case, plan resource management.

30.   All of the following are inputs to manage a team except

  a) Project management plan

  b) Project documents updates

  c) Work performance reports

  d) Team performance

Answer: b. Project document updates is an output.

31.   A project has five stakeholders, when an additional project member gets added, how many communication channels exist?

  a) 14

  b) 15

  c) 6

  d) 20

Answer: b. Remember the formula $n(n-1)/2$

32.   Antonio is a new project manager on an existing project. The project has been in its execute stage. The process that has just been completed is estimate costs. As a project manager, which process will Antonio do next?

  a) Define scope

  b) Control costs

c) Data gathering

d) Create WBS

Answer: b. Control costs is the process that would be performed next since the project is in the execute phase; money is being spent, so the cost must be controlled. When execute starts, then the monitor control process starts. Data gathering is a tool and technique. Define scope and create WBS are planning processes.

33.   What is the correct order of team development?

   a) Performing, storming, norming, forming, and adjourning

   b) Forming, storming, norming, performing, and adjourning

   c) Forming, norming, storming, performing, and adjourning

   d)   Performing, storming, adjourning, forming, and norming

Answer: b. Only b is in the correct order.

34.   Sabrina is a new project manager on an existing project. The project has been canceled by senior management without cause. As a project manager, what will Sabrina do next?

   a) Negotiate with management to keep the project going

   b) Negotiate with the sponsor to keep the project going for a few more weeks because things can be turned around

   c) Begin the closing process immediately

   d) Continue the project until she has heard from the sponsor

Answer: c. Once the project manager has been notified by senior management or the sponsor that the project is being canceled, then the closing procedure must begin immediately.

35.   The process of defining how to estimate, acquire, manage, and utilize physical and team resources is

   a) Develop team

   b) Team Charter

   c) Organizational theory

d) Plan resource management

Answer: d. The fact that the question asks "how to" indicates the project is in the planning stage. Develop team is a process in the execute stage. Organizational theory and team charter are not processes.

36.   Mark is a new project manager on an existing project. The project has moved beyond the planning stage. The vendor chosen to complete a portion of the project has started work. As a project manager, what will Mark do next?

   a) Plan what is expected of outside vendors

   b) Ask the vendor for closing reports and place in archives

   c) Control procurements

   d) Continue the project until he has heard from the sponsor

Answer: c. Once the contractor has started work, they will be monitored and tracked to make sure the results are being established according to the project plan and the vendor contract. Closing reports for archive comes in the closing phase. Planning what is expected of the vendor would have been performed in the planning stage.

37.   Pepper is a new project manager for TF Banking Services. Pepper is in the process of acquiring resources. All are tools and techniques Pepper can use to aid in her search except

   a) Virtual teams

   b) Multicriteria analysis

   c) Resource management plan

   d) Negotiation

Answer: c. The resource management plan is a document and is the output of plan resource management.

38.   The process of defining how to estimate, acquire, manage, and utilize physical and team resources is

   a) Develop team

   b) Plan resource management

   c) Organizational theory

d) Team charter

Answer: b. Plan resource management is part of the planning stage and answers the question of how to estimate, acquire, manage, and utilize physical and team resources. Develop team is also a process but in the execute stage and would best fit training a resource. Choices c and d are not processes.

39. John is a new project manager on an existing project. The project is now in the execute stage. John and his project team know the plan resources they need, what the resources will do, and how long the work will take. As a project manager, what will John do next?

    a) Control resources

    b) Develop team

    c) Manage team

    d) Acquire resources

Answer: d. Since the project is now in the execute stage, the order of what occurs next is acquire resources, develop team, and manage resources.

40. Your team has been together for a while and have settled into their roles. Now they are just beginning to work on the project efficiently and effectively. What stage of team development are they in?

    a) Performing

    b) Norming

    c) Storming

    d) Forming

Answer: a. Performing – For Project Human Resource Management, you need to know some Management 101 terms and definitions.

41. Luther is a new project manager on an existing project. The project is now in the execute stage. Luther and his project team know the plan resources they need, what the resources will do, and how long the work will take. As a project manager, what will Luther do next?

    a) Control resources

b) Develop team

c) Manage team

d) Determine stakeholders

Answer: b. Develop team will be the project manager's next task. Since the project is now in the execute stage, the order of what occurs next is acquire resources, develop team, and manage resources.

42. As a project manager for a multi-family housing construction project, you decided to phase your project for ease of management. In your discussions with your sponsor and potential vendors, you are taking suggestions for names of the phases so everyone can understand the project. You have whittled the list down to the following four suggestions. Which one of the following would you not choose?

a) Design, Site, Development, Infrastructure, Construction

b) Initiating, Planning, Executing, Monitoring and Controlling, Closing

c) Approval, Design, Site construction, Building construction

d) Design, Site development, Infrastructure, Structure construction

Answer: b. Project phases can be named anything that the performing organization and the stakeholders understand or desire. Answer D is a list of the names of the process groups in project management and therefore would not be used.

43. Ashley is a new project manager on an existing project. The project has now in the execute stage. Ashley and his project team know the plan resources they need, what the resources will do, and how long the work will take. As a project manager, what will Ashley do next?

a) Control resources

b) Train management

c) Lay out a grand plan for the project

d) Determine stakeholders

Answer: a. Control resources will be the project manager's next task. Since the project is now in the execute stage, the order of what occurs next is acquire resources, develop team, and manage resources. However, since none of these options are there, the choice that best answers the question is control resources.

44. Michelle is a project manager for a bookseller. One of her projects is improving the ways books can be found without assistance from the staff. Michelle needs to introduce a new member to the project team. What is the correct order of team development?

    a) Performing, storming, norming, forming, and adjourning

    b) Performing, storming, adjourning, forming, and norming

    c) Forming, norming, storming, performing, and adjourning

    d) Forming, storming, norming, performing, and adjourning

Answer: d. Only d is in the correct order.

45. The process of defining how to estimate, acquire, manage, and utilize physical and team resources is

    a) Develop team

    b) Organizational theory

    c) Plan resource management

    d) Team charter

Answer: c. Plan resource management defines how to estimate, acquire, manage, and utilize physical and team resources.

46. Pepper is a new project manager for TF Banking Services. Pepper is in the process of acquiring resources. All are tools and techniques Pepper can use to aid in her search except

    a) Virtual teams

    b) Multicriteria analysis

    c) Resource management plan

    d) Negotiation

Answer: c. The resource management plan is an output of plan resource management.

47. David is a new project manager for Monorail Enterprises. David wants to get off to the best start in understanding the project, people, and environment. Interpersonal and team skills is a tool and technique of which process?

   a) Meetings

   b) Develop project charter

   c) Organizational process assets

   d) Planning

Answer: b. Develop project charter is the only process on this list. Meetings is a tool and technique for many processes. Organizational process assets are an input to many processes, and planning is a process group.

48. All the following are inputs to the develop project charter process except

   a) SOW

   b) Enterprise environmental factors

   c) Organizational process assets

   d) Data gathering

Answer: d. Data gathering is a tool and technique, not an input.

49. You are a new project manager for an existing project with issues. What document do you need to determine the project goals, high-level risks, and high-level constraints?

   a) Communication plan

   b) Project management plan

   c) SOW

   d) Project charter

Answer: d. The communication plan is a document for planning communication of the project. The project management plan plans the overall activities of the project and contains detailed requirements of the project. The SOW is the statement of work, which includes the objectives of the project. The project charter contains the high-level requirements of the project.

50. Which is an output of the validate scope process?

   a) Work performance data

   b) Acceptable deliverables

   c) Verified deliverables

   d) Work performance information

Answer: b. The output of validate scope is acceptable deliverables. Validate scope formalizes the acceptance of the completed project deliverables. Verified deliverables are the output of the project tasks. Work performance data is raw data that is reported on change requests. Work performance information is the work performance data that has been transformed for example, number of change requests or forecast estimates.

51. Samantha is a new project manager on an existing project. After the project kickoff, Samantha and her project team have completed collection of all requirements and determined the scope. The project plan has been approved. As a project manager, what will Samantha do next?

   a) Create WBS

   b) Validate scope

   c) Lay out a grand plan for the project

   d) Negotiate with the sponsor for overtime

Answer: b. Validate scope is the best option here. Create WBS is performed in the planning process, in which the project plan has already been approved. Answer c is the approved project plan. The negotiation with a sponsor for overtime response is already answered in the project plan with the creation and approval of the schedule baseline.

52. Which answer best describes the stakeholder engagement plan?

   a) The process of developing approaches to involve project stakeholders based on their needs and expectations, addressing issues, and fostering appropriate stakeholder engagement involvement

   b) The process of monitoring project stakeholder relationships and tailoring strategies for engaging stakeholders through the modification of engagement strategies and plans

   c) The process of communicating and working with stakeholders to meet their needs and expectations

d) The process of not communicating and working with stakeholders to meet their needs and expectations

Answer: a. If the question asks for a plan, then b is not the answer. Answer c is executing the plan. Answer d is not correct because you always want to communicate in project management. The process of developing is a "plan" type of answer.

53. William is a new project manager on an existing project. Before the project kickoff, William and his project team have completed the plan procurement management process. The project plan has not been approved. As a project manager, what will William do next?

   a) Create WBS

   b) Validate scope

   c) Plan stakeholder engagement

   d) Negotiate with the sponsor for overtime

Answer: c. The next step in the planning stage after plan procurement management is to plan the stakeholder engagement process. Create WBS happens earlier in the planning stage, and validate scope is in the execute stage. Project managers will not negotiate with the sponsor.

54. Tomas is a junior project manager for a pharmaceutical company. One of Tomas's roles is to assist in the development of a project charter. What document is from the plan stakeholder engagement process?

   a) Assumption and constraint analysis

   b) Stakeholder engagement plan

   c) Project management plan

   d) Process improvement plan

Answer: b. Assumption and constraint analysis is a tool and technique. Choices c and d are outputs of other processes.

55. One of the duties of a project manager is the process of communicating and working with stakeholders to meet their needs and expectations, address issues, and foster appropriate involvement. As a project manager, what do you do next?

   a) Manage stakeholder engagement

b) Monitor communications

c) Manage communications

d) Monitor stakeholder engagement

Answer: a. The difference between monitoring and managing is that monitoring is watching or observing. Managing is an action in which you are actually doing something. In this case, it is the "process of communicating and working with stakeholders."

56. Jesus is a new project manager on an existing project. After the project kickoff, Jesus and his project team have completed the plan stakeholder engagement process and are managing the stakeholder engagements. The project plan has been approved. As a project manager, what will Jesus do next?

a) Create WBS

b) Validate scope

c) Plan stakeholder engagement

d) Monitor stakeholder engagement

Answer: d. The next thing the project manager will do is monitor the stakeholder engagement as part of the project plan.

57. Kazem is a project manager with many years of experience. Kazem knows how important customer communication and satisfaction are to project management. What is the best definition of the monitor stakeholder engagement process?

a) The process of identifying project stakeholders regularly and analyzing and documenting relevant information regarding their interests, involvement, interdependencies, influence, and impact on project success

b) The process of communicating and working with stakeholders to meet their needs and expectations, address issues, and foster appropriate stakeholder engagement

c) The process of providing an overview of the project stakeholder management process

d) The process of monitoring project stakeholder relationships and tailoring strategies for engaging stakeholders through the modification of engagement strategies and plans

Answer: d. Option a is identifying stakeholders, b is manage stakeholder engagement, and c does not exist.

58. Joaquim is a very seasoned and energetic project manager. Recently, Joaquim's emails to some stakeholders have gone unanswered. When some stakeholders do respond, Joaquim must decide how to answer their concerns. Joaquim should do all the following in monitor stakeholder engagement except

   a) Managing stakeholder relationships

   b) Ignoring the stakeholders until they go away

   c) Engaging with the stakeholders

   d) Formulating strategies with the stakeholders

Answer: b. You would think answer b would be common sense, but it is surprising how many testers will miss a question like this on the exam. You never ignore stakeholders because communication, collaboration, and compromise are primary tools of a project manager.

59. Jeffrey is a project manager responsible for the delivery of a solar car prototype. There are many moving parts to a project on the cutting edge of technology. Resources such as people and equipment for solar technology are not as common. Jeffrey must learn the language of solar technology to deliver the project successfully. As project manager, which of the following is Jeffery not going to use as an input to manage team?

   a) Project management plan

   b) Project documents updates

   c) Work performance reports

   d) Team performance

Answer: b. Project document updates is an output. All others are inputs to one or more processes.

60. Andy is a project manager on an existing project. After the project kickoff, Andy and his project team have completed the acquire resources process. The project plan has been approved. As a project manager, what will Andy do next?

   a) Create WBS

   b) Develop team

   c) Plan stakeholder engagement

   d) Monitor stakeholder engagement

Answer: b. Once the project plan has been approved or kickoff has been performed then as project manager your start in the execute stage. Develop team is in the execute stage. The next thing the project manager will do is develop a team as part of the project plan.

61. In your project you believe the current variances occurred because of extraneous factors, and you do not expect similar variances to occur in future. The information you have is BAC = $300,000; AC = $100,000; EV = $150,000; CPI = 1.5. What is the estimate at completion (EAC) for your project?

    a) $200,000

    b) $250,000

    c) $100,000

    d) $280,000

Answer: b. The formula for EAC when variances are atypical and you do not expect the variances to continue in the future is, AC + (BAC - EV). So, plugging in the numbers we have $100,000 + ($300,000 - $150,000)=$250,000.

62. Andy is a project manager on an existing project at the PASSMAX company, which sells passports. After the project kickoff, Andy and his project team are in the managing team resources process. The project plan has been approved. As a project manager, what will Andy do next?

    a) Create WBS

    b) Develop team

    c) Control resources

    d) Monitor stakeholder engagement

Answer: c. The next thing the project manager will do is control resources as part of the project plan. At this time, the resources have already been trained and develop. The team is producing results. As a project manager, you want to make sure the results are per the project plan.

63. As a project manager, Sandy must introduce new team members because either the previous contract did not work out, there was more work than current team members could handle, or the new team members had skills the current team members were lacking. What is the correct order of team development?

    a) Performing, storming, norming, forming, and adjourning

b) Performing, storming, adjourning, forming, and norming

c) Forming, norming, storming, performing, and adjourning

d) Forming, storming, norming, performing, and adjourning

Answer: d. Only d is in the correct order.

64. Joseph is a senior project manager on an existing project for building boats. The project is currently in the execute stage. Which document will Joseph not need as an input to the manage team process?

a) Project management plan

b) Project documents updates

c) Work performance reports

d) Team performance

Answer: b. Project documents updates is an output.

65. Your company is developing a new financial vehicle to sell to clients. The project team is in the process of identifying risks. Which of the following would not be classified as a risk?

a) A decision by the Federal Reserve to increase lending rates to banks

b) The economy

c) An eight-point increase in the unemployment rate

d) A sudden drop in the stock market

Answer: b. A risk is defined as an uncertain event or condition that, if it occurs, will cause an impact on one or more of your project objectives. Answers A, C, and D are all possible risk events. Answer B is a category of risk events, and not a specifically identified risk vent.

66. Norman is a project manager for a ventilator company for delivery to hospitals. Norman is replacing a team member because of quality and performance issues. The new team member is getting up to speed quickly to begin producing. As the project manager, in what order will Norman perform the steps of team development?

a) Performing, storming, norming, forming, and adjourning

b) Performing, storming, adjourning, forming, and norming

c) Forming, norming, storming, performing, and adjourning

d) Forming, storming, norming, performing, and adjourning

Answer: d. Only d is in the correct order.

67. Miss Jones is a project manager on an existing project at the Best Acting Company, Inc, which sells dreams. After the project kickoff, Miss Jones and her project team are in the managing team resources process. The project plan has been approved. As a project manager, what will Miss Jones do next?

a) Performing team development

b) Create WBS

c) Develop team

d) Monitor stakeholder engagement

Answer: c. Develop team is the next step for the project manager.

68. Your project team has just completed the final component of a three-year long project that cost $20 million. The final product has been transitioned to operations and maintenance, a final lessons learned meeting has been held, all contracts have been closed and all post-project support requirements have been identified, documented and agreed upon with the customer. You have been offered a promotion due to the resounding success of this project. As part of project closure what is the next thing you will do?

a) Release project team

b) Create the final project closure documents

c) Hold a celebration event to toast the team's success

d) Thank the project team for their work and let them know you got promoted for it

Answer: b. Creating the final project closure documents would be next. Since the team will assist with developing these, Answer D is one of the last things that would be done. While we may hold a celebration for the project team, that would happen after the project is completely closed.

69. Mr. Greene is a project manager on an existing project at the Ultimate Real Estate Company, which sells passports. After the project kickoff, Mr. Greene and his project team are in the manage team resources process. The project plan has been approved. As a project manager, what will Mr. Greene do next?

   a) Control resources

   b) Create WBS

   c) Develop team

   d) Monitor stakeholder engagement

Answer: a. The next thing the project manager will do is control resources as part of the project plan. At this time, the resources have already been trained and developed. The team is producing results. As a project manager, you want to make sure the results are per the project plan.

70. Olivia is a project manager at the corporation MAOHC. MAOHC has numerous affiliates and thousands of ongoing projects. Olivia is introducing a new team member to handle quality assurance on her project. As the project manager, in what order should Olivia perform the steps of team development?

   a) Performing, storming, norming, forming, and adjourning

   b) Performing, storming, adjourning, forming, and norming

   c) Forming, norming, storming, performing, and adjourning

   d) Forming, storming, norming, performing, and adjourning

Answer: d. Only d is in the correct order.

71. Noah is a project manager at Emca, a producer of animated characters for worldwide distribution to children as consumers. Which tool and technique should Noah use next in the plan communications management process to create the communication management plan?

   a) Change log

   b) Project management plan

   c) Manage quality

   d) Interpersonal and team skills

Answer: d. Option a is an output, b is an input, and c is a process.

72. Emma is a project manager for Guidance Cybernetics, a maker of exoskeletons for those who have lost the use of their limbs or are paralyzed from spinal injuries. Emma's project has suffered both material and people resource setbacks. As the project manager, what should Emma choose as the best tool and technique of the plan communication management process to create the communication management plan document?

    a) Change log

    b) Project management plan

    c) Manage quality

    d) Communication technology

Answer: d. Change log and project management plan are never a tool and technique. Manage quality is a process.

73. Ava is a junior project manager learning the ropes for the company Dadcorp. Dadcorp is a company that performs the to-do list for families or single parents and other things around the home of the consumer. Conversations and meetings are part of which tool and technique?

    a) Communications analysis

    b) Communications technology

    c) Communications model

    d) Communications method

Answer: b. Communications analysis describes what is needed to maximize the value of information for project stakeholders. Communications technology includes shared portals, emails, and databases. The communications model is the encoding and decoding of messages. And the communication method is the interaction of information, such as one-way or multidirectional conversations.

74. Which best describes the manage communications process?

    a) Project management plan

    b) The process of ensuring timely and appropriate collection, creation, distribution, storage, retrieval, management, monitoring, and the ultimate disposition of project information

    c) Work performance reports

    d) Team performance

Answer: b. The project management plan describes the project, work performance reports describe the status of the project, and team performance is the evaluation of the effectiveness of the team.

75. Kazem is a project manager with many years of experience. Kazem knows how important customer communication and satisfaction are to project management. What is the best definition of the monitor stakeholder engagement process?

    a) The process of identifying project stakeholders regularly and analyzing and documenting relevant information regarding their interests, involvement, interdependencies, influence, and impact on project success

    b) The process of communicating and working with stakeholders to meet their needs and expectations, address issues, and foster appropriate stakeholder engagement

    c) The process of providing an overview of the project stakeholder management process

    d) The process of monitoring project stakeholder relationships and tailoring strategies for engaging stakeholders through the modification of engagement strategies and plans

Answer: d. Option a is identifying stakeholders, b is manage stakeholder engagement, and c does not exist.

76. The following describe monitor stakeholder engagement except

    a) Managing stakeholder relationships

    b) Ignoring the stakeholders until they go away

    c) Engaging with the stakeholders

    d) Formulating strategies with the stakeholders

Answer: b. You would think answer b would be common sense, but it is surprising how many testers will miss a question like this on the exam. You never ignore stakeholders because communication, collaboration, and compromise are primary tools of a project manager.

77. The process of communicating and working with stakeholders to meet their needs and expectations, address issues, and foster appropriate involvement is

    a) Manage stakeholder engagement

    b) Monitor communications

    c) Manage communications

    d) Monitor stakeholder engagement

Answer: a. The difference between monitoring and managing is that monitoring is watching or observing. Managing is an action in which you are actually doing something. In this case, it is the "process of communicating and working with stakeholders."

78. Elijah is a project manager at Poor Man's Industries, a maker of economical products that look expensive. As the project manager, Elijah will supply all the inputs to manage a team except

    a) Project management plan

    b) Project documents updates

    c) Work performance reports

    d) Team performance

Answer: b. Project document updates is an output.

79. You are assisting the PMO director in project selection. The executive steering committee has identified four possible projects but can only do one with the remaining funds in this fiscal year. Project A has an internal rate of return (IRR) of 21% and an NPV of $200,000. Project B has an IRR of 20% and an NPV of $180,000. Project C has an IRR of 7% and an NPV of $180,000. Project D has an IRR of 13% and an NPV of $110,000. Based on this information which project would you recommend and what is the opportunity cost?

    a) Project A, $180,000

    b) Project D, $110,000

    c) Project B, $290,000

    d) Project A, $470,000

Answer: b. When selecting between project options, always select the one with the highest internal rate of return. Opportunity cost is the value of the next highest option in the list of projects. Therefore, project A has the highest rate of return in the next highest option in the list as an NPV of $180,000.

80. What is the correct order of team development?

    a) Forming, storming, norming, performing, and adjourning

    b) Performing, storming, adjourning, forming, and norming

    c) Forming, norming, storming, performing, and adjourning

    d) Performing, storming, norming, forming, and adjourning

Answer: a. Only a is in the correct order.

81. David is a project manager on an existing project at the Unified Passports, Incorporated, which sells passports. After the project kickoff, David and his project team are in the managing team resources process. The project plan has been approved. As a project manager, what will David do next?

    a) Create WBS

    b) Control resources

    c) Develop team

    d) Monitor stakeholder engagement

Answer: b. The next thing the project manager will do is control resources as part of the project plan. At this time, the resources have already been trained and developed. The team is producing results. As a project manager, you want to make sure the results are per the project plan.

82. Daryl is a project manager on an existing project at the Best Acting Company Inc., which sells dreams. Before the project kickoff, Daryl and her project team are planning to perform qualitative risk analysis. The project plan has not been approved. As a project manager, what will Daryl do next?

    a) Plan risk management

    b) Create WBS

    c) Control resources

    d) Monitor stakeholder engagement

Answer: a. Plan risk management is the next step for the project manager.

83. Daryl is a project manager on an existing project at the Best Acting Company Inc., which sells dreams. Before the project kickoff, Daryl and her project team are planning to perform qualitative risk analysis. The project plan has not been approved. As a project manager, what does Daryl do prior to performing qualitative risk analysis?

    a) Implement risk responses

    b) Plan risk responses

    c) Control resources

    d) Plan communication management

Answer: b. Plan communication management is the step that comes before planning to perform qualitative risk analysis.

84. Daryl is a project manager on an existing project at the Best Acting Company, Inc, which sells dreams. Before the project kickoff, Daryl and her project team are planning to perform qualitative risk analysis. The project plan has not been approved. As a project manager, what will Daryl do prior to qualitative risk analysis?

   a) Create WBS

   b) Control resources

   c) Monitor stakeholder engagement

   d) Plan risk management

Answer: d. Plan risk management is the next step for the project manager.

16 Questions on Business

1. Daniel is a new project manager for IT Providers LLC. Daniel wants to get off to the best start understanding the project, people, and environment. Interpersonal and team skills are a tool and technique of which process?

    a) Meetings

    b) Develop project charter

    c) OPA

    d) Planning

Answer: b. Meetings are the only tool and technique on this list. Develop project charter is a process. OPA is input, and planning alone is a word, not a tool and technique.

2. Mia is a new project manager for Warbuck LLC. Mia and her team inherited a project with many assumptions and constraints. All the requirements are not available, and the deliverables do not match up with client expectations. Mia wants to get off to the best start understanding the project, people, and environment. All the following are inputs to develop project charter except

    a) SOW

    b) Assumptions and constraints

    c) OPA

    d) Data analysis

Answer: d. SOW, assumptions, and constraints and OPA are all inputs to the project charter. Data analysis is a tool and technique.

3. Lucas is a new project manager for a computer company. As a new project manager who documents the develop project charter process, which documents does Lucas needs to examine?

    a) Project management plan and requirements plan

    b) Project charter and assumptions log

    c) Quality management plan and change management plan

    d) Stakeholder management plan

Answer: b. The output when developing a charter is a project charter and assumptions log.

4. David is a new project manager for Unique Homes Corp. David wants to get off to the best start in understanding the project, people, and environment. Interpersonal and team skills are a tool and technique of which process?

   a) Meetings

   b) Develop project charter

   c) Organizational process assets

   d) Planning

Answer: b. Develop project charter is the only process on this list. Meetings is a tool and technique for many processes. Organizational process assets are an input to many processes, and planning is a process group.

5. All the following are inputs to the develop project charter process except

   a) SOW

   b) Enterprise environmental factors

   c) Organizational process assets

   d) Data gathering

Answer: d. Data gathering is a tool and technique, not an input.

6. Priscilla is a project manager for an existing project with issues. What document does the project manager need to determine the project goals, high-level risks, and high-level constraints?

   a) Communication plan

   b) Project management plan

   c) SOW

   d) Project charter

Answer: d. The communication plan is a document for planning communication of the project. The project management plan plans the overall activities of the project and contains detailed requirements of the project. The SOW is the statement of work, which includes the objectives of the project. The project charter contains the high-level requirements of the project.

7. Daryl is a senior project manager for a book publishing company. Daryl wants to identify all current stakeholders for the project. All the documents below are inputs to the identify stakeholders process except

   a) Project charter

   b) EEF

   c) Expert judgments

   d) Organizational process assets

Answer: c. Expert judgments is a tool and technique.

8. Asheem is a project manager working remotely, so some of his team is in different locations performing their work. As project manager, Asheem determines the output of the develop project management plan process is

   a) Project charter

   b) Enterprise environmental factors

   c) Project management plan

   d) Organizational process assets

Answer: c. Project charter, EEF, and OPA are all inputs to the process.

9. Thomas has been working as a project manager for over 20 years. He has recently acquired his project management professional certificate. Which document does Thomas need to examine that maps the project deliverables to its requirements?

   a) OPA

   b) Requirements traceability matrix

   c) Project management plan

   d) Data analysis

Answer: b. The requirements traceability matrix maps the project deliverables to its requirements. The OPA and project management plan are inputs. Data analysis is a tool and technique.

10. Adrianne is a transferred project manager on loan from another department. Adrianne's first task is to develop a schedule management plan. Which order will Adrianne use for inputs to the plan schedule management process?

   a) Project charter, project management plan, scope management plan, development approached, and OPA

   b) Perform qualitative risk analysis, perform quantitative risk analysis, and plan risk responses

   c) Project management plan, project documents, approved change requests, EEF, and OPA

   d) Project charter, project management plan, quality management plan, project life cycle development, EEF, and OPA

Answer: a. Choice b describes plan risk management, and c describes direct and manage projects. As stated earlier, knowing the sequences of the planning group in all knowledge areas is crucial to passing the PMP exam.

11. Isabella is a project manager for Soylent Purple Corporation. As the project manager, which of the following will she use as an output of the process implement risk response plan?

   a) Change requests

   b) Data analysis

   c) Approved changes

   d) OPA

Answer: a. Data analysis is a tool and technique of most processes. Approved changes are an output of performed integrated change control and an input to direct and manage project work. OPA is an input to most processes.

12. Oliver is a project manager for the Very Tough Corporation of America. As project manager, he will use all the following as inputs to develop project charter except

   a) SOW

   b) Assumptions and constraints

   c) OPA

   d) Data analysis

Answer: d. Data analysis is a tool and technique. Statement of work, assumptions and constraints, and organizational process assets are inputs to the project charter.

13. Megan is a new project manager for an existing project with issues. What document does Megan need to determine the project goals, high-level risks, and high-level constraints?

    a) Communication plan

    b) Project management plan

    c) SOW

    d) Project charter

Answer: d. The project management plan has the overall activities of the project and contains detailed requirements of the project. The SOW is the statement of work, which contains the objectives of the project. The project charter contains the high-level requirements of the project.

14. Mason is a new project manager for Tube Socks LLC. Mason wants to get off to the best start understanding the project, people, and environment. As the project manager, Mason would choose all as inputs to the identify stakeholders process except

    a) Project charter

    b) EEF

    c) Expert judgments

    d) Organizational process assets

Answer: c. Expert judgments is always a tool and technique.

15. Jamis is a new project manager for the World-Eaters Corp. World-Eaters Corp is a company that terraforms planets so humans can live there comfortably. As a project manager, Jamis will use all tools and techniques to determine budget except

    a) Expert judgments

    b) Historical information review

    c) Funding limit reconciliation

    d) Business case

Answer: d. Expert judgments, historical information review, and funding limit reconciliation are all tools and techniques that can be used to determine the budget.

16. Sophia is a new project manager for Flatliners Inc., a company that makes and sells defibrillators to the medical industry. Sophia wants to get off to the best start understanding the company environment. As the project manager, which output would she choose for the determine budget process?

    a) Cost baseline

    b) Alternative analysis

    c) Business need

    d) Voting

Answer: a. Options b, c, and d are not outputs.

100 Questions on Process

1.	Patrick is a new project manager for NoTouchTV LLC. Patrick wants to get off to the best start understanding the project, people, and environment. As a project manager, what process will Patrick perform that contains the project's objectives, assumptions, constraints, and high-level requirements?

	a)	Meetings

	b)	Develop project charter

	c)	OPA

	d)	Planning

Answer: b. Develop project charter is the process that creates the project charter document, which contains the project's objectives, assumptions, constraints, and high-level requirements. Meetings is a tool and technique. OPA is the organization policies, procedures, and practices, and planning is not a process. Develop project plan is a process.

2.	Promise is a project manager at MoreBooks Inc. Promise wants to get off to the best start on her project. Promise will accept all the following as inputs to develop project charter except

	a)	SOW

	b)	Assumptions and constraints

	c)	OPA

	d)	Data analysis

Answer: d. Data analysis is a tool and technique. SOW, OPA, and assumptions and constraints are used in the develop project charter process.

3.	Paul is a project manager with many years of experience in developing projects, managing personnel, document distribution, and bringing projects in on time and under budget. Paul needs to get started on this project and come up to speed immediately because senior management and the sponsor are getting anxious. As a project manager, what does Paul determine are the outputs of the develop project charter process?

	a)	Project management plan and requirements plan

b) Project charter and assumptions log

c) Quality management plan and change management plan

d) Stakeholder management plan

Answer: b. The project charter and assumptions log are the outputs of the develop charter process.

4.	Zoey is a new project manager for HoverMobiles. Zoey wants to get off to the best start understanding the project, people, and environment. All are inputs to the identify stakeholder group except

a) Project charter

b) EEF

c) Expert judgment

d) OPA

Answer: c. Expert judgment is a tool and technique. Project charter, EEF, and OPA are inputs to most identify stakeholder processes.

5.	Logan is a new project manager for iClassified LLC, an internet newspaper company that specializes in online advertisements. Logan wants to understand his new project, so he must secure the right documents and have meetings with the right people. As the project manager, Logan would ask for all documents that pertain to the project charter except those that

a) Formally authorize the existence of a project

b) Provide the project manager the authority to apply organizational resources to the project

c) State the high-level constraints and assumptions of the project

d) State the details of project deliverables

Answer: d. The project charter does not have detailed information. Options a, b, and c all describe the project charter.

6. Amelia is a new project manager for Tyronn Toys LLC. Amelia wants to get off to the best start understanding the project, people, and environment. Which best describes the develop project charter process?

   a) The process of developing a document that formally authorizes the existence of a project and provides the project manager with the authority to apply organizational resources to project activities

   b) The process of documenting how the project and product scope will be defined, validated, and controlled throughout the project

   c) The process of developing detailed descriptions of the project and products, which is what the project includes and excludes

   d) The process of estimating the number of work periods needed to complete activities with the estimated resources

Answer: a. Choice b better describes plan scope management. Choice c, develop charter, does process detailed information. Choices b, c, and d are performed in the planning stage of the project.

7. Frances is starting a new project that involves infrastructure and database migration. Frances needs to create documents for the best plan of communication for the team. Deliverables are an output of which process group?

   a) OPA

   b) EEF

   c) Final report

   d) Direct and manage project work

Answer: d. OPA and EEF are inputs to other processes, and the final report is an output of close process.

8. Samuel is a new project manager with good experience in change management to do the necessary work. All the following are inputs to process direct and manage project work except

   a) Approved changes

   b) Project management plan

   c) Deliverables

   d) OPA

Answer: c. Deliverables is an output of direct and manage the project work process. Options a, b and c are inputs to direct and manage project work.

9.   Charlotte is a senior project manager for Grayson Enterprises. Charlotte wants to avoid scope creep and gold plating on this project. Which choice best describes the direct and manage project work process?

    a)   The process of leading and performing the work defined in the project plan and implementing the approved changes to achieve the project objectives

    b)   The process of improving the competencies of team members and the overall team environment to enhance project performance

    c)   The process of obtaining seller responses, selecting sellers, and awarding a contract

    d)   The process of documenting project decisions, specifying the approach, and identifying potential sellers

Answer: a. Choice b is the develop team process, and c and d involve procurements.

10.   The output of create WBS is

    a)   Decomposition

    b)   Scope baseline

    c)   Project management plan

    d)   Product scope statement

Answer: b. Decomposition is a tool and technique. The project management plan is an output of develop project plan process

11.   James is a fresh project manager hired from a competitor. James has a friend who wants to be chosen as a contractor for this project. The bidding for the project does not start until next spring. Which best describes the create WBS process??

    a)   The process of developing a detailed description of the project and product

    b)   The process of creating a scope management plan that documents how the project and product scope will be defined, validated, and controlled

    c)   The process of subdividing project deliverables and project work into smaller, more manageable components

d) The process of monitoring the status of the project and product scope and managing changes in the scope baseline

Answer: c. Option b describes plan scope management and d describes monitor and control project work.

12. Harper is a new project manager hired from a competitor. Harper wants to get off to the best start understanding the project, people, and environment. Which are number systems in the WBS dictionary and WBS, respectively?

    a) Code of account identifier and (1.0, 1.1, 1.1.1)

    b) Chart of accounts and (a, ab, abc)

    c) Control chart and (1, 2, 3)

    d) All of the above

Answer: a. Code of account identifier and (1.0, 1.1, 1.1.1) are the correct number systems.

13. Henri is a new project manager for the ElitePens Company. Henri wants to get off to the best start understanding the project, people, and environment. What is the output of plan communication management?

    a) Project management plan

    b) Project documents

    c) Communications management plan

    d) Communication baseline

Answer: c. The project management plan is the output of develop project plan. Communication baseline does not exist in PMBOK.

14. Charles is a seasoned project manager and is a wizard at communication management. Which answer below best fits the tools and technique of plan communication management?

    a) Change log

    b) Project management plan

    c) Manage quality

    d) Interpersonal and team skills

Answer: d. Interpersonal and team skills are the only tools and techniques in the list. The project management plan is an output of the develop project plan. Manage quality is a process. The change log is an output of perform integrated change control.

15. Ethan is a new project manager for VirtuNext, a maker of virtual games play systems. Ethan wants to get off to the best start understanding the project, people, and environment. What tool and technique of plan communication management would Ethan use next?

   a) Change log

   b) Project management plan

   c) Manage quality

   d) Communication technology

Answer: d. Communication technology is the only tool and technique on the list. The project management plan is an output of the develop project plan. Manage quality is a process. The change log is an output of perform integrated change control.

16. Ella is a new project manager for the PlanetEx Corporation. Ella wants to avoid team conflicts in meetings by setting up ground rules. As the project manager, which tool and technique would Ella choose next for the manage communications process?

   a) Change log

   b) Project management plan

   c) Manage quality

   d) Interpersonal and team skills

Answer: d. Interpersonal and team skills are only tool and technique on the list. The project management plan is an output of develop project plan. Manage quality is a process. The change log is an output of perform integrated change control.

17. Mateo is a new project manager for the Canopy Corp. Mateo, like all project managers, wants to manage the perfect project: on time, under budget, great quality to the customers' satisfaction. Manage communication is a process of which knowledge area?

   a) Plan communications management

   b) Project quality management

   c) Manage tools and techniques

   d) Project communications management

Answer: d. There are ten knowledge areas in the *PMBOK* 6th edition. You can get a quick glance at all ten knowledge areas in *PMBOK*, page 25.

18. Luna is a new project manager for Clark Enterprises. Luna wants to avoid quality issues that cause defects and require rework. Luna and his team carefully design and monitor quality into the project plan. Which best describes the manage communications process?

　　a) Project management plan

　　b) The process of ensuring timely and appropriate collection, creation, distribution, storage, retrieval, management, monitoring, and the ultimate disposition of project information

　　c) Work performance reports

　　d) Team performance

Answer: b. Manage communications is the process of ensuring timely and appropriate collection, creation, distribution, storage, retrieval, management, monitoring, and the ultimate disposition of project information.

19. Sebastian is a new project manager for Prince International. Sebastian wants to build team cohesiveness, so he schedules team company parties so that the team can bond with games and be better together as workers. Which process would Sebastian use next to communicate and work with stakeholders to meet their needs and expectations, address issues, and foster appropriate involvement?

　　a) Manage stakeholder engagement

　　b) Monitor communications

　　c) Manage communications

　　d) Monitor stakeholder engagement

Answer: a. Manage stakeholder engagement is the correct response. Revisit glossary for definitions.

20. Jack is a new project manager for the Stonewall Corp. Jack's team is tasked with improving a business process within the organization. Which answer best describes the manage communications process?

　　a) The process of developing an appropriate approach and plan for project communication activities based on the information needs of each stakeholder, the available organizational assets, and the needs of the project

　　b) The document that includes information on staff acquisition and release, resource calendars, recognition and rewards, compliance, and safety

c) The process of ensuring timely and appropriate collection, creation, distribution, storage, retrieval, management, monitoring, and the ultimate disposition of project information

d) The process of ensuring the information needs of the project and its stakeholders

Answer: c. Manage communications is the process of ensuring timely and appropriate collection, creation, distribution, storage, retrieval, management, monitoring, and the ultimate disposition of project information.

21. Camila is a new project manager for the Oneil Oil Company. Camila wants to get off to the best start understanding the project, people, and environment. The process of communicating and working with stakeholders to meet their needs and expectations, address issues, and foster appropriate involvement is

a) Monitor communications

b) Manage stakeholder engagement

c) Manage communications

d) Monitor stakeholder engagement

Answer: b. The process described is manage stakeholder engagement.

22. Jackson is a new project manager for the Atlanta Airlines Corporation. Jackson wants to get off to the best start understanding the project, people, and environment. Which answer best describes monitor communications?

a) The process of developing an appropriate approach and plan for project communication activities based on the information needs of each stakeholder, the available organizational assets, and the needs of the project

b) The document that includes information on staff acquisition and release, resource calendars, recognition and rewards, and compliance and safety

c) The process of monitoring communications and the process of ensuring the information needs of the project and its stakeholders are met

d) The process of ensuring the information needs of the project and its stakeholders are met

Answer: c. This choice best describes monitor communications.

23.   Aria is a new project manager for Yoda Propulsion Systems. Aria wants to avoid equipment delays and improve worker performance, so Aria registers with a company application that monitors all facets of scheduling from order to delivery. Aria also has daily stand up meetings to make sure there is always progress in the project. As the project manager, what description of the resource management plan should best suit Aria?

a)   The process of developing an appropriate approach and plan for project communication activities based on the information needs of each stakeholder, the available organizational assets, and the needs of the project

b)   The document that includes information on staff acquisition and release, resource calendars, recognition and rewards, and compliance and safety

c)   The process of monitoring communications and the process of ensuring the information needs of the project and its stakeholders are met

d)   The process of ensuring the information needs of the project and its stakeholders are met

Answer: b. Option b best describes the resource management plan.

24.   Linda is a new project manager with some experience in risk analysis to do the necessary work. What is the output of plan risk management?

a)   Communication management plan

b)   Configuration management plan

c)   Home improvement plan

d)   Risk management plan

Answer: d. The risk management plan is the output of plan risk management.

25.   Elizabeth is starting a new project that involves infrastructure and database upgrades. What description best identifies plan risk management?

a)   The process of defining how to conduct risk management activities

b)   The process of using existing knowledge and creating new knowledge to achieve the project's objectives and contribute to organizational learning

c)   The process of translating the quality management plan into executable project activities that incorporate the organization's quality policies

d) Risk baseline

Answer: a. Option a best describes plan risk management. Option c is plan quality management, and d does not exist in PMBOK.

26. Mila is a new project manager for the CyberWorld Corp. Mila wants to impress the managers who hired her by performing well on day one on a massive project that will take a year to complete. As the project manager, which document will Mila create from the plan risk management process?

   a) Cost management plan

   b) Risk management plan

   c) Scope baseline

   d) Risk baseline

Answer: b. Answer a is the output of plan cost management. Answer c is the output of define scope, and d does not exist in PMBOK.

27. Benjamin is a new project manager for Anaconda Copper. Benjamin wants to get off to the best start understanding the project, people, and environment. Which process best describes identify risk?

   a) The process of identifying individual risks as well as sources of overall project risks and documenting their characteristics

   b) Data analysis and interpersonal skills

   c) Project management plan

   d) The process of defining how to estimate, acquire, manage, and utilize physical and team resources

Answer: a. Option b is a tool and technique, c is a document, and d is plan resource management.

28. Kenneth is a new project manager with minimal experience in acquiring proper resources to do the necessary work. Which description best fits perform qualitative risk analysis?

   a) The process of prioritizing individual project risks for further analysis by assessing their probability of occurrence and impact

   b) The process of numerically analyzing the effects of identified risks on overall project objects

   c) Identify risks, perform a qualitative risk analysis, perform a quantitative risk analysis, and plan risk responses

d) Plan schedule management, define activities, sequence activities, and develop schedules

Answer: a. Answer b is perform quantitative risk analysis. Answer c is project risk management, and d is project schedule management.

29. Aurora is a new project manager for Kool Klothes LLC. Aurora wants to get off to the best start understanding the project, people, and environment. Which answer is the best description of perform quantitative risk analysis?

a) The process of numerically analyzing the effects of identified risks on overall project objects

b) Identify risks, perform a qualitative risk analysis, perform a quantitative risk analysis, and plan risk responses

c) Plan schedule management, define activities, sequence activities, estimate activity resources, estimate activity costs, and develop schedules

d) Estimate costs and determine budget

Answer: a. Option a best describes perform quantitative risk analysis.

30. Kenneth is a new project manager with minimal experience in acquiring proper resources to do the necessary work. Which description best describes perform qualitative risk analysis?

a) The process of numerically analyzing the effects of identified risks on overall project objects

b) Identify risks, perform qualitative risk analysis, perform quantitative risk analysis, and plan risk responses

c) The process of prioritizing individual project risks for further analysis by assessing their probability of occurrence and impact

d) Plan schedule management, define activities, sequence activities, estimate activity resources, estimate activity costs, and develop schedule

Answer: c. Choice c best describes perform qualitative risk analysis.

31. Ellie is a new project manager for TinHooks LLC. Ellie's team is tasked with acquiring and installing a new computer and hardware system for use in the organization. Which answer is the best description of perform quantitative risk analysis?

a) The process of numerically analyzing the effects of identified risks on overall project objects

b) Identify risks, perform qualitative risk analysis, perform quantitative risk analysis, and plan risk responses

c) Plan schedule management, define activities, sequence activities, estimate activity resources, estimate activity costs, and develop schedule

d) Estimate costs and determine budget

Answer: a. Option a best describes perform quantitative risk analysis.

32. Carter is a new project manager for Blazed Enterprises. He is managing a project that develops a new pharmaceutical compound to bring to market. As a project manager, which input would Carter choose for the perform qualitative risk analysis process?

a) Project management plan

b) Alternative analysis

c) OPA updates

d) EEF updates

Answer: a. Choice b is a tool and technique. Choices c and d are outputs to other processes.

33. Robert is one of the best project managers the company has. Lately, Robert has seen a switch in management style. SMEs are being switched from one project to another without explanation or permission. Which answer is the best description of perform quantitative risk analysis?

a) It is the process of numerically analyzing the effects of identified risks on overall project objects.

b) It is the process by which we identify risks, perform qualitative risk analysis, perform quantitative risk analysis, and plan risk responses.

c) It is the process by which we plan schedule management, define activities, sequence activities, estimate activity resources, estimate activity costs, and develop schedules.

d) It involves estimating costs and determining the budget.

Answer: a. Choice a is the best description for perform quantitative risk analysis.

34.	The project management plan plans the overall activities of the project and contains detailed requirements of the project. The SOW is the statement of work, which contains the objectives of the project. The project charter contains the high-level requirements of the project. All are inputs to the identify stakeholders process except

a)	Project charter

b)	EEF

c)	Expert judgments

d)	Organizational process assets

Answer: c. Expert judgments is a tool and technique.

35.	Alysia is a new project manager for Headgear Inc. Alysia wants to show the company they have made the correct decision by asking for the right documents to get up to speed and asking the right questions in meetings. What is the output of plan stakeholder management?

a)	Stakeholder management plan

b)	Stakeholder baseline

c)	Risk register

d)	RBS

Answer: a. Answer b does not exist in PMBOK. Answer c is an output of identify risks. Answer d could be either a risk breakdown structure or resource breakdown structure, neither of which is the answer.

36.	The process of communicating and working with stakeholders to meet their needs and expectations, address issues, and foster appropriate involvement describes which process?

a)	Manage stakeholder engagement

b)	Monitor communications

c)	Manage communications

d)	Monitor stakeholder engagement

Answer: a. The difference between monitoring and managing is that monitoring is watching or observing. Managing is an action in which you are actually doing something. In this case, it is the "process of communicating and working with stakeholders."

37. Kazem is a project manager with many years of experience. Kazem knows how important customer communication and satisfaction are to project management. What is the best definition of the monitor stakeholder engagement process?

   a) The process of identifying project stakeholders regularly and analyzing and documenting relevant information regarding their interests, involvement, interdependencies, influence, and impact on project success

   b) The process of communicating and working with stakeholders to meet their needs and expectations, address issues, and foster appropriate stakeholder engagement

   c) The process of providing an overview of the project stakeholder management process

   d) The process of monitoring project stakeholder relationships and tailoring strategies for engaging stakeholders through the modification of engagement strategies and plans

Answer: d. Option a is identifying stakeholders, b is managing stakeholder engagement, and c does not exist.

38. Avery is a project manager newly hired from a competitor. Avery wants to show the company they have made the correct decision by asking for the right documents to get up to speed and asking the right questions in meetings. The following describe monitor stakeholder engagement except

   a) Managing stakeholder relationships

   b) Ignoring the stakeholders until they go away

   c) Engaging with the stakeholders

   d) Formulating strategies with the stakeholders

Answer: b. You would think answer b would be common sense, but it is surprising how many testers will miss a question like this on the exam. You never ignore stakeholders because communication, collaboration, and compromise are primary tools of a project manager.

39. Grayson is a senior project manager for Nearlight Enterprises. Grayson's team is tasked with modifying a computer software program used in the organization. As the project manager, which definition would Grayson choose as the best description of plan cost management?

   a) The process of defining how the project cost will be estimated, budgeted, managed, monitored, and controlled

   b) The process of defining how to estimate, acquire, manage, and utilize physical and team resources

c) The process of defining how to conduct risk management activities

d) The process of identifying the relationships among project activities

Answer: a. Option b is plan resource management. Option c is manage risks.

40. Abigail is a project manager for a new underwater concept company. Abigail's team is tasked with conducting research to develop a new manufacturing process for the organization. As the project manager, which output of the plan cost management process would Abigail choose?

a) Risk management plan

b) Cost baseline

c) Cost management plan

d) Schedule baseline

Answer: c. Option b is an output of plan risk management. Option c is an output of plan cost management. Option d is an output of define scope.

41. Leo is a new project manager for a security software company that protects against hackers and credit card scams. Leo team is tasked with building a complete enterprise system to meet the sponsor's vision. Which is the best description of estimate costs?

a) The process of analyzing sequences, durations, resource requirements, and schedule constraints to create a project model for project executions, monitoring, and controlling

b) The process of developing an approximation of the monetary resources needed to complete the work

c) The process of developing an approach and plan for project communications activities based on the information needs of each stakeholder and the project

d) The process of defining how to estimate, acquire, manage, and utilize physical and team resources

Answer: b. Option a is plan schedule management. Option d is plan resource management.

42. Sofia is a new project manager for a computer animation company. Sofia's team has the task of acquiring resources and computer equipment and installing and configuring software so

developers can program. Which of the following depicts the order of activities in project cost management?

a) Collect requirements, define scope, and create WBS

b) Identify risks, perform qualitative risk analysis, perform quantitative risk analysis, and plan risk responses

c) Plan schedule management, define activities, sequence activities, estimate activity durations, and develop schedule

d) Estimate costs and determine budget

Answer: d. The order is plan cost management, estimate costs, and determine budget.

43. As a project manager, you are planning the activities in the project schedule. Which of the following depicts the order of activities in plan cost management?

a) Collect requirements, define scope, and create WBS

b) Identify risks, perform qualitative risk analysis, perform quantitative risk analysis, and plan risk responses

c) Plan schedule management, define activities, sequence activities, estimate activity resources, estimate activity costs, and develop schedule

d) Estimate costs and determine budget

Answer: d. Option a describes scope management, b defines risk management, and c is schedule management.

44. Which is not a tool and technique used in the estimate activity durations process?

a) Analogous estimating

b) Bottom-up estimating

c) Three-point estimating

d) Duration estimates

Answer: d. Analogous, bottom-up, and three-point estimating are tools and techniques for the estimate activity durations process.

45. Mary is a project manager for a real estate company. Using the PERT beta distribution formula, how long will it take Mary to complete the project if most likely = 32, optimistic = 20, and pessimistic = 50?

a) 44

b) 33

c) 34

d) 32

Answer: b. $(P+(4(M)+O)/6=(20 + 32(4) + 50) / 6 = 33$

46. The project manager continues to put numbers together for cost and schedule. Using the triangular distribution method, how long will it take the project manager to complete the project if most likely = 32, optimistic = 20, and pessimistic = 50?

a) 44

b) 33

c) 34

d) 32

Answer: c. $(P+M+O)/3= (32 + 20 + 50) / 3 = 34$

47. The following are all tools and techniques that can be used to determine budget except

a) Expert judgments

b) Historical information review

c) Funding limit reconciliation

d) Business documents

Answer: d. Expert judgments, historical information review, and funding limit reconciliation are all tools and techniques that can be used to determine the budget.

48. Which is an output of the determine budget process?

a) Cost baseline

b) Alternative analysis

c) Project management plan

d) Voting

Answer: a. Options b, c, and d are not outputs.

49. As a project manager, you are planning the activities in the project schedule. What is the output of plan schedule management?

   a) Collect requirements, define scope, and create WBS

   b) Identify risks, perform qualitative risk analysis, perform quantitative risk analysis, and plan risk responses

   c) Create the schedule management plan

   d) Estimate costs and determine the budget

Answer: c. Option a describes scope management, b describes defining risk management, and d is cost management.

50. As the project manager, which inputs would you choose for the plan schedule management process?

   a) Project charter, project management plan, scope management plan, development approach, EEF, and OPA

   b) Perform qualitative risk analysis, perform quantitative risk analysis, and plan risk responses

   c) Project management plan, project documents, approved change requests, EEF, and OPA

   d) Project charter, project management plan, quality management plan, project life cycle development, EEF, and OPA

Answer: a. Choice b describes plan risk management, and c describes direct and manage projects. As stated earlier, knowing the sequences of the planning group in all knowledge areas is crucial to passing the PMP exam.

51. Which of the following depicts the order of activities in schedule management?

   a) Collect requirements, define scope, and create the WBS

   b) Identify risks, perform qualitative risk analysis, perform quantitative risk analysis, and plan risk responses

c) Plan schedule management, define activities, sequence activities, estimate activity durations, and develop schedules

d) Estimate costs and determine budget

Answer: c. Option a describes scope management, b defines risk management, and d is cost management.

52. As the project manager in the define activities process, work is decomposed into which of the following?

a) Work packages

b) WBS

c) Activities

d) WBS and activities

Answer: c. Decomposition into activities occurs in the define activities process. Decomposition into work packages occurs in the create WBS process. Answer d is a typical PMP exam trick to trip you up because it combines processes like WBS and activities.

53. Jason is a new project manager who is currently in the planning phase of a project. Jason has defined the activities—what should he do next?

a) Sequence activities

b) Estimate costs

c) Collect requirements

d) Identify risks

Answer: a. The question clearly states that Jason is still in the planning process, so what process occurs after the sequence that is in the list of choices and part of the planning process group? Define activities, sequence activities, estimate activity duration, et cetera. Knowing the order of processes in the planning process group is crucial to passing the exam. *Memorize the order of processes in the planning process group!*

54. Jason is a new project manager who is currently in the planning phase of a project. Jason has defined the activities. As a project manager, what did Jason do before defining the activities?

a) Sequence activities

b) Estimate costs

c) Plan schedule management

d) Identify risks

Answer: c. See the order of processes in the planning process group.

55. As the project manager, which of the four types of PDM relationships will you use least often?

a) Finish to Start (FS)

b) Finish to Finish (FF)

c) Start to Finish (SF)

d) Start to Start (SS)

Answer: c. Start to Finish (SF) is very rarely used.

56. As the project manager, which of the four types of PDM relationships will you use most often?

a) Finish to Start (FS)

b) Finish to Finish (FF)

c) Start to Finish (SF)

d) Start to Start (SS)

Answer: a. Finish to Start (FS) is the most commonly used.

57. As a project manager, you are planning the activities in the project schedule. Which of the following depicts the order of activities in cost management?

a) Collect requirements, define scope, and create WBS

b) Identify risks, perform qualitative risk analysis, perform quantitative risk analysis, and plan risk responses

c) Plan schedule management, define activities, sequence activities, estimate activity resources, estimate activity costs, and develop schedule

d) Estimate costs and determine budget

Answer: d. Option a describes scope management, b defines risk management, and c is schedule management.

58. Which is not a tool and technique used in the estimate activity durations process?

    a) Analogous estimating

    b) Bottom-up estimating

    c) Three-point estimating

    d) Duration estimates

Answer: d. Analogous, bottom-up, and three-point estimating are tools and techniques for the estimate activity durations process.

59. As the project manager, when using the PERT beta distribution formula, how long will it take Mary to complete the project if most likely = 32, optimistic = 20, and pessimistic = 50?

    a) 44

    b) 33

    c) 34

    d) 32

Answer: b. $(P+(4(M)+O)/6=(20 + 32(4) + 50) / 6 = 33$

60. Mary is a project manager for a biochemical firm. By using the triangular distribution method, how long will it take Mary to complete the project if most likely = 32, optimistic = 20, and pessimistic = 50?

    a) 44

    b) 33

    c) 34

    d) 32

Answer: c. $(P+M+O)/3= (32 + 20 + 50) / 3 = 34$

61. Which of the following depicts the order of activities in schedule management?

    a) Collect requirements, define scope, and create WBS

    b) Identify risks, perform qualitative risk analysis, perform quantitative risk analysis, and plan risk responses

    c) Plan schedule management, define activities, sequence activities, estimate activity durations and develop schedule

    d) Estimate costs and determine budget

Answer: c. Choice a is plan scope management, b is plan risk management, and d is plan cost management.

62.   All are tools and techniques of the develop schedule process except

    a) Schedule compression

    b) Data analysis

    c) Project documents

    d) Critical path method

Answer: c. Project documents are inputs.

63.   Judy is a superb project manager at her firm. She is currently working on a project in which a fix is necessary. As a project manager, what should Judy do next?

    a) Check the release documents

    b) Notify the sponsor

    c) Evaluate the impact of the change

    d) Implement the risk response plan

Answer: c. She should evaluate the impact of the change.

64.   Judy is a top project manager at her firm. She is currently working on a project in which a fix *might be* necessary. As a project manager, what should Judy do next?

    a) Prevent changes from occurring

    b) Notify the sponsor

    c) Evaluate the impact of the change

    d) Implement the risk response plan

Answer: a. She should prevent changes from occurring.

65. Mitchell is a project manager for a solar car company on a new project that has not started. He wants to know where he can get information about projects like the one, he is about to start. Where would Mitchell go first to get this information?

    a) Program manager

    b) PMO

    c) Portfolio office

    d) Sponsor

Answer: b. Answer b is the best choice. Answer a is an option as the **project manager** can go to the program manager; however, the program manager will go to the PMO and then give the information to the PM. There is no portfolio office. The sponsor would not be an option.

66. Jeffrey is a new project manager for Apocrypha Inc., a producer of religious books and artifacts. As the new project manager, he must have a plan in which many criteria are met for the condition of the books and artifacts. As a project manager, what document must Jeffrey create to set guidelines in criteria?

    a) Project management plan

    b) Project documents

    c) Risk management plan

    d) Quality management plan

Answer: d. Option a is the output of develop project plan, b is not the output of the plan quality management process, and c is the output of plan risk management.

67. Marshall is a project manager for the Action Solar Company, a maker of sun car parts. Quality is important in the company. Which best describes the plan quality management process?

    a) The process of identifying quality requirements and standards for the project and its deliverables and documenting how the project will demonstrate compliance with quality requirements and standards

    b) The process of monitoring and recording the results of executing the quality management activities to assess performance and ensure the project outputs are complete, correct, and meet customer requirements

    c) The process of translating the quality management plan into executable quality activities that incorporate the organization's quality policies into the project

    d) None of the above

Answer: a. Option b is monitoring quality. Option c is managing quality, and d is not the answer.

68. Which of the following is an input to the manage quality process?

    a) Quality reports

    b) Quality metrics

    c) Data gathering

    d) Enterprise environmental factors

Answer: b. Quality reports are an output; enterprise environmental factors are not input in this process, and data gathering is a tool and technique.

69. Terri is a new project manager at a manufacturing firm. She has completed the planning stage. Her team has begun implementing the work according to the project plan. One of Terri's team members has noticed a problem with her task but has not yet found a fix. What tools can be used to determine the cause of the problem?

    a) Prototypes

    b) An oscilloscope

    c) Fishbone

    d) Bottom-up estimating

Answer: c. An oscilloscope is outside the scope of PMP. Prototypes are used to find problems in the design, and bottom-up estimating is used to estimate the time and cost of a project.

70. David is a new project manager for Voice Activated Systems Enterprises. He wants to get off to the best start understanding ways to deliver a quality product. David and his team are planning for accuracy in quality. Which of the following tools is one of the seven rules of quality control?

    a) Analysis technique

    b) Cause-and-effect diagram

    c) Data representation

d) Manage quality

Answer: b. Only the cause-and-effect diagram is one of the seven rules of quality control.

71. Emma is a project manager at a paper factory. Before the project starts, she requests information about political influence and public opinion. Which of these are influences out of the project manager's control?

   a) Enterprise environmental factors

   b) Organizational process assets

   c) Evolution environmental factors

   d) Extreme environmental factors

Answer: a. Enterprise environmental factors are influences outside the project manager's control. Organizational process assets are factors within the organization's and project team's control. And c and d are not part of the project management plan.

72. Susan is a project manager with many years of experience. Her current project is especially difficult because of problems with the timeline getting extended many times. This could be because the scope is not well defined, and the delays are causing increases in cost because of increased hours of work on the project for fixes. Susan can find all of the following in the project charter except

   a) Project purpose

   b) High-level requirements

   c) Detailed requirements

   d) Key stakeholder list

Answer: c. The project charter does not contain detailed information of any type. Detailed information is found in the project management plan.

73. Bradford is the new project manager at Green Thumb Nursery. His current project has constantly run into delays because of new deliverables that must be added for the project to be a success. As a project manager, which documents should Bradford check first to determine deliverables?

   a) Scope management plan and requirements management plan

   b) Project charter and project management plan

c) Quality management plan and process improvement plan

d) Risk management plan and risk response plan

Answer: b. The project charter will contain the vision of what is expected from the project. The project management plan will include the WBS, which will include project deliverables.

74. Jamerson is the project manager of Aqua Rooms, which are short-term underwater apartments. The project Jamerson is managing is consistently encountering incomplete requirements. As a project manager, he would use all tools and techniques to collect requirements except

a) Data analysis

b) Decision-making

c) Organizational process assets

d) Interpersonal skills and team skills

Answer: c. Organizational process assets are inputs. But a, b, and d are all tools and techniques.

75. Jamal is a senior project manager at a major pharmaceutical company. The project involves the testing of a new drug to halt aging. The project data is currently being collected. As a senior project manager, which requirement will Jamal not capture as an input to collect requirements?

a) Project management plan

b) Communication management plan

c) Project documents

d) EEF

Answer: b. The communication management plan is not an input to collect requirements. The communication management plan is a guide on how the project team will send, receive, distribute, store, and dispose of communication material.

76. Maria is a newly hired contract project manager who wants all documents related to the current project. Which document will Maria most want to map deliverables to their respective requirements?

a) OPA

b) Requirements traceability matrix

c) Project management plan

d) Data analysis

Answer: b. The requirements traceability matrix maps deliverables to their respective requirements. The OPA and project management plan are inputs. Data analysis is a tool and technique.

77. Which answer best describes the define scope process?

   a) The process of developing a detailed description of the project and product

   b) The process of creating a scope management plan that documents how the project and product scope will be defined, validated, and controlled

   c) The process of subdividing project deliverables and project work into smaller, more manageable components

   d) The process of monitoring the status of the project and product scope and managing changes in the scope baseline

Answer: a. Answer b describes the plan scope management process. Answer c describes the create WBS process. Answer d best describes monitoring and controlling a process.

78. Work that is outside the scope of the project is demanded by a sponsor, senior management, or stakeholders other than the project team. Which answer best describes this scenario?

   a) Gold plating

   b) Work that is necessary

   c) Work that is unnecessary

   d) Scope creep

Answer: d. Scope creep is work ask for by sponsors, senior management, or other stakeholders which are not on the project team, outside the scope of the project, and deemed unnecessary by the project team. Answers b and c are general concepts that help narrow down the scope of the project.

79. There is work performed outside the scope of the project and suggested by the project team. Which answer best describes this action?

   a) Gold plating

   b) Work that is necessary

c) Work that is unnecessary

d) Scope creep

Answer: a. Gold plating occurs when project team members make unnecessary and unwanted changes to the project.

80.   Which process best exemplifies monitoring and control in project integration?

   a) Direct and manage project work

   b) Monitor and control project work

   c) Manage project knowledge

   d) Perform integrated change control

Answer: b. Direct and manage project work is in the execute process groups and describe the performance of work. Manage project knowledge manages documents found, generated, compiled, or created because of the work. Perform integrated change control is a process that occurs when the original work plan must deviate with an approved change.

81.   Harry is a contractor responsible for the refurbishment of an automobile showroom. The estimated refurbishment cost is $500 per square foot. The total showroom area that needs to be refurbished is 1,000 square feet. Based on his past experience, he knows his team can refurbish 100 square feet per week. As a project manager, how would Harry report how the project is performing?

   a) On schedule and on budget

   b) Behind schedule and over budget

   c) Ahead of schedule and over budget

   d) Behind schedule and ahead of budget

Answer: c. As a project manager, you report the fact at the time and not what you know or assume will happen later. Harry would report the project as ahead of schedule and over budget.

| Cost Variance | (EV - AC) = $25,000.00 |
| Schedule Variance | (EV - PV) = $25,000.00 |

82.   Harry is a contractor responsible for the refurbishment of an automobile showroom. The estimated refurbishment cost is $500 per square foot. The total showroom area that needs to be refurbished is 1,000 square feet. Based on his past experience, he knows his team can refurbish 100 square

feet per week. As the project manager, Harry will report the steady-state value of the project as

a) $525,000

b) $375,000

c) $555,555.56

d) $475,000

Answer: c. The steady-state value of the project is computed with the formula below.

Estimate at Completion (typical, steady-state, or continuous)	(BAC / CPI) = $555,555.56

83. Jacob is a contractor responsible for the refurbishment of an automobile showroom. The estimated refurbishment cost is $500 per square foot. The total showroom area that needs to be refurbished is 1,000 square feet. Based on his past experience, he knows his team can refurbish 100 square feet per week. As a project manager, what does Jacob compute the estimate at completion to be?

a) $525,000

b) $375,000

c) $555,555.56

d) $516,224.19

Answer: d. The estimate at completion formula is (AC + (BAC-EV)) / (CPI * SPI). (AC + (BAC-EV)) / (CPI * SPI) = $516,224.19

Complete table solutions below:

Estimated refurbishment cost $500.00 per square foot

Total showroom area   1,000.00 square feet

Refurbishment pace   100.00 square feet per week

Term	Value
Budget at Completion	($500 x 1,000) = $500,000.00
Planned Value	(4 / 10 x BAC) = $200,000.00
Earned Value	(45% x BAC) = $225,000.00
Actual Cost	$250,000.00

Cost Variance	(EV - AC) = $25,000.00
Schedule Variance	(EV - PV) = $25,000.00
Cost Performance Index	(EV / AC) = 0.90
Schedule Performance Index	(EV / PV) = 1.13
Estimate at Completion (atypical)	(AC + (BAC - EV)) = 525,000
Estimate at Completion (forecast)	(AC+ (BAC - EV)) / (CPI * SPI) = 516,224.19
Estimate at Completion (typical, steady-state or continuous)	(BAC / CPI) = $555,555.56
Estimate to Complete	(EAC - AC) = $305,555.56
Variance at Completion	(BAC - EAC) = $55,555.56

Total duration (1,000 / 100)   = 10.00 weeks

Duration Elapsed   = 4.00 weeks

Percentage completion   = 45%

84.   Judy is a superb project manager at her firm. She is currently working on a project in which a fix is necessary. As a project manager, what should Judy do next?

   a)   Check the release documents

   b)   Notify the sponsor

   c)   Evaluate the impact of the change

   d)   Implement the risk response plan

Answer: c. If the fix is necessary, then checking release documents has already occurred. Implementing the risk response plan would occur if a risk previously planned had occurred. Notifying sponsor might occur if a fix was not previously planned for, and the issue that necessitated the fix would impact the project adversely either in cost, schedule, or quality.

85.   Patricia is a top project manager at her firm. She is currently working on a project in which a fix *might be* necessary. As a project manager, what should Patricia do next?

   a)   Prevent changes from occurring

   b)   Notify the sponsor

   c)   Evaluate the impact of the change

   d)   Implement the risk response plan

Answer: a. The project manager would want to prevent the change from occurring and seek alternative solutions. However, if the change must occur, then evaluate the impact of the change. Implement the risk response plan would occur if a risk previously planned had occurred. Notify sponsor might occur if the fix was not previously planned for, and the issue that necessitated the fix would impact the project adversely, either in cost, schedule, or quality.

86. Jeffrey is a project manager and wants to define how to estimate, acquire, manage, and utilize physical and team resources. Which process fits the definition for Jeffrey?

    a) Develop team

    b) Plan resource management

    c) Organizational theory

    d) Team charter

Answer: b. The keyword here is "how," which describes the plan—in this case, plan resource management. Develop team is in the execute process group, and you would see terms such as "manager," "administer," "train," and "translate." Organization theory and team charter describe the organization and the team, respectively, and would not utilize "how."

87. In your project for a new interplanetary, space-based telescope the team is performing quality testing. The telescope's focusing mount is out of adjustment causing inaccurate data during the test. You call the team together to discuss the root cause of the problem as well as options and the impact they could have on the rest of the project. Which of the following documents would you create to discover the underlying problem?

    a) Affinity diagram

    b) Ishikawa diagram

    c) Pareto chart

    d) Histogram

Answer: b. In this instance you have found a problem and are trying to discover the root cause of the problem. The document used to uncover the possible root causes of a problem is called an Ishikawa diagram, a cause-and-effect or fishbone diagram.

88. You take over a project from another project manager. You would like to understand the meeting cadence and membership. Where will you find this information?

a) The human resource management plan

b) The meeting management plan

c) The survey of the organization's environment

d) The communication management plan

Answer: d. You would find the information in the communication management plan, as it outlines all communication activities for the project.

89. Which answer best describes the process to manage communications?

a) Project management plan

b) The process of ensuring timely and appropriate collection, creation, distribution, storage, retrieval, management, monitoring, and the ultimate disposition of project information

c) Work performance reports

d) Team performance

Answer: b. The project management plan describes the project, work performance reports describe the status of the project, and team performance is the evaluation of the effectiveness of the team.

90. The process of communicating and working with stakeholders to meet their needs and expectations, address issues, and foster appropriate involvement is

a) Manage stakeholder engagement

b) Monitor communications

c) Manage communications

d) Monitor stakeholder engagement

Answer: a. The difference between monitoring and managing is that monitoring is watching or observing. Managing is an action in which you are actually doing something. In this case, it is the "process of communicating and working with stakeholders."

91. Frank is a project manager with Carmon Lip Balm LLC. He and his project team meticulously put together a project plan that captured and strategized for many risks. One of the risks has just materialized. As a project manager, what should Frank do next?

a) Plan risk management

b) Monitor risks

c) Use his interpersonal and team management skills

d) Implement risk responses

Answer: d. Plan risk management is a process to first create the risk management plan document. Interpersonal skills is a tool and technique. Risks are being monitored to see if any occur. If a risk does occur, the next step as a project manager is to implement the risk response strategy.

92. Debbie is a project manager at Cool Socks Inc. She is in the planning process for a new project and has completed the sequence activities process. The kickoff of the project occurred three months ago. The project team is currently managing the project. As a project manager, what would Debbie do next?

a) Estimate activity durations

b) Close the project

c) Control schedule

d) Identify stakeholders

Answer: c. We are clearly in the execute phase of the project. We have already estimated durations because we have entered the execute phase. There is no mention of project close or cancellation. Identifying stakeholders is going on throughout the life cycle of the project. The best answer is control schedule.

93. Which of the following is an output of the process implement risk response plan?

a) Change requests

b) Data analysis

c) Approved changes

d) OPA

Answer: a. Data analysis is a tool and technique of most processes. Approved changes are outputs of performed integrated change control and inputs to direct and manage project work. OPA is an input to most processes.

94. Joseph is a project manager with Carmon Lip Balm LLC. He and his project team meticulously put together a project plan that captured and strategized for many risks. One of the risks has just materialized. As a project manager, what should Joseph do next?

    a) Plan risk management

    b) Monitor risks

    c) Use his interpersonal and team management skills

    d) Implement risk responses

Answer: d. Plan risk management is a process to first create the risk management plan document. Interpersonal skills is a tool and technique. Risks are being monitored to see if any occur. If a risk does occur, the next step as a project manager is to implement the risk response strategy.

95. Mila is a project manager at Cool Socks Inc. She is in the planning process for a new project and has completed the sequence activities process. The kickoff of the project occurred three months ago. The project team is currently managing the project. As a project manager, what would Mila do next?

    a) Estimate activity durations

    b) Close the project

    c) Control schedule

    d) Identify stakeholders

Answer: c. We are clearly in the execute phase of the project. We have already estimated durations because we have entered the execute phase. There is no mention of project close or cancellation. Identifying stakeholders is going on throughout the life cycle of the project. The best answer is control schedule.

96. Which of the following is an output of the process implement risk response plan?

    a) Change requests

    b) Data analysis

    c) Approved changes

    d) OPA

Answer: a. Data analysis is a tool and technique of most processes. Approved changes are outputs of performed integrated change control and inputs to direct and manage project work. OPA is an input to most processes.

97.   All are components of tools and techniques in the manage project knowledge process except

    a)   Knowledge management

    b)   Information management

    c)   Interpersonal and team skills

    d)   Lessons learned register

Answer: d. The lessons learned register is an input.

98.   Which of the following is an input to the manage project knowledge process?

    a)   Alternative analysis

    b)   Deliverables

    c)   OPA updates

    d)   Project management plan updates

Answer: b. Choice a is a tool and technique of another process; c and d are outputs to other processes.

99.   What is the output of the validate scope process?

    a)   Work performance data

    b)   Acceptable deliverables

    c)   Verified deliverables

    d)   Work performance information

Answer: b. Acceptable deliverables is the output of the validate scope process.

100. Susan is a first-time project manager; however, she is excited to make a good impression. Halfway through her project, Susan gets an email from the client that the project will be canceled because of a funding issue. What should Susan do next?

    a)   Try to negotiate with the client and suggest where to find additional funding

    b)   Prepare the final project report

c) Tell the team this is only a temporary setback; it happened before on a similar project, but the problem was cleared shortly

d) Ask senior management to talk to the client

Answer: b. Susan should immediately begin the closing process. Prepare the final report is the only answer that is part of the closing process.

Mock Exam—Concentration Simplified – Retake Test for Higher Score

1. Ali is a new project manager for Remote Lawnmowers LLC. Ali wants to get off to the best start understanding the project, people, and environment. Interpersonal and team skills is a tool and technique of which process?

    a) Meetings

    b) Develop project charter

    c) OPA

    d) Planning

2. All the following are inputs to develop project charter except

    a) SOW

    b) Assumptions and constraints

    c) OPA

    d) Data analysis

3. The outputs to develop project charter are

    a) Project management plan and requirements plan

    b) Project charter and assumptions log

    c) Quality management plan and change management plan

    d) Stakeholder management plan

4. All are inputs to identify stakeholder group except

    a) Project charter

    b) EEF

c) Expert judgment

d) OPA

5. All describe a project charter except

    a) Formally authorizes the existence of a project

    b) Provides project manager the authority to apply organizational resources to the project

    c) States the high-level constraints and assumptions of the project

    d) States the details of project deliverables

6. Which best describes the develop project charter process?

    a) The process of developing a document that formally authorizes the existence of a project and provides the project manager with the authority to apply organizational resources to project activities

    b) The process of documenting how the project and product scope will be defined, validated, and controlled throughout the project

    c) The process of developing detailed descriptions of the project and products, which is what the project includes and excludes

    d) The process of estimating the number of work periods needed to complete activities with the estimated resources

7. Which tool and technique would a project manager use to collect information about a potential project during project integration management?

    a) Data analysis

    b) Data representation

    c) Manage quality

    d) Data gathering

8. All are tools and techniques in the identify stakeholders process except

   a) Brainstorming

   b) Data analysis

   c) Change requests

   d) Data representation

9. What is the output of the identify stakeholders process?

   a) Project management plan

   b) Stakeholder register

   c) Quality management plan

   d) Requirements management plan

10. The output of the develop project management plan is

   a) Change management plan

   b) Configuration management plan

   c) Project management plan

   d) Stakeholder baseline

11. Which is the correct definition of the develop project management plan?

   a) The process of developing a document that formally authorizes the existence of a project and provides the project manager with the authority to apply organizational resources to project activities

   b) The process of documenting how the project and product scope will be defined, validated, and controlled throughout the project

   c) The process of developing detailed descriptions of the project and products, which is what the project includes and excludes

d) The process of what needs to be done to define, prepare, and coordinate all subsidiary activities to produce a document that defines the project

12. All are part of develop project management plan except

a) Define all subsidiary activities

b) State high-level requirements

c) Prepare all subsidiary activities

d) Coordinate all subsidiary activities

13. All are part of a project management plan except

a) How work will be executed

b) How work will be monitored

c) Implementing project work

d) How work will be closed

14. Which is the best definition of the project management plan?

a) The process of developing a document that formally authorizes the existence of a project and provides the project manager with the authority to apply organizational resources to project activities

b) The document that describes how work will be executed, monitored, and controlled, and closed

c) The process of developing detailed descriptions of the project and products, which is what the project includes and excludes

d) The process of what needs to be done to define, prepare, and coordinate all subsidiary activities to produce a document that defines the project

15. All are contained in plan scope management except

a) How the project and product scope will be defined

b) Implementing change requests

c) How the project and product scope will be validated

d) How the project and product scope will be controlled throughout the project

16. Which best describes the plan scope management process?

a) The process of developing a document that formally authorizes the existence of a project and provides the project manager with the authority to apply organizational resources to project activities

b) The process of documenting how the project and product scope will be defined, validated, and controlled throughout the project

c) The process of developing detailed descriptions of the project and products which is what the project includes and excludes

d) The process of estimating the number of work periods needed to complete activities with the estimated resources

17. All are contained in the define scope process except

a) What the project includes and excludes

b) The output of the project scope statement

c) A detailed description of the project and products

d) How the project and product scope will be validated

18. Which best describes the define scope process?

a) The process of developing a document that formally authorizes the existence of a project and provides the project manager with the authority to apply organizational resources to project activities

b) The process of documenting how the project and product scope will be defined, validated, and controlled throughout the project

c) The process of developing detailed descriptions of the project and products, which is what the project includes and excludes

d) The process of estimating the number of work periods needed to complete activities with the estimated resources

19. All the following describe estimate activity durations except

    a) Determine risks

    b) The process of estimating work periods

    c) The work periods to complete activities

    d) Estimated resources to complete activities

20. Which best describes the estimate activity durations process?

    a) The process of developing a document that formally authorizes the existence of a project and provides the project manager with the authority to apply organizational resources to project activities

    b) The process of documenting how the project and product scope will be defined, validated, and controlled throughout the project

    c) The process of developing detailed descriptions of the project and products, which is what the project includes and excludes

    d) The process of estimating the number of work periods needed to complete activities with the estimated resources

21. The output of develop project management plan is

    a) Project charter

    b) EEF

    c) Project management plan

    d) OPA

22. The outputs of plan scope management are

    a) Scope management plan and requirements management plan

    b) Quality management plan and process improvement plan

    c) Resource management plan and resource breakdown structure

    d) Risk management plan and risk improvement plan

23. The _____ are influences out of the project manager's control.

   a) Enterprise environmental factors

   b) OPA

   c) Evolution environmental factors

   d) Extreme environmental factors

24. _____ are factors internal to the organization that affect the project.

   a) Optimal process assets

   b) Omni process assets

   c) Organization process assets

   d) Optical process assets

25. Ahmal is a project manager with many years of experience. His current project is especially difficult because of problems with the timeline getting extended many times. This could be because the scope is not well defined, causing increases in cost because of increased hours of work on the project for fixes. All may be found in the project charter except

   a) Project purpose

   b) High-level requirements

   c) Detail requirements

   d) Key stakeholder list

26. Susan is a project manager with many years of experience. Susan's current project is especially difficult because of problems with the timeline getting extended many times. This could be because the scope is not well defined, causing increases in cost because of increased hours of work on the project for fixes. Which best describes the collect requirements process?

   a) Project purpose

   b) The process to determine, document, and manage stakeholder needs and requirements to meet project objectives

c) Detail requirements

d) Key stakeholder list

27. Susan is a project manager with many years of experience. Susan's current project is especially difficult because of problems with the timeline getting extended many times. This could be because the scope is not well defined, causing increases in cost because of increased hours of work on the project for fixes. Which tool and technique links product requirements from their origins to the deliverables that satisfy them?

a) Project purpose

b) Requirements traceability matrix

c) Detail requirements

d) Key stakeholder list

28. The output of define scope is

a) Project documents

b) Data analysis

c) Project scope statement

d) Risk management plan

29. David is a project manager with many years of experience. David's current project is especially difficult because of problems with the timeline getting extended many times. This could be because the scope is not well defined, causing increases in cost because of increased hours of work on the project for fixes. Which best describes the define scope process?

a) Project purpose

b) The process to determine, document, and manage stakeholder needs and requirements to meet project objectives

c) Detail requirements

d) The process of developing detailed descriptions of the project and products

30. Susan is a project manager with many years of experience. Susan's current project is especially difficult because of problems with the timeline getting extended many times. This could be because the scope is not well defined, causing increases in cost because of increased hours of work on the project for fixes. What is the output of define scope?

   a) Project scope statement and project document updates

   b) The process of determining, documenting, and managing stakeholder needs and requirements to meet project objectives

   c) Detail requirements

   d) The process of developing detailed descriptions of the project and products

31. Which best describes the define scope process?

   a) The process of developing a detailed description of the project and product

   b) The process of creating a scope management plan that documents how the project and product scope will be defined, validated, and controlled

   c) The process of subdividing project deliverables and project work into smaller, more manageable components

   d) The process of monitoring the status of the project and product scope and managing changes in the scope baseline

32. The output of create WBS is

   a) Decomposition

   b) Scope baseline

   c) Project management plan

   d) Product scope statement

33. Which process best describes create WBS?

   a) The process of developing a detailed description of the project and product

   b) The process of creating a scope management plan that documents how the project and product scope will be defined, validated, and controlled

c) The process of subdividing project deliverables and project work into smaller, more manageable components

d) The process of monitoring the status of the project and product scope and managing changes in the scope baseline

34. Which are number systems in the WBS dictionary and WBS, respectively?

a) Code of account identifier and $(1.0, 1.1, 1.1.1)$

b) Chart of accounts and (a, ab, abc)

c) Control chart and $(1, 2, 3)$

d) All of the above

35. The scope baseline consists of

a) The process of developing a detailed description of the project and product

b) The project scope statement, WBS, WBS dictionary, and planning package

c) The process of subdividing project deliverables and project work into smaller, more manageable components

d) The process of monitoring the status of the project and product scope and managing changes in the scope baseline

36. The output of plan schedule management is

a) Cost baseline

b) Scope baseline

c) Schedule baseline

d) Schedule management plan

37. All describe project schedule management except

a) Define activities

b) Sequence activities

c) Change requests

d) Estimate activity durations

38. As a project manager, James is planning the activities in the project schedule management. Which of the following depicts the order of activities in schedule management?

   a) Collect requirements, define scope, create WBS

   b) Identify risks, perform qualitative risk analysis, perform quantitative risk analysis, and plan risk responses

   c) Plan schedule management, define activities, sequence activities, estimate activity durations, and develop schedule

   d) Estimate costs and determine budget

39. Jason is a new project manager currently in the planning phase of a project. He has defined the activities. As a project manager, what should Jason do next?

   a) Sequence activities

   b) Estimate costs

   c) Plan schedule management

   d) Identify risks

40. Peter is a new project manager currently in the planning phase of a project. He has defined the activities. As a project manager, what did Peter do prior to defining activities?

   a) Sequence activities

   b) Estimate costs

   c) Plan schedule management

   d) Identify risks

41. As a senior project manager, you are planning the activities in the project schedule. What is the output of plan schedule management?

   a) Collect requirements, define scope, create WBS

b) Identify risks, perform qualitative risk analysis, perform quantitative risk analysis, plan risk responses

c) Schedule management plan

d) Estimate costs, determine budget

42. The output of define activities is

a) Activity list, milestone list, activity attributes, and change requests

b) Identify risks, perform qualitative risk analysis, perform quantitative risk analysis, and plan risk responses

c) Plan schedule management, define activities, sequence activities, estimate activity resources, estimate activity costs, and develop schedule

d) Estimate costs and determine budget

43. As a junior project manager, you are planning the activities in the project schedule. Which of the following depicts the order of activities in schedule management?

a) Collect requirements, define scope, and create WBS

b) Identify risks, perform qualitative risk analysis, perform quantitative risk analysis, and plan risk responses

c) Plan schedule management, define activities, sequence activities, estimate activity durations, and develop schedule

d) Estimate costs and determine budget

44. The output of define activity consists of all except

a) Activity list

b) Milestone list

c) Rolling wave

d) Activity attributes

45. The output of sequence activities is

   a) Change request

   b) Project management plan

   c) Project schedule network diagram

   d) Data analysis

46. Jason is a new project manager currently in the planning phase of a project. He has defined the activities. As a project manager, what should Jason do next?

   a) Sequence activities

   b) Estimate costs

   c) Collect requirements

   d) Identify risks

47. John is one of the top project managers in the company. He is concerned about the order of some of the sequenced activities. Of the four types of PDM relationships, which are used most often?

   a) Finish to Start (FS)

   b) Finish to Finish (FF)

   c) Start to Finish (SF)

   d) Start to Start (SS)

48. Robert is a junior project manager at a consulting firm. He has been signed to a high-profile project and needs to be sure the sequence of activities is accurate. Of the four types of PDM relationships, which is used least often?

   a) Finish to Start (FS)

   b) Finish to Finish (FF)

   c) Start to Finish (SF)

   d) Start to Start (SS)

49. Which is one of the tools and techniques for estimating activity duration?

    a) Parametric analogous

    b) Schedule compression

    c) Critical path method

    d) EEF

50. The best description of estimate activity duration is

    a) The process of estimating the number of work periods needed to complete activities with the estimated resources

    b) The process of defining how the project cost will be estimated, budgeted, managed, monitored, and controlled

    c) The process of identifying quality requirements and standards for the project and its deliverables and documenting how the project will demonstrate compliance with quality requirements

    d) The process of estimating team resources and quantity of materials, equipment, and supplies necessary to perform project work

51. What is the output of estimate activity duration?

    a) Duration estimates

    b) Change requests

    c) Project management plan

    d) Data analysis

52. Which process best describes develop schedule?

    a) The process of analyzing sequences, durations, resource requirements, and schedule constraints to create a project model for project executions, monitoring, and controlling

    b) Critical path method

c) Project documents

d) Schedule baseline

53. All are tools and techniques for develop schedule except

a) Critical path

b) Resource optimization

c) Schedule data

d) Schedule compression

54. What is the critical path in days of a project in which the following activities are defined as follows: activity A has a duration of 5 days and starts the project; activities B and C have durations of 3 and 4 days, respectively, and follow A; activity E has a duration of 2 days and follows activity B; activity F has a duration of 2 days and follows activity E; activity D has a duration of 2 days and follows activity C; and activity G has a duration of 5 days and follows F and D.

a) 17 days

b) 16 days

c) 18 days

d) 14 days

55. Now, what is the critical path of a project in which the following activities are defined as follows: activity A has a duration of 5 days and starts the project; activities B and C have durations of 3 and 4 days, respectively, and follow A; activity E has a duration of 2 days and follows activity B; activity F has a duration of 2 days and follows activity E; activity D has a duration of 2 days and follows activity C; and activity G has a duration of 5 days and follows F and D.

a) ABEFG

b) ACDG

c) There is no critical path.

d) The critical path can be reduced or changed.

56. What is the float in days of project activities E and C, respectively, where activities are defined as follows : activity A has a duration of 5 days and starts the project; activities B and C have durations of 3 and 4 days, respectively, and follow A; activity E has a duration of 2 days and follows activity B; activity F has a duration of 2 days and follows activity E; activity D has a duration of 2 days and follows activity C; and activity G has a duration of 5 days and follows F and D.

    a) 0, 1

    b) 1, 0

    c) Float is negative, so the project is ahead of schedule.

    d) Float is negative, so activity is ahead of schedule.

57. The best description of plan cost management is

    a) The process of defining how the project cost will be estimated, budgeted, managed, monitored, and controlled

    b) The process of defining how to estimate, acquire, manage, and utilize physical and team resources

    c) The process of defining how to conduct risk management activities

    d) The process of identifying the relationships among project activities

58. The output of plan cost management is

    a) Risk management plan

    b) Cost baseline

    c) Cost management plan

    d) Schedule baseline

59. Which is not a tool and technique used in estimate activity duration?

    a) Analogous estimating

    b) Bottom-up estimating

c) Three-point estimating (PERT)

d) Duration estimates

60. The best description of estimate costs is

a) The process of analyzing sequences, durations, resource requirements, and schedule constraints to create a project model for project executions, monitoring, and controlling

b) The process of developing an approximation of the monetary resources needed to complete the work

c) The process of developing an approach and plan for project communications activities based on the information needs of each stakeholder and the project

d) The process of defining how to estimate, acquire, manage, and utilize physical and team resources

61. The best description of determine budget process is

a) The process of aggregating the estimated costs of individual activities or work packages to establish an authorized cost baseline

b) The process of developing an approximation of the monetary resources needed to complete the work

c) The process of developing options, selecting strategies, and agreeing on actions to address project risk exposure

d) The process of documenting project decisions, specifying the approach, and identifying potential sellers

62. All are outputs of determine budget except

a) Cost baseline

b) Project funding

c) Data analysis

d) Cost estimates

63. As a project manager III, Michael is planning the activities in the project schedule. Which of the following depicts the order of activities in plan cost management?

   a) Collect requirements, define scope, and create WBS

   b) Identify risks, perform qualitative risk analysis, perform quantitative risk analysis, and plan risk responses

   c) Plan schedule management, define activities, sequence activities, estimate activity resources, estimate activity costs, and develop schedule

   d) Estimate costs and determine budget

64. Which best describes plan quality management?

   a) The process of identifying quality requirements and standards for the project and its deliverables and documenting how the project will demonstrate compliance with quality requirements and/or standards

   b) The process of monitoring and recording the results of executing the quality management activities to assess performance and ensure the project outputs are complete and correct and meet customer requirements

   c) The process of translating the quality management plan into executable quality activities that incorporate the organization's quality policies into the project

   d) None of the above

65. There has been a concern about too many issues after each completed activity in the project. William is a project manager and wants to fix this problem. Which is a part of the cost of conformance?

   a) Rework

   b) Testing

   c) Internal failure costs

   d) Liabilities

66. David is a project manager for a top-five IT consulting firm. David believes issues of activities failing can be averted. Which is a part of the cost of nonconformance?

a) Training

b) Destructive testing loss

c) Inspections

d) Lost business

67. Richard is excited about his first full-time project manager role. He is assigned to multiple projects. Nonconformance issues continue to be a problem on one of Richard's projects. All are a part of preventive costs except

a) Time to do it right

b) Training

c) Inspections

d) Document processes

68. As a project manager, it is a good practice to have as many tools as possible to track whether the quality is occurring at a high level on a project. Which of the following is not one of the seven basic quality tools?

a) Flowcharts

b) Control charts

c) Risk management

d) Check sheets

69. Joseph has been a project manager for 12 years. The process of defining how to estimate, acquire, manage, and utilize physical and team resources is

a) Develop team

b) Plan resource management

c) Organizational theory

d) Team charter

70. Which tool and technique of plan resource management identifies responsible, accountable, consult, and inform parties of tasks/activities?

   a) RBS

   b) RACI charts

   c) Responsibility assignment matrix

   d) Organizational theory

71. The following resources necessary to perform work could be represented in estimate activity resource except

   a) Team resources and quantity of materials

   b) Equipment

   c) Supplies necessary

   d) Analogous estimating

72. Which answer represents the best definition of an estimate activity resource?

   a) The process of developing approaches to involve project stakeholders based on their needs, expectations, interests, and potential impact on the project

   b) The process of estimating team resources and the quantity of materials, equipment, and supplies necessary to perform project work

   c) The process of translating the quality management plan into executable project activities that incorporate the organization's quality policies

   d) The process of numerically analyzing the combined effects of identified individual project risks

73. Thomas is a new project manager with minimal experience in acquiring proper resources to do the necessary work. The following tools and techniques can assist Thomas in estimating resources except

   a) Bottom-up estimating

   b) Analogous estimating

   c) Parametric estimating

d) Resource breakdown structure (RBS)

74. Which process best describes estimate activity resources?

a) The process of estimating team resources and the quantity of materials, equipment, and supplies necessary to perform project work

b) The process of defining how to estimate, acquire, manage, and utilize physical and team resources

c) The process of identifying quality requirements and standards for the project and its deliverables and documenting how the project will demonstrate compliance with quality requirements

d) The process of defining how to conduct risk management activities

75. Charles is a seasoned project manager and a wizard at communication management. Which answer below best fits the tool and technique of plan communication management?

a) Change log

b) Project management plan

c) Manage quality

d) Interpersonal and team skills

76. Patricia is starting a new project that involves infrastructure and database migration. She needs to create documents for the best plan of communication for the team. Which answer best describes a communications management plan?

a) The process of developing an appropriate approach and plan for project communication activities based on the information needs of each stakeholder, available organizational assets, and the needs of the project

b) The document that includes information on staff acquisition and release, resource calendars, recognition and rewards, compliance, and safety

c) The process of ensuring timely and appropriate collection, creation, distribution, storage, retrieval, management, monitoring, and ultimate disposition of project information

d) The process of ensuring the information needs of the project and its stakeholders

77. What is the output of plan communication management?

   a) Project management plan

   b) Project documents

   c) Communications management plan

   d) Communication baseline

78. Jennifer is an IT project manager at an airline's electronics company. The project is behind schedule, and additional people will need to be brought onto the project to get it back on schedule. What tools and techniques can the project manager use to determine the number of communication channels?

   a) EV - AC

   b) PERT

   c) AC + (BAC - EV)

   d) $N(n+1) / 2$

79. As a project manager, you are planning the activities in the project schedule. Which of the following depicts the order of activities in risk management?

   a) Collect requirements, define scope, and create WBS

   b) Identify risks, perform qualitative risk analysis, perform quantitative risk analysis, and plan risk responses

   c) Plan schedule management, define activities, sequence activities, estimate activity resources, estimate activity costs, and develop schedule

   d) Estimate costs and determine budget

80. Linda is a new project manager with some experience in risk analysis to do the necessary work. What is the output of plan risk management?

   a) Communication management plan

   b) Configuration management plan

   c) Home improvement plan

   d) Risk management plan

81. Elizabeth is starting a new project that involves infrastructure and database upgrades. What description best identifies plan risk management?

   a) The process of defining how to conduct risk management activities

   b) The process of using existing knowledge and creating new knowledge to achieve the project's objectives and contribute to organizational learning

   c) The process of translating the quality management plan into executable project activities that incorporate the organization's quality policies

   d) Risk baseline

82. Which process best describes plan communications management?

   a) The process of numerically analyzing the combined effect of identified individual project risks

   b) The process of developing an approach and plan for project communications activities based on the information needs of each stakeholder and the project

   c) Plan-Do-Check-Act

   d) The process of prioritizing individual project risks for further analysis by assessing their probability of occurrence and impact

83. Which process best describes project risk management?

   a) The process of prioritizing individual project risks for further analysis by assessing their probability of occurrence and impact

b) The process of defining how to estimate, acquire, manage, and utilize physical and team resources

c) The process of defining how to conduct risk management activities

d) The process of identifying individual risks as well as sources of overall project risks and documenting their characteristics

84. The output of plan risk management is

a) Cost management plan

b) Risk management plan

c) Scope baseline

d) Risk baseline

85. Which process best describes identify risk?

a) The process of identifying individual risks as well as sources of overall project risks and documenting their characteristics

b) Data analysis and interpersonal skills

c) Project management plan

d) The process of defining how to estimate, acquire, manage, and utilize physical and team resources

86. Barbara is starting a new project that involves application and database migration. A tool and technique that can be used in assessing risk impact is

a) Project management plan

b) Project document updates

c) Risk probability and impact assessment

d) Risk register

87. Kenneth is a new project manager with minimal experience in acquiring proper resources to do the necessary work. Which description best describes perform qualitative risk analysis?

   a) The process of prioritizing individual project risks for further analysis by assessing their probability of occurrence and impact

   b) The process of numerically analyzing the effect of identified risks on overall project objects

   c) Identify risks, perform qualitative risk analysis, perform quantitative risk analysis, and plan risk responses

   d) Plan schedule management, define activities, sequence activities, estimate activity resources, estimate activity costs, and develop schedule

88. Which answer is the best description of perform quantitative risk analysis?

   a) The process of numerically analyzing the effect of identified risks on overall project objects

   b) Identify risks, perform qualitative risk analysis, perform quantitative risk analysis, and plan risk responses

   c) Plan schedule management, define activities, sequence activities, estimate activity resources, estimate activity costs, and develop schedule

   d) Estimate costs and determine budget

89. The following are tools and techniques to perform quantitative risk analysis except

   a) Simulations

   b) EEF

   c) Tornado diagram

   d) Facilitation

90. Sandra is a senior project manager at a solar auto electronics company. This new role brings many new challenges she has rarely faced before. The following are strategies for negative risks/threats except

   a) Avoid

   b) Mitigate

c) Share

d) Transfer

91. All are strategies for positive risks/threats except

a) Exploit

b) Mitigate

c) Share

d) Enhance

92. Dorothy is a project manager at a local marketing firm. Dorothy needs to perform a risk analysis, which includes quantitative and qualitative risk analysis. All are tools and techniques to plan risk responses except

a) Expert judgment

b) Interpersonal and team skills

c) Contingency response strategy

d) Change requests

93. Which best describes the plan procurement management process?

a) The process of documenting project decisions, specifying the approach, and identifying potential sellers

b) The process of using existing knowledge and creating new knowledge to achieve the project's objectives and contribute to organizational learning

c) The process of obtaining team members, facilities, equipment, materials, supplies, and other resources necessary to complete the project work

d) The process of developing an approach and plan for project communications activities based on the information needs of each stakeholder and the project

94. Andrew is a seasoned project manager and a wizard at an electric automobile company. The process of documenting project procurement decisions, specifying the approach, and identifying potential sellers is

   a) Data analysis

   b) Procurement management plan

   c) OPA

   d) Plan procurement management

95. The following are contract types in plan procurement management except

   a) Fixed-priced contracts

   b) Time and material contracts

   c) Standard contracts

   d) Cost-reimbursable contracts

96. Which answer best describes plan stakeholder engagement?

   a) The process of developing approaches to involve project stakeholders based on their needs and expectations, addressing issues, and fostering appropriate stakeholder engagement

   b) The process of monitoring project stakeholder relationships and tailoring strategies for engaging stakeholders through the modification of engagement strategies and plans

   c) The process of communicating and working with stakeholders to meet their needs and expectations

   d) The process of not communicating and working with stakeholders to meet their needs and expectations

97. What is the output of plan stakeholder management?

   a) Stakeholder management plan

   b) Stakeholder baseline

   c) Risk register

d) RBS

98. Bill is an experienced project manager who wants to be sure his team collects all the necessary requirements. Which best describes plan scope management?

a) The process of developing a detailed description of the project and product

b) The process of creating a scope management plan that documents how the project and product scope will be defined, validated, and controlled

c) The process of subdividing project deliverables and project work into smaller, more manageable components

d) The process of monitoring the status of the project and product scope and managing changes in the scope baseline

99. The output of the plan scope management process is

a) Scope baseline

b) Requirements plan

c) Scope management plan

d) EEF

100. Bill is an experienced project manager who wants to be sure his team collects all the necessary requirements. Which best describes WBS?

a) The process of developing a detailed description of the project and product

b) The process of creating a scope management plan that documents how the project and product scope will be defined, validated, and controlled

c) The process of subdividing project deliverables and project work into smaller, more manageable components

d) The process of monitoring the status of the project and product scope and managing changes in the scope baseline

101. Bill is an experienced project manager who wants to be sure his team collects all the necessary requirements. Which best describes controlling scope?

    a) The process of developing a detailed description of the project and product

    b) The process of creating a scope management plan that documents how the project and product scope will be defined, validated, and controlled

    c) The process of subdividing project deliverables and project work into smaller, more manageable components

    d) The process of monitoring the status of the project and product scope and managing changes in the scope baseline

102. Bill is an experienced project manager who wants to be sure his team collects all the necessary requirements. What are the outputs to plan scope management?

    a) Accepted deliverables and change requests

    b) Requirements documentation and requirements traceability matrix

    c) The process of subdividing project deliverables and project work into smaller, more manageable components

    d) Scope management plan and requirements management plan

103. What are the tools and techniques to collect requirements?

    a) Prototypes

    b) Project documents

    c) Requirements documentation

    d) Project management plan

104. The output of the collect requirements process is

    a) OPA

    b) Data analysis

    c) Requirements documentation

d) Subject matter expert

105. Bill is an experienced project manager who wants to be sure his team collects all the necessary requirements. All are ways to collect requirements during project planning except

a) Prototypes

b) Data analysis

c) Project documents

d) Expert judgments

106. Which of the following best defines collect requirements?

a) The process to determine, document, and manage stakeholder needs and requirements to meet project objectives

b) Requirements baseline

c) The process of identifying the relationships among project activities

d) Decompose into lower-level components

107. Steven is a new project manager with minimal experience in project management to do the necessary work. Which best describes the define scope process?

a) The process of developing a detailed description of the project and product

b) The process of creating a scope management plan that documents how the project and product scope will be defined, validated, and controlled

c) The process of subdividing project deliverables and project work into smaller, more manageable components

d) The process of monitoring the status of the project and product scope and managing changes in the scope baseline

108. Kimberly is a project manager responsible for adding a new structure to a building. Which process best describes create WBS?

   a) The process of developing a detailed description of the project and product

   b) The process of creating a scope management plan that documents how the project and product scope will be defined, validated, and controlled

   c) The process of subdividing project deliverables and project work into smaller, more manageable components

   d) The process of monitoring the status of the project and product scope and managing changes in the scope baseline

109. Senior management called the project manager, Emily, into a meeting to talk about cost concerns. Senior management wants Emily to take as much time as needed. However, they do want the most accurate estimate of the current cost. Which cost management tool and technique will provide the most accurate cost estimates?

   a) Bottom-up estimating

   b) Analogous estimating

   c) Parametric estimating

   d) EVM

110. Amanda is a new project manager at a manufacturing firm. Senior management wants the most accurate information from Amanda to determine what the project will cost and how long the project will take. Amanda has been instructed to take as long as she needs. What tool and technique would Amanda use to satisfy this requirement from senior management?

   a) Prototypes

   b) An oscilloscope

   c) Fishbone

   d) Bottom-up estimating

111. Raymond is a top-level project manager at a construction company. During the implementation phase of a project, there was an atypical issue that caused a minor setback for Raymond and his team. Then BAC = 120, EV = 10, PV = 12, AC = 11. What is the EAC of the project?

    a) 132

    b) 120

    c) 121

    d) 156.2

112. Joyce is a top-level project manager at a construction company. During the implementation phase of a project, there was a typical issue that caused a minor setback for Joyce and her team. Then BAC = 120, EV = 10, PV = 12, AC = 11. What is the EAC of the project?

    a) 132

    b) 120

    c) 144

    d) 156.2

113. Nathan is a top-level project manager as a construction company. Then BAC = 120, EV = 10, PV = 12, AC = 11. What is the EAC forecast earning of the project?

    a) 132

    b) 120

    c) 121

    d) 156.2

114. Lauren is a seasoned project manager and is very good at solving projects that are not in conformance. Which is a part of the cost of conformance?

    a) Rework

    b) Testing

    c) Internal failure costs

    d) Liabilities

115. Douglas is a project manager with some experience in quality project management to do the necessary work. Which is a part of the cost of nonconformance?

   a) Training

   b) Destructive testing loss

   c) Inspections

   d) Lost business

116. Jeremy is a project manager at a local marketing firm. Jeremy needs to perform a quality audit. All are a part of preventive costs except

   a) Time to do it right

   b) Training

   c) Inspections

   d) Document processes

117. Gerald is a project manager responsible for adding a new structure to a building. The process of defining how to estimate, acquire, manage, and utilize physical and team is

   a) Develop team

   b) Plan resource management

   c) Organizational theory

   d) Team charter

118. Which answer below best fits the tools and techniques of manage communications?

   a) Change log

   b) Project management plan

   c) Manage quality

   d) Interpersonal and team skills

119. As a project manager, Jacob is planning the activities in risk management. Which of the following depicts the order of activities in risk management?

    a) Collect requirements, define scope, and create WBS

    b) Identify risks, perform qualitative risk analysis, perform quantitative risk analysis, and plan risk responses

    c) Plan schedule management, define activities, sequence activities, estimate activity resources, estimate activity costs, and develop schedule

    d) Estimate costs and determine budget

120. The process of documenting project procurement decisions, specifying the approach, and identifying potential sellers is

    a) Data analysis

    b) Procurement management plan

    c) OPA

    d) Plan procurement management

121. Janine is a longtime project manager at Aspire LLC. Janine needs to work with the procurement department to secure people with sufficient skills. Which answer best describes plan stakeholder engagement?

    a) The process of developing approaches to involve project stakeholders based on their needs and expectations, address issues, and foster appropriate stakeholder engagement

    b) Templates for the risk management plan, risk register, and risk report

    c) The process of managing procurement relationships, monitoring contract performance, making changes and corrections as appropriate, and closing out contracts

    d) The process of obtaining seller responses, selecting a seller, and awarding a contract

122. Frances is starting a new project that involves infrastructure and database migration. Frances needs to create documents for the best plan of communication for the team. Deliverables are an output of which process group?

    a) OPA

    b) EEF

    c) Final report

    d) Direct and manage project work

123. Samuel is a new project manager with good experience in change management to do the necessary work. The following are inputs to the direct and manage project work process except

    a) Approved changes

    b) Project management plan

    c) Deliverables

    d) OPA

124. Which of the following best describes the process direct and manage project work?

    a) The process of leading and performing the work defined in the project plan and implementing the approved changes to achieve the project objectives

    b) The process of improving the competencies of team members and the overall team environment to enhance project performance

    c) The process of obtaining seller responses, selecting sellers, and awarding a contract

    d) The process of documenting project decisions, specifying the approach, and identifying potential sellers

125. Jose is a project manager with great people skills. Interpersonal and team skills involve all of the following except

    a) Active listening

    b) Expert judgment

c) Networking

d) Political awareness

126. The following are a part of tools and techniques in manage project knowledge except

a) Knowledge management

b) Information management

c) Interpersonal and team skills

d) Lessons learned register

127. Which process best describes manage project knowledge?

a) The process of using existing knowledge and creating new knowledge to achieve the project's objectives and contribute to organizational learning

b) The process of communicating and working with stakeholders to meet their needs, expectations, interests, and potential impact on the project

c) The process of developing a document that formally authorizes the existence of a project and provides the project manager with authority to apply organizational resources to project activities

d) The process of what needs to be done to define, prepare, and coordinate all subsidiary activities to produce a document that defines the project

128. All are tools and techniques to manage project knowledge except

a) Information management

b) Active listening

c) Deliverables

d) Knowledge management

129. The following are inputs of the manage quality process except

   a) Project documents

   b) Project management plan

   c) EEF

   d) OPA

130. Which of the following is an input to the manage quality process?

   a) Quality reports

   b) Quality metrics

   c) Data gathering

   d) EEF

131. Which description best identifies the manage quality process?

   a) The process of obtaining seller responses, selecting sellers, and awarding a contract

   b) The process of translating the quality management plan into executable project activities that incorporate the organization's quality policies

   c) The process of communicating and working with stakeholders to meet their needs, expectations, interests, and potential impact on the project

   d) The process of leading and performing the work defined in the project plan and implementing the approved changes to achieve the project objectives

132. All are quality management styles except

   a) Philip Crosby

   b) Kaizen

   c) Deming

   d) Maslow

133. Pepper is a new project manager for TF Banking Services. Pepper is in the process of acquiring resources. All are tools and techniques Pepper can use to aid in her search except

    a) Virtual teams

    b) Multicriteria analysis

    c) Resource management plan

    d) Negotiation

134. Which process best describes acquire resources?

    a) The process of improving the competencies of team members and the overall team environment to enhance project performance

    b) The process of obtaining team members, facilities, equipment, materials, supplies, and other resources necessary to complete the project work

    c) The process of tracking team member performance, providing feedback, resolving issues, and managing team changes to optimize project performance

    d) The process of defining how to estimate, acquire, manage, and utilize physical and team resources

135. What is the correct order of Tuckman's ladder?

    a) Forming, storming, norming, performing, adjourning

    b) Adjourning, forming, storming, norming, performing

    c) Performing, forming, storming, norming, adjourning

    d) Storming, norming, forming, performing, adjourning

136. When developing teams, what is the most desired location of team members?

    a) Virtual teams

    b) Colocation

    c) Meetings

    d) Team performance assessments

137. When developing teams, what is the most desired location of team members?

   a) Virtual teams

   b) Colocation

   c) Meetings

   d) Team performance assessments

138. All the following are inputs to manage team except

   a) PMP

   b) Project documents updates

   c) Work performance reports

   d) Team performance

139. Which description best defines develop team?

   a) The process of tracking team member performance, providing feedback, resolving issues, and managing team changes to optimize project performance

   b) The process of ensuring timely and appropriate collection, creation, distribution, storage, retrieval, management, monitoring, and ultimate disposition of project information

   c) The process of leading and performing the work defined in the project plan and implementing the approved changes to achieve the project objectives

   d) The process of improving the competencies of team members and the overall team environment to enhance project performance

140. Of the four types of conflict management, which is considered the best outcome?

   a) Avoid

   b) Force

   c) Compromise

   d) Collaborate

141. Which best describes the manage resources process?

   a) The process of reviewing all change requests; approving changes; managing changes to deliverables, project documents, and the project management plan; and communicating decisions

   b) The process of tracking team member performance, providing feedback, resolving issues, and managing team changes to optimize project performance

   c) The process of obtaining team members, facilities, equipment, materials, supplies, and other resources necessary to complete the project work

   d) The process of translating the quality management plan into executable project activities that incorporate the organization's quality policies

142. Of the four types of conflict management, which is considered the worst outcome?

   a) Avoid

   b) Force

   c) Compromise

   d) Collaborate

143. Manage communication is a process of which knowledge area?

   a) Plan communications management

   b) Project quality management

   c) Manage communications is not a process.

   d) Project communications management

144. Which best describes the manage communications process?

   a) PMP

   b) The process of ensuring timely and appropriate collection, creation, distribution, storage, retrieval, management, monitoring, and the ultimate disposition of project information

   c) Work performance reports

   d) Team performance

145. All are traits of interpersonal and team skills except

    a) Active listening

    b) Conflict management

    c) Political awareness

    d) Change requests

146. Frank is a project manager with Carmon Lip Balm LLC. He and his project team meticulously put together a project plan which captured and strategized for many risks. One of them has just materialized. As a project manager, what should Frank do next?

    a) Plan risk management

    b) Monitor risks

    c) Use his interpersonal skills and team management

    d) Implement risk responses

147. Which definition correctly defines implement risk responses?

    a) The process of implementing the agreed-upon risk response

    b) The process of obtaining seller responses, selecting sellers, and awarding a contract

    c) The process of monitoring the status of the project and product scope and managing changes to the scope baseline

    d) The process of improving the competencies of team members and the overall team environment to enhance project performance

148. Which of the following is an output of implement risk response?

    a) Expert judgment

    b) Risk management plan

    c) Interpersonal skills

    d) Change requests

149. The process of obtaining seller responses, selecting a seller, and awarding a contract is

   a) Plan procurement management

   b) Conduct procurements

   c) Control procurements

   d) Project procurement management

150. All are tools and techniques to select a seller except

   a) Advertising

   b) Bidder conference

   c) Proposal evaluation

   d) Asking your best friend

151. Which definition accurately describes the conduct procurements process?

   a) The process of obtaining seller responses, selecting sellers, and awarding a contract

   b) The process of formalizing acceptance of the completed project deliverables

   c) The process of performing integrated change control

   d) The process of monitoring and recording the results of executing the quality management plan activities to assess performance and ensure project outputs are complete, correct, and meet customer expectations

152. The process of communicating and working with stakeholders to meet their needs and expectations, address issues, and foster appropriate involvement is

   a) Manage stakeholder engagement

   b) Monitor communications

   c) Manage communications

   d) Monitor stakeholder engagement

153. All are tools and techniques of manage stakeholder engagement except

   a) Feedback

   b) Negotiation

   c) Ground rules

   d) Change request

154. The output of manage stakeholder engagement is

   a) EEF

   b) Expert judgment

   c) Change request

   d) Change log

155. Which process best exemplifies monitoring and control in project integration?

   a) Direct and manage project work

   b) Monitor and control project work

   c) Manage project knowledge

   d) Perform integrated change control

156. What is the best definition of monitoring and control?

   a) The process of tracking, reviewing, and reporting the overall progress to meet performance objectives defined in the project management plan

   b) The process of reviewing all change requests; approving changes; managing changes to deliverables, project documents, and the project management plan; and communicating decisions

   c) The process of formalizing acceptance of the completed project deliverables

   d) The process of monitoring the status of the project and product scope and managing changes to the scope baseline

157. Judy is a top project manager at her firm. She is currently working on a project in which a fix is necessary. As a project manager, what should Judy do next?

    a) Check the release documents

    b) Notify the sponsor

    c) Evaluate the impact of the change

    d) Implement the risk response plan

158. What is the best definition of perform integrated change control?

    a) The process of tracking, reviewing, and reporting the overall progress to meet performance objectives defined in the project management plan

    b) The process of reviewing all change requests; approving changes; managing changes to deliverables, project documents, and the project management plan; and communicating decisions

    c) The process of formalizing acceptance of the completed project deliverables

    d) The process of monitoring the status of the project and product scope and managing changes to the scope baseline

159. All are tools and techniques of the perform integrated change control process except

    a) Meetings

    b) Expert judgment

    c) Project management updates

    d) Multicriteria decision analysis

160. What is the best definition of validate scope?

    a) The process of tracking, reviewing, and reporting the overall progress to meet performance objectives defined in the project management plan

    b) The process of reviewing all change requests; approving changes; managing changes to deliverables, project documents, and the project management plan; and communicating decisions

c) The process of formalizing acceptance of the completed project deliverables

d) The process of monitoring the status of the project and product scope and managing changes to the scope baseline

161. Which is the output of validate scope?

   a) Work performance data

   b) Acceptable deliverables

   c) Verified deliverables

   d) Work performance information

162. Which is an input to validate scope?

   a) Verified deliverables

   b) Acceptable deliverables

   c) Inspection

   d) Scope baseline

163. What is the best definition of perform integrated change control?

   a) The process of tracking, reviewing, and reporting the overall progress to meet performance objectives defined in the project management plan

   b) The process of reviewing all change requests; approving changes; managing changes to deliverables, project documents, and the project management plan; and communicating decisions

   c) The process of formalizing acceptance of the completed project deliverables

   d) The process of monitoring the status of the project and product scope and managing changes to the scope baseline

164. All are inputs to control scope except

   a) Scope management plan

   b) Change management plan

   c) Change requests

   d) Scope baseline

165. Which is a tool and technique for control scope?

   a) Trend analysis

   b) EEF

   c) Work performance information

   d) Project document updates

166. What is the best definition of control schedule?

   a) The process of monitoring the status of the project and product scope and managing changes to the scope baseline

   b) The process of monitoring project costs to the cost baseline

   c) The process of monitoring and recording the results of executing the quality management plan activities to assess performance and ensure project outputs are complete, correct, and meet customer expectations

   d) The process of ensuring the physical resources assigned and allocated to the project are available as planned versus actual utilization of resources and taking corrective actions as necessary

167. The following are tools and techniques used in control schedule except

   a) Critical path method

   b) PMIS

   c) Resource optimization

   d) Change requests

168. All are outputs for the control schedule process except

   a) Schedule forecasts

   b) Change requests

   c) Work performance information

   d) PMIS

169. What is the best definition of control costs?

   a) The process of monitoring the status of the project and product scope and managing changes to the scope baseline

   b) The process of monitoring project costs to the cost baseline

   c) The process of monitoring and recording the results of executing the quality management plan activities to assess performance and ensure project outputs are complete, correct, and meet customer expectations

   d) The process of ensuring the physical resources assigned and allocated to the project are available as planned versus actual utilization of resources and taking corrective actions as necessary

170. All are tools and techniques of control costs except

   a) Earned value analysis

   b) Trend analysis

   c) TCPI

   d) PERT

171. Which of the following is an output of control costs?

   a) Cost forecasts

   b) PMIS

   c) Cost management plan

   d) OPA

172. What is the best definition of control quality?

a) The process of monitoring the status of the project and product scope and managing changes to the scope baseline

b) The process of monitoring the status of the project to update the project schedule and manage changes to the schedule baseline

c) The process of monitoring and recording the results of executing the quality management plan activities to assess performance and ensure project outputs are complete, correct, and meet customer expectations

d) The process of ensuring the physical resources assigned and allocated to the project are available as planned versus actual utilization of resources and taking corrective actions as necessary

173. Which description best describes control quality?

a) The process of monitoring and recording the results of executing the quality management plan activities to assess performance and ensure project outputs are complete, correct, and meet customer expectations

b) EVM

c) PERT

d) The process of finalizing all activities for the project, phase, or contract

174. Terri is a new project manager at a manufacturing firm. She has currently completed the planning stage. Her team has begun implementing the work according to the project plan. One of Terri's team members has noticed a problem with her task but has not yet found a fix. What tools can be used to determine the cause of the problem?

a) Prototypes

b) An oscilloscope

c) Fishbone

d) Bottom-up estimating

175. David is a new project manager for Hydro-Autos Enterprises. He wants to get off to the best start understanding ways to deliver a quality product. David and his team are planning for accuracy in quality. Which of the following tools is one of the seven rules of quality control?

    a) Analysis technique

    b) Cause-and-effect diagram

    c) Data representation

    d) Quality audit

176. Susan is a new project manager for Bikes Incorporated. She wants to get off to the best start understanding ways to deliver a quality product. She and her team are planning for accuracy in quality. They can check for quality using each of these rules of quality control except

    a) Control chart

    b) Quality audit

    c) Pareto chart

    d) Scatter diagram

177. Aaron is the project manager at a communication company that builds precision devices. His team has produced a device that is consistently measured with the same output value with little scattering, but the output is not close to the true value. This is an example of what?

    a) Accuracy

    b) Cost of quality

    c) Prevention over inspection

    d) Precision

178. What is the best definition of control resources?

    a) The process of monitoring the status of the project and product scope and managing changes to the scope baseline

    b) The process of monitoring project costs to the cost baseline

c) The process of monitoring and recording the results of executing the quality management plan activities to assess performance and ensure project outputs are complete, correct, and meet customer expectations

d) The process of ensuring the physical resources assigned and allocated to the project are available as planned versus actual utilization of resources and taking corrective actions as necessary

179. Robert is a new project manager at Use It or Lose It! Inc. Robert does not trust his employees to do their jobs, so he must monitor their every action to make sure he gets the results he wants. Robert is practicing

a) RAM

b) McGregor's Theory X

c) Expectancy Theory

d) McGregor's Theory Y

180. What is the correct order of team development?

a) Performing, storming, norming, forming, and adjourning

b) Performing, storming, adjourning, forming, and norming

c) Forming, norming, storming, performing, and adjourning

d) Forming, storming, norming, performing, and adjourning

181. What are the least and most desired methods of conflict resolution?

a) Avoidance and collaboration

b) Compromise and smoothing

c) Force and avoidance

d) Compromise and collaboration

182. The document that includes information on staff acquisition and release, resource calendars, recognition and rewards, compliance, and safety is

    a) Resource plan

    b) Project management plan

    c) Staffing management plan

    d) Project resource plan

183. Which answer best describes the manage communications process?

    a) The process of developing an appropriate approach and plan for project communication activities based on the information needs of each stakeholder, the available organizational assets, and the needs of the project

    b) The document that includes information on staff acquisition and release, resource calendars, recognition and rewards, compliance, and safety

    c) The process of ensuring timely and appropriate collection, creation, distribution, storage, retrieval, management, monitoring, and the ultimate disposition of project information

    d) The process of ensuring the information needs of the project and its stakeholders

184. Which answer best describes monitor communications?

    a) The process of developing an appropriate approach and plan for project communication activities based on the information needs of each stakeholder, the available organizational assets, and the needs of the project

    b) The document that includes information on staff acquisition and release, resource calendars, recognition and rewards, compliance, and safety

    c) The process of ensuring timely and appropriate collection, creation, distribution, storage, retrieval, management, monitoring, and the ultimate disposition of project information

    d) The process of ensuring the information needs of the project and its stakeholders are met

185. Francis is a new project manager for World Force, Inc. Francis's team consisted of 6 members, including Tom; 2 new members have just been added. What is the number of channels of communication?

    a) 13

    b) 12

    c) 15

    d) 28

186. Francis is a new project manager for World Force, Inc. Francis's team consisted of 6 members, including Tom; 2 new members have just been added. How many more channels of communication are there now?

    a) 13

    b) 12

    c) 15

    d) 28

187. Which best identifies the monitor risks process?

    a) The process of monitoring the implementation of the agreed-upon risk response plan, tracking identified risks, analyzing new risks, and evaluating the risk process

    b) The process of formalizing acceptance of the completed project deliverables

    c) The process of tracking, reviewing, and reporting the overall progress to meet performance objectives defined in the project management plan

    d) Data analysis

188. Joe is a project manager who has a sponsor who does not like risk, so Joe must identify the risks and list the probability of occurrence. What answer best describes the risk management plan?

    a) It is all the requirements of the project.

    b) It is the process of defining how to conduct risk management activities for a project.

    c) It is not a desirable choice when managing large projects.

d) It is a grid for mapping the probability of each risk occurrence and the impact on project objectives if the risk occurs.

189. Joe is a project manager who has a sponsor who does not like risk, so Joe must identify the risks and list the probability of occurrence. Which answer best describes the probability impact matrix?

a) It is all the requirements of the project.

b) It is the process of defining how to conduct risk management activities for a project.

c) It is not a desirable choice when managing large projects.

d) It is a grid for mapping the probability of each risk occurrence and the impact on project objectives if the risk occurs.

190. Janine is a longtime project manager at Aspire LLC. Janine needs to work with the procurement department to secure people with sufficient skills. Which answer best describes control procurements management?

a) The process of documenting project decisions, specifying the approach, and identifying potential sellers

b) Templates for the risk management plan, risk register, and risk report

c) The process of managing procurement relationships, monitoring contract performance, making changes and corrections as appropriate, and closing out contracts

d) The process of obtaining seller responses, selecting a seller, and awarding a contract

191. Which process best describes conduct procurements?

a) The process of documenting project decisions, specifying the approach, and identifying potential sellers

b) The process of communicating and working with stakeholders to meet their needs and expectations, address issues, and foster appropriate stakeholder engagement

c) The process of obtaining seller responses, selecting sellers, and awarding a contract

d) Templates for the risk management plan, risk register, and risk report

192. Which statement best describes the control procurements process?

   a) The process of documenting project decisions, specifying the approach, and identifying potential sellers

   b) Templates for the risk management plan, risk register, and risk report

   c) The process of managing procurement relationships, monitoring contract performance, making changes and corrections as appropriate, and closing out contracts

   d) The process of communicating and working with stakeholders to meet their needs and expectations, address issues, and foster appropriate stakeholder engagement

193. Kazem is a project manager with many years of experience. Kazem knows how important customer communication and satisfaction are to how a project is managed. What is the best definition of monitor stakeholder engagement?

   a) The process of identifying project stakeholders regularly and analyzing and documenting relevant information regarding their interests, involvement, interdependencies, influence, and impact on project success

   b) The process of communicating and working with stakeholders to meet their needs and expectations, address issues, and foster appropriate stakeholder engagement

   c) The process of providing an overview of the project stakeholder management process

   d) The process of monitoring project stakeholder relationships and tailoring strategies for engaging stakeholders through the modification of engagement strategies and plans

194. The following describe monitor stakeholder engagement except

   a) Managing stakeholder relationships

   b) Ignoring the stakeholders until they go away

   c) Engaging with the stakeholders

   d) Formulating strategies with the stakeholders

195. The sponsor is not very happy with the progress of the project. The sponsor says to stop all efforts on the project immediately. As a project manager, what would you do next?

   a) Start the closing process

   b) Gain formal acceptance

   c) Release the team

   d) Close the project

196. What is the best definition of the close process?

   a) The process of finalizing all activities for the project, phase, or contract

   b) The process of monitoring project costs to the cost baseline

   c) The process of monitoring the status of the project and product scope and managing changes to the scope baseline

   d) The process of ensuring the information needs of the project and its stakeholders are met

197. The sponsor has accepted all deliverables of the project. As a project manager, what would you do next?

   a) Close the project

   b) Gain formal acceptance

   c) Document lessons learned

   d) Release the team

198. All are part of the closing process except

   a) Obtain stakeholder satisfaction

   b) Release the team

   c) EEF

   d) Prepare final project report

199. The sponsor has accepted all deliverables of the project. As a project manager, what would you do next?

   a) Release the team

b) Gain formal acceptance

c) Document lessons learned

d) Close the project

200. The following are part of the closing process except

a) Obtain stakeholder satisfaction

b) Release the team

c) EEF updates

d) Prepare final project report

Mock Exam—Concentration Solutions – Retake Test for Higher Score

1.	b	2.	d	3.	b	4.	c
5.	d	6.	a	7.	d	8.	c
9.	b	10.	c	11.	a	12.	b
13.	c	14.	a	15.	b	16.	b
17.	d	18.	c	19.	a	20.	d
21.	c	22.	a	23.	a	24.	c
25.	c	26.	b	27.	b	28.	c
29.	d	30.	a	31.	a	32.	b
33.	c	34.	a	35.	b	36.	d
37.	c	38.	c	39.	a	40.	c
41.	c	42.	a	43.	c	44.	c
45.	c	46.	a	47.	a	48.	c
49.	a	50.	a	51.	a	52.	a
53.	a	54.	a	55.	a	56.	a
57.	a	58.	c	59.	d	60.	b
61.	a	62.	c	63.	d	64.	a
65.	b	66.	d	67.	c	68.	c
69.	b	70.	b	71.	d	72.	b
73.	d	74.	a	75.	d	76.	a
77.	c	78.	d	79.	b	80.	d
81.	b	82.	b	83.	c	84.	b
85.	a	86.	c	87.	b	88.	a
89.	b	90.	c	91.	b	92.	d
93.	a	94.	d	95.	c	96.	a
97.	a	98.	b	99.	c	100.	c

101.	d	102.	d	103.	a	104.	c
105.	c	106.	a	107.	a	108.	c
109.	a	110.	d	111.	c	112.	a
113.	d	114.	b	115.	d	116.	c
117.	b	118.	d	119.	b	120.	d
121.	a	122.	d	123.	c	124.	a
125.	b	126.	d	127.	a	128.	c
129.	c	130.	b	131.	b	132.	d
133.	c	134.	b	135.	a	136.	b
137.	b	138.	b	139.	d	140.	d
141.	b	142.	a	143.	d	144.	b
145.	d	146.	d	147.	a	148.	d
149.	b	150.	d	151.	a	152.	a
153.	d	154.	c	155.	b	156.	a
157.	c	158.	b	159.	c	160.	c
161.	b	162.	a	163.	b	164.	c
165.	a	166.	a	167.	d	168.	d
169.	b	170.	d	171.	a	172.	c
173.	a	174.	c	175.	b	176.	b
177.	d	178.	d	179.	b	180.	d
181.	a	182.	c	183.	c	184.	d
185.	d	186.	a	187.	a	188.	b
189.	d	190.	c	191.	c	192.	c
193.	d	194.	b	195.	a	196.	a
197.	c	198.	c	199.	c	200.	a

Mock Exam Two – Retake Test for Higher Score
200 Questions—4 Hours

1. Assume a project costs $10,000 today and will return $2,500 per year for 5 years. Your required return on investments is 10%. As a project manager, should you do the project?

   a) No, because the project will make a great profit.

   b) No, because the payback period is four years.

   c) No, because "the required return on investments is 10%."

   d) Yes, because the project meets the organization's strategic goals.

2. Lauren is a contractor responsible for the refurbishment of an automobile showroom. The estimated refurbishment cost is $500 per square foot. The total showroom area that needs to be refurbished is 1,000 square feet. Based on Lauren's past experience, she knows the project team can refurbish 100 square feet per week. What is the steady-state value?

   a) $525,000

   b) $375,000

   c) $555,555.56

   d) $475,000

3. Walter is a new project manager for SelectMates LLC. He wants to get off to the best start in understanding the project, people, and environment. Interpersonal and team skills is a tool and technique of which process?

   a) Meetings

   b) Develop project charter

   c) Organizational process assets

   d) Planning

4. Megan is a new project manager for an existing project with issues. What document does she need to determine the project goals, high-level risks, and high-level constraints?

   a) Communication plan

   b) Project management plan

   c) SOW

   d) Project charter

5. If a stakeholder has high interest but low power, what is the best way to manage the stakeholder?

   a) Keep satisfied

   b) Manage closely

   c) Keep informed

   d) Monitor

6. The output of the develop project management plan process is

   a) Project charter

   b) Enterprise environmental factors

   c) Project management plan

   d) Organizational process assets

7. The following are tools and techniques for the develop project management plan process except

   a) Meetings

   b) Project management plan

   c) Interpersonal and team skills

   d) Expert judgments

8. Which of the following is an input to develop the project management plan?

    a) Data gathering

    b) Project management plan

    c) Inspection

    d) Project charter

9. The _____ are influences out of the project manager's control.

    a) Enterprise environmental factors

    b) Organizational process assets

    c) Evolution environmental factors

    d) Extreme environmental factors

10. Susan is a project manager with many years of experience. Her current project is especially difficult because of problems with the timeline getting extended many times. This could be because the scope is not well defined, and the delays are causing increases in cost because of increased hours of work on the project for fixes. All are found in the project charter except

    a) Project purpose

    b) High-level requirements

    c) Detailed requirements

    d) Key stakeholder list

11. Which of the following are outputs to the plan scope management process?

    a) Scope management plan and requirements management plan

    b) Project charter and project management plan

    c) Quality management plan and process improvement plan

    d) Risk management plan and risk response plan

12. Which document would the project manager use to achieve the plan benefits of timeline, tools, and resources to ensure benefits are fully realized?

   a) Project management plan

   b) Benefits management plan

   c) Projects documents

   d) OPA

13. Which of the following is an output of the collect requirements process?

   a) OPA

   b) Requirements traceability matrix

   c) Project management plan

   d) Data analysis

14. Which best describes the define scope process?

   a) The process of developing a detailed description of the project and product

   b) The process of creating a scope management plan that documents how the project and product scope will be defined, validated, and controlled

   c) The process of subdividing project deliverables and project work into smaller, more manageable components

   d) The process of monitoring the status of the project and product scope and managing changes in the scope baseline

15. Work that is performed that is outside the scope of the project but is demanded by a sponsor, senior management, or stakeholders other than the project team is called

   a) Gold plating

   b) Work that is necessary

   c) Work that is unnecessary

   d) Scope creep

16. Which are number systems in the WBS dictionary and WBS, respectively?

   a) Code of account identifier and (1.0, 1.1, 1.1.1)

   b) Chart of accounts and (a, ab, abc)

   c) Control chart and (1, 2, 3)

   d) All of the above

17. The following are tools and techniques used to collect requirements except

   a) Data analysis

   b) Decision-making

   c) Organizational process assets

   d) Interpersonal skills and team skills

18. The scope baseline consists of

   a) The process of developing a detailed description of the project and product

   b) The project scope statement, WBS, WBS dictionary, and planning package

   c) The process of subdividing project deliverables and project work into smaller, more manageable components

   d) The process of monitoring the status of the project and product scope and managing changes in the scope baseline

19. As a project manager, you are planning the activities in the project schedule. What is the output of plan schedule management?

   a) Collect requirements, define scope, and create WBS

   b) Identify risks, perform qualitative risk analysis, perform quantitative risk analysis, and plan risk responses

   c) Create the schedule management plan

   d) Estimate costs and determine the budget

20. The inputs to the plan schedule management process are

    a) Project charter, project management plan, scope management plan, development approach, EEF, and OPA

    b) Perform qualitative risk analysis, perform quantitative risk analysis, and plan risk responses

    c) Project management plan, project documents, approved change requests, EEF, and OPA

    d) Project charter, project management plan, quality management plan, project life cycle, development, EEF, and OPA

21. Susan is a first-time project manager; however, she is excited to make a good impression. Halfway through her project, Susan gets an email from the client that the project will be canceled because of a funding issue. What should she do next?

    a) Try to negotiate with the client and suggest where to find additional funding

    b) Prepare the final project report

    c) Tell the team this is only a temporary setback; it happened before on a similar project, but the problem was cleared shortly.

    d) Ask senior management to talk to the client

22. Which of the following depicts the order of activities in schedule management?

    a) Collect requirements, define scope, and create the WBS

    b) Identify risks, perform qualitative risk analysis, perform quantitative risk analysis, and plan risk responses

    c) Plan schedule management, define activities, sequence activities, estimate activity durations, and develop schedules

    d) Estimate costs and determine budget

23. In the define activities process, work is decomposed into which of the following?

   a) Work packages

   b) WBS

   c) Activities

   d) WBS and activities

24. Carl is a new project manager who is currently in the planning phase of a project. He has defined the activities—what should he do next?

   a) Sequence activities

   b) Estimate costs

   c) Collect requirements

   d) Identify risks

25. The work performed outside of scope and suggested by the project team is called

   a) Gold plating

   b) Work that is necessary

   c) Work that is unnecessary

   d) Scope creep

26. The following are inputs to collect requirements except

   a) Project management plan

   b) Communication management plan

   c) Project documents

   d) EEF

27. Jesse is a new project manager who is currently in the planning phase of a project. He has defined the activities. As a project manager, what did Jesse do before defining the activities?

a) Sequence activities

b) Estimate costs

c) Plan schedule management

d) Identify risks

28. Madison is a project manager responsible for adding a new structure to a building. Of the four types of PDM relationships, which are used most often?

   a) Finish to Start (FS)

   b) Finish to Finish (FF)

   c) Start to Finish (SF)

   d) Start to Start (SS)

29. Jacqueline is a project manager at a local marketing firm. She needs to perform a sequence of activities. Which of the following depicts the order of activities in schedule management?

   a) Collect requirements, define scope, and create WBS

   b) Identify risks, perform qualitative risk analysis, perform quantitative risk analysis, and plan risk responses

   c) Plan schedule management, define activities, sequence activities, estimate activity durations, and develop schedule

   d) Estimate costs and determine budget

30. Which answer best represents the order of plan scope management?

   a) Identify risks, perform qualitative risk analysis, perform quantitative risk analysis, and plan risk responses

   b) Collect requirements, define scope, and create WBS

   c) Plan schedule management, define activities, sequence activities, estimate activity durations, and develop schedule

   d) Estimate costs and determine budget

31. The following are tools and techniques of the develop schedule process except

    a) Schedule compression

    b) Data analysis

    c) Project documents

    d) Critical path method

32. Which is a tool and technique of the plan cost management process?

    a) Alternative analysis

    b) Project documents

    c) Project plan updates

    d) Rolling wave technique

33. Mary is a new project manager. How much will it cost for Mary to complete the project if most likely = $2,000, optimistic = $1,000, and pessimistic = $3,000, using three-point estimation?

    a) $44

    b) $2,000

    c) $2,167

    d) $32

34. The following are tools and techniques that can be used to determine budget except

    a) Expert judgments

    b) Historical information review

    c) Funding limit reconciliation

    d) Business documents

35. Which is an output of the determine budget process?

   a) Cost baseline

   b) Alternative analysis

   c) Project management plan

   d) Voting

36. What is the output of the plan quality management process?

   a) Project management plan

   b) Project documents

   c) Risk management plan

   d) Quality management plan

37. Which best describes the plan quality management process?

   a) The process of identifying quality requirements and standards for the project and its deliverables and documenting how the project will demonstrate compliance with quality requirements and standards

   b) The process of monitoring and recording the results of executing the quality management activities to assess performance and ensure the project outputs are complete, correct, and meet customer requirements

   c) The process of translating the quality management plan into executable quality activities that incorporate the organization's quality policies into the project

   d) None of the above

38. Terry is a new project manager at a telecommunication company. She has a lot of experience in project management to do the necessary work. The process of defining how to estimate, acquire, manage, and utilize physical and team resources is

    a) Develop team

    b) Plan resource management

    c) Organizational theory

    d) Team charter

39. Theodore is a new project manager with minimal experience in acquiring proper resources to do the necessary work. The following tools and techniques can assist Theodore in estimating resources except

    a) Bottom-up estimating

    b) Analogous estimating

    c) Parametric estimating

    d) Resource breakdown structure (RBS)

40. Christian is a project manager at a local marketing firm. He needs to manage the project team to prevent scope creep and gold plating. All the following are inputs to manage a team except

    a) Project management plan

    b) Project documents updates

    c) Work performance reports

    d) Team performance

41. Which is a tool and technique of plan communications management?

    a) Change log

    b) Project management plan

    c) Manage quality

d) Interpersonal and team skills

42. Which answer below best fits the tools and techniques of plan communication management?

   a) Change log

   b) Project management plan

   c) Manage quality

   d) Communication technology

43. Conversations and meetings are part of which tool and technique?

   a) Communications analysis

   b) Communications technology

   c) Communications model

   d) Communications method

44. Of the four types of PDM relationships, which is used least often?

   a) Finish to Start (FS)

   b) Finish to Finish (FF)

   c) Start to Finish (SF)

   d) Start to Start (SS)

45. Which of the following depicts the order of activities in estimate costs?

   a) Collect requirements, define scope, and create WBS

   b) Identify risks, perform qualitative risk analysis, perform quantitative risk analysis, and plan risk responses

   c) Plan schedule management, define activities, sequence activities, estimate activity durations, and develop schedule

   d) Estimate costs and determine budget

46. Which of the following depicts the order of activities in plan risk management?

    a) Collect requirements, define scope, and create WBS

    b) Identify risks, perform qualitative risk analysis, perform quantitative risk analysis, and plan risk responses

    c) Plan schedule management, define activities, sequence activities, estimate activity resources, estimate activity costs, and develop schedule

    d) Estimate costs and determine budget

47. Which is a tool and technique of plan risk management?

    a) Stakeholder analysis

    b) Project documents

    c) Decomposition

    d) Project management plan updates

48. The output of identify risk is

    a) Project management plan

    b) Procurement plan

    c) Project documents

    d) Risk register

49. Which is an output of the plan risk management process?

    a) Project management plan

    b) Communications management plan

    c) Data analysis

    d) Risk management plan

50. A tool and technique that can be used in assessing risk impact is

   a) Project management plan

   b) Project document updates

   c) Risk probability and impact assessment

   d) Risk register

51. Which is an input to the perform qualitative risk analysis process?

   a) Project management plan

   b) Alternative analysis

   c) OPA updates

   d) EEF updates

52. Which answer is the best description of perform quantitative risk analysis?

   a) It is the process of numerically analyzing the effect of identified risks on overall project objects.

   b) It is the process by which we identify risks, perform qualitative risk analysis, perform quantitative risk analysis, and plan risk responses.

   c) It is the process by which we plan schedule management, define activities, sequence activities, estimate activity resources, estimate activity costs, and develop schedules.

   d) It involves estimating costs and determining budget.

53. Which is both an input and output of the process perform quantitative risk analysis?

   a) Risk report

   b) Analysis report

   c) Rolling wave

   d) Decomposition

54. All are tools and techniques of the plan risk responses process except

   a) Expert judgments

   b) Interpersonal and team skills

   c) Contingency response strategy

   d) Change requests

55. Which is a tool or technique of the plan risk response process?

   a) Interpersonal and team skills

   b) Process improvement plan

   c) Project management plan

   d) Quality management plan

56. The process of documenting project procurement decisions, specifying the approach, and identifying potential sellers is

   a) Data analysis

   b) Procurement management plan

   c) Organizational process assets

   d) Plan procurement management

57. The output of the plan procurement management process is

   a) Procurement management plan

   b) Project management plan

   c) Conduct procurement

   d) Control procurement

58. Which answer best describes the plan stakeholder engagement process?

   a) The process of developing approaches to involve project stakeholders based on their needs and expectations, addressing issues, and fostering appropriate stakeholder involvement

b) The process of monitoring project stakeholder relationships and tailoring strategies for engaging stakeholders through the modification of engagement strategies and plans

c) The process of communicating and working with stakeholders to meet their needs and expectations

d) The process of not communicating and working with stakeholders to meet their needs and expectations

59. The output of plan stakeholder engagement is

a) Assumption and constraint analysis

b) Stakeholder engagement plan

c) Project management plan

d) Process improvement plan

60. Deliverables are an output of which process group?

a) Organizational process assets

b) Enterprise environmental factors

c) Final report

d) Direct and manage project work

61. The following are components of tools and techniques in the manage project knowledge process except

a) Knowledge management

b) Information management

c) Interpersonal and team skills

d) Lessons learned register

62. Which of the following is an input to the manage project knowledge process?

    a) Alternative analysis

    b) Deliverables

    c) OPA updates

    d) Project management plan updates

63. Which of the following is an input to the manage quality process?

    a) Quality reports

    b) Quality metrics

    c) Data gathering

    d) Enterprise environmental factors

64. Pepper is a new project manager for TF Banking Services. She is in the process of acquiring resources. All are tools and techniques Pepper can use to aid in her search except

    a) Virtual teams

    b) Multicriteria analysis

    c) Resource management plan

    d) Negotiation

65. What is the correct order of Tuckman's ladder?

    a) Forming, storming, norming, performing, adjourning

    b) Adjourning, forming, storming, norming, performing

    c) Performing, forming, storming, norming, adjourning

    d) Storming, norming, forming, performing, adjourning

66. All of the following are inputs to manage a team except

    a) Project management plan

b) Project documents updates

c) Work performance reports

d) Team performance

67. Which best describes the process to manage communications?

a) Project management plan

b) The process of ensuring timely and appropriate collection, creation, distribution, storage, retrieval, management, monitoring, and the ultimate disposition of project information

c) Work performance reports

d) Team performance

68. Frank is a project manager with Carmon Lip Balm LLC. He and his project team meticulously put together a project plan which captured and strategized for many risks. One of the risks has just materialized. As a project manager, what should Frank do next?

a) Plan risk management

b) Monitor risks

c) Use his interpersonal and team management skills

d) Implement risk responses

69. Debbie is a project manager at Cool Socks Inc. She is in the planning process for a new project and has completed the sequence activities process. The kickoff of the project occurred three months ago. The project team is currently managing the project. As a project manager, what should she do next?

a) Estimate activity durations

b) Close the project

c) Control schedule

d) Identify stakeholders

70. Which of the following is an output of the implement risk response plan process?

    a) Change requests

    b) Data analysis

    c) Approved changes

    d) OPA

71. The process of obtaining seller responses, selecting a seller, and awarding a contract is

    a) Plan procurement management

    b) Conduct procurements

    c) Control procurements

    d) Project procurement management

72. All are tools and techniques to select a seller except

    a) Advertising

    b) Bidder conference

    c) Proposal evaluation

    d) Asking your best friend

73. The process of communicating and working with stakeholders to meet their needs and expectations, address issues, and foster appropriate involvement is

    a) Manage stakeholder engagement

    b) Monitor communications

    c) Manage communications

    d) Monitor stakeholder engagement

74. Which process best exemplifies monitoring and controlling in project integration?

    a) Direct and manage project work

    b) Monitor and control project work

    c) Manage project knowledge

    d) Perform integrated change control

75. Harry is a contractor responsible for the refurbishment of an automobile showroom. The estimated refurbishment cost is $500 per square foot. The total showroom area that needs to be refurbished is 1,000 square feet. Based on his past experience, he knows his team can refurbish 100 square feet per week. How is the project performing?

    a) On schedule and on budget

    b) Behind schedule and over budget

    c) Ahead of schedule and over budget

    d) Behind schedule and ahead of budget

76. Which of the following is a tool and technique of direct and manage project work?

    a) Change requests

    b) PMIS

    c) Project management plan

    d) OPA updates

77. Judy is a superb project manager at her firm. She is currently working on a project in which a fix is necessary. As a project manager, what should Judy do next?

    a) Check the release documents

    b) Notify the sponsor

    c) Evaluate the impact of the change

    d) Implement the risk response plan

78. Judy is a top project manager at her firm. She is currently working on a project in which a fix *might be* necessary. As a project manager, what should Judy do next?

    a) Prevent changes from occurring

    b) Notify the sponsor

    c) Evaluate the impact of the change

    d) Implement the risk response plan

79. What is the output of the validate scope process?

    a) Work performance data

    b) Acceptable deliverables

    c) Verified deliverables

    d) Work performance information

80. All are inputs to control scope except

    a) Scope management plan

    b) Change management plan

    c) Change requests

    d) Scope baseline

81. All are tools and techniques used in the control schedule process except

    a) Critical path method

    b) PMIS

    c) Resource optimization

    d) Change requests

82. Which tool/technique is best for controlling cost and schedule?

    a) EVM

    b) PERT

    c) PMIS

    d) Cost forecast

83. Which tool/technique is best for planning cost and schedule?

    a) EVM

    b) PERT

    c) PMIS

    d) Cost forecast

84. Terri is a new project manager at a manufacturing firm. She currently has completed the planning stage. Her team has begun implementing the work according to the project plan. One of Terri's team members has noticed a problem with her task but has not yet found a fix. What tools can be used to determine the cause of the problem?

    a) Prototypes

    b) An oscilloscope

    c) Fishbone

    d) Bottom-up estimating

85. David is a new project manager for Combo-Wash/Dry Services. He wants to get off to the best start understanding ways to deliver a quality product. David and his team are planning for accuracy in quality. Which of the following tools is one of the seven rules of quality control?

    a) Analysis technique

    b) Cause-and-effect diagram

    c) Data representation

    d) Quality audit

86. Robert is a new project manager at Use It or Lose It! Inc. Robert does not trust his employees to do their jobs, so he must monitor their every action to make sure he gets the results he wants. Robert is practicing

   a) RAM

   b) McGregor's Theory X

   c) Expectancy Theory

   d) McGregor's Theory Y

87. What is the correct order of team development?

   a) Performing, storming, norming, forming, and adjourning

   b) Performing, storming, adjourning, forming, and norming

   c) Forming, norming, storming, performing, and adjourning

   d) Forming, storming, norming, performing, and adjourning

88. Which answer best describes monitor communications?

   a) The process of developing an appropriate approach and plan for project communication activities based on the information needs of each stakeholder, the available organizational assets, and the needs of the project

   b) The document that includes information on staff acquisition and release, resource calendars, recognition and rewards, and compliance and safety

   c) The process of monitoring communications and the process of ensuring the information needs of the project and its stakeholders are met

   d) The process of ensuring the information needs of the project and its stakeholders are met

89. Lydell is a new project manager for Sportsman, Inc. His team consisted of 6 members, including Lydell. Two new members have just been added. What is the number of channels of communication?

   a) 13

   b) 12

c) 15

d) 28

90. Tom is a new project manager for Worldenders Enterprise. Tom's team consisted of 6 members, including Tom. Two new members have just been added. How many more channels of communication are there now

   a) 13

   b) 12

   c) 15

   d) 28

91. Which answer best describes the risk management plan?

   a) It contains all the requirements of the project.

   b) It is the process of defining how to conduct risk management activities for a project.

   c) It is not a desirable choice when managing large projects.

   d) It is used for mapping the probability of each risk occurrence and the impact on project objectives if the risk occurs.

92. Joe is a project manager and has a sponsor who does not like risk, so Joe must identify the risks and list the probability of occurrence. Which answer best describes the probability and impact matrix?

   a) It contains all the requirements of the project.

   b) It is the process of defining how to conduct risk management activities for a project.

   c) It is not a desirable choice when managing large projects.

   d) It is used for mapping the probability of each risk occurrence and the impact on project objectives if the risk occurs.

93. Janine is a longtime project manager at Aspire LLC. She needs to work with the procurement department to secure people with sufficient skills. Which answer best describes the control procurements process?

a) The process of documenting project decisions, specifying the approach, and identifying potential sellers

b) The process of creating templates for the risk management plan, risk register, and risk report

c) The process of managing procurement relationships, monitoring contract performance, making changes and corrections as appropriate, and closing out contracts

d) The process of obtaining seller responses, selecting a seller and awarding a contract

94. Which is a tool or technique of the control procurements process?

a) Project management plan

b) Communication management plan

c) Change requests

d) Claims administration

95. Kazem is a project manager with many years of experience. He knows how important customer communication and satisfaction are to how a project is managed. What is the best definition of the monitor stakeholder engagement process?

a) The process of identifying project stakeholders regularly and analyzing and documenting relevant information regarding their interests, involvement, interdependencies, influence, and impact on project success

b) The process of communicating and working with stakeholders to meet their needs and expectations, address issues, and foster appropriate stakeholder engagement

c) The process of providing an overview of the project stakeholder management process

d) The process of monitoring project stakeholder relationships and tailoring strategies for engaging stakeholders through the modification of engagement strategies and plans

96. The following describe monitor stakeholder engagement except

a) Managing stakeholder relationships

b) Ignoring the stakeholders until they go away

c) Engaging with the stakeholders

d) Formulating strategies with the stakeholders

97. Susan is a first-time project manager; however, she is excited to make a good impression. Halfway through her project, Susan gets an email from the client that the project will be canceled because of a funding issue. What should she do next?

a) Try to negotiate with the client and suggest where to find additional funding

b) Prepare the final project report

c) Tell the team this is only a temporary setback; it happened before on a similar project, but the problem was cleared shortly.

d) Ask senior management to talk to the client

98. Which is a tool and technique of the close project or phase process?

a) Regression analysis

b) OPA

c) EEF

d) Deliverables

99. Judy is a superb project manager at her firm. She is currently working on a project in which a fix is necessary. As a project manager, what should Judy do next?

a) Check the release documents

b) Notify the sponsor

c) Evaluate the impact of the change

d) Implement the risk response plan

100. Judy is a top project manager at her firm. She is currently working on a project in which a fix *might be* necessary. As a project manager, what should Judy do next?

   a) Prevent changes from occurring

   b) Notify the sponsor

   c) Evaluate the impact of the change

   d) Implement the risk response plan

101. What is the output of the validate scope process?

   a) Work performance data

   b) Acceptable deliverables

   c) Verified deliverables

   d) Work performance information

102. All are inputs to control scope except

   a) Scope management plan

   b) Change management plan

   c) Change requests

   d) Scope baseline

103. All tools and techniques used in the control schedule process except

   a) Critical path method

   b) PMIS

   c) Resource optimization

   d) Change requests

104. Which tool/technique is best for controlling cost and schedule?

   a) EVM

   b) PERT

   c) PMIS

   d) Cost forecast

105. Which tool/technique is best for planning cost and schedule?

   a) EVM

   b) PERT

   c) PMIS

   d) Cost forecast

106. Terri is a new project manager at a manufacturing firm. She currently has completed the planning stage. Her team has begun implementing the work according to the project plan. One of Terri's team members has noticed a problem with her task but has not yet found a fix. What tools can be used to determine the cause of the problem?

   a) Prototypes

   b) An oscilloscope

   c) Fishbone

   d) Bottom-up estimating

107. David is a new project manager for Dog Dispenser Corp. He wants to get off to the best start understanding ways to deliver a quality product. David and his team are planning for accuracy in quality. Which of the following tools is one of the seven rules of quality control?

   a) Analysis technique

   b) Cause-and-effect diagram

   c) Data representation

   d) Quality audit

108. Robert is a new project manager at Use It or Lose It! Inc., He does not trust his employees to do their jobs, so he must monitor their every action to make sure he gets the results he wants. Robert is practicing

    a) RAM

    b) McGregor's Theory X

    c) Expectancy Theory

    d) McGregor's Theory Y

109. What is the correct order of team development?

    a) Performing, storming, norming, forming, and adjourning

    b) Performing, storming, adjourning, forming, and norming

    c) Forming, norming, storming, performing, and adjourning

    d) Forming, storming, norming, performing, and adjourning

110. Which answer best describes monitor communications?

    a) The process of developing an appropriate approach and plan for project communication activities based on the information needs of each stakeholder, the available organizational assets, and the needs of the project

    b) The document that includes information on staff acquisition and release, resource calendars, recognition and rewards, and compliance and safety

    c) The process of monitoring communications and the process of ensuring the information needs of the project and its stakeholders are met

    d) The process of ensuring the information needs of the project and its stakeholders are met

111. Tom is a new project manager for World Force Inc. Tom's team consisted of 6 members, including Tom; 2 new members have just been added. What is the number of channels of communications now?

    a) 13

    b) 12

    c) 15

    d) 28

112. Tom is a new project manager for World Force Inc. Tom's team consisted of 6 members, including Tom; 2 new members have just been added. How many more channels of communication are there now?

    a) 13

    b) 12

    c) 15

    d) 28

113. Which of the following depicts the order of activities in cost management?

    a) Collect requirements, define scope, and create WBS

    b) Identify risks, perform qualitative risk analysis, perform quantitative risk analysis, and plan risk responses

    c) Plan schedule management, define activities, sequence activities, estimate activity resources, estimate activity costs, and develop schedule

    d) Estimate costs and determine budget

114. Joe is a project manager and has a sponsor who does not like risk, so Joe must identify the risks and list the probability of occurrence. Which answer best describes the probability and impact matrix?

    a) It contains all the requirements of the project.

    b) It is the process of defining how to conduct risk management activities for a project.

    c) It is not a desirable choice when managing large projects.

    d) It is used for mapping the probability of each risk occurrence and the impact on project objectives if the risk occurs.

115. Janine is a longtime project manager at Aspire LLC. She needs to work with the procurement department to secure people with sufficient skills. Which answer best describes the control procurements process?

    a) The process of documenting project decisions, specifying the approach, and identifying potential sellers

    b) The process of creating templates for the risk management plan, risk register, and risk report

    c) The process of managing procurement relationships, monitoring contract performance, making changes and corrections as appropriate, and closing out contracts

    d) The process of obtaining seller responses, selecting a seller, and awarding a contract

116. The project management plan plans the overall activities of the project and contains detailed requirements of the project. The SOW is the statement of work, which contains the objects of the project. The project charter contains the high-level requirements of the project. All are inputs to the identify stakeholders process except

    a) Project charter

    b) EEF

    c) Expert judgments

    d) Organizational process assets

117. Which is a tool or technique of the control procurements process?

   a) Project management plan

   b) Communication management plan

   c) Change requests

   d) Claims administration

118. Kazem is a project manager with many years of experience. He knows how important customer communication and satisfaction are to how a project is managed. What is the best definition of the monitor stakeholder engagement process?

   a) The process of identifying project stakeholders regularly and analyzing and documenting relevant information regarding their interests, involvement, interdependencies, influence, and impact on project success

   b) The process of communicating and working with stakeholders to meet their needs and expectations, address issues, and foster appropriate stakeholder engagement

   c) The process of providing an overview of the project stakeholder management process

   d) The process of monitoring project stakeholder relationships and tailoring strategies for engaging stakeholders through the modification of engagement strategies and plans

119. The following describe monitor stakeholder engagement except

   a) Managing stakeholder relationships

   b) Ignoring the stakeholder until they go away

   c) Engaging with the stakeholders

   d) Formulating strategies with the stakeholders

120. Which is a tool and technique of the close project or phase process?

   a) Regression analysis

   b) OPA

   c) EEF

   d) Deliverables

121. Senior management is attempting to decide on which project to invest. Which one would you recommend?

    a) It has a present value of $1,157.00.

    b) The payback period is four years.

    c) The net present value will be -$523.03.

    d) IRR will be 7.93%.

122. All the following are inputs to the develop project charter process except

    a) SOW

    b) Enterprise environmental factors

    c) Organizational process assets

    d) Data gathering

123. The following are part of the closing process except

    a) Obtain stakeholder satisfaction

    b) Release the team

    c) EEF

    d) Prepare the final project report

124. The sponsor has accepted all deliverables of the project. As a project manager, what would you do next?

    a) Release the team

    b) Gain formal acceptance

    c) Document lessons learned

    d) Close the project

125. The following are part of the closing process except

    a) Obtain stakeholder satisfaction

b) Release the team

c) EEF updates

d) Prepare final project report

126. The outputs to develop project charter are

   a) Project management plan and requirements plan

   b) Project charter and assumptions log

   c) Quality management plan and change management plan

   d) Stakeholder management plan

127. All are inputs to identify stakeholder group except

   a) Project charter

   b) EEF

   c) Expert judgment

   d) OPA

128. All describe a project charter except

   a) Formally authorizes the existence of a project

   b) Provides project manager the authority to apply organizational resources to the project

   c) States the deliverables of the project

   d) States the details of project deliverables

129. Which best identifies the monitor risks process?

   a) The process of monitoring the implementation of the agreed-upon risk response plan, tracking identified risks, analyzing new risks, and evaluating the risk process

   b) The process of formalizing acceptance of the completed project deliverables

   c) The process of tracking, reviewing, and reporting the overall progress to meet performance objectives defined in the project management plan

   d) Data analysis

130. Joe is a project manager who has a sponsor who does not like risk, so Joe must identify the risk and list the probability of occurrence. Which answer best describes the risk management plan?

a) It is all the requirements of the project.

b) It is the process of defining how to conduct risk management activities for a project.

c) It is not a desirable choice when managing large projects.

d) It is a grid for mapping the probability of each risk occurrence and the impact on project objectives if the risk occurs.

131. Which best describes the process plan scope management?

a) The process of developing a document that formally authorizes the existence of a project and provides the project manager with the authority to apply organizational resources to project activities.

b) The process of how the project and product scope will be defined, validated and controlled throughout the project.

c) The process of developing detailed descriptions of the project and products. This is what the project includes and excludes.

d) The process of estimating the number of work periods needed to complete activities with the estimated resources.

132. All are contained in the define scope process except

a) What the project includes and excludes

b) The output is the project scope statement

c) A detailed description of the project and products

d) How the project and product scope will be validated

133. Joe is a project manager who has a sponsor who does not like risk, so Joe must identify the risk and list the probability of occurrence. Which answer best describes the probability impact matrix?

a) It is all the requirements of the project.

b) It is the process of defining how to conduct risk management activities for a project.

c) It is not a desirable choice when managing large projects.

d) It is a grid for mapping the probability of each risk occurrence and the impact on project objectives if the risk occurs.

134. Which best describes the define scope process?

a) The process of developing a document that formally authorizes the existence of a project and provides the project manager with authority to apply organizational resources to project activities

b) The process of how the project and product scope will be defined, validated, and controlled throughout the project

c) The process of developing detailed descriptions of the project and products, which is what the project includes and excludes

d) The process of estimating the number of work periods needed to complete activities with the estimated resources

135. All the following describe estimate activity durations except

a) Determine risks

b) The process of estimating work periods

c) The work periods to complete activities

d) Estimated resources to complete activities

136. Which answer best describes the manage communications process?

a) The process of developing an appropriate approach and plan for project communication activities based on the information needs of each stakeholder, the available organizational assets, and the needs of the project

b) The document that includes information on staff acquisition and release, resource calendars, recognition, rewards, compliance, and safety

c) The process of ensuring timely and appropriate collection, creation, distribution, storage, retrieval, management, monitoring, and the ultimate disposition of project information

d) The process of ensuring the information needs of the project and its stakeholders

137. Which answer best describes monitor communications?

a) The process of developing an appropriate approach and plan for project communication activities based on the information needs of each stakeholder, the available organizational assets, and the needs of the project

b) The document that includes information on staff acquisition and release, resource calendars, recognition, rewards, compliance, and safety

c) The process of ensuring timely and appropriate collection, creation, distribution, storage, retrieval, management, monitoring, and the ultimate disposition of project information

d) The process of ensuring the information needs of the project and its stakeholders are met

138. Tom is a new project manager for World Force Inc. His team consisted of 6 members, including Tom; 2 new members have just been added. What is the number of channels of communication?

a) 13

b) 12

c) 15

d) 28

139. Tom is a new project manager for World Force Inc. Tom's team consisted of 6 members, including Tom; 2 new members have just been added. How many more channels of communication are there now?

a) 13

b) 12

c) 15

d) 28

140. Which best describes the estimate activity durations process?

a) The process of developing a document that formally authorizes the existence of a project and provides the project manager with authority to apply organizational resources to project activities

b) The process of how the project and product scope will be defined, validated, and controlled throughout the project

c) The process of developing detailed descriptions of the project and products. This is what the project includes and excludes

d) The process of estimating the number of work periods needed to complete activities with the estimated resources

141. The output of develop project management plan is

a) Project charter

b) EEF

c) Project management plan

d) OPA

142. The outputs of plan scope management are

a) Scope management plan and requirements management plan

b) Quality management plan and process improvement plan

c) Resource management plan and resource breakdown structure

d) Risk management plan and risk improvement plan

143. The _____ are influences out of the project manager's control.

a) Enterprise environmental factors

b) OPA

c) Evolution environmental factors

d) Extreme environmental factors

144. _____ are factors internal to the organization that affect the project.

   a) Optimal process assets

   b) Omni process assets

   c) Organization process assets

   d) Optical process assets

145. Susan is a new project manager for Bikes Incorporated. She wants to get off to the best start understanding ways to deliver a quality product. Susan and her team are planning for accuracy in quality. They can check for quality using each of these rules of quality control except

   a) Control chart

   b) Quality audit

   c) Pareto chart

   d) Scatter diagram

146. Aaron is the project manager at a communication company that builds precision devices. His team has produced a device that is consistently measured with the same output value with little scattering, but the output is not close to the true value. This is an example of what?

   a) Accuracy

   b) Cost of quality

   c) Prevention over inspection

   d) Precision

147. What is the best definition of control resources?

   a) The process of monitoring the status of the project and product scope and managing changes to the scope baseline

   b) The process of monitoring project costs to the cost baseline

   c) The process of monitoring and recording the results of executing the quality management plan activities to assess performance and ensure project outputs are complete, correct, and meet customer expectations

d) The process of ensuring the physical resources assigned and allocated to the project are available as planned versus actual utilization of resources and taking corrective actions as necessary

148. Robert is a new project manager at Use It or Lose It! Inc. Robert does not trust his employees to do their jobs, so he must monitor their every action to make sure he gets the results he wants. Robert is practicing

   a) RAM

   b) McGregor's Theory X

   c) Expectancy Theory

   d) McGregor's Theory Y

149. What is the correct order of team development?

   a) Performing, storming, norming, forming, and adjourning

   b) Performing, storming, adjourning, forming, and norming

   c) Forming, norming, storming, performing, and adjourning

   d) Forming, storming, norming, performing, and adjourning

150. What are the least and most desired methods of conflict resolution?

   a) Avoidance and collaboration

   b) Compromise and smoothing

   c) Force and avoidance

   d) Compromise and collaboration

151. The document that includes information on staff acquisition and release, resource calendars, recognition, rewards, compliance, and safety is

   a) Resource plan

   b) Project management plan

c) Staffing management plan

d) Project resource plan

152. Deliverables are an output of which process group?

a) OPA

b) EEF

c) Final report

d) Direct and manage project work

153. The following are inputs to the direct and manage project work process except

a) Approved changes

b) Project management plan

c) Deliverables

d) OPA

154. Which of the following best describes the direct and manage project work process?

a) The process of leading and performing the work defined in the project plan and implementing the approved changes to achieve the project objectives

b) The process of improving the competencies of team members and the overall team environment to enhance project performance

c) The process of obtaining seller responses, selecting sellers, and awarding a contract

d) The process of documenting project decisions, specifying the approach, and identifying potential sellers

155. Interpersonal and team skills involve all except

a) Active listening

b) Expert judgment

c) Networking

d) Political awareness

156. The following are a part of tools and techniques in manage project knowledge except

   a) Knowledge management

   b) Information management

   c) Interpersonal and team skills

   d) Lessons learned register

157. Which process best exemplifies monitoring and control in project integration?

   a) Direct and manage project work

   b) Monitor and control project work

   c) Manage project knowledge

   d) Perform integrated change control

158. What is the best definition of monitoring and control?

   a) The process of tracking, reviewing, and reporting the overall progress to meet performance objectives defined in the project management plan

   b) The process of reviewing all change requests; approving changes; managing changes to deliverables, project documents and the project management plan; and communicating decisions

   c) The process of formalizing acceptance of the completed project deliverables

   d) The process of monitoring the status of the project and product scope and managing changes to the scope baseline

159. Judy is a top project manager at her firm. She is currently working on a project in which a fix is necessary. As a project manager, what should Judy do next?

   a) Check the release documents

b) Notify the sponsor

c) Evaluate the impact of the change

d) Implement the risk response plan

160. What is the best definition of perform integrated change control?

a) The process of tracking, reviewing, and reporting the overall progress to meet performance objectives defined in the project management plan

b) The process of reviewing all change requests; approving changes; managing changes to deliverables, project documents, and the project management plan; and communicating decisions

c) The process of formalizing acceptance of the completed project deliverables

d) The process of monitoring the status of the project and product scope and managing changes to the scope baseline

161. All are tools and techniques of the perform integrated change control process except

a) Meetings

b) Expert judgment

c) Project management updates

d) Multicriteria decision analysis

162. Of the four types of conflict management, which is considered the worst outcome?

a) Avoid

b) Force

c) Compromise

d) Collaborate

163. Manage communication is a process of which knowledge area?

a) Plan communications management

b) Project quality management

c) Manage communications is not a process

d) Project communications management

164. Which best describes the manage communications process?

a) PMP

b) The process of ensuring timely and appropriate collection, creation, distribution, storage, retrieval, management, monitoring, and the ultimate disposition of project information

c) Work performance reports

d) Team performance

165. All are traits of interpersonal and team skills except

a) Active listening

b) Conflict management

c) Political awareness

d) Change requests

166. Frank is a project manager with Carmon Lip Balm LLC. He and his project team meticulously put together a project plan that captured and strategized for many risks. One of them has just materialized. As a project manager, what should Frank do next?

a) Plan risk management

b) Monitor risks

c) Use his interpersonal skills and team management

d) Implement risk responses

167. Which of the following correctly defines implement risk responses?

a) The process of implementing the agreed-upon risk response

b) The process of obtaining seller responses, selecting sellers, and awarding a contract

c) The process of monitoring the status of the project and product scope and managing changes

to the scope baseline

d) The process of improving the competencies of team members and the overall team environment to enhance project performance

168. Which of the following is an output of implement risk response?

a) Expert judgment

b) Risk management plan

c) Interpersonal skills

d) Change requests

169. The output of plan risk management is

a) Cost management plan

b) Risk management plan

c) Scope baseline

d) Risk baseline

170. Which process best describes identify risk?

a) The process of identifying individual risks as well as sources of overall project risks and documenting their characteristics

b) Data analysis and interpersonal skills

c) Project management plan

d) The process of defining how to estimate, acquire, manage, and utilize physical and team resources

171. A tool and technique that can be used in assessing risk impact is

a) Project management plan

b) Project document updates

c) Risk probability and impact assessment

d) Risk register

172. Which of the following best describes perform qualitative risk analysis?

    a) The process of prioritizing individual project risks for further analysis by assessing their probability of occurrence and impact

    b) The process of numerically analyzing the effect of identified risks on overall project objects

    c) Identify risks, perform qualitative risk analysis, perform quantitative risk analysis, and plan risk responses

    d) Plan schedule management, define activities, sequence activities, estimate activity resources, estimate activity costs, and develop schedule

173. Which answer is the best description of perform quantitative risk analysis?

    a) The process of numerically analyzing the effect of identified risks on overall project objects

    b) Identify risks, perform qualitative risk analysis, perform quantitative risk analysis, and plan risk responses

    c) Plan schedule management, define activities, sequence activities, estimate activity resources, estimate activity costs, and develop schedule

    d) Estimate costs and determine budget

174. The following are tools and techniques to perform quantitative risk analysis except

    a) Simulations

    b) EEF

    c) Tornado diagram

    d) Facilitation

175. The following are strategies for negative risks/threats except

 a) Avoid

 b) Mitigate

 c) Share

 d) Transfer

176. The following are strategies for positive risks/threats except

 a) Exploit

 b) Mitigate

 c) Share

 d) Enhance

177. All are tools and techniques to plan risk responses except

 a) Expert judgment

 b) Interpersonal and team skills

 c) Contingency response strategy

 d) Change requests

178. Senior management called the project manager into a meeting to talk about cost concerns. Senior management wants the project manager to take as much time as needed. However, they do want the most accurate estimate of the current cost. Which cost management tool and technique will provide the most accurate cost estimates?

 a) Bottom-up estimating

 b) Analogous estimating

 c) Parametric estimating

 d) EVM

179. Terri is a new project manager at a manufacturing firm. Senior management wants her to determine the most accurate costs and the time the project will take. Terri has been instructed to take as long as she needs. What tool and technique would Terri use to satisfy this requirement from senior management?

    a) Prototypes

    b) An oscilloscope

    c) Fishbone

    d) Bottom-up estimating

180. Jim is a top-level project manager at a construction company. During the implementation phase of a project, there was an atypical issue that caused a minor setback for Jim and his team. Then BAC = 150, EV =10, PV = 12, AC = 11. What is the EAC of the project?

    a) 132

    b) 120

    c) 151

    d) 156.2

181. Richard is a junior project manager at a construction company. During the implementation phase of a project, there was an atypical issue that caused a minor setback for Richard and his team. Then BAC = 120, EV =10, PV = 12, AC = 11. What is the ETC of the project?

    a) 132

    b) 120

    c) 110

    d) 156.2

182. Kimberly is a top-level project manager at a construction company. For her project, BAC = 120, EV = 10, PV = 12, AC = 11. What is the EAC forecast earning of the project?

   a) 132

   b) 120

   c) 110.833

   d) 156.2

183. Which is a part of the cost of conformance?

   a) Rework

   b) Testing

   c) Internal failure costs

   d) Liabilities

184. Which is a part of the cost of nonconformance?

   a) Training

   b) Destructive testing loss

   c) Inspections

   d) Lost business

185. All are a part of preventive costs except

   a) Time to do it right

   b) Training

   c) Inspections

   d) Document processes

186. Which is a part of the cost of conformance?

    a) Rework

    b) Testing

    c) Internal failure costs

    d) Liabilities

187. Which is a part of the cost of nonconformance?

    a) Training

    b) Destructive testing loss

    c) Inspections

    d) Lost business

188. All are a part of preventive costs except

    a) Time to do it right

    b) Training

    c) Inspections

    d) Document processes

189. Which of the following is not one of the seven basic quality tools?

    a) Flowcharts

    b) Control charts

    c) Risk management

    d) Check sheets

190. Which answer best describes a communications plan?

   a) The process of developing an appropriate approach and plan for project communication activities based on the information needs of each stakeholder, the available organizational assets, and the needs of the project

   b) The document that includes information on staff acquisition and release, resource calendars, recognition, rewards, compliance, and safety

   c) The process of ensuring timely and appropriate collection, creation, distribution, storage, retrieval, management, monitoring, and the ultimate disposition of project information

   d) The process of ensuring the information needs of the project and its stakeholders

191. What is the output of plan communications management?

   a) Project management plan

   b) Project documents

   c) Communications management plan

   d) Communication baseline

192. What tool and technique can the project manager use to determine the number of communication channels?

   a) EV - AC

   b) PERT

   c) AC + (BAC - EV)

   d) N (n + 1) / 2

193. As a project manager, you are planning the activities in the project schedule. Which of the following depicts the order of activities in risk management?

   a) Collect requirements, define scope, and create WBS

   b) Identify risks, perform qualitative risk analysis, perform quantitative risk analysis, and plan risk responses

c) Plan schedule management, define activities, sequence activities, estimate activity resources, estimate activity costs, and develop schedule

d) Estimate costs and determine budget

194. What is the output of plan risk management?

a) Communication management plan

b) Configuration management plan

c) Home improvement plan

d) Risk management plan

195. What description best identifies plan risk management?

a) The process of defining how to conduct risk management activities

b) The process of using existing knowledge and creating new knowledge to achieve the project's objectives and contribute to organizational learning

c) The process of translating the quality management plan into executable project activities that incorporate the organization's quality policies

d) Risk baseline

196. Which process best describes plan communications management?

a) The process of numerically analyzing the combined effects of identified individual project risks

b) The process of developing an approach and plan for project communications activities based on the information needs of each stakeholder and the project

c) Plan-Do-Check-Act

d) The process of prioritizing individual project risks for further analysis by assessing their probability of occurrence and impact

197. Rajish is a new project manager for OpenSystem LLC. Rajish wants to get off to the best start understanding the project, people, and environment. Interpersonal and team skills is a tool and technique of which process?

    a) Meetings

    b) Develop project charter

    c) OPA

    d) Planning

198. All the following are inputs to develop project charter except

    a) SOW

    b) EEF

    c) OPA

    d) Data analysis

199. Henry is a project manager with many years of experience. He wants to understand the objectives of the sponsor of this project. The outputs to develop project charter are

    a) Project management plan and requirements plan

    b) Project charter and assumptions log

    c) Quality management plan and change management plan

    d) Stakeholder management plan

200. What is the output of the plan quality management process?

    a) Project management plan

    b) Project documents

    c) Risk management plan

    d) Quality management plan

Mock Exam Two – Retake Test for Higher Score
200 Questions—4 Hours Solutions

1.   Answer: *c*. No, because "the required return on investments is 10%."

2.   Answer: *c*.

Estimate at Completion (typical, steady-state or continuous)	(BAC / CPI) = 555,555.56 dollars

3.   Answer: *b*. Develop project charter is the only process in this list. Meetings is a tool and technique for many processes. Organizational process assets are input to many processes, and planning is a process group.

4.   Answer: *d*. The communication plan is a document for planning the communication of the project.

5.   Answer: *c*. Keep informed.

6.   Answer: *c*. Project charter, EEF, and OPA are all inputs to the process.

7.   Answer: *b*. The project management plan is the output of the process, not a tool and technique.

8.   Answer: *d*. The project charter contains the objectives and other information needed to create the PMP. Data gathering and inspection are tools and techniques. The project management plan is the output of the process.

9.   Answer: *a*. Enterprise environmental factors are influences out of the project manager's control. Organizational process assets are factors within the organization's and project team's control. And *c* and *d* are not part of the project management plan.

10.   Answer: *c*. The project charter does not contain detailed information of any type. Detailed information is found in the project management plan.

      Note: This is a typical PMP exam question. The problem has nothing to do with the answer. Focus on the "ask" which is "All are found in the project charter except."

11. Answer: *a*. Scope management plan and requirements management plan are outputs to the plan scope management process. The project charter and project management plan are outputs of earlier stages. Answers *c* and *d* are plan quality management and plan risk management, respectively.

12. Answer: *b*. The benefits management plan is a document outlining the activities necessary for achieving the planned benefits. It shows a timeline and the tools and resources necessary to ensure the benefits are fully realized over time.

13. Answer: *b*. The OPA and project management plan are inputs. Data analysis is a tool and technique.

14. Answer: *a*. Answer *b* describes the plan scope management process, *c* describes the create WBS process, and *d* best describes monitoring and controlling a process.

15. Answer: *d*. Gold-plating is work outside the scope of the project deemed necessary by the project team. Answers *b* and *c* are general concepts that help narrow down the scope of the project.

16. Answer: *a*. Code of account is A numbering system used to uniquely identify each component of the work breakdown structure. A chart of accounts is a created list of the accounts used by an organization to define each class of items for which money or its equivalent is spent or received. Control charts are a statistical process control tool used to determine if a manufacturing or business process is in a state of control.

17. Answer: *c*. Organizational process assets is an input. But *a*, *b*, and *d* are all tools and techniques.

18. Answer: *b*. Answer *a* describes project management plan, and *c* is create WBS.

19. Answer: *c*. Option *a* describes scope management, *b* describes defining risk management, and *d* is cost management.

20. Answer: *a*. Choice *b* describes plan risk management, and *c* is direct and manage projects. As stated earlier, knowing the sequences of the planning group in all knowledge areas is crucial to passing the PMP exam.

21. Answer: *b*. Susan should immediately begin the closing process. Prepare final report is the only answer that is part of the closing process.

22. Answer: *c*. Option *a* describes scope management, *b* defines risk management, and *d* is cost management.

23. Answer: *c*. Decomposition into activities occurs in the define activities process. Decomposition into work packages occurs in the create WBS process. Answer *d* is a typical PMP exam trick to trip you up because it is combining processes like WBS and activities.

24. Answer: *a*. The question clearly states that Jason is still in the planning process, so what process comes after sequence that is in the list of choices and part on the planning process group. Define activities, sequence activities, estimate activity duration, et cetera. Knowing the order of processes in the planning process group is crucial to passing the exam. Memorize the order of processes in the planning process group!

25. Answer: *a*. Gold plating is the practice of making changes to a project that are outside of the original agreed-upon scope.

26. Answer: *b*. The communication management plan is not an input to collect requirements. The communication management plan is a guide on how the project team will send, receive, distribute, store, and dispose of communication material.

27. Answer: *c*. See the order of processes in the planning process group.

28. Answer: *a*. Finish to start (FS) is the most commonly used.

29. Answer: *c*. Answer 'a' is project scope management, answer 'b' is Project risk management and answer 'd' is Project cost management

30. Answer: *b*. Answer 'a' is project risk management, answer 'c' is project schedule management and answer 'd' is project cost management

31. Answer: *c*. Project documents are inputs to several processes

32. Answer: *a*. Project documents is an input, project plan updates is an output, and rolling wave is a technique in another process.

33. Answer: *b*. 1000+2000(4) + 3000 / 6=12000

    12000 / 6=2000

34. Answer: *d*. Expert judgments, historical information review, and funding limit reconciliation are all tools and techniques that can be used to determine spending budget.

35. Answer: *a*. Choices *b*, *c*, and *d* are not outputs.

36. Answer: *d*. Choice *a* is an output for develop project plan, *c* is an output for plan risk management, and *b* is not the output for the plan quality management process.

37. Answer: *a*. Choice *b* is monitoring quality, *c* is manage quality, and *d* is not the answer.

38. Answer: *b*. Develop team is the process of improving competencies, team member interaction, and overall team environment to enhance project performance. A team charter is a document that is developed in a group setting that clarifies team direction while establishing boundaries.

39. Answer: *d*. Resource breakdown structure is not used to estimate resources. In project management, the resource breakdown structure is a hierarchical list of resources related by function and resource type that is used to facilitate planning and controlling of project work.

40. Answer: *d*. Team Performance Assessment is defined as teamwork which is key to effective performance in any work group and is a tool and technique.

41. Answer: *d*. Choice *b* is an input, *c* is process, and *a* is an output.

42. Answer: *d*. Change log is an output; project management plan is an input and manage quality is a process.

43. Answer: *b*. Communication technology consists includes shared portals, video and conferencing, chats, databases, social media, email, and websites. Communications model includes encoding and decoding of messages. Communication analysis does not exist in pmbok 6th. Communications requirements analysis combines communications types and formats as needed to maximize value of the information for project stakeholders.

44. Answer: *c*. Start to finish (SF) is very rarely used.

45. Answer: *d*. Estimate costs. 'b' is project risk management, 'c' is project schedule management and 'd' is project cost management.

46. Answer: *b*. Identify risks, perform qualitative risk analysis, perform quantitative risk analysis, and plan risk responses.

47. Answer: *a*. Project documents is an input, decomposition is a tool and technique of create WBS, and define activities and project management plan updates is an output of other processes.

48. Answer: *d*. a, b, and c are inputs to other processes.

49. Answer: *d*. Answers *a* and *b* are outputs to develop project plan and plan communication management, respectively; *c* is a tool and technique to other processes.

50. Answer: *c*. Risk probability and impact assessment. Project management plan is a document to follow to track project progress. Project document updates include many other documents. Risk register is a document of identified risks.

51. Answer: *a*. Project management plan is an input this process. Alternative analysis is a tool and technique, OPA updates and EEF updates can be output to processes

52. Answer: *a*. It is the process of numerically analyzing the effect of identified risks on overall project objects.

53. Answer: *a*. Risk report. Rolling wave and decomposition are tool and techniques

54. Answer: *d*. Change requests is an output to processes in monitoring and control process group and input to direct and manage project work process.

55. Answer: *a*. Interpersonal skills. Process improvement plan, project management plan and quality management plan are inputs and outputs to their respective processes.

56. Answer: *Plan procurement management*. Data analysis is a tool and technique, Organizational process assets is an input and procurement management plan define activities to be undertaken during the procurement process such as the type of bidding and how the project is funded.

57. Answer: *a*. Procurement management plan. Project management plan is the output of develop project management plan. Conduct procurement and Control procurement are process in the execute process group and monitor and control process group respectively.

58. Answer: *a*. The process of developing approaches to involve project stakeholders based on their needs and expectations, addressing issues, and fostering appropriate stakeholder involvement.

59. Answer: *b*. Stakeholder engagement plan

60. Answer: *d*. Direct and manage project work. Organizational process assets and enterprise environmental factors are inputs to many process groups. Final report is an output of the close project or phase process group.

61. Answer: *d*. The lessons learned register is an input.

62. Answer *b*. Choice *a* is a tool and technique of another process; *c* and *d* are outputs to other processes.

63. Answer: *b*. Quality reports is an output; enterprise environmental factors is not an input in this process, and data gathering is a tool and technique.

64. Answer: *c*. Resource management plan is a document created by the process plan resource management.

65. Answer: *a*. Forming, storming, norming, performing, adjourning is the correct order.

66. Answer: *b*. Project documents updates is an output.

67. Answer: *b*. The process of ensuring timely and appropriate collection, creation, distribution, storage, retrieval, management, monitoring, and the ultimate disposition of project information

68. Answer: *d*. Implement risk responses. The question clearly states ". project team meticulously put together a project plan which captured and strategized for many risks." The risk has been monitored from start of the project and has been ongoing. Once the risk materializes then the project manager must implement the risk responses.

69. Answer: *c*. the project is clearly in the execute phase of the project. The project manager has already estimate durations because the project has entered the execute phase. There is no mention of project close or cancellation. Identifying stakeholders is going on throughout the life cycle. The best answer is control schedule.

70. Answer: *a*. Data analysis is a tool and technique of most processes. Approved changes are an output to performed integrated change control and an input to direct and manage project work. OPA is an input to most processes.

71. Answer: *b*. Conduct procurements is the process of obtaining seller responses, selecting a seller, and awarding a contract. The key benefit of this process is that it provides alignment of internal and external stakeholder expectations through established agreements.

72. Answer: *d*. This is an easy one. Asking your best friend may work in real-world, but always wrong on the PMP exam.

73. Answer: *a*. Manage stakeholder engagement. Monitor communications is reading emails, answering phone calls and responding to chats in social media. Manage communications is the process of creating, collecting, distributing, storing, retrieving, and the ultimate disposition of project information in accordance to the communications management plan.

74. Answer: *b*. Monitor and control project work. Direct and Manage Project Work is the process of leading and performing the work defined in the project management plan and implementing approved changes to achieve the project's objectives. Manage Project Knowledge is the process of using existing knowledge and creating new knowledge to achieve the project's objectives and contribute to organization's learning. Perform Integrated Change Control is the process of reviewing all change requests; approving changes and managing changes to deliverables, organizational process assets, project documents, and the project management plan; and communicating their disposition.

75. Answer: *c.* Ahead of schedule and over budget

Cost Variance	(EV – AC) = (25,000.00) dollars
Schedule Variance	(EV - PV) = 25,000.00 dollars

76. Answer: *b.* change requests can be an input or output, project management plan is a document, and OPA updates is an output.

77. Answer: *c.* Evaluate the impact of the change. Review the order of the closing process.

78. Answer: *a.* Prevent changes from occurring if possible. If change cannot be prevented, then evaluate the impact of the change.

79. Answer: *b.* Work performance information

80. Answer: *c.* Change requests is an output to control scope.

81. Answer: *d.* Change requests can be an output or input

82. Answer: *c.* Project management software because costs and schedule can be updated automatically and provides project simulation.

83. Answer: *b.* PERT stands for Program Evaluation Review Technique. PERT is a project management planning tool used to calculate the amount of time it will take to realistically finish a project.

84. Answer: *c.* Fishbone. Prototyping is a method of obtaining early feedback on requirements by providing a model of the expected product before building it. Bottom-up estimating is a project management technique in which the people who are going to do the work take part in the estimating process

85. Answer: *b.* Cause-and-effect diagram

86. Answer: *b.* McGregor's Theory X assumes that the typical worker has little ambition, avoids responsibility, and is individual-goal oriented. McGregor's Theory Y assumes employees are

568

internally motivated, enjoy their job, and work to better themselves without a direct reward in return.

87. Answer: *d.* Forming, storming, norming, performing, and adjourning

88. Answer: *c.* The process of monitoring communications and the process of ensuring the information needs of the project and its stakeholders are met.

89. Answer: *d.* The communication channel formula is n (n + 1) / 2. (Where n = the number of people on the project). 6 + 2 = 8. 8(7) = 56. 56 / 2 = 28.

90. Answer: *a.* The communication channel formula is n x (n - 1)/2. (Where n = the number of people on the project). Previous channels for 6 members. 6x(6-1)/2 = 6x5/2 = 15. Add 2 members. Additional channels = 8x(8-1)/2 = (56/2) = 28. More Channels = (Additional channels - Previous channels) = 28-15 = 13.

91. Answer: *b.* Option *a* describes requirements documentation; *c* is not the choice because you want a risk management plan, and *d* describes the probability impact matrix.

92. Answer: *d.* It is used for mapping the probability of each risk occurrence and the impact on project objectives if the risk occurs.

93. Answer: *c.* The process of managing procurement relationships, monitoring contract performance, making changes and corrections as appropriate, and closing out contracts.

94. Answer: *d.* Claims administration. Project management plan and communication management plan are documents and change request can be an input or output.

95. Answer: *d.* Choice *a* is identifying stakeholders, *b* is manage stakeholder engagement, and *c* does not exist.

96. Answer: *b.* you must never ignore stakeholders.

97. Answer: *b.* Susan should immediately begin the closing process. Prepare final report is the only answer that is part of the closing process.

98. Answer: *a.* Regression analysis. Regression analysis is a technique that involves examining the series of input variables in relations to the corresponding output results. OPA, EEF and deliverables are inputs

99. Answer: *c.* Evaluate the impact of the change

100. Answer: *a.* Prevent changes from occurring

101. Answer: *b.* Acceptable deliverables

102. Answer: *c.* Change requests is an output to control scope.

103. Answer: *d.* Change requests is an output.

104. Answer: *c.* Project management software

105. Answer: *b.* PERT

106. Answer: *c.* Fishbone

107. Answer: *b.* Cause-and-effect diagram

108. Answer: *b.* McGregor's Theory X assumes that the typical worker has little ambition, avoids responsibility, and is individual-goal oriented. McGregor's Theory Y assumes employees are internally motivated, enjoy their job, and work to better themselves without a direct reward in return.

109. Answer: *d.* Forming, storming, norming, performing, and adjourning

110. Answer: *c.* The process of monitoring communications and the process of ensuring the information needs of the project and its stakeholders are met

111. Answer: *d.* 28 Solution:
6 +2 = 8 (6 current team members plus 2 new team members)
n = 8

n(n-1) / 2
8(7) / 2 = 56
56 / 2=28

112. Answer: *a*. 13 In this question, you will need to get the new number of channels and subtract the current number of channels from it.
New - current
(8(7) / 2 - (6(5) / 2)
28 - 15 = 13

113. Answer: *d*. Option *a* describes scope management, *b* defines risk management, and *c* is schedule management.

114. Answer: *d*. It is used for mapping the probability of each risk occurrence and the impact on project objectives if the risk occurs.

115. Answer: *c*. The process of managing procurement relationships, monitoring contract performance, making changes and corrections as appropriate, and closing out contracts

116. Answer: *c*. Expert judgments is a tool and technique.

117. Answer: *d*. Claims administration

118. Answer: *d*. Choice *a* is identifying stakeholders, *b* is manage stakeholder engagement, and *c* does not exist.

119. Answer: *b*. Ignoring the stakeholder until they go away

120. Answer: *a*. Regression analysis

121. Answer: *d*. IRR will be 7.93%. On the PMP exam, you should always choose the project with the highest return. In this example, answer '*a*' only gives a dollar value. Answer *b* is just a payback period, which yields no return. And answer *c* is in the negative range.

122. Answer: *d*. Data analysis is a tool and technique, not an input.

123. Answer: *c*. EEF. The order of the closing process is: Obtain acceptance of deliverables, conduct post-project or phase-end review, Record impact of tailoring any process, Document lessons learned, Apply appropriate updates to organizational process assets (OPA), Archive all relevant project documents, Close out all procurement activities and Perform team member assessments.

124. Answer: *c*. Document lessons learned

125. Answer: *b*. Obtain customer satisfaction is not a closing process list. Obtain customer acceptance is in the closing process list.

126. Answer: *b*. Project charter and assumptions log

127. Answer: *c*. Expert judgement is always a tool and technique.

128. Answer: *d*. The project charter never states the details of project deliverables.

129. Answer: *a*. The process of monitoring the implementation of the agreed-upon risk response plan, tracking identified risks, analyzing new risks, and evaluating the risk process

130. Answer: *b*. It is the process of defining how to conduct risk management activities for a project.

131. Answer: *b*. The process of how the project and product scope will be defined, validated and controlled throughout the project.

132. Answer: *d*. How the project and product scope will be validated.

133. Answer: *d*. It is a grid for mapping the probability of each risk occurrence and the impact on project objectives if the risk occurs.

134. Answer: *c*. The process of developing detailed descriptions of the project and products, which is what the project includes and excludes

135. Answer: *a*. Determine risks does not exists in Pmbok 6th edition

136. Answer: *c.* The process of ensuring timely and appropriate collection, creation, distribution, storage, retrieval, management, monitoring, and the ultimate disposition of project information

137. Answer: *d.* The process of ensuring the information needs of the project and its stakeholders are met

138. Answer: *d.* 28

139. Answer: *a.* 13

140. Answer: *d.* The process of estimating the number of work periods needed to complete activities with the estimated resources

141. Answer: *c.* Project management plan

142. Answer: *a.* Scope management plan and requirements management plan

143. Answer: a. Enterprise environmental factors are influences out of the project manager's control.

144. Answer: c. Only organization process assets are a valid PMP lexicon and is internal to the organization that affects the project.

145. Answer: *b.* Quality audit

146. Answer: *d.* Precision. Accuracy is measurements are closer to true value.

147. Answer: *d.* The process of ensuring the physical resources assigned and allocated to the project are available as planned versus actual utilization of resources and taking corrective actions as necessary

148. Answer: *b.* McGregor's Theory X. McGregor stated that those employees who are separated into Theory X need to be micromanaged. Theory X believes that employees are inherently lazy and without constant supervision, they will not complete their work. Conversely, McGregor stated that those employees who are separated into Theory Y should be left to complete their work independently. Theory Y believes that employees are inherently motivated and want to produce quality work.

149. Answer: *d*. Forming, storming, norming, performing, and adjourning

150. Answer: *a*. Avoidance and collaboration

151. Answer: *c*. Staffing management plan

152. Answer: *d*. OPA and EEF are inputs to many process groups. Final report is an output to the close project or phase process group.

153. Answer: *c*. Staffing management plan

154. Answer: *a*. The process of leading and performing the work defined in the project plan and implementing the approved changes to achieve the project objectives

155. Answer: *a*. Active listening. Interpersonal and team skills are used to communicate effectively with team members, sponsors, and others either face to face or via email or other communication methods. Interpersonal and team skills will include conflict resolution methods, facilitation, and meeting management. Interpersonal skills are used in conflict management, facilitation, and meeting management.

156. Answer: *d*. Lessons learned register

157. Answer: *b*. Monitor and control project work

158. Answer *a*. Answer *d* looks tempting, but the key word was *best*. The process of tracking, reviewing, and reporting the overall progress to meet performance objectives defined in the project management plan

159. Answer: *c*. Evaluate the impact of the change

160. Answer: *b*. The process of reviewing all change requests; approving changes; managing changes to deliverables, project documents, and the project management plan; and communicating decisions

161. Answer: *c*. Project management plan updates is an output.

162. Answer: *a*. Avoid is the worst of the four conflict management types.

163. Answer: *d*. Project communications management

164. Answer: *b*. The process of ensuring timely and appropriate collection, creation, distribution, storage, retrieval, management, monitoring, and the ultimate disposition of project information

165. Answer: *d*. Change requests

166. Answer: *d*. Implement risk responses

167. Answer: *a*. The process of implementing the agreed-upon risk response

168. Answer *d*. Change requests

169. Answer *b*. Risk management plan

170. Answer *a*. The process of identifying individual risks as well as sources of overall project risks and documenting their characteristics

171. Answer *c*. Risk probability and impact assessment

172. Answer: *a*. The process of prioritizing individual project risks for further analysis by assessing their probability of occurrence and impact

173. Answer: *a*. The process of numerically analyzing the effect of identified risks on overall project objects

174. Answer: *a*. Simulations

175. Answer: *c*. Share

176. Answer: *b*. Mitigate

177. Answer: *d*. Change requests

178. Answer: *a*. Bottom-up estimating.

179. Answer: *d* Bottom-up estimating

180. Answer: *c*. ATYPICAL: EAC= AC + (BAC-EV) = 11+(150-10) = 151

181. Answer: *c*. ETC = EAC - AC = 11+(120-10) - 11 = 110

182. Answer: *c.* AC + [[BAC-EV)/(CPI*SPI)] = 11 + [[120-10)/ ((10/11) *(10/12))] = 11+ (110/ (.909) *(.833)) = 110.833

183. Answer: *b.* Testing. Rework and Liabilities are part of non-conformance

184. Answer: *d.* Lost business

185. Answer: *c.* Inspections

186. Answer: *b.* Testing

187. Answer: *d.* Lost business

188. Answer: *c.* inspections

189. Answer: *c.* Risk management

190. Answer: *c.* The process of ensuring timely and appropriate collection, creation, distribution, storage, retrieval, management, monitoring, and the ultimate disposition of project information

191. Answer: *c.* Communications management plan

192. Answer: *d.* N (n + 1) / 2

193. Answer: *b.* Identify risks, perform qualitative risk analysis, perform quantitative risk analysis, and plan risk responses

194. Answer: *d.* Risk management plan

195. Answer: *a.* The process of defining how to conduct risk management activities

196. Answer: *b.* The process of developing an approach and plan for project communications activities based on the information needs of each stakeholder and the project

197. Answer: *b.* Develop project charter

198. Answer: *d.* Data analysis.

199. Answer: *d.* Project charter and assumptions log

200. Answer: *d.* Quality management plan

Mock Exam Three
200 Questions—4 Hours Advanced

1. Quasar is a project manager who wants to run an efficient project that completes on time and under budget to the client's satisfaction. When performing the develop project plan process, what will be the output document the project manager will want the most?

    a) Project management plan

    b) Project documents updates

    c) Work performance reports

    d) Team performance

2. A project is expected to result in $2 million in five years. The current interest rate is 5%. What is the PV of the project?

    a) $1,567,398

    b) $1,359,252

    c) $2 million

    d) $1,784,972

3. Your team members are arguing about the acceptable budget range for a particular deliverable. Jim says the acceptable range is +/- 5%, and Katherine says the acceptable range is +/- 10%. Where should Jim and Katherine look to determine the acceptable quality metric?

    a) Schedule Metrics

    b) Cost Metrics

    c) Quality Metrics

    d) Scope Metrics

4. Jonathan is a project manager at a solar car company. Jonathan wants to develop a document that will give him the best chance of managing the project from start to completion. Which document does the project manager need to create next?

   a) Project management plan

   b) Project documents updates

   c) Work performance reports

   d) Team performance

5. Lucia is a new project manager for Razor LLC. Lucia wants to get off to the best start in understanding the project, people, and environment. Meetings are a tool and technique of which process?

   a) Meetings

   b) Develop project charter

   c) Organizational process assets

   d) Planning

6. All are components of tools and techniques in the manage project knowledge process except

   a) Knowledge management

   b) Information management

   c) Interpersonal and team skills

   d) Lessons learned register

7. Barron is a new project manager for Best Cereal Products LLC. Barron wants to get off to the best start in understanding the project, people, and environment. All the following are inputs to the develop project charter process except

   a) SOW

   b) Enterprise environmental factors

c) Organizational process assets

d) Data gathering

8. Mila is a project manager at Cool Socks Inc. She is in the planning process for a new project and has completed the sequence activities process. The kickoff of the project occurred three months ago. The project team is currently managing the project. As a project manager, what would Mila do next?

   a) Estimate activity durations

   b) Close the project

   c) Control schedule

   d) Identify stakeholders

9. Candy is a seasoned project manager at a pickle factory. The project manager needs which tool and technique to collect information?

   a) SOW

   b) Enterprise environmental factors

   c) Organizational process assets

   d) Data gathering

10. You are a new project manager for an existing project with issues. What document does the project manager need to determine the project goals, high-level risks, and high-level constraints?

    a) Communication plan

    b) Project management plan

    c) SOW

    d) Project charter

11. The process of communicating and working with stakeholders to meet their needs and expectations, address issues, and foster appropriate involvement is

a) Manage stakeholder engagement

b) Monitor communications

c) Manage communications

d) Monitor stakeholder engagement

12. Jonathan is the senior project manager for a High-energy company. In the beginning stages of the project, Jonathan spends much of his time conversing with the sponsor and senior management to develop a document that gives the project manager authority to commit resources to the project. What is the output of the develop project charter process?

a) Project charter

b) Enterprise environmental factors

c) Project management plan

d) Organizational process assets

13. Judy is a superb project manager at her firm. She is currently working on a project in which a fix is necessary. As a project manager, what should Judy do next?

a) Check the release documents

b) Notify the sponsor

c) Evaluate the impact of the change

d) Implement the risk response plan

14. The following are tools and techniques for the develop project management plan process except

a) Meetings

b) Project management plan

c) Interpersonal and team skills

d) Expert judgments

15. Harry is a contractor responsible for the refurbishment of an automobile showroom. The estimated refurbishment cost is $500 per square foot. The total showroom area that needs to be refurbished is 1,000 square feet. Based on Harry's experience, he knows his team can refurbish 100 square feet per week. As a project manager, how should Harry report how the project is performing?

    a) On schedule and on budget

    b) Behind schedule and over budget

    c) Ahead of schedule and over budget

    d) Behind schedule and ahead of budget

Cost Variance	(EV – AC) = ($25,000.00)
Schedule Variance	(EV – PV) = $25,000.00

16. Patricia is a top project manager at her firm. She is currently working on a project in which a fix *might be* necessary. As a project manager, what should Patricia do next?

    a) Prevent changes from occurring

    b) Notify the sponsor

    c) Evaluate the impact of the change

    d) Implement the risk response plan

17. Ulysses is a new project manager on an existing project. The project has been in its planning stage. The process that has just been completed is collect requirements. As a project manager, what would you do next?

    a) Define scope

    b) Project management plan

    c) Plan scope management

    d) Expert judgments

18. Danny is a new project manager on an existing project. The project has been in its planning stage. The process that has just been completed is collect requirements. As a project manager, what would you do next?

    a) Project management plan

    b) Define activities

    c) Plan scope management

    d) Expert judgments

19. Deliverables are an output of which process group?

    a) Organizational process assets

    b) Enterprise environmental factors

    c) Final report

    d) Direct and manage project work

20. Luke is a new project manager on an existing project. The project has been in its planning stage. The process that has just completed is define activities. As a project manager, what process did you determine was done previously to define activities?

    a) Define scope

    b) Project management plan

    c) Plan schedule management

    d) Expert judgments

21. Which of the following is a tool and technique of direct and manage project work?

    a) Change requests

    b) PMIS

    c) Project management plan

    d) OPA updates

22. Shaq is a new project manager on an existing project. The project has been in its planning stage. The process that has just been completed is define activities. As a project manager, what process did he determine was done prior to define activities?

    a) Define scope

    b) Project management plan

    c) Data gathering

    d) Create WBS

23. Which process best exemplifies monitoring and control in project integration?

    a) Direct and manage project work

    b) Monitor and control project work

    c) Manage project knowledge

    d) Perform integrated change control

24. Glover is a new project manager on an existing project. The project has been in its execute stage. The process that has just been completed is define activities. As a project manager, which process will he do next?

    a) Define scope

    b) Validate scope

    c) Data gathering

    d) Create WBS

25. You are a new project manager for an existing project with issues. As the project manager, what document do you need to determine how, when, and the level of authority the stakeholders communicate with?

    a) Communication management plan

    b) Project management plan

    c) SOW

    d) Project charter

26. The process of defining how to estimate, acquire, manage, and utilize physical and team resources is

    a) Develop team

    b) Plan resource management

    c) Organizational theory

    d) Team charter

27. Jeffrey is a contractor responsible for the refurbishment of an automobile showroom. The estimated refurbishment cost is $500 per square foot. The total showroom area that needs to be refurbished is 1,000 square feet. Based on Jeffrey's experience, he knows his team can refurbish 100 square feet per week. As a project manager, how should Jeffrey report the forecast estimate at completion to senior management?

    a) $525,000

    b) $375,000

    c) $555,555.56

    d) $516,224.19

28. The process of defining how to estimate, acquire, manage, and utilize physical and team resources is

    a) Develop team

    b) Plan resource management

    c) Organizational theory

    d) Team charter

29. Jonathan is a new project manager at Warm Hands Glove Company Inc. Jonathan does not trust his employees to do their jobs, so he must monitor their every action to make sure he gets the results he wants. Jonathan is practicing

    a) RAM

    b) McGregor's Theory X

c) Expectancy Theory

d) McGregor's Theory Y

30. Antonio is a new project manager on an existing project. The project has been is its execute stage. The process that has just been completed is estimate costs. As a project manager, which process will Antonio do next?

a) Define scope

b) Control costs

c) Data gathering

d) Create WBS

31. What is the correct order of team development?

a) Performing, storming, norming, forming, and adjourning

b) Forming, storming, norming, performing, and adjourning

c) Forming, norming, storming, performing, and adjourning

d) Performing, storming, adjourning, forming, and norming

32. Sabrina is a new project manager on an existing project. The project has been canceled by senior management without cause. As a project manager, what will Sabrina do next?

a) Negotiate with management to keep the project going

b) Negotiate with the sponsor to keep the project going for a few more weeks because things can be turned around

c) Begin the closing process immediately

d) Continue the project until she has heard from the sponsor

33. Michelle is a project manager for a bookseller. One of her projects is improving the ways books can be found without assistance from the staff. Michelle needs to introduce a new member to the project team. What is the correct order of team development?

    a) Performing, storming, norming, forming, and adjourning

    b) Performing, storming, adjourning, forming, and norming

    c) Forming, norming, storming, performing, and adjourning

    d) Forming, storming, norming, performing, and adjourning

34. The process of defining how to estimate, acquire, manage, and utilize physical and team resources is

    a) Develop team

    b) Team Charter Plan resource management

    c) Organizational theory

    d) Plan resource management Team charter

35. Mark is a new project manager on an existing project. The project has moved beyond the planning stage. The vendor chosen to complete a portion of the project has started work. As a project manager, what will Mark do next?

    a) Plan what is expected of outside vendors

    b) Ask the vendor for closing reports and place in archives

    c) Control procurements

    d) Continue the project until he has heard from the sponsor

36. Pepper is a new project manager for TF Banking Services. Pepper is in the process of acquiring resources. All are tools and techniques Pepper can use to aid in her search except

    a) Virtual teams

    b) Multicriteria analysis

    c) Resource management plan

    d) Negotiation

37. Sophia is a contractor responsible for the refurbishment of an automobile showroom. The estimated refurbishment cost is $500 per square foot. The total showroom area that needs to be refurbished is 1,000 square feet. Based on Sophia's past experience, she knows her team can refurbish 100 square feet per week. As the project manager, how should Sophia report the steady-state progress of the project?

    a) $525,000

    b) $375,000

    c) $555,555.56

    d) $475,000

Estimate at Completion (typical, steady-state, or continuous)	(BAC / CPI) = $555,555.56

38. All of the following are inputs to manage a team except

    a) Project management plan

    b) Project documents updates

    c) Work performance reports

    d) Team performance

39. Which is an output of the validate scope process?

    a) Work performance data

    b) Acceptable deliverables

    c) Verified deliverables

    d) Work performance information

40. John is a new project manager on an existing project. The project is now in the execute stage. John and his project team know the plan resources they need, what the resources will do, and how long the work will take. As a project manager, what will John do next?

    a) Control resources

    b) Develop team

    c) Manage team

    d) Acquire resources

41. The target weight of a widget is three pounds. You as the project manager take a sample and find that the weights of the five widgets are 3.4, 3.41, 3.4, 3.39, and 3.4 pounds each. You would describe the weight of the widgets as:

    a) Precise but not accurate

    b) Accurate and precise

    c) Accurate but not precise

    d) Neither accurate nor precise.

42. Which of the following are items to consider during stakeholder management:

    a) Communicate the same to every stakeholder

    b) Over-deliver on expectations

    c) Avoid challenging stakeholders

    d) Identify the needs of all stakeholders

43. Robert is a new project manager at Fresh Minds, Inc. Robert does not trust his employees to do their jobs, so he must monitor their every action to make sure he gets the results he wants. Robert is practicing

    a) RAM

    b) McGregor's Theory X

c) Expectancy Theory

d) McGregor's Theory Y

44. Ashley is a new project manager on an existing project. The project has now in the execute stage. Ashley and his project team know the plan resources they need, what the resources will do, and how long the work will take. As a project manager, what will Ashley do next?

a) Control resources

b) Train management

c) Lay out a grand plan for the project

d) Determine stakeholders

45. Harry is a contractor responsible for the refurbishment of an automobile showroom. The estimated refurbishment cost is $500 per square foot. The total showroom area that needs to be refurbished is 1,000 square feet. Based on his past experience, he knows his team can refurbish 100 square feet per week. As a project manager, how would Harry report how the project is performing?

a) On schedule and on budget

b) Behind schedule and over budget

c) Ahead of schedule and over budget

d) Behind schedule and ahead of budget

Cost Variance	(EV - AC) = $25,000.00
Schedule Variance	(EV - PV) = $25,000.00

46. Tomas is a junior project manager for a pharmaceutical company. One of Tomas's roles is to assist in the development of a project charter. What document is from the plan stakeholder engagement process?

a) Assumption and constraint analysis

b) Stakeholder engagement plan

c) Project management plan

d) Process improvement plan

47. The process of defining how to estimate, acquire, manage, and utilize physical and team resources is

a) Develop team

b) Organizational theory

c) Plan resource management

d) Team charter

48. You are a new project manager for an existing project with issues. What document do you need to determine the project goals, high-level risks, and high-level constraints?

a) Communication plan

b) Project management plan

c) SOW

d) Project charter

49. Abraham is a project manager on an existing project at the Best Acting Company Inc., which sells dreams. After the project kickoff, Abraham and his project team are managing the team resources process. The project plan has been approved. As a project manager, what will Abraham do next?

a) Create WBS

b) Control resources

c) Perform team development

d) Monitor stakeholder engagement

50. Samantha is a new project manager on an existing project. After the project kickoff, Samantha and her project team have completed collection of all requirements and determined the scope. The project plan has been approved. As a project manager, what will Samantha do next?

a) Create WBS

b) Validate scope

c) Lay out a grand plan for the project

d) Negotiate with the sponsor for overtime

51. All the following are inputs to the develop project charter process except

a) SOW

b) Enterprise environmental factors

c) Organizational process assets

d) Data gathering

52. Which answer best describes the stakeholder engagement plan?

a) The process of developing approaches to involve project stakeholders based on their needs and expectations, addressing issues, and fostering appropriate stakeholder engagement involvement

b) The process of monitoring project stakeholder relationships and tailoring strategies for engaging stakeholders through the modification of engagement strategies and plans

c) The process of communicating and working with stakeholders to meet their needs and expectations

d) The process of not communicating and working with stakeholders to meet their needs and expectations

53. What is the output of the validate scope process?

a) Work performance data

b) Acceptable deliverables

c) Verified deliverables

d) Work performance information

54. Luther is a new project manager on an existing project. The project is now in the execute stage. Luther and his project team know the plan resources they need, what the resources will do, and how long the work will take. As a project manager, what will Luther do next?

   a) Control resources

   b) Develop team

   c) Manage team

   d) Determine stakeholders

55. Jesus is a new project manager on an existing project. After the project kickoff, Jesus and his project team have completed the plan stakeholder engagement process and are managing the stakeholder engagements. The project plan has been approved. As a project manager, what will Jesus do next?

   a) Create WBS

   b) Validate scope

   c) Plan stakeholder engagement

   d) Monitor stakeholder engagement

56. Kazem is a project manager with many years of experience. Kazem knows how important customer communication and satisfaction are to project management. What is the best definition of the monitor stakeholder engagement process?

   a) The process of identifying project stakeholders regularly and analyzing and documenting relevant information regarding their interests, involvement, interdependencies, influence, and impact on project success

   b) The process of communicating and working with stakeholders to meet their needs and expectations, address issues, and foster appropriate stakeholder engagement

   c) The process of providing an overview of the project stakeholder management process

   d) The process of monitoring project stakeholder relationships and tailoring strategies for engaging stakeholders through the modification of engagement strategies and plans

57. Joaquim is a very seasoned and energetic project manager. Recently, Joaquim's emails to some stakeholders have gone unanswered. When some stakeholders do respond, Joaquim must decide how to answer their concerns. Joaquim should do all the following in monitor stakeholder engagement except

    a) Managing stakeholder relationships

    b) Ignoring the stakeholders until they go away

    c) Engaging with the stakeholders

    d) Formulating strategies with the stakeholders

58. Jeffrey is a project manager responsible for the delivery of a solar car prototype. There are many moving parts to a project on the cutting edge of technology. Resources such as people and equipment for solar technology are not as common. Jeffrey must learn the language of solar technology to deliver the project successfully. As project manager, which of the following is Jeffery not going to use as an input to manage team?

    a) Project management plan

    b) Project documents updates

    c) Work performance reports

    d) Team performance

59. David is a new project manager for Monorail Enterprises. David wants to get off to the best start in understanding the project, people, and environment. Interpersonal and team skills is a tool and technique of which process?

    a) Meetings

    b) Develop project charter

    c) Organizational process assets

    d) Planning

60. William is a new project manager on an existing project. After the project kickoff, William and his project team have completed the plan procurement management process. The project plan has not been approved. As a project manager, what will William do next?

    a) Create WBS

    b) Validate scope

    c) Plan stakeholder engagement

    d) Negotiate with the sponsor for overtime

61. Emma is a project manager for Guidance Cybernetics, a maker of exoskeletons for those who have lost the use of their limbs or are paralyzed from spinal injuries. Emma's project has suffered both material and people resource setbacks. As the project manager, what should Emma choose as the best tool and technique of the plan communication management process to create the communication management plan document?

    a) Change log

    b) Project management plan

    c) Manage quality

    d) Communication technology

62. Robert is a new project manager at No Fear Inc. Robert does not trust his employees to do their jobs, so he must monitor their every action to make sure he gets the results he wants. What is Robert is practicing?

    a) RAM

    b) McGregor's Theory X

    c) Expectancy Theory

    d) McGregor's Theory Y

63. One of the duties of a project manager is the process of communicating and working with stakeholders to meet their needs and expectations, address issues, and foster appropriate involvement. As a project manager, what do you do next?

    a) Manage stakeholder engagement

    b) Monitor communications

    c) Manage communications

    d) Monitor stakeholder engagement

64. Jerry is a new project manager at Cool Car Seats, Inc. Jerry does not trust his employees to do their jobs, so he must monitor their every action to make sure he gets the results he wants. Jerry is practicing

    a) RAM

    b) McGregor's Theory X

    c) Expectancy Theory

    d) McGregor's Theory Y

65. Norman is a project manager for a ventilator company for delivery to hospitals. Norman is replacing a team member because of quality and performance issues. The new team member is getting up to speed quickly to begin producing. As the project manager, in what order will Norman perform the steps of team development?

    a) Performing, storming, norming, forming, and adjourning

    b) Performing, storming, adjourning, forming, and norming

    c) Forming, norming, storming, performing, and adjourning

    d) Forming, storming, norming, performing, and adjourning

66. Miss Jones is a project manager on an existing project at the Best Acting Company, Inc, which sells dreams. After the project kickoff, Miss Jones and her project team are in the managing team resources process. The project plan has been approved. As a project manager, what will Miss Jones do next?

    a) Performing team development

    b) Create WBS

    c) Develop team

    d) Monitor stakeholder engagement

67. Lavell is a new project manager at Prove It to Me Inc. Lavell does not trust his employees to do their jobs, so he must monitor their every action to make sure he gets the results he wants. What is Lavell practicing?

    a) RAM

    b) McGregor's Theory X

    c) Expectancy Theory

    d) McGregor's Theory Y

68. The following describe monitor stakeholder engagement except

    a) Managing stakeholder relationships

    b) Ignoring the stakeholders until they go away

    c) Engaging with the stakeholders

    d) Formulating strategies with the stakeholders

69. Mr. Greene is a project manager on an existing project at the Ultimate Real Estate Company, which sells passports. After the project kickoff, Mr. Greene and his project team are in the manage team resources process. The project plan has been approved. As a project manager, what will Mr. Greene do next?

    a) Control resources

b) Create WBS

c) Develop team

d) Monitor stakeholder engagement

70. Noah is a project manager at Emca, a producer of animated characters for worldwide distribution to children as consumers. Which tool and technique should Noah use next in the plan communications management process to create the communication management plan?

    a) Change log

    b) Project management plan

    c) Manage quality

    d) Interpersonal and team skills

71. Andy is a project manager on an existing project. After the project kickoff, Andy and his project team have completed the acquire resources process. The project plan has been approved. As a project manager, what will Andy do next?

    a) Create WBS

    b) Develop team

    c) Plan stakeholder engagement

    d) Monitor stakeholder engagement

72. Which best describes the manage communications process?

    a) Project management plan

    b) The process of ensuring timely and appropriate collection, creation, distribution, storage, retrieval, management, monitoring, and the ultimate disposition of project information

    c) Work performance reports

    d) Team performance

73. Kazem is a project manager with many years of experience. Kazem knows how important customer communication and satisfaction are to project management. What is the best definition of the monitor stakeholder engagement process?

   a) The process of identifying project stakeholders regularly and analyzing and documenting relevant information regarding their interests, involvement, interdependencies, influence, and impact on project success

   b) The process of communicating and working with stakeholders to meet their needs and expectations, address issues, and foster appropriate stakeholder engagement

   c) The process of providing an overview of the project stakeholder management process

   d) The process of monitoring project stakeholder relationships and tailoring strategies for engaging stakeholders through the modification of engagement strategies and plans

74. The process of communicating and working with stakeholders to meet their needs and expectations, address issues, and foster appropriate involvement is

   a) Manage stakeholder engagement

   b) Monitor communications

   c) Manage communications

   d) Monitor stakeholder engagement

75. Elijah is a project manager at Poor Man's Industries, a maker of economical products that look expensive. As the project manager, Elijah will supply all the inputs to manage a team except

   a) Project management plan

   b) Project documents updates

   c) Work performance reports

   d) Team performance

76. Andy is a project manager on an existing project at the PASSMAX company, which sells passports. After the project kickoff, Andy and his project team are in the managing team resources process. The project plan has been approved. As a project manager, what will Andy do next?

   a) Create WBS

   b) Develop team

   c) Control resources

   d) Monitor stakeholder engagement

77. Robert is a new project manager at MAX Testosterone Support, Inc. Robert does not trust his employees to do their jobs, so he must monitor their every action to make sure he gets the results he wants. Robert is practicing

   a) RAM

   b) McGregor's Theory X

   c) Expectancy Theory

   d) McGregor's Theory Y

78. What is the correct order of team development?

   a) Forming, storming, norming, performing, and adjourning

   b) Performing, storming, adjourning, forming, and norming

   c) Forming, norming, storming, performing, and adjourning

   d) Performing, storming, norming, forming, and adjourning

79. Daryl is a project manager on an existing project at the Best Acting Company Inc., which sells dreams. Before the project kickoff, Daryl and her project team are planning to perform qualitative risk analysis. The project plan has not been approved. As a project manager, what will Daryl do next?

   a) Plan risk management

   b) Create WBS

   c) Control resources

   d) Monitor stakeholder engagement

80. Joseph is a senior project manager on an existing project for building boats. The project is currently in the execute stage. Which document will Joseph not need as an input to the manage team process?

    a) Project management plan

    b) Project documents updates

    c) Work performance reports

    d) Team performance

81. Daryl is a project manager on an existing project at the Best Acting Company Inc., which sells dreams. Before the project kickoff, Daryl and her project team are planning to perform qualitative risk analysis. The project plan has not been approved. As a project manager, what does Daryl do prior to performing qualitative risk analysis?

    a) Implement risk responses

    b) Plan risk responses

    c) Control resources

    d) Plan communication management

82. Ava is a junior project manager learning the ropes for the company Dadcorp. Dadcorp is a company that performs the to-do list for families or single parents and other things around the home of the consumer. Conversations and meetings are part of which tool and technique?

    a) Communications analysis

    b) Communications technology

    c) Communications model

    d) Communications method

83. Daryl is a project manager on an existing project at the Best Acting Company, Inc, which sells dreams. Before the project kickoff, Daryl and her project team are planning to perform qualitative risk analysis. The project plan has not been approved. As a project manager, what will Daryl do next?

    a) Create WBS

    b) Control resources

c) Monitor stakeholder engagement

d) Plan risk management

84. David is a project manager on an existing project at the Passport Makers Company, which sells passports. After the project kickoff, David and his project team are in the managing team resources process. The project plan has been approved. As a project manager, what will David do next?

   a) Create WBS

   b) Control resources

   c) Develop team

   d) Monitor stakeholder engagement

85. Daniel is a new project manager for IT Providers LLC. Daniel wants to get off to the best start understanding the project, people, and environment. Interpersonal and team skills are a tool and technique of which process?

   a) Meetings

   b) Develop project charter

   c) OPA

   d) Planning

86. Mia is a new project manager for Warbuck LLC. Mia and her team inherited a project with many assumptions and constraints. All the requirements are not available, and the deliverables do not match up with client expectations. Mia wants to get off to the best start understanding the project, people, and environment. All the following are inputs to develop project charter except:

   a) SOW

   b) Assumptions and constraints

   c) OPA

   d) Data analysis

87. Olivia is a project manager at the corporation MAOHC. MAOHC has numerous affiliates and thousands of ongoing projects. Olivia is introducing a new team member to handle quality assurance on her project. As the project manager, in what order should Olivia perform the steps of team development?

    a) Performing, storming, norming, forming, and adjourning

    b) Performing, storming, adjourning, forming, and norming

    c) Forming, norming, storming, performing, and adjourning

    d) Forming, storming, norming, performing, and adjourning

88. Lucas is a new project manager for a computer company. As a new project manager who documents the develop project charter process, which documents does Lucas needs to examine?

    a) Project management plan and requirements plan

    b) Project charter and assumptions log

    c) Quality management plan and change management plan

    d) Stakeholder management plan

89. David is a new project manager for Unique Homes Corp. David wants to get off to the best start in understanding the project, people, and environment. Interpersonal and team skills are a tool and technique of which process?

    a) Meetings

    b) Develop project charter

    c) Organizational process assets

    d) Planning

90. All the following are inputs to the develop project charter process except

    a) SOW

    b) Enterprise environmental factors

    c) Organizational process assets

d) Data gathering

91. David is a project manager on an existing project at the In Dream of Escape LLC, which sells passports. After the project kickoff, David and his project team are in the managing team resources process. The project plan has been approved. As a project manager, what will David do next?

    a) Create WBS

    b) Control resources

    c) Develop team

    d) Monitor stakeholder engagement

92. Priscilla is a project manager for an existing project with issues. What document does the project manager need to determine the project goals, high-level risks, and high-level constraints?

    a) Communication plan

    b) Project management plan

    c) SOW

    d) Project charter

93. Daryl is a senior project manager for a book publishing company. Daryl wants to identify all current stakeholders for the project. All the documents below are inputs to the identify stakeholders process except

    a) Project charter

    b) EEF

    c) Expert judgments

    d) Organizational process assets

94. Asheem is a project manager working remotely, so some of his team is in different locations performing their work. As project manager, Asheem determines the output of the develop project management plan process is

   a) Project charter

   b) Enterprise environmental factors

   c) Project management plan

   d) Organizational process assets

95. Pepper is a new project manager for TF Banking Services. Pepper is in the process of acquiring resources. All are tools and techniques Pepper can use to aid in her search except

   a) Virtual teams

   b) Multicriteria analysis

   c) Resource management plan

   d) Negotiation

96. Thomas has been working as a project manager for over 20 years. He has recently acquired his project management professional certificate. Which document does Thomas need to examine that maps the project deliverables to its requirements?

   a) OPA

   b) Requirements traceability matrix

   c) Project management plan

   d) Data analysis

97. Adrianne is a transferred project manager on loan from another department. Adrianne's first task is to develop a schedule management plan. Which order will Adrianne use for inputs to the plan schedule management process?

   a) Project charter, project management plan, scope management plan, development approach, EEF, and OPA

b) Perform qualitative risk analysis, perform quantitative risk analysis, and plan risk responses

c) Project management plan, project documents, approved change requests, EEF, and OPA

d) Project charter, project management plan, quality management plan, project life cycle development, EEF, and OPA

98. Isabella is a project manager for Soylent Purple Corporation. As the project manager, which of the following will she use as an output of the process implement risk response plan?

a) Change requests

b) Data analysis

c) Approved changes

d) OPA

99. Oliver is a project manager for the Very Tough Corporation of America. As project manager, he will use all the following as inputs to develop project charter except

a) SOW

b) Assumptions and constraints

c) OPA

d) Data analysis

100. Megan is a new project manager for an existing project with issues. What document does Megan need to determine the project goals, high-level risks, and high-level constraints?

a) Communication plan

b) Project management plan

c) SOW

d) Project charter

101. Mason is a new project manager for Tube Socks LLC. Mason wants to get off to the best start understanding the project, people, and environment. As the project manager, Mason would choose all as inputs to the identify stakeholders process except

   a) Project charter

   b) EEF

   c) Expert judgments

   d) Organizational process assets

102. Jamis is a new project manager for the World-Eaters Corp. World-Eaters Corp is a company that terraforms planets so humans can live there comfortably. As a project manager, Jamis will use all tools and techniques to determine budget except

   a) Expert judgments

   b) Historical information review

   c) Funding limit reconciliation

   d) Business case

103. Jacob is a contractor responsible for the refurbishment of an automobile showroom. The estimated refurbishment cost is $500 per square foot. The total showroom area that needs to be refurbished is 1,000 square feet. Based on his past experience, he knows his team can refurbish 100 square feet per week. As a project manager, what does Jacob compute the estimate at completion to be?

   a) $525,000

   b) $375,000

   c) $555,555.56

   d) $516,224.19

104. Sophia is a new project manager for Flatliners Inc., a company that makes and sells defibrillators to the medical industry. Sophia wants to get off to the best start understanding the company environment. As the project manager, which output would she choose for the determine budget process?

   a) Cost baseline

b) Alternative analysis

c) Business need

d) Voting

105. Patrick is a new project manager for NoTouchTV LLC. Patrick wants to get off to the best start understanding the project, people, and environment. As a project manager, what process will Patrick perform that contains the project's objectives, assumptions, constraints, and high-level requirements?

a) Meetings

b) Develop project charter

c) OPA

d) Planning

106. Promise is a project manager at MoreBooks Inc. Promise wants to get off to the best start on her project. Promise will accept all the following as inputs to develop project charter except

a) SOW

b) Assumptions and constraints

c) OPA

d) Data analysis

107. Paul is a project manager with many years of experience in developing projects, managing personnel, document distribution, and bringing projects in on time and under budget. Paul needs to get started on this project and come up to speed immediately because senior management and the sponsor are getting anxious. As a project manager, what does Paul determine are the outputs of the develop project charter process?

a) Project management plan and requirements plan

b) Project charter and assumptions log

c) Quality management plan and change management plan

d) Stakeholder management plan

108. Zoey is a new project manager for HoverMobiles. Zoey wants to get off to the best start understanding the project, people, and environment. All are inputs to the identify stakeholder group except

a) Project charter

b) EEF

c) Expert judgment

d) OPA

109. Logan is a new project manager for iClassified LLC, an internet newspaper company that specializes in online advertisements. Logan wants to understand his new project, so he must secure the right documents and have meetings with the right people. As the project manager, Logan would ask for all documents that pertain to the project charter except those that

a) Formally authorize the existence of a project

b) Provide the project manager the authority to apply organizational resources to the project

c) State the high-level constraints and assumptions of the project

d) State the details of project deliverables

110. Amelia is a new project manager for Tyronn Toys LLC. Amelia wants to get off to the best start understanding the project, people, and environment. Which best describes the develop project charter process?

a) The process of developing a document that formally authorizes the existence of a project and provides the project manager with the authority to apply organizational resources to project activities

b) The process of documenting how the project and product scope will be defined, validated, and controlled throughout the project

c) The process of developing detailed descriptions of the project and products, which is what the project includes and excludes

d) The process of estimating the number of work periods needed to complete activities with the estimated resources

111. Frances is starting a new project that involves infrastructure and database migration. Frances needs to create documents for the best plan of communication for the team. Deliverables are an output of which process group?

    a) OPA

    b) EEF

    c) Final report

    d) Direct and manage project work

112. Samuel is a new project manager with good experience in change management to do the necessary work. All the following are inputs to process direct and manage project work except

    a) Approved changes

    b) Project management plan

    c) Deliverables

    d) OPA

113. Charlotte is a senior project manager for Grayson Enterprises. Charlotte wants to avoid scope creep and gold plating on this project. Which choice best describes the direct and manage project work process?

    a) The process of leading and performing the work defined in the project plan and implementing the approved changes to achieve the project objectives

    b) The process of improving the competencies of team members and the overall team environment to enhance project performance

    c) The process of obtaining seller responses, selecting sellers, and awarding a contract

    d) The process of documenting project decisions, specifying the approach, and identifying potential sellers

114. The output of create WBS is

    a) Decomposition

    b) Scope baseline

c) Project management plan

d) Product scope statement

115. James is a fresh project manager hired from a competitor. James has a friend who wants to be chosen as a contractor for this project. The bidding for the project does not start until next spring. Which best describes the create WBS process??

a) The process of developing a detailed description of the project and product

b) The process of creating a scope management plan that documents how the project and product scope will be defined, validated, and controlled

c) The process of subdividing project deliverables and project work into smaller, more manageable components

d) The process of monitoring the status of the project and product scope and managing changes in the scope baseline

116. Harper is a new project manager hired from a competitor. Harper wants to get off to the best start understanding the project, people, and environment. Which are number systems in the WBS dictionary and WBS, respectively?

a) Code of account identifier and (1.0, 1.1, 1.1.1)

b) Chart of accounts and (a, ab, abc)

c) Control chart and (1, 2, 3)

d) All of the above

117. Henri is a new project manager for the ElitePens Company. Henri wants to get off to the best start understanding the project, people, and environment. What is the output of plan communication management?

a) Project management plan

b) Project documents

c) Communications management plan

d) Communication baseline

118. Charles is a seasoned project manager and is a wizard at communication management. Which answer below best fits the tools and technique of plan communication management?

    a) Change log

    b) Project management plan

    c) Manage quality

    d) Interpersonal and team skills

119. Ethan is a new project manager for VirtuNext, a maker of virtual games play systems. Ethan wants to get off to the best start understanding the project, people, and environment. What tool and technique of plan communication management would Ethan use next?

    a) Change log

    b) Project management plan

    c) Manage quality

    d) Communication technology

120. Ella is a new project manager for the PlanetEx Corporation. Ella wants to avoid team conflicts in meetings by setting up ground rules. As the project manager, which tool and technique would Ella choose next for the manage communications process?

    a) Change log

    b) Project management plan

    c) Manage quality

    d) Interpersonal and team skills

121. Mateo is a new project manager for the Canopy Corp. Mateo, like all project managers, wants to manage the perfect project: on time, under budget, great quality to the customers' satisfaction. Manage communication is a process of which knowledge area?

    a) Plan communications management

    b) Project quality management

c) Manage tools and techniques

d) Project communications management

122. Luna is a new project manager for Clark Enterprises. Luna wants to avoid quality issues that cause defects and require rework. Luna and his team carefully design and monitor quality into the project plan. Which best describes the manage communications process?

a) Project management plan

b) The process of ensuring timely and appropriate collection, creation, distribution, storage, retrieval, management, monitoring, and the ultimate disposition of project information

c) Work performance reports

d) Team performance

123. Sebastian is a new project manager for Prince International. Sebastian wants to build team cohesiveness, so he schedules team company parties so that the team can bond with games and be better together as workers. Which process would Sebastian use next to communicate and work with stakeholders to meet their needs and expectations, address issues, and foster appropriate involvement?

a) Manage stakeholder engagement

b) Monitor communications

c) Manage communications

d) Monitor stakeholder engagement

124. Jack is a new project manager for the Stonewall Corp. Jack's team is tasked with improving a business process within the organization. Which answer best describes the manage communications process?

a) The process of developing an appropriate approach and plan for project communication activities based on the information needs of each stakeholder, the available organizational assets, and the needs of the project

b) The document that includes information on staff acquisition and release, resource calendars, recognition and rewards, compliance, and safety

c) The process of ensuring timely and appropriate collection, creation, distribution, storage, retrieval, management, monitoring, and the ultimate disposition of project information

d) The process of ensuring the information needs of the project and its stakeholders

125. Camila is a new project manager for the Oneil Oil Company. Camila wants to get off to the best start understanding the project, people, and environment. The process of communicating and working with stakeholders to meet their needs and expectations, address issues, and foster appropriate involvement is

a) Monitor communications

b) Manage stakeholder engagement

c) Manage communications

d) Monitor stakeholder engagement

126. Jackson is a new project manager for the Atlanta Airlines Corporation. Jackson wants to get off to the best start understanding the project, people, and environment. Which answer best describes monitor communications?

a) The process of developing an appropriate approach and plan for project communication activities based on the information needs of each stakeholder, the available organizational assets, and the needs of the project

b) The document that includes information on staff acquisition and release, resource calendars, recognition and rewards, and compliance and safety

c) The process of monitoring communications and the process of ensuring the information needs of the project and its stakeholders are met

d) The process of ensuring the information needs of the project and its stakeholders are met

127. Aria is a new project manager for Yoda Propulsion Systems. Aria wants to avoid equipment delays and improve worker performance, so Aria registers with a company application that monitors all facets of scheduling from order to delivery. Aria also has daily standup meetings to make sure there is always progress in the project. As the project manager, what description of the resource management plan should best suit Aria?

a) The process of developing an appropriate approach and plan for project communication activities based on the information needs of each stakeholder, the available organizational assets, and the needs of the project

b) The document that includes information on staff acquisition and release, resource calendars, recognition and rewards, and compliance and safety

c) The process of monitoring communications and the process of ensuring the information needs of the project and its stakeholders are met

d) The process of ensuring the information needs of the project and its stakeholders are met

128. Linda is a new project manager with some experience in risk analysis to do the necessary work. What is the output of plan risk management?

a) Communication management plan

b) Configuration management plan

c) Home improvement plan

d) Risk management plan

129. Elizabeth is starting a new project that involves infrastructure and database upgrades. What description best identifies plan risk management?

a) The process of defining how to conduct risk management activities

b) The process of using existing knowledge and creating new knowledge to achieve the project's objectives and contribute to organizational learning

c) The process of translating the quality management plan into executable project activities that incorporate the organization's quality policies

d) Risk baseline

130. Mila is a new project manager for the CyberWorld Corp. Mila wants to impress the managers who hired her by performing well on day one on a massive project that will take a year to complete. As the project manager, which document will Mila create from the plan risk management process?

a) Cost management plan

b) Risk management plan

c) Scope baseline

d) Risk baseline

131. Benjamin is a new project manager for Anaconda Copper. Benjamin wants to get off to the best start understanding the project, people, and environment. Which process best describes identify risk?

   a) The process of identifying individual risks as well as sources of overall project risks and documenting their characteristics

   b) Data analysis and interpersonal skills

   c) Project management plan

   d) The process of defining how to estimate, acquire, manage, and utilize physical and team resources

132. Kenneth is a new project manager with minimal experience in acquiring proper resources to do the necessary work. Which description best fits perform qualitative risk analysis?

   a) The process of prioritizing individual project risks for further analysis by assessing their probability of occurrence and impact

   b) The process of numerically analyzing the effects of identified risks on overall project objects

   c) Identify risks, perform a qualitative risk analysis, perform a quantitative risk analysis, and plan risk responses

   d) Plan schedule management, define activities, sequence activities, and develop schedules

133. Aurora is a new project manager for Kool Klothes LLC. Aurora wants to get off to the best start understanding the project, people, and environment. Which answer is the best description of perform quantitative risk analysis?

   a) The process of numerically analyzing the effects of identified risks on overall project objects

   b) Identify risks, perform a qualitative risk analysis, perform a quantitative risk analysis, and plan risk responses

c) Plan schedule management, define activities, sequence activities, estimate activity resources, estimate activity costs, and develop schedules

d) Estimate costs and determine budget

134. Kenneth is a new project manager with minimal experience in acquiring proper resources to do the necessary work. Which description best describes perform qualitative risk analysis?

a) The process of numerically analyzing the effects of identified risks on overall project objects

b) Identify risks, perform qualitative risk analysis, perform quantitative risk analysis, and plan risk responses

c) The process of prioritizing individual project risks for further analysis by assessing their probability of occurrence and impact

d) Plan schedule management, define activities, sequence activities, estimate activity resources, estimate activity costs, and develop schedule

135. Ellie is a new project manager for TinHooks LLC. Ellie's team is tasked with acquiring and installing a new computer and hardware system for use in the organization. Which answer is the best description of perform quantitative risk analysis?

a) The process of numerically analyzing the effects of identified risks on overall project objects

b) Identify risks, perform qualitative risk analysis, perform quantitative risk analysis, and plan risk responses

c) Plan schedule management, define activities, sequence activities, estimate activity resources, estimate activity costs, and develop schedule

d) Estimate costs and determine budget

136. Carter is a new project manager for Blazed Enterprises. He is managing a project that develops a new pharmaceutical compound to bring to market. As a project manager, which input would Carter choose for the perform qualitative risk analysis process?

a) Project management plan

b) Alternative analysis

c) OPA updates

d) EEF updates

137. Robert is one of the best project managers the company has. Lately, Robert has seen a switch in management style. SMEs are being switched from one project to another without explanation or permission. Which answer is the best description of perform quantitative risk analysis?

    a) It is the process of numerically analyzing the effects of identified risks on overall project objects.

    b) It is the process by which we identify risks, perform qualitative risk analysis, perform quantitative risk analysis, and plan risk responses.

    c) It is the process by which we plan schedule management, define activities, sequence activities, estimate activity resources, estimate activity costs, and develop schedules.

    d) It involves estimating costs and determining the budget.

138. The project management plan plans the overall activities of the project and contains detailed requirements of the project. The SOW is the statement of work, which contains the objectives of the project. The project charter contains the high-level requirements of the project. All are inputs to the identify stakeholders process except

    a) Project charter

    b) EEF

    c) Expert judgments

    d) Organizational process assets

139. Alysia is a new project manager for Headgear Inc. Alysia wants to show the company they have made the correct decision by asking for the right documents to get up to speed and asking the right questions in meetings. What is the output of plan stakeholder management?

    a) Stakeholder management plan

    b) Stakeholder baseline

    c) Risk register

    d) RBS

140. The process of communicating and working with stakeholders to meet their needs and expectations, address issues, and foster appropriate involvement describes which process?

    a) Manage stakeholder engagement

    b) Monitor communications

    c) Manage communications

    d) Monitor stakeholder engagement

141. Kazem is a project manager with many years of experience. Kazem knows how important customer communication and satisfaction are to project management. What is the best definition of the monitor stakeholder engagement process?

    a) The process of identifying project stakeholders regularly and analyzing and documenting relevant information regarding their interests, involvement, interdependencies, influence, and impact on project success

    b) The process of communicating and working with stakeholders to meet their needs and expectations, address issues, and foster appropriate stakeholder engagement

    c) The process of providing an overview of the project stakeholder management process

    d) The process of monitoring project stakeholder relationships and tailoring strategies for engaging stakeholders through the modification of engagement strategies and plans

142. Avery is a project manager newly hired from a competitor. Avery wants to show the company they have made the correct decision by asking for the right documents to get up to speed and asking the right questions in meetings. The following describe monitor stakeholder engagement except

    a) Managing stakeholder relationships

    b) Ignoring the stakeholders until they go away

    c) Engaging with the stakeholders

    d) Formulating strategies with the stakeholders

143. Grayson is a senior project manager for Nearlight Enterprises. Grayson's team is tasked with modifying a computer software program used in the organization. As the project manager, which definition would Grayson choose as the best description of plan cost management?

   a) The process of defining how the project cost will be estimated, budgeted, managed, monitored, and controlled

   b) The process of defining how to estimate, acquire, manage, and utilize physical and team resources

   c) The process of defining how to conduct risk management activities

   d) The process of identifying the relationships among project activities

144. Abigail is a project manager for a new underwater concept company. Abigail's team is tasked with conducting research to develop a new manufacturing process for the organization. As the project manager, which output of the plan cost management process would Abigail choose?

   a) Risk management plan

   b) Cost baseline

   c) Cost management plan

   d) Schedule baseline

145. Leo is a new project manager for a security software company that protects against hackers and credit card scams. Leo team is tasked with building a complete enterprise system to meet the sponsor's vision. Which is the best description of estimate costs?

   a) The process of analyzing sequences, durations, resource requirements, and schedule constraints to create a project model for project executions, monitoring, and controlling

   b) The process of developing an approximation of the monetary resources needed to complete the work

   c) The process of developing an approach and plan for project communications activities based on the information needs of each stakeholder and the project

   d) The process of defining how to estimate, acquire, manage, and utilize physical and team resources

146. Sofia is a new project manager for a computer animation company. Sofia's team has the task of acquiring resources and computer equipment and installing and configuring software so developers can program. Which of the following depicts the order of activities in project cost management?

   a) Collect requirements, define scope, and create WBS

   b) Identify risks, perform qualitative risk analysis, perform quantitative risk analysis, and plan risk responses

   c) Plan schedule management, define activities, sequence activities, estimate activity durations, and develop schedule

   d) Estimate costs and determine budget

147. As a project manager, you are planning the activities in the project schedule. Which of the following depicts the order of activities in plan cost management?

   a) Collect requirements, define scope, and create WBS

   b) Identify risks, perform qualitative risk analysis, perform quantitative risk analysis, and plan risk responses

   c) Plan schedule management, define activities, sequence activities, estimate activity resources, estimate activity costs, and develop schedule

   d) Estimate costs and determine budget

148. Which is not a tool and technique used in the estimate activity durations process?

   a) Analogous estimating

   b) Bottom-up estimating

   c) Three-point estimating

   d) Duration estimates

149. Mary is a project manager for a real estate company. Using the PERT beta distribution formula, how long will it take Mary to complete the project if most likely = 32, optimistic = 20, and pessimistic = 50?

   a) 44

   b) 33

   c) 34

   d) 32

150. The project manager continues to put numbers together for cost and schedule. Using the triangular distribution method, how long will it take the project manager to complete the project if most likely = 32, optimistic = 20, and pessimistic = 50?

   a) 44

   b) 33

   c) 34

   d) 32

151. The following are all tools and techniques that can be used to determine budget except

   a) Expert judgments

   b) Historical information review

   c) Funding limit reconciliation

   d) Business documents

152. Which is an output of the determine budget process?

   a) Cost baseline

   b) Alternative analysis

   c) Project management plan

   d) Voting

153. As a project manager, you are planning the activities in the project schedule. What is the output of plan schedule management?

    a) Collect requirements, define scope, and create WBS

    b) Identify risks, perform qualitative risk analysis, perform quantitative risk analysis, and plan risk responses

    c) Create the schedule management plan

    d) Estimate costs and determine the budget

154. As the project manager, which inputs would you choose for the plan schedule management process?

    a) Project charter, project management plan, scope management plan, development approach, EEF, and OPA

    b) Perform qualitative risk analysis, perform quantitative risk analysis, and plan risk responses

    c) Project management plan, project documents, approved change requests, EEF, and OPA

    d) Project charter, project management plan, quality management plan, project life cycle development, EEF, and OPA

155. Which of the following depicts the order of activities in schedule management?

    a) Collect requirements, define scope, and create the WBS

    b) Identify risks, perform qualitative risk analysis, perform quantitative risk analysis, and plan risk responses

    c) Plan schedule management, define activities, sequence activities, estimate activity durations, and develop schedules

    d) Estimate costs and determine budget

156. As the project manager in the define activities process, work is decomposed into which of the following?

    a) Work packages

    b) WBS

c) Activities

d) WBS and activities

157. Jason is a new project manager who is currently in the planning phase of a project. Jason has defined the activities—what should he do next?

a) Sequence activities

b) Estimate costs

c) Collect requirements

d) Identify risks

158. Jason is a new project manager who is currently in the planning phase of a project. Jason has defined the activities. As a project manager, what did Jason do before defining the activities?

a) Sequence activities

b) Estimate costs

c) Plan schedule management

d) Identify risks

159. As the project manager, which of the four types of PDM relationships will you use least often?

a) Finish to Start (FS)

b) Finish to Finish (FF)

c) Start to Finish (SF)

d) Start to Start (SS)

160. As the project manager, which of the four types of PDM relationships will you use most often?

a) Finish to Start (FS)

b) Finish to Finish (FF)

c) Start to Finish (SF)

d) Start to Start (SS)

161. As a project manager, you are planning the activities in the project schedule. Which of the following depicts the order of activities in cost management?

    a) Collect requirements, define scope, and create WBS

    b) Identify risks, perform qualitative risk analysis, perform quantitative risk analysis, and plan risk responses

    c) Plan schedule management, define activities, sequence activities, estimate activity resources, estimate activity costs, and develop schedule

    d) Estimate costs and determine budget

162. Which is not a tool and technique used in the estimate activity durations process?

    a) Analogous estimating

    b) Bottom-up estimating

    c) Three-point estimating

    d) Duration estimates

163. As the project manager, when using the PERT beta distribution formula, how long will it take Mary to complete the project if most likely = 32, optimistic = 20, and pessimistic = 50?

    a) 44

    b) 33

    c) 34

    d) 32

164. Mary is a project manager for a biochemical firm. By using the triangular distribution method, how long will it take Mary to complete the project if most likely = 32, optimistic = 20, and pessimistic = 50?

    a) 44

    b) 33

c) 34

d) 32

165. Which of the following depicts the order of activities in schedule management?

    a) Collect requirements, define scope, and create WBS

    b) Identify risks, perform qualitative risk analysis, perform quantitative risk analysis, and plan risk responses

    c) Plan schedule management, define activities, sequence activities, estimate activity durations and develop schedule

    d) Estimate costs and determine budget

166. All are tools and techniques of the develop schedule process except

    a) Schedule compression

    b) Data analysis

    c) Project documents

    d) Critical path method

167. Judy is a superb project manager at her firm. She is currently working on a project in which a fix is necessary. As a project manager, what should Judy do next?

    a) Check the release documents

    b) Notify the sponsor

    c) Evaluate the impact of the change

    d) Implement the risk response plan

168. Judy is a top project manager at her firm. She is currently working on a project in which a fix *might be* necessary. As a project manager, what should Judy do next?

    a) Prevent changes from occurring

b) Notify the sponsor

c) Evaluate the impact of the change

d) Implement the risk response plan

169. Mitchell is a project manager for a solar car company on a new project that has not started. He wants to know where he can get information about projects like the one, he is about to start. Where would Mitchell go first to get this information?

a) Program manager

b) PMO

c) Portfolio office

d) Sponsor

170. Jeffrey is a new project manager for Apocrypha Inc., a producer of religious books and artifacts. As the new project manager, he must have a plan in which many criteria are met for the condition of the books and artifacts. As a project manager, what document must Jeffrey create to set guidelines in criteria?

a) Project management plan

b) Project documents

c) Risk management plan

d) Quality management plan

171. Marshall is a project manager for the Action Solar Company, a maker of sun car parts. Quality is important in the company. Which best describes the plan quality management process?

a) The process of identifying quality requirements and standards for the project and its deliverables and documenting how the project will demonstrate compliance with quality requirements and standards

b) The process of monitoring and recording the results of executing the quality management activities to assess performance and ensure the project outputs are complete, correct, and meet customer requirements

c) The process of translating the quality management plan into executable quality activities that incorporate the organization's quality policies into the project

d) None of the above

172. Which of the following is an input to the manage quality process?

    a) Quality reports

    b) Quality metrics

    c) Data gathering

    d) Enterprise environmental factors

173. Terri is a new project manager at a manufacturing firm. She has completed the planning stage. Her team has begun implementing the work according to the project plan. One of Terri's team members has noticed a problem with her task but has not yet found a fix. What tools can be used to determine the cause of the problem?

    a) Prototypes

    b) An oscilloscope

    c) Fishbone

    d) Bottom-up estimating

174. David is a new project manager for Voice Activated Systems Enterprises. He wants to get off to the best start understanding ways to deliver a quality product. David and his team are planning for accuracy in quality. Which of the following tools is one of the seven rules of quality control?

    a) Analysis technique

    b) Cause-and-effect diagram

    c) Data representation

    d) Manage quality

175. Emma is a project manager at a paper factory. Before the project starts, she requests information about political influence and public opinion. Which of these are influences out of the project manager's control?

    a) Enterprise environmental factors

    b) Organizational process assets

    c) Evolution environmental factors

    d) Extreme environmental factors

176. Susan is a project manager with many years of experience. Her current project is especially difficult because of problems with the timeline getting extended many times. This could be because the scope is not well defined, and the delays are causing increases in cost because of increased hours of work on the project for fixes. Susan can find all of the following in the project charter except

    a) Project purpose

    b) High-level requirements

    c) Detailed requirements

    d) Key stakeholder list

177. Bradford is the new project manager at Green Thumb Nursery. His current project has constantly run into delays because of new deliverables that must be added for the project to be a success. As a project manager, which documents should Bradford check first to determine deliverables?

    a) Scope management plan and requirements management plan

    b) Project charter and project management plan

    c) Quality management plan and process improvement plan

    d) Risk management plan and risk response plan

178. Jamerson is the project manager of Aqua Rooms, which are short-term underwater apartments. The project Jamerson is managing is consistently encountering incomplete requirements. As a project manager, he would use all tools and techniques to collect requirements except

    a) Data analysis

    b) Decision-making

c) Organizational process assets

d) Interpersonal skills and team skills

179. Jamal is a senior project manager at a major pharmaceutical company. The project involves the testing of a new drug to halt aging. The project data is currently being collected. As a senior project manager, which requirement will Jamal not capture as an input to collect requirements?

a) Project management plan

b) Communication management plan

c) Project documents

d) EEF

180. Maria is a newly hired contract project manager who wants all documents related to the current project. Which document will Maria most want to map deliverables to their respective requirements?

a) OPA

b) Requirements traceability matrix

c) Project management plan

d) Data analysis

181. Which answer best describes the define scope process?

a) The process of developing a detailed description of the project and product

b) The process of creating a scope management plan that documents how the project and product scope will be defined, validated, and controlled

c) The process of subdividing project deliverables and project work into smaller, more manageable components

d) The process of monitoring the status of the project and product scope and managing changes in the scope baseline

182. Work that is outside the scope of the project is demanded by a sponsor, senior management, or stakeholders other than the project team. Which answer best describes this scenario?

    a) Gold plating

    b) Work that is necessary

    c) Work that is unnecessary

    d) Scope creep

183. There is work performed outside the scope of the project and suggested by the project team. Which answer best describes this action?

    a) Gold plating

    b) Work that is necessary

    c) Work that is unnecessary

    d) Scope creep

184. Which process best exemplifies monitoring and control in project integration?

    a) Direct and manage project work

    b) Monitor and control project work

    c) Manage project knowledge

    d) Perform integrated change control

185. Harry is a contractor responsible for the refurbishment of an automobile showroom. The estimated refurbishment cost is $500 per square foot. The total showroom area that needs to be refurbished is 1,000 square feet. Based on his past experience, he knows his team can refurbish 100 square feet per week. As the project manager, Harry will report the steady-state value of the project as

    a) $525,000

    b) $375,000

    c) $555,555.56

    d) $475,000

186. David has been a project manager for many years. David has been communicating with the sponsor and senior management, combining SOW, assumptions, initial stakeholders, and high-level risk into one document. As the project manager, which of the following documents is he creating?

a) Data gathering

b) Project management plan

c) Inspection

d) Project charter

187. Jeffrey is a project manager and wants to define how to estimate, acquire, manage, and utilize physical and team resources. Which process fits the definition for Jeffrey?

a) Develop team

b) Plan resource management

c) Organizational theory

d) Team charter

188. Priscilla is a project manager who transferred from another department. One of the documents Priscilla must create is vital to the success of the project in meeting its deliverables. Which document is created from the output of the develop project management plan process?

a) Project charter

b) Enterprise environmental factors

c) Project management plan

d) Organizational process assets

189. Robert is a new project manager at Use It or Lose It! Inc. Robert does not trust his employees to do their jobs, so he must monitor their every action to make sure he gets the results he wants. As a project manager, what management type is Robert practicing?

a) RAM

b) McGregor's Theory X

    c) Expectancy Theory

    d) McGregor's Theory Y

190. David has been a project manager for many years. David has been communicating with the sponsor and senior management, combining SOW, assumptions, initial stakeholders, and high-level risk into one document. As the project manager, which of the following documents is he creating?

    a) Data gathering

    b) Project management plan

    c) Inspection

    d) Project charter

191. The project manager is responsible for all of the following during stakeholder management except:

    a) Communication

    b) Establishing relationships with stakeholders

    c) Determining stakeholder unique requirements

    d) Hand selecting the stakeholders

192. Which answer best describes the process to manage communications?

    a) Project management plan

    b) The process of ensuring timely and appropriate collection, creation, distribution, storage, retrieval, management, monitoring, and the ultimate disposition of project information

    c) Work performance reports

    d) Team performance

193. David is a new project manager for New Brand Cola LLC. David wants to get off to the best start in understanding the project, people, and environment. As a project manager, David has discovered interpersonal and team skills as a tool and technique of which process?

    a) Meetings

    b) Develop project charter

    c) Organizational process assets

d) Planning

194. Frank is a project manager with Carmon Lip Balm LLC. He and his project team meticulously put together a project plan that captured and strategized for many risks. One of the risks has just materialized. As a project manager, what should Frank do next?

    a) Plan risk management

    b) Monitor risks

    c) Use his interpersonal and team management skills

    d) Implement risk responses

195. Debbie is a project manager at Cool Socks Inc. She is in the planning process for a new project and has completed the sequence activities process. The kickoff of the project occurred three months ago. The project team is currently managing the project. As a project manager, what would Debbie do next?

    a) Estimate activity durations

    b) Close the project

    c) Control schedule

    d) Identify stakeholders

196. Olivia is a new project manager at World of Crowe Inc. Olivia trusts her employees to do their jobs, so she does not monitor their every action to make sure she gets the results she wants. What is the project manager practicing?

    a) RAM

    b) McGregor's Theory X

    c) Expectancy Theory

    d) McGregor's Theory Y

197. Which of the following is an output of the process implement risk response plan?

    a) Change requests

b) Data analysis

c) Approved changes

d) OPA

198. Joseph is a project manager with Carmon Lip Balm LLC. He and his project team meticulously put together a project plan that captured and strategized for many risks. One of the risks has just materialized. As a project manager, what should Joseph do next?

a) Plan risk management

b) Monitor risks

c) Use his interpersonal and team management skills

d) Implement risk responses

199. Which of the following is an output of the process implement risk response plan?

a) Change requests

b) Data analysis

c) Approved changes

d) OPA

200. Which of the following is an input to the manage project knowledge process?

a) Alternative analysis

b) Deliverables

c) OPA updates

d) Project management plan updates

Mock Exam Three
200 Questions—4 Hours Advanced Solutions

1. **Answer: a**. The project management plan is the document the project manager will want most.

2. **Answer: a**. Only a is in the correct order.

3. **Answer: a**. Only a has all the correct elements. Starting, adjusting, and closing are not part of Tuckman's ladder.

4. **Answer: a**. Jonathan needs to create a project management plan which is used by the project manager to manage the project from start to completion. Project documents is not used to track project from start to completion. Work performance reports is a document that shows how well project is performing.

5. **Answer: b**. Develop project charter is the only process on this list. Meetings is a tool and technique for many processes. Organizational process assets are input to many processes, and planning is a process group.

6. **Answer: d**. The lessons learned register is an input.

7. **Answer: d**. Data gathering is a tool and technique, not an input.

8. **Answer: c**. We are clearly in the execute phase of the project. We have already estimated durations because we have entered the execute phase. There is no mention of project close or cancellation. Identifying stakeholders is going on throughout the life cycle of the project. The best answer is control schedule.

9. **Answer: d**. Data gathering is a tool and technique. SOW, enterprise environmental factors, and organizational process assets are inputs for develop project charter.

10. **Answer: d**. The communication plan is a document for planning communication of the project. The project management plan plans the overall activities of the project and contains detailed requirements of the project. The SOW is the statement of work, which includes the objectives of the project. The project charter contains the high-level requirements of the project.

11. **Answer: a**. The difference between monitoring and managing is that monitoring is watching or observing. Managing is an action in which you are actually doing something. In this case, it is the "process of communicating and working with stakeholders."

12. **Answer: a**. The project management plan is the output of the process to develop the project management plan. EEF and OPA are inputs of other processes.

13. **Answer: c**. If the fix is necessary, then checking release documents has already occurred. Implementing the risk response plan would occur if a risk previously planned had occurred. Notifying sponsor might occur if a fix was not previously planned for, and the issue that necessitated the fix would impact the project adversely either in cost, schedule, or quality.

14. **Answer: b**. The project management plan is the output of the process, not a tool and technique.

15. **Answer: c**. Harry will report the project ahead of schedule and over budget.

Cost Variance	(EV - AC) = ($25,000.00)
Schedule Variance	(EV - PV) = $25,000.00

16. **Answer: a**. The project manager would want to prevent the change from occurring and seek alternative solutions. However, if the change must occur, then evaluate the impact of the change. Implement the risk response plan would occur if a risk previously planned had occurred. Notify sponsor might occur if the fix was not previously planned for, and the issue that necessitated the fix would impact the project adversely, either in cost, schedule, or quality.

17. **Answer: a**. Define scope is the planning process that would be performed next. The project management plan is an output of develop project management plan. Plan scope management would have been done previously to collect requirements. Expert judgments is a tool and technique.

18. **Answer: b**. Define activities is the planning process that would be performed next. The project management plan is an output of develop project management plan. Plan scope management would have been done previously to collect requirements. Expert judgments are a tool and technique.

19. **Answer: d**. Organizational process assets and enterprise environmental factors are inputs to many process groups. The final report is an output of the close project or phase process group.

20. **Answer: c**. Plan schedule management is the planning process that would have been performed prior to define activities. The project management plan is an output of develop project management plan. Plan scope management would have been done previously to collect requirements. Expert judgments is a tool and technique.

21. **Answer: b**. Change requests are an output of perform integrated change control process, the project management plan is an output of develop project plan process, and OPA updates are outputs of other processes. Only b is a tool and technique.

22. **Answer: d**. Create WBS is the planning process that would have been performed prior to define activities. The project management plan is an output of develop project management plan. Plan scope management would have been done prior to collect requirements. Data gathering is a tool

and technique.

23. **Answer: d**. Choices a, c, and d are not the best exemplification of monitoring and control in project integration.

24. **Answer: b**. Validate scope is the process that would be performed next because the project is in the execute phase. When execute starts, then the monitor control process starts. Project management and plan scope management are planning processes. Data gathering is a tool and technique.

25. **Answer: a**. The communication management plan is a document for planning communication of the project. The project management plan plans the overall activities of the project and contains detailed requirements of the project. The SOW is the statement of work, which includes the objectives of the project. The project charter contains the high-level requirements of the project.

26. **Answer: b**. Plan resource management is part of the planning stage and answers the question of how to estimate, acquire, manage, and utilize physical and team resources. Develop team is also a process but in the execute stage and would best fit training a resource. Choices c and d are not processes.

27. **Answer: d**. Jeffrey should report the estimate at completion as $516,224.19.

28. **Answer: b**. The keyword here is "how," which describes the plan—in this case, plan resource management.

29. **Answer: b**. McGregor's Theory X assumes that the typical worker has little ambition, avoids responsibility, and is individual-goal oriented. McGregor's Theory Y assumes employees are internally motivated, enjoy their jobs, and work to better themselves without a direct reward in return.

30. **Answer: b**. Control costs is the process that would be performed next since the project is in the execute phase; money is being spent, so the cost must be controlled. When execute starts, then the monitor control process starts. Data gathering is a tool and technique. Define scope and create WBS are planning processes.

31. **Answer: b**. Only b is in the correct order.

32. **Answer: c**. Once the project manager has been notified by senior management or the sponsor that the project is being canceled, then the closing procedure must begin immediately.

33. **Answer: d**. Only d is in the correct order.

34. **Answer: d**. The fact that the question asks "how to" indicates the project is in the planning stage. Develop team is a process in the execute stage. Organizational theory and team charter are not processes.

35. **Answer: c**. Once the contractor has started work, they will be monitored and tracked to make sure the results are being established according to the project plan and the vendor contract. Closing reports for archive comes in the closing phase. Planning what is expected of the vendor would have been performed in the planning stage.

36. **Answer: c**. The resource management plan is a document and is the output of plan resource management.

37. **Answer: c**. Sophia will report the steady-state as $555,555.56.

Estimate at Completion (typical, steady-state, or continuous)	(BAC / CPI) = $555,555.56

38. **Answer: b**. Project document updates is an output.

39. **Answer: b**. The output of validate scope is acceptable deliverables. Validate scope formalizes the acceptance of the completed project deliverables. Verified deliverables are the output of the project tasks. Work performance data is raw data that is reported on change requests. Work performance information is the work performance data that has been transformed for example, number of change requests or forecast estimates.

40. **Answer: d**. Since the project is now in the execute stage, the order of what occurs next is acquire resources, develop team, and manage resources.

41. **Answer: a**. Choices b, c, and d are not in the correct order.

42. **Answer: d**. Only d is in the correct order.

43. **Answer: b**. McGregor's Theory X assumes that the typical worker has little ambition, avoids responsibility, and is individual-goal oriented. McGregor's Theory Y assumes employees are internally motivated, enjoy their jobs, and work to better themselves without a direct reward in return.

44. **Answer: a**. Control resources will be the project manager's next task. Since the project is now in the execute stage, the order of what occurs next is acquire resources, develop team, and manage resources. However, since none of these options are there, the choice that best answers the question is control resources.

45. **Answer: c**. As a project manager, you report the fact at the time and not what you know or assume will happen later. Harry would report the project as ahead of schedule and over budget.

Cost Variance	(EV - AC) = $25,000.00
Schedule Variance	(EV - PV) = $25,000.00

46. **Answer: b**. Assumption and constraint analysis is a tool and technique. Choices c and d are outputs of other processes.

47. **Answer: c.** Plan resource management defines how to estimate, acquire, manage, and utilize physical and team resources.

48. **Answer: d**. The communication plan is a document for planning communication of the project. The project management plan plans the overall activities of the project and contains detailed requirements of the project. The SOW is the statement of work, which includes the objectives of the project. The project charter contains the high-level requirements of the project.

49. **Answer: c**. Performing team development is the next step for the project manager. After the project kickoff the project is in the Execute phase. Create WBS is in the planning phase. Control resources and stakeholder engagement are in the monitoring and control phase.

50. **Answer: b**. Validate scope is the best option here. Create WBS is performed in the planning process, in which the project plan has already been approved. Answer c is the approved project plan. The negotiation with a sponsor for overtime response is already answered in the project plan with the creation and approval of the schedule baseline.

51. **Answer: d**. Data gathering is a tool and technique, not an input.

52. **Answer: a**. If the question asks for a plan, then b is not the answer. Answer c is executing the plan. Answer d is not correct because you always want to communicate in project management. The process of developing is a "plan" type of answer.

53. **Answer: b**. Acceptable deliverables is the output of the validate scope process.

54. **Answer: c**. Develop team will be the project manager's next task. Since the project is now in the execute stage, the order of what occurs next is acquire resources, develop team, and manage resources.

55. **Answer: d**. The next thing the project manager will do is monitor the stakeholder engagement as part of the project plan.

56. **Answer: d**. Option a is identifying stakeholders, b is manage stakeholder engagement, and c does not exist.

57. **Answer: b**. You would think answer b would be common sense, but it is surprising how many testers will miss a question like this on the exam. You never ignore stakeholders because communication, collaboration, and compromise are primary tools of a project manager.

58. **Answer: b**. Project document updates is an output. All others are inputs to one or more processes.

59. **Answer: b**. Develop project charter is the only process on this list. Meetings is a tool and technique for many processes. Organizational process assets are an input to many processes, and planning is a process group.

60. **Answer: c**. The next step in the planning stage after plan procurement management is to plan the stakeholder engagement process. Create WBS happens earlier in the planning stage, and validate scope is in the execute stage. Project managers will not negotiate with the sponsor.

61. **Answer: d**. Change log and project management plan are never a tool and technique. Manage quality is a process.

62. **Answer: b**. McGregor's Theory X assumes that the typical worker has little ambition, avoids responsibility, and is individual-goal oriented. McGregor's Theory Y assumes employees are internally motivated, enjoy their jobs, and work to better themselves without a direct reward in return.

63. **Answer: a**. The difference between monitoring and managing is that monitoring is watching or observing. Managing is an action in which you are actually doing something. In this case, it is the "process of communicating and working with stakeholders."

64. **Answer: b**. McGregor's Theory X assumes that the typical worker has little ambition, avoids responsibility, and is individual-goal oriented. McGregor's Theory Y assumes employees are internally motivated, enjoy their jobs, and work to better themselves without a direct reward in return.

65. **Answer: d**. Only d is in the correct order.

66. **Answer**: **d**. Develop team is the next step for the project manager.

67. **Answer: b**. McGregor's Theory X assumes that the typical worker has little ambition, avoids responsibility, and is individual-goal oriented. McGregor's Theory Y assumes employees are internally motivated, enjoy their jobs, and work to better themselves without a direct reward in return.

68. **Answer: b**. You would think answer b would be common sense, but it is surprising how many testers will miss a question like this on the exam. You never ignore stakeholders because communication, collaboration, and compromise are primary tools of a project manager.

69. **Answer: a**. The next thing the project manager will do is control resources as part of the project plan. At this time, the resources have already been trained and developed. The team is producing results. As a project manager, you want to make sure the results are per the project plan.

70. **Answer: d**. Option a is an output, b is an input, and c is a process.

71. **Answer: b**. The next thing the project manager will do is develop a team as part of the project

plan.

72. **Answer: b.** The project management plan describes the project, work performance reports describe the status of the project, and team performance is the evaluation of the effectiveness of the team.

73. **Answer: d.** Option a is identifying stakeholders, b is manage stakeholder engagement, and c does not exist.

74. **Answer: a.** The difference between monitoring and managing is that monitoring is watching or observing. Managing is an action in which you are actually doing something. In this case, it is the "process of communicating and working with stakeholders."

75. **Answer: b.** Project document updates is an output.

76. **Answer: c.** The next thing the project manager will do is control resources as part of the project plan. At this time, the resources have already been trained and develop. The team is producing results. As a project manager, you want to make sure the results are per the project plan.

77. **Answer: b.** McGregor's Theory X assumes that the typical worker has little ambition, avoids responsibility, and is individual-goal oriented. McGregor's Theory Y assumes employees are internally motivated, enjoy their jobs, and work to better themselves without a direct reward in return.

78. **Answer: a.** Only a is in the correct order.

79. **Answer: a.** Plan risk management is the next step for the project manager.

80. **Answer: b.** Project documents updates is an output.

81. **Answer: b.** Plan communication management is the step that comes before planning to perform qualitative risk analysis.

82. **Answer: b.** Communications analysis describes what is needed to maximize the value of information for project stakeholders. Communications technology includes shared portals, emails, and databases. The communications model is the encoding and decoding of messages. And the communication method is the interaction of information, such as one-way or multidirectional conversations.

83. **Answer: d.** Plan risk management is the next step for the project manager.

84. **Answer: b.** The next thing the project manager will do is control resources as part of the project plan. At this time, the resources have already been trained and developed. The team is producing results. As a project manager, you want to make sure the results are per the project plan.

85. **Answer: a.** Meetings are the only tool and technique on this list. Develop project charter is a

process. OPA is input, and planning alone is a word, not a tool and technique.

86. **Answer: d**. SOW, assumptions, and constraints and OPA are all inputs to the project charter. Data analysis is a tool and technique.

87. **Answer: d**. Only d is in the correct order.

88. **Answer: b**. The output when developing a charter is a project charter and assumptions log.

89. **Answer: b**. Develop project charter is the only process on this list. Meetings is a tool and technique for many processes. Organizational process assets are an input to many processes, and planning is a process group.

90. **Answer: d**. Data gathering is a tool and technique, not an input.

91. **Answer: b**. The next thing the project manager will do is control resources as part of the project plan. At this time, the resources have already been trained and developed. The team is producing results. As a project manager, you want to make sure the results are per the project plan.

92. **Answer: d**. The communication plan is a document for planning communication of the project. The project management plan plans the overall activities of the project and contains detailed requirements of the project. The SOW is the statement of work, which includes the objectives of the project. The project charter contains the high-level requirements of the project.

93. **Answer: c**. Expert judgments is a tool and technique.

94. **Answer: c**. Project charter, EEF, and OPA are all inputs to the process.

95. **Answer: c**. The resource management plan is an output of plan resource management.

96. **Answer: b**. The requirements traceability matrix maps the project deliverables to its requirements. The OPA and project management plan are inputs. Data analysis is a tool and technique.

97. **Answer: a**. Choice b describes plan risk management, and c describes direct and manage projects. As stated earlier, knowing the sequences of the planning group in all knowledge areas is crucial to passing the PMP exam.

98. **Answer: a**. Data analysis is a tool and technique of most processes. Approved changes are an output of performed integrated change control and an input to direct and manage project work. OPA is an input to most processes.

99. **Answer: d**. Data analysis is a tool and technique. Statement of work, assumptions and constraints, and organizational process assets are inputs to the project charter.

100. **Answer: d**. The project management plan has the overall activities of the project and contains detailed requirements of the project. The SOW is the statement of work, which contains the

objectives of the project. The project charter contains the high-level requirements of the project.

101. **Answer: c**. Expert judgments is always a tool and technique.

102. **Answer: d**. Expert judgments, historical information review, and funding limit reconciliation are all tools and techniques that can be used to determine the budget.

103. **Answer: d**. The estimate at completion formula is (AC + (BAC-EV)) / (CPI * SPI). (AC + (BAC-EV)) / (CPI * SPI) = $516,224.19

Complete table solutions below:

Estimated refurbishment cost	$500.00 per square foot
Total showroom area	1,000.00 square feet
Refurbishment pace	100.00 square feet per week

Term	Value
Budget at Completion	($500 x 1,000) = $500,000.00
Planned Value	(4 / 10 x BAC) = $200,000.00
Earned Value	(45% x BAC) = $225,000.00
Actual Cost	$250,000.00
Cost Variance	(EV - AC) = $25,000.00
Schedule Variance	(EV - PV) = $25,000.00
Cost Performance Index	(EV / AC) = 0.90
Schedule Performance Index	(EV / PV) = 1.13
Estimate at Completion (atypical)	(AC + (BAC - EV)) = 525,000
Estimate at Completion (forecast)	(AC+ (BAC - EV)) / (CPI * SPI) = 516,224.19
Estimate at Completion (typical, steady-state or continuous)	(BAC / CPI) = $555,555.56
Estimate to Complete	(EAC - AC) = $305,555.56
Variance at Completion	(BAC - EAC) = $55,555.56

Total duration (1,000 / 100)	= 10.00 weeks
Duration Elapsed	= 4.00 weeks
Percentage completion	= 45%

104. **Answer: a**. Options b, c, and d are not outputs.

105. **Answer: b**. Develop project charter is the process that creates the project charter document, which contains the project's objectives, assumptions, constraints, and high-level requirements. Meetings is a tool and technique. OPA is the organization policies, procedures, and practices, and planning is not a process. Develop project plan is a process.

106. **Answer: d**. Data analysis is a tool and technique. SOW, OPA, and assumptions and constraints are used in the develop project charter process.

107. **Answer: b**. The project charter and assumptions log are the outputs of the develop charter process.

108. **Answer: c**. Expert judgment is a tool and technique. Project charter, EEF, and OPA are inputs to most identify stakeholder processes.

109. **Answer: d**. The project charter does not have detailed information. Options a, b, and c all describe the project charter.

110. **Answer: a**. Choice b better describes plan scope management. Choice c, develop charter, does process detailed information. Choices b, c, and d are performed in the planning stage of the project.

111. **Answer: d**. OPA and EEF are inputs to other processes, and the final report is an output of close process.

112. **Answer: c**. Deliverables is an output of direct and manage the project work process. Options a, b and c are inputs to direct and manage project work.

113. **Answer: a**. Choice b is the develop team process, and c and d involve procurements.

114. **Answer: b**. Decomposition is a tool and technique. The project management plan is an output of develop project plan process

115. **Answer: c**. Option b describes plan scope management and d describes monitor and control project work.

116. **Answer: a**. Code of account identifier and (1.0, 1.1, 1.1.1) are the correct number systems.

117. **Answer: c**. The project management plan is the output of develop project plan. Communication baseline does not exist in PMBOK.

118. **Answer: d**. Interpersonal and team skills are the only tools and techniques in the list. The project management plan is an output of the develop project plan. Manage quality is a process. The change log is an output of perform integrated change control.

119. **Answer: d**. Communication technology is the only tool and technique on the list. The project

management plan is an output of the develop project plan. Manage quality is a process. The change log is an output of perform integrated change control.

120. **Answer: d**. Interpersonal and team skills are only tool and technique on the list. The project management plan is an output of develop project plan. Manage quality is a process. The change log is an output of perform integrated change control.

121. **Answer: d**. There are ten knowledge areas in the *PMBOK* 6th edition. You can get a quick glance at all ten knowledge areas in *PMBOK*, page 25.

122. **Answer: b**. Manage communications is the process of ensuring timely and appropriate collection, creation, distribution, storage, retrieval, management, monitoring, and the ultimate disposition of project information.

123. **Answer: a**. Manage stakeholder engagement is the correct response. Revisit glossary for definitions.

124. **Answer: c**. Manage communications is the process of ensuring timely and appropriate collection, creation, distribution, storage, retrieval, management, monitoring, and the ultimate disposition of project information.

125. **Answer: b**. The process described is manage stakeholder engagement.

126. **Answer: c**. This choice best describes monitor communications.

127. **Answer: b**. Option b best describes the resource management plan.

128. **Answer: d**. The risk management plan is the output of plan risk management.

129. **Answer: a**. Option a best describes plan risk management. Option c is plan quality management, and d does not exist in PMBOK.

130. **Answer: b**. Answer a is the output of plan cost management. Answer c is the output of define scope, and d does not exist in PMBOK.

131. **Answer: a**. Option b is a tool and technique, c is a document, and d is plan resource management.

132. **Answer: a**. Choice b is perform quantitative risk analysis. Answer c is project risk management, and d is project schedule management.

133. **Answer: a**. Option a best describes perform quantitative risk analysis.

134. **Answer: c**. Choice c best describes perform qualitative risk analysis.

135. **Answer: a**. Option a best describes perform quantitative risk analysis.

136. **Answer: a**. Choice b is a tool and technique. Choices c and d are outputs to other processes.

137. **Answer: a**. Choice a is the best description for perform quantitative risk analysis.

138. **Answer: c.** Expert judgments is a tool and technique.

139. **Answer: a.** Answer b does not exist in PMBOK. Answer c is an output of identify risks. Answer d could be either a risk breakdown structure or resource breakdown structure, neither of which is the answer.

140. **Answer: a.** The difference between monitoring and managing is that monitoring is watching or observing. Managing is an action in which you are actually doing something. In this case, it is the "process of communicating and working with stakeholders."

141. **Answer: d.** Option a is identifying stakeholders, b is managing stakeholder engagement, and c does not exist.

142. **Answer: b.** You would think answer b would be common sense, but it is surprising how many testers will miss a question like this on the exam. You never ignore stakeholders because communication, collaboration, and compromise are primary tools of a project manager.

143. **Answer: a.** Option b is plan resource management. Option c is manage risks.

144. **Answer: c.** Option b is an output of plan risk management. Option c is an output of plan cost management. Option d is an output of define scope.

145. **Answer: b.** Option a is plan schedule management. Option d is plan resource management.

146. **Answer: d.** The order is plan cost management, estimate costs, and determine budget.

147. **Answer: d.** Option a describes scope management, b defines risk management, and c is schedule management.

148. **Answer: d.** Analogous, bottom-up, and three-point estimating are tools and techniques for the estimate activity durations process.

149. **Answer: b.** (P+(4(M)+O)/6=(20 + 32(4) + 50) / 6 = 33

150. **Answer: c.** (P+M+O)/3= (32 + 20 + 50) / 3 = 34

151. **Answer: d.** Expert judgments, historical information review, and funding limit reconciliation are all tools and techniques that can be used to determine the budget.

152. **Answer: a.** Options b, c, and d are not outputs.

153. **Answer: c.** Option a describes scope management, b describes defining risk management, and d is cost management.

154. **Answer: a.** Choice b describes plan risk management, and c describes direct and manage projects. As stated earlier, knowing the sequences of the planning group in all knowledge areas is crucial to passing the PMP exam.

155. **Answer: c.** Option a describes scope management, b defines risk management, and d is cost management.

156. **Answer: c.** Decomposition into activities occurs in the define activities process. Decomposition into work packages occurs in the create WBS process. Answer d is a typical PMP exam trick to trip you up because it combines processes like WBS and activities.

157. **Answer: a.** The question clearly states that Jason is still in the planning process, so what process occurs after the sequence that is in the list of choices and part of the planning process group? Define activities, sequence activities, estimate activity duration, et cetera. Knowing the order of processes in the planning process group is crucial to passing the exam. ***Memorize the order of processes in the planning process group!***

158. **Answer: c.** See the order of processes in the planning process group.

159. **Answer: c.** Start to Finish (SF) is very rarely used.

160. **Answer: a.** Finish to Start (FS) is the most commonly used.

161. **Answer: d.** Option a describes scope management, b defines risk management, and c is schedule management.

162. **Answer: d.** Analogous, bottom-up, and three-point estimating are tools and techniques for the estimate activity durations process.

163. **Answer: b.** (P+(4(M)+O)/6=(20 + 32(4) + 50) / 6 = 33

164. **Answer: c.** (P+M+O)/3= (32 + 20 + 50) / 3 = 34

165. **Answer: c.** Choice a is plan scope management, b is plan risk management, and d is plan cost management.

166. **Answer: c.** Project documents are inputs.

167. **Answer: c.** She should evaluate the impact of the change.

168. **Answer: a.** She should prevent changes from occurring.

169. **Answer: b.** Answer b is the best choice. Answer a is an option as the **project manager** can go to the program manager; however, the program manager will go to the PMO and then give the information to the PM. There is no portfolio office. The sponsor would not be an option.

170. **Answer: d.** Option a is the output of develop project plan, b is not the output of the plan quality management process, and c is the output of plan risk management.

171. **Answer: a.** Option b is monitoring quality. Option c is managing quality, and d is not the answer.

172. **Answer: b.** Quality reports are an output; enterprise environmental factors are not input in this

process, and data gathering is a tool and technique.

173. **Answer: c**. An oscilloscope is outside the scope of PMP. Prototypes are used to find problems in the design, and bottom-up estimating is used to estimate the time and cost of a project.

174. **Answer: b**. Only the cause-and-effect diagram is one of the seven rules of quality control.

175. **Answer: a**. Enterprise environmental factors are influences outside the project manager's control. Organizational process assets are factors within the organization's and project team's control. And c and d are not part of the project management plan.

176. **Answer: c**. The project charter does not contain detailed information of any type. Detailed information is found in the project management plan.

177. **Answer: b**. The project charter will contain the vision of what is expected from the project. The project management plan will include the WBS, which will include project deliverables.

178. **Answer: c**. Organizational process assets are inputs. But a, b, and d are all tools and techniques.

179. **Answer: b**. The communication management plan is not an input to collect requirements. The communication management plan is a guide on how the project team will send, receive, distribute, store, and dispose of communication material.

180. **Answer: b**. The requirements traceability matrix maps deliverables to their respective requirements. The OPA and project management plan are inputs. Data analysis is a tool and technique.

181. **Answer: a**. Answer b describes the plan scope management process. Answer c describes the create WBS process. Answer d best describes monitoring and controlling a process.

182. **Answer: d**. Gold plating is work outside the scope of the project but deemed necessary by the project team. Answers b and c are general concepts that help narrow down the scope of the project.

183. **Answer: a**. Gold plating occurs when project team members make unnecessary and unwanted changes to the project.

184. **Answer: b**. Direct and manage project work is in the execute process groups and describe the performance of work. Manage project knowledge manages documents found, generated, compiled, or created because of the work. Perform integrated change control is a process that occurs when the original work plan must deviate with an approved change.

185. **Answer: c**. The steady-state value of the project is computed with the formula below.

Estimate at Completion (typical, steady-state, or continuous)	(BAC / CPI) = $555,555.56

186. **Answer: d**. The project charter contains the objectives and other information needed to create the PMP. Data gathering and inspection are tools and techniques. The project management plan is the output of the process.

187. **Answer: b**. The keyword here is "how," which describes the plan—in this case, plan resource management. Develop team is in the execute process group, and you would see terms such as "manager," "administer," "train," and "translate." Organization theory and team charter describe the organization and the team, respectively, and would not utilize "how."

188. **Answer: c**. Project charter, EEF, and OPA are all inputs to the process.

189. **Answer: b**. McGregor's Theory X assumes that the typical worker has little ambition, avoids responsibility, and is individual-goal oriented. McGregor's Theory Y assumes employees are internally motivated, enjoy their jobs, and work to better themselves without a direct reward in return.

190. **Answer: d**. The project charter contains the objectives and other information needed to create the PMP. Data gathering and inspection are tools and techniques. The project management plan is the output of the process.

191. **Answer: d**. Only d is in the correct order. All others are not in the correct order, according to Tuckman's ladder.

192. **Answer: b**. The project management plan describes the project, work performance reports describe the status of the project, and team performance is the evaluation of the effectiveness of the team.

193. **Answer: b**. Develop project charter is the only process on this list. Meetings is a tool and technique for many processes. Organizational process assets are input to many processes, and planning is a process group.

194. **Answer: d**. Plan risk management is a process to first create the risk management plan document. Interpersonal skills is a tool and technique. Risks are being monitored to see if any occur. If a risk does occur, the next step as a project manager is to implement the risk response strategy.

195. **Answer: c**. We are clearly in the execute phase of the project. We have already estimated durations because we have entered the execute phase. There is no mention of project close or cancellation. Identifying stakeholders is going on throughout the life cycle of the project. The best answer is control schedule.

196. **Answer: d**. McGregor's Theory Y assumes employees are internally motivated, enjoy their jobs, and work to better themselves without a direct reward in return. McGregor's Theory X assumes that the typical worker has little ambition, avoids responsibility, and is individual-goal oriented.

197. **Answer: a**. Data analysis is a tool and technique of most processes. Approved changes are outputs of performed integrated change control and inputs to direct and manage project work. OPA is an input to most processes.

198. **Answer: d**. Plan risk management is a process to first create the risk management plan document. Interpersonal skills is a tool and technique. Risks are being monitored to see if any occur. If a risk does occur, the next step as a project manager is to implement the risk response strategy.

199. **Answer: a**. Data analysis is a tool and technique of most processes. Approved changes are outputs of performed integrated change control and inputs to direct and manage project work. OPA is an input to most processes.

200. **Answer: b**. Choice a is a tool and technique of another process; c and d are outputs to other processes.

Pamphlet:

PMP Reference Guide

How to use this Booklet

Glance through quickly in the morning before work, at lunch and before bed. It will be on your mind 24/7 making you an expert PMP before and after the exam.

July 2020 Exam Updates

Exam content will not change but percentage weight of questions will increase to 42 percent and 8 percent in people and business domain respectively and process will decrease to 50 percent.

Mapping Domains to Project Processes

Domain	Percentage of Items on Test
I. People	42%
II. Process	50%
III. Business Environment	8%
Total	100%

Domains, Tasks, and Enablers:

- » Domain: Domain is defined as the high-level knowledge area that is essential to the practice of project management.
- » Tasks: Tasks are the underlying responsibilities of the project manager within each domain area.
- » Enablers: Illustrative examples of the work associated with the task. Please note that enablers are not meant to be an exhaustive list but instead offer a few examples to help demonstrate what the task encompasses.

Fundamental Concepts

Project: Projects are defined as unique, temporary endeavors with a specific beginning and end.

Program: A *program* is a group of related projects, subprograms, and program activities managed in a coordinated way to obtain benefits not available from managing them individually.

Project Management: Project management is the application of knowledge, skills, tools, and techniques to complete project activities to meet project requirements.

Progressive elaboration: involves continuously improving and detailing a plan as more detailed and specific information and more accurate estimates become available.

Process: 1 of 49 processes consisting of *inputs, tools & techniques* to produce specific *outputs* for the project

Project Life Cycle: description determines the phases a project passes through from one inception to another.

Operations Management: constitute an organization's ongoing, repetitive activities, such as accounting or production.

Project Phase: is a collection of logically related project activities that culminates in the completion of one or more deliverables.

Baseline documents: The original plan plus all approved changes to scope, schedule or cost.

Project management business documents: These are documents such as benefits management plan and business case created which captures data for the intent of the business.

Lessons Learned: documented variances used to avoid variances in future projects

Portfolio: refers to projects, programs, subportfolios, and operations managed as a group to achieve strategic objectives.

Project Data and Information: These are the Work performance data, Work performance information, and Work performance reports documents created for the various stakeholder it is intended.

Project Roles

Project manager: The project manager has the responsibility of leading and managing the project throughout its entire life cycle.

Project coordinator: Maintaining and monitoring project plans, project schedules, work hours, budgets and expenditures.

Project expeditor: checks for problems, monitoring changes in the project, ensuring that the schedule is followed and tracking the status of all tasks to assure the the project deliverables will be ready on time and within budget.

Program Manager: directing all efforts of the projects and project managers.

Project sponsor: is primarily concerned with ensuring that the project delivers the agreed business benefits.

Senior management: is responsible for planning and directing the work of a group of individuals.

Stakeholder: have responsibilities to businesses that include educating developers, financing projects, creating scheduling parameters and setting milestone dates.

Functional Manager: manages and owns the resources in a specific department, such as IT, engineering, public relations, or marketing, and generally directs the technical work of individuals from that functional area who are working on the project.

Project Management Office: is a central place to make sure company standards, procedures and practices are being followed to ensure projects are successful.

653

Organization Types & Project Manager Power	Diagram Of Matrix Organizational types
Functional Matrix. This is the practice of managing individuals with more than one reporting line. **Weak Matrix.** In this form of organization, the functional manager retains most of the power; they "own" the people and resources. In a weak/functional matrix, the project manager is not very powerful. **Balanced Matrix.** A two-dimensional management structure (matrix) in which employees are assigned to two organizational groups: a functional group based on skill sets, which has a functional manager (vertical), and a specific project group, in which employees report to a product manager (horizontal). **Strong Matrix** or **Project Matrix.** The project manager has most of the power, resources, and control over the work.	

Process Framework	Common Inputs, Tools, and Outputs	Integration Management Diagram
Process Groups (5) Initiating processes Planning processes Executing processes Monitoring and controlling processes Closing processes Knowledge Areas (10) Integration Management Scope Management Schedule Management Cost Management Quality Management Human resource Management Communication Management Risk Management Procurement Management Stakeholder Management	**Inputs**: Organizational Process Assets (OPA), Enterprise Environmental Factors (EEF), Project Management Plan, Risk Register, Work Performance Data, Work Performance Reports **Tools**: Expert Judgement, Meetings, Analytical Techniques, Facilitation Techniques, Project Management Information Systems (PMIS) **Outputs**: Change Requests, Updates (Project Management Plan, Projects documents, and OPA) Work Performance Information	

Project Management Process Groups (49)					
Knowledge Areas	Initiating	Planning	Executing	Monitoring and Controlling	Closing
[4] Project Integration Management	4.1 Develop Project Charter	4.2 Develop Project Management Plan	4.3 Direct and Manage Project Work 4.4 Manage Project Knowledge	4.5 Monitor and Control Project Work 4.6 Perform Integrated Change Control	4.7 Close Project or Phase
[5] Project Scope Management		5.1 Plan Scope Management 5.2 Collect Requirements 5.3 Define Scope 5.4 Create WBS		5.5 Validate Scope 5.6 Control Scope	
[6] Project Schedule Management		6.1 Plan Schedule Management 6.2 Define Activities 6.3 Sequence Activities 6.4 Estimate Activity Durations 6.5 Develop Schedule		6.6 Control Schedule	
[7] Project Cost Management		7.1 Plan Cost Management 7.2 Estimate Costs 7.3 Determine Budget		7.4 Control Costs	
[8] Project Quality Management		8.1 Plan Quality Management	8.2 Manage Quality	8.3 Control Quality	

[9] Project Resource Management		9.1 Plan Resource Management 9.2 Estimate Activity Resources	9.3 Acquire Resources 9.4 Develop Team 9.5 Manage Team	9.6 Control Resources	
[10] Project Communications Management		10.1 Plan Communications Management	10.2 Manage Communications	10.3 Monitor Communications	
[11] Project Risk Management		11.1 Plan Risk Management 11.2 Identify Risks 11.3 Perform Qualitative Risk Analysis 11.4 Perform Quantitative Risk Analysis 11.5 Plan Risk Responses	11.6 Implement Risk Responses	11.7 Monitor Risks	
[12] Project Procurement Management		12.1 Plan Procurement Management	12.2 Conduct Procurements	12.3 Control Procurements	
[13] Project Stakeholder Management	13.1 Identify Stakeholders	13.2 Plan Stakeholder Engagement	13.3 Manage Stakeholder Engagement	13.4 Monitor Stakeholder Engagement	

Project Integration Management

Process	Inputs	Tools and Techniques	Outputs
4.1 Develop Project Charter	Business documents	Expert Judgments Data gathering Interpersonal skills Meetings	Project charter Assumptions log

Process	Inputs	Tools and Techniques	Outputs
4.2 Develop Project Management Plan	Project charter Outputs from other processes EEF	Expert Judgments Data gathering	Project management plan

Process	Inputs	Tools and Techniques	Outputs
4.3 Direct and Manage Project Work	Project management plan Project documents » Change log » Lessons learned register » Milestones list » Project communications » Project schedule » Requirements traceability matrix » Risk register » Risk report Approved change requests OPA EEF	Expert Judgments PMIS Meetings	Deliverables Work performance data Issues log Change requests PMP updates Project documents updates Activity list Assumptions log Lessons learned register Requirements documentation Risk register Stakeholder register OPA updates

Process	Inputs	Tools and Techniques	Outputs
4.4 Manage Project Knowledge	Project management plan Project documents » Lessons learned register » Project team assignments » Resource breakdown structure » Stakeholder register Deliverables OPA EEF	Expert Judgments Knowledge Management Information Management Interpersonal and team skills » Active listening » Facilitation » Leadership » Networking » Political awareness	Lessons learned register PMP updates OPA updates

Process	Inputs	Tools and Techniques	Outputs
13.4 Monitor Stakeholder Engagement	Project management plan » Scope management plan » Schedule management plan » Costs management plan » Quality management plan » Human resources management plan » Risks management plan » Communication management plan » Procurement management plan » Stakeholder management plan » Requirements management plan » Scope baseline » Schedule baseline » Cost baseline Project documents » Assumptions log » Basis of estimates » Cost forecasts » Issues log » Quality report » Lessons learned register » Milestone list » Risk register » Risk report » Schedule forecast Work performance information » Deliverables » Implementation status for change requests » Forecast estimates to complete EEF OPA	Data analysis » Alternative analysis » Cost-benefit analysis » Earned value analysis » Root cause analysis » Trend analysis » Variance analysis Estimate at completion Schedule forecasts Cost forecasts Decision-making Meetings	Work performance reports » Status reports » Progress reports » Change requests » Project management plan updates » Resource management plan » Communications management plan » Stakeholder engagement plan Project documents updates » Cost forecasts » Issues log » Lessons learned register » Project communications » Risk register » Stakeholder register » Schedule forecasts

Process	Inputs	Tools and Techniques	Outputs
4.6 Perform Integrated Change Control	Project management plan » Change management plan » Configuration management plan » Cost baseline » Schedule baseline » Scope baseline Project documents » Basis of estimates » Requirement traceability matrix » Risk report Work performance reports Change requests OPA EEF	Expert judgments Change control tools Data analysis » Alternative analysis » Cost-benefit analysis Decision-making » Voting » Autocratic decision-making » Multicriteria decision analysis Meetings	Approved change requests Project management plan updates Project documents updates

Process	Inputs	Tools and Techniques	Outputs
4.7 Close Project or Phase	Project charter Project management plan All components Project documents » Assumptions log » Basis of estimates » Change log » Issues log » Lessons learned register » Milestone list » Project communications » Quality control measurements » Quality report » Requirements documentation » Risk register » Risk report » Accepted deliverables » Business documents » Business case » Benefits management plan Agreements Procurement documents OPA	Expert judgments Data analysis » Document analysis » Regression analysis » Trend analysis » Variance analysis Meetings	Final product documents Final product, service, or result Final report OPA updates

Remarks about INTEGRATION MANAGEMENT

Business case describes why the project is necessary and includes information on funding the project.

Project selection methods offer a set of time-tested techniques based on sound logical reasoning to arrive at a choice of project and filter out undesirable projects with a very low likelihood of success.

Project Charter is a statement of the scope, objectives, and participants in a project. It provides a preliminary delineation of roles and responsibilities, outlines the project objectives, identifies the main stakeholders, and defines the authority of the project manager. It serves as a reference of authority for the future of the project.

Change requests may be necessary if you find that some activities were not initially discovered through progressive elaboration.

Closing process group is to conclude all activities across all project management process groups and formally complete the project, phase, or contractual obligations.

Project Scope Management

Process	Inputs	Tools and Techniques	Outputs
5.1 Plan Scope Management	Project charter Project management plan Quality management plan Project life cycle description Development approach EEF OPA	Expert judgments Data analysis » Alternative analysis for collecting requirements Meetings	Scope management plan Requirements management plan

Process	Inputs	Tools and Techniques	Outputs
5.2 Collect Requirements	Project charter Project management plan Project documents Business documents Agreements EEF OPA	Expert judgments Data gathering » Benchmarking Data analysis » Document analysis Decision-making » Voting » Multicriteria analysis Data representation » Affinity diagram » Mind mapping Interpersonal and team skills Context diagram Prototypes	Requirements documentation Requirements traceability matrix

Process	Inputs	Tools and Techniques	Outputs
5.3 Define Scope	Project charter Project management plan » Scope management plan Project documents EEF OPA	Expert judgments Data analysis » Alternative analysis Decision-making » Multicriteria decision analysis Interpersonal and team skills » Facilitation Product analysis	Project scope statement Project document updates

Process	Inputs	Tools and Techniques	Outputs
5.4 Create WBS	Project management plan » Scope management plan Project documents » Project scope statement » Requirements document EEF OPA	Expert judgments Decomposition	Scope baseline Project scope statement WBS Work package WBS dictionary Planning package Project document updates

Process	Inputs	Tools and Techniques	Outputs
5.5 Validate Scope	Project management plan » Scope management plan » Requirements management plan Project documents » Lessons learned register » Quality report » Requirements documentation » Requirements traceability matrix » Verified deliverables » Work performance data	Inspection Decision-making » Voting	Acceptable deliverables Work performance information Change requests Project documents updates » Lessons learned register » Requirements documentation » Requirements traceability matrix

Process	Inputs	Tools and Techniques	Outputs
5.6 Control Scope	Project management plan » Scope management plan » Requirements management plan » Change management plan » Configuration management plan » Scope baseline Performance measurement baseline Project documents » Lessons learned register » Requirements documentation » Requirements traceability matrix Work performance data OPA	Data analysis » Variance analysis » Trend analysis	Work performance information Change requests Project management plan updates » Scope management plan » Schedule baseline » Cost baseline » Scope baseline » Performance measurement baseline Project documents » Lessons learned register » Requirements documentation » Requirements traceability matrix

Remarks about SCOPE MANAGEMENT

Delphi technique is used to solicit information anonymously and gather honest feedback by eliminating intimidation.

Data analysis includes the stakeholder analysis of its interests, legal rights, ownership, knowledge, and contribution. It may also include analyzing documents from previous projects.

Data representation is an exercise in which the stakeholders are represented in a model such as a power/interest grid, a power influence grid, or an impact/influence grid. (See the figure below.)

Alternative analysis is the evaluation of the different choices available to achieve a particular project management objective.

Variance analysis is used to compare the baseline to the actual results.

Trend analysis is used to determine if there is a pattern such as whether the performance is improving or deteriorating over time.

WBS Diagrams on the Exam

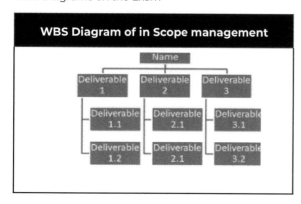

WBS Diagram of in Scope management

Project Schedule Management

Process	Inputs	Tools and Techniques	Outputs
6.1 Plan Schedule Management	Project charter Project management plan » Scope management plan Development approach EEF OPA	Expert judgments Data analysis » Alternative analysis » Rolling wave Meetings	Schedule management plan

Process	Inputs	Tools and Techniques	Outputs
6.2 Define Activities	Project management plan » Schedule management plan » Scope baseline EEF OPA	Expert judgments Decomposition Rolling wave planning Meetings	Activity list Activity attributes Milestone list Change requests PMP updates » Schedule baseline » Cost baseline

Process	Inputs	Tools and Techniques	Outputs
6.3 Sequence Activities	Project management plan » Schedule management plan » Scope baseline Project documents EEF OPA	Precedence diagramming method (PDM) Dependency determination and integration » Mandatory dependency » Discretionary dependency » External dependencies » Internal dependencies Leads and lags PMIS	Project schedule network diagram Project documents updates

Process	Inputs	Tools and Techniques	Outputs
6.4 Estimate Activity Durations	Project management plan Project documents » Activity attributes, activity list, assumption log » Lessons learned register » Milestone list » Project team assignments » Resource breakdown structure (RBS) » Resource calendars » Resource requirements » Risk register EEF OPA	Expert judgments Analogous estimating Parametric estimating Three point estimating Bottom-up estimating Data analysis » Alternative analysis » Reserve analysis Decision-making Meetings	Duration estimates Basis estimates Project documents updates Activity attributes Assumption log Lessons learned register

Process	Inputs	Tools and Techniques	Outputs
6.5 Develop Schedule	Project management plan » Schedule management plan » Scope baseline Project documents » Activity attributes, activity list, assumption log » Basis of estimates » Duration estimates » Lessons learned register » Milestone list » Project schedule network diagrams » Project team assignments » Resource breakdown structure (RBS) » Resource calendars » Resource requirements » Risk register » Agreements EEF OPA	Schedule network analysis » Critical path method » Resource optimization Data analysis » What-if scenario analysis » Monte Carlo simulation Leads and lags Schedule compression PMIS Agile release planning	Schedule baseline Project schedule » Schedule data » Project calendars » Change requests Project management plan updates » Schedule management plan » Cost baseline Project documents updates » Activity attributes, activity list, assumption log » Duration estimates » Lessons learned register » Resource requirements » Risk register

Process	Inputs	Tools and Techniques	Outputs
6.6 Control Schedule	Project management plan » Schedule management plan » Scope baseline » Schedule baseline » Performance measurement baseline Project documents » Lessons learned register » Project calendars » Project schedule » Resource calendars » Schedule data Work performance data OPA	Data analysis » Earned value analysis » Iteration burndown chart » Performance reviews » Trend analysis » Variance analysis » What-if scenario analysis Project management software Critical path method PMIS Resource optimization Leads and lags Schedule compression	Work performance information Schedule forecasts Change requests Project management plan updates » Schedule management plan » Schedule baseline » Performance measurement baseline Cost baseline » Project documents updates » Assumption log » Basis of estimates » Lessons learned register » Project schedule » Resource calendars » Schedule data

Remarks about SCHEDULE MANAGEMENT

Decomposition is the process of creating WBS work packages into activities.

Rolling wave planning is a technique wherein work to be completed in the near term is planned in detail, while work further in the future is planned at a higher level.

Milestone list is a list of significant points or events in a project.

critical path is the sequence of activities that represents the longest path through a project, which determines the shortest duration.

Resource optimization is used to adjust the start and finish dates of activities to match adjusted planned resource availability. Adjusting the schedule for resource optimization includes either resource leveling or resource smoothing.

Resource leveling is used when shared or critically required resources are only available at certain times or in limited quantities or are overallocated, such as when a resource has been assigned to two or more projects during the same time.

Resource smoothing does not change the critical path, and the completion date may not be delayed because with resource smoothing, the activities are adjusted on the schedule model so the requirements for resources on the project do not exceed certain predefined resource limits.

What-if scenario analysis is the process of changing the values in cells to see how those changes will affect the outcome of formulas on the worksheet.

Monte Carlo simulation is a quantitative risk-analysis technique used to identify the risk level of completing the project.

Schedule compression is used to shorten the schedule duration without reducing the project scope to meet imposed constraints.

Crashing shortens schedule duration by adding resources, such as approving overtime or paying to expedite delivery to activities on the critical path.

Fast-tracking is when activities normally done in sequence are performed in parallel for at least a portion of their duration.

Precedence Diagram Method (PDM)

Analogous estimating is cost estimating based on a previous project similar to the current one.

Parametric estimating uses a similar previous project with a statistical relationship between historical data and variables.

Bottom-up estimating is the most accurate way to estimate costs because each work package in the WBS is analyzed.

Three-point estimating uses a formula based on most likely, optimistic, and pessimistic time estimates.

Reserve analysis estimates include contingency reserves. As more information becomes available through progressive elaboration, the contingency reserve is changed, reduced, and possibly eliminated.

Voting is used to select for best response involving project team members when discussing cost estimates.

Schedule forecasts are the computed time estimates of the earn value management (EVM) compared against schedule baseline.

Project Cost Management

Process	Inputs	Tools and Techniques	Outputs
7.1 Plan Cost Management	Project charter Project management plan » Schedule management plan » Risk management plan EEF OPA	Expert judgments Data analysis » Alternative analysis Self-funding Funding with equity or debt Making resources Purchasing resources Renting resources Leasing resources Meetings	Cost management plan » Units of measure » Level of precision » Level of accuracy » Control threshold Strategic funding choices Procedures for fluctuations in currency Procedure for project cost recording

Process	Inputs	Tools and Techniques	Outputs
7.2 Estimate Costs	Project management plan » Cost management plan » Quality management plan » Scope baseline » Project scope statement » WBS » WBS dictionary Project documents » Lessons learned » Project schedules » Resource requirements » Risk register EEF OPA	Expert judgments Analogous estimating Parameter estimating Bottom up estimating Three point estimating Data analysis » Alternative analysis » Reserve analysis » Cost of quality PMIS Decision-making » voting	Cost estimates » Quantitative assessments » Contingency amounts » Basis of estimates Project documents updates » Lessons learned » Project schedule » Risk register

Process	Inputs	Tools and Techniques	Outputs
7.3 Determine Budget	Project management plan » Cost management plan » Resource management plan » Scope baseline Project documents » Basis estimates » Cost estimates » Project schedule » Risk register Business documents » Business case » Benefits management plan Agreement s EEF OPA	Expert judgments Cost aggregation Data analysis » Reserve analysis Historical information review » Analogous estimates » Parametric estimates Funding limitation reconciliation Financing	Cost baseline Project funding requirements Project documents updates » Cost estimates » Project schedule » Risk register

Process	Inputs	Tools and Techniques	Outputs
6.6 Control costs	Project management plan » Cost management plan » Cost baseline » Performance measurement baseline Project documents » Lessons learned register » Project funding requirements » Work performance data OPA	Expert judgments Data Analysis » Earned value analysis » Variance analysis » Trend analysis » What if scenario analysis » To-complete performance index (TCPI) PMIS	Work performance information Cost forecasts Change requests Project management plan updates » Cost management plan » Cost baseline » Performance measurement baseline Project documents updates » Assumption log » Basis of estimates » Cost estimates » Lessons learned register » Risk register

Remarks about COST MANAGEMENT

Cost forecasts are the computed cost estimates of the earn value management (EVM) compared against cost baseline.

Earned value analysis is used to capture information on schedule forecasts and cost forecasts.

Estimate at completion (EAC) is a forecast of the project's final cost.

Estimate to Completion (ETC) is how long until completion which is the EAC – AC.

Earn Value Management Formulas and Meanings		
Abbr.	Terminology	Formula
CV	Cost Variance	EV - AC
SV	Schedule Variance	EV - PV
CPI	Cost Performance Index	EV / AC
SPI	Schedule Performance Index	EV / PV
EAC	Estimate at Completion	AC + (BAC - EV)
		BAC / CPI
		AC + [(BAC-EV) / (CPI*SPI)]
ETC	Estimate to Completion	EAC - AC
VAC	Variance at Completion	BAC - EAC
TCPI	To Complete Performance Index	(BAC - EV) / (BAC - AC)
		(BAC - EV) / (EAC - AC)

To Complete Performance Index (TCPI) is the Cost performance needed to complete work Assumes original budget cannot be met which is BAC - EV) / (BAC - AC) or (BAC - EV) / (EAC - AC)

Variance at Completion (VAC) determine is forecast to be over or under budget for the project which is BAC-EAC.

Cost Performance Index (CPI) determine rate the project is spending money which is calculated with EV / AC=CPI

Schedule Performance Index (SPI) determines rate the project team is working which is calculate with EV / PV=SPI

Cost variance (CV) is defined as the "difference between earned value and actual costs. (CV = EV – AC)

Schedule variance (SV), which measures the difference between the earned value (EV) (the value of work actually performed) and the planned value (PV), so SV = EV – PV

Planned Value (PV) is the authorized budget assigned to work to be accomplished for an activity

Budget at Completion (BAC) refers to the sum of all **budget** values that have been previously established for the work to be performed on a project, or on components within a project

Cost baseline is used as an example in which cost performance is measured and monitored to gauge the importance of the project. This cost baseline is created by estimating the costs by the period in which the project would be completed.

669

Process	Inputs	Tools and Techniques	Outputs
8.1 Plan Quality Management	Project charter Project management plan » Requirements management plan » Risk management plan » Stakeholder engagement plan » Scope baseline Project documents » Assumptions log » Requirements documentation » Requirements traceability matrix » Risk register » Stakeholder register OPA EEF	Expert judgments Data gathering » Benchmarking » Brainstorming » Interviews Data analysis » Cost-benefit analysis » Cost of quality Data representation » Flowcharts » Logical model » Matrix diagrams » Mind mapping » Decision-making » Multicriteria analysis » Test and inspection Meetings	Quality management plan PMP updates » Risk management plan » Scope baseline Quality metrics Project documents updates » Lessons learned register » Requirements traceability matrix » Risk register » Stakeholder register

Process	Inputs	Tools and Techniques	Outputs
8.2 Manage Quality	Project management plan » Quality management plan Project documents » Lessons learned register » Quality control measurements » Quality metrics » Risk report OPA	Data gathering » Checklists Data analysis » Alternative analysis » Document analysis » Process analysis » Root cause analysis Decision-making » Multicriteria decision analysis Data representation » Affinity diagrams » Cause-and-effect diagrams » Flowcharts » Histograms » Matrix diagrams » Scatter diagrams Audits Design for X Problem-solving Quality improvement methods	Quality reports Test and evaluation documents Change requests PMP updates » Quality management plan » Scope baseline » Schedule baseline » Cost baseline » Project documents updates » Issues log » Lessons learned register » Risk register

Process	Inputs	Tools and Techniques	Outputs
8.3 Control Quality	Project management plan » Quality management plan » Project documents » Lessons learned register » Quality metrics » Test and evaluation documents » Approved change requests » Deliverables Work performance data OPA EEF	Data Gathering » Checklists » Check sheets/tally sheets » Statistical gathering » Questionnaires/surveys Data analysis » Performance reviews » Root cause analysis Inspection Testing/product evaluations Data representation » Cause-and-effect diagrams » Flowcharts » Check sheets » Pareto diagrams » Histograms » Control charts » Scatter diagrams Meetings	Quality control measurements Verified deliverables Work performance information Change requests Project Management plan updates » Quality management plan Project documents updates » Issues log » Lessons learned register » Risk register » Test and evaluation documents

Remarks about QUALITY MANAGEMENT

Cost of quality (COQ) refers to the total costs needed to bring products or services up to standards defined by project management professionals.

Inspection is when the contractor performs the structural review of the work—either a review of the deliverables or a physical review.

"Prevention over inspection" means that it costs less to prevent quality issues than it does to correct; meaning better control over your budgets.

One Sigma 68% of the observations in a process would be within one standard deviation

Two Sigma 95% of the observations in a process would be within two standard deviation

Three Sigma 99.73 of the observations in a process would be within three standard deviation

Six Sigma method focuses on understanding customers' requirements better and eliminating defects and waste. 3.4 defects per million; 99.99966% meet specifications

Quality control measurements are the documented results of control quality.

Seven Basic tools diagram in Quality management	Quality Management control tools
1. **Check sheets** are simple tally sheets that are used to gather data. Use this template when categorizing how often a problem occurs. 2. **Pareto diagram** is a chart that consists of a vertical bar and sometimes a bar-and-line graph. The vertical bar represents the frequency of defects from most to least, and the line represents a cumulative percentage of the defects. 3. **Histogram chart** is a bar graph that illustrates the frequency of an event occurring using the height of the bar as an indicator. 4. **Scatter diagrams** allow you to analyze the relationship between two variables. 5. **Control chart** is a graphic display of process data over time and against established control limits that has a centerline that assists in detecting a trend of plotted values toward control limit. 6. **Cause-and-effect diagram, Fishbone, Ishakawa** is a tool that can help you perform a cause-and effect analysis for a problem you are trying to solve. This type of analysis enables you to discover the root cause of a problem. 7. **Flowcharts** above provide visual representations of project processes.	

Project Human Resources Management

Process	Inputs	Tools and Techniques	Outputs
9.1 Plan Resource Management	Project charter Project management plan » Quality management plan » Scope baseline » Project documents » Project schedule » Requirements documentation Risk register Stakeholder register OPA EEF	Expert judgments Data representation » Hierarchical charts » Responsibility assignment matrix » Text-oriented formats » Organizational theory Meetings	Resource management plan Team charter PMP updates » Assumption log » Risk register

Process	Inputs	Tools and Techniques	Outputs
9.2 Estimate Activity Resources	Project management plan » Resource management plan » Scope baseline Project documents » Activity attributes » Activity list » Assumption log » Cost estimates » Resource calendars » Risk register OPA EEF	Expert judgments Analogous estimating Parametric estimating Three point estimating Bottom-up estimating Data analysis	Resource requirements Basis estimates Resource breakdown structure (RBS) Project document updates » Activity attributes » Assumption log » Lessons learned register

Process	Inputs	Tools and Techniques	Outputs
9.3 Acquire Resources	Project management plan » Resource management plan » Procurement management plan » Cost baseline Project documents » Project schedule » Resource calendars » Resource requirements » Stakeholder register OPA EEF	Decision-making » Multicriteria analysis Interpersonal skills » Negotiation Pre-assignment Virtual teams	Physical resource assignments Project team assignments Resource calendars Change requests PMP updates » Resource management plan » Cost baseline Project documents updates » Lessons learned register » Project schedule » RBS » Resource requirements » Risk register » Stakeholder register EEF updates OPA updates

Process	Inputs	Tools and Techniques	Outputs
9.4 Develop Team	Project management plan » Resource management plan Project documents » Lessons learned register » Project schedule » Project team assignments » Resource calendars » Team charter OPA EEF	Colocation Virtual teams Mixed locations Communication technology Interpersonal and team skills » Conflict management » Influencing » Motivation » Negotiation » Team building Recognition and rewards Training Individual and team assessments Meetings	Team performance assessments Change requests PMP updates » Resource management plan Project documents updates » Lessons learned register » Project schedule » Project team assignments » Resource calendars » Team charter » EEF updates » OPA updates

Process	Inputs	Tools and Techniques	Outputs
9.5 Manage Team	Project management plan » Resource management plan Project documents » Issues log » Lessons learned register » Project team assignments » Team charter Work performance report Team performance OPA EEF	Interpersonal and team skills » Conflict management » Decision-making » Emotional intelligence » Influencing » Leadership PMIS	Change requests PMP updates » Resource management plan » Cost baseline » Schedule baseline Project documents updates » Issues log » Lessons learned register » Project team assignments EEF updates

Process	Inputs	Tools and Techniques	Outputs
9.6 Control Resources	Project management plan » Resource management plan Project documents » Issues log » Lessons learned register » Physical resource assignments » Project schedule » Resource breakdown structure » Resource requirements » Risk register Work performance data Agreements OPA	Data Analysis » Alternative analysis » Cost-benefit analysis » Performance reviews » Trend analysis » Problem-solving Interpersonal and team skills » Negotiation » Influencing PMIS	Work performance information Change requests PMP updates » Resource management plan » Schedule baseline » Cost baseline Project documents updates » Assumption log » Issues log » Lessons learned register » Physical resource assignments » Resource breakdown structure » Risk register

Remarks about HUMAN RESOURCE MANAGEMENT

Herzberg's motivation-hygiene theory - states that there are certain factors in the workplace that cause job satisfaction while a separate set of factors cause dissatisfaction, all of which act independently of each other.

Project Communications Management

Process	Inputs	Tools and Techniques	Outputs
10.1 Plan Communications Management	Project charter Project management plan » Resource management plan » Stakeholder engagement plan Project documents » Requirements documentation » Stakeholder register OPA EEF	Expert judgments Communications requirements analysis Communication technology Communication models Communication skills PMIS Project reporting Interpersonal and team skills » Communication styles assessment » Political awareness » Cultural awareness Data Representation » Stakeholder engagement assessment matrix Meetings	Communications management plan PMP updates » Stakeholder engagement plan Project documents updates » Project schedule » Stakeholder register Organizational process assets updates

Process	Inputs	Tools and Techniques	Outputs
10.2 Manage Communications	Project management plan » Requirements management plan » Communications management plan » Stakeholder engagement plan Project documents » Change log » Issues log » Lessons learned register » Quality report » Risk report » Stakeholder register Work performance reports OPA EEF	Communications technology Communications methods Communications skills » Communications competence » Feedback » Nonverbal » Presentations PMIS Project reporting Interpersonal and team skills » Active listening » Conflict management » Cultural awareness » Meeting management » Networking » Political awareness Meetings	Project communications PMP updates » Communications management plan » Stakeholder engagement plan Project documents updates » Issues log » Lessons learned register » Project schedule » Risk register » Stakeholder register OPA updates

Process	Inputs	Tools and Techniques	Outputs
10.3 Monitor Communications	Project management plan » Resource management plan » Communications management plan » Stakeholder engagement plan Project documents » Issues log » Lessons learned register » Project communications Work performance data OPA EEF	Expert judgments PMIS Data analysis » Stakeholder engagement assessment matrix Interpersonal and team skills » Observation » Conversation skills Meetings	Work performance information Change requests Project management plan updates » Communications management plan » Stakeholder engagement plan Project document updates » Issues log » Lessons learned register

Remarks about COMMUNICATIONS MANAGEMENT

Communication channels is the number of communication channels be calculated using the formula N (N - 1) / 2; where N = the number of people.

Communication methods are interactive (multidirectional conversations), push (emails), and pull (shared storage, portals, or websites).

Communication models include encoding, which is transmitting the message, and decoding, which is receiving the message.

Communication technology includes shared portals, video and conferencing, chats, databases, social media, email, and websites.

Communications requirements analysis combines communications types and formats as needed to maximize the value of the information for project stakeholders.

Project Risk Management

Process	Inputs	Tools and Techniques	Outputs
11.1 Plan Risk Management	Project charter Project management plan » All subsidiary plans Project documents » Stakeholder register EEF OPA	Expert judgments Data analysis Meetings	Risk management plan » Methodology » Roles and responsibilities » Funding » Timing » Risk categories Probability and impact matrix Revised stakeholder tolerances Tracking

Process	Inputs	Tools and Techniques	Outputs
11.2 Identify Risks	Project management plan » Requirements management plan » Schedule management plan » Cost management plan » Quality management plan » Resource management plan » Risk management plan » Scope baseline » Schedule baseline » Cost baseline Project documents » Assumptions log » Cost estimates » Duration estimates » Issues log » Lessons learned register » Requirements documentation » Stakeholder register Agreements Procurement documents EEF OPA	Expert judgments Data gathering » Brainstorming » Checklists » Interviews Data analysis » Root cause analysis » Assumption and constraint analysis » SWOT analysis » Document analysis Interpersonal and team skills Facilitation Prompt lists Meetings	Risk register Risk report Project documents updates » Assumption log » Issues log » Lessons learned register

Process	Inputs	Tools and Techniques	Outputs
11.3 Perform Qualitative Risk Analysis	Project management plan » Risk management plan Project documents » Assumptions log » Risk register » Stakeholder register OPA EEF	Expert judgments Data gathering » Interviews of » Data analysts » Risk data quality assessment » Risk probability and impact assessment » Assessment of other risk parameters Interpersonal and team skills » Facilitation Risk categorization Data representation » Probability and impact matrix » Hierarchical charts	Project documents updates » Assumptions log » Issues log » Risk register » Risk report

Process	Inputs	Tools and Techniques	Outputs
11.4 Perform Quantitative Risk Analysis	Project management plan » Risk management plan » Scope baseline » Schedule baseline » Cost baseline Project documents » Assumption log » Basis of estimates » Cost estimates » Cost forecasts » Duration estimates » Milestone list » Risk register » Risk report » Schedule forecasts OPA EEF	Expert judgments Data gathering » Interviews Interpersonal and team skills » Facilitation Representations of uncertainty Data analysis » Simulations » Sensitivity analysis » Decision tree analysis » Influence diagrams	Project documents updates » Risk report » Assessment of overall project risks » Detail probabilistic analysis of project » Prioritized list of individual project risks » Trends in the quantitative risk analysis results » Recommended risk responses

Process	Inputs	Tools and Techniques	Outputs
11.5 Plan Risk Responses	Project management plan » Resource management plan » Risk management plan » Cost baseline Project documents » Lessons learned register » Project schedule » Project team assignments » Resource calendars » Risk register » Risk report » Stakeholder register OPA EEF	Expert judgments Data gathering » Interviews Interpersonal and team skills » Facilitation Data analysis » Alternative analysis Decision-making » Multicriteria decision analysis Contingency response strategies Strategies for overall project risk » Strategies for threats » Strategies for opportunities	Change requests Project management plan updates » Schedule management plan » Cost management plan » Quality management plan » Resource management plan » Procurement management plan » Scope baseline » Schedule baseline » Cost baseline Project documents updates » Assumptions log » Cost forecasts » Lessons learned register » Project schedule » Project team assignments » Risk register » Risk report

679

Process	Inputs	Tools and Techniques	Outputs
11.6 Implement Risk Response	Project management plan » Risk management plan Project documents » Lessons learned register » Risk register » Risk report OPA	Expert judgments Interpersonal skills Influencing PMIS	Change requests Project document updates » Issues log » Lessons learned register » Project team assignments » Risk register » Risk report

Process	Inputs	Tools and Techniques	Outputs
11.7 Monitor Risks	Project management plan » Risk management plan Project documents » Issues log » Lessons learned register » Risk register » Risk report Work performance data Work performance reports	Data analysis » Technical performance analysis » Reserve analysis Audits Meetings	Work performance information Change requests Project management updates Project documents updates » Assumptions log » Issues log » Lessons learned register » Risk register » Risk report OPA updates

Remarks about RISK MANAGEMENT

SWOT analysis analyzes the project's strengths, weaknesses, opportunities, and threats.

Risk categorization or grouping of risks is usually structured with a risk breakdown structure (RBS).

Probability impact matrix is the process of assessing the probabilities and consequences of risk events if they are realized.

Strategies for Threats	Strategies for Opportunities	Strategies for Project Risk	Contingent Response Strategies
» **Escalating** is appropriate when the threat is outside the scope of the project and at the program, portfolio, or another organizational level, but not at the project level.	» **Escalation** is appropriate when the opportunity is outside the scope of the project and at the program, portfolio, or other organizational levels, but not at the project level.	» To avoid risk when a team member is not working out, that person must be released. Another cross-trained team member should take their place until a suitable replacement can be found.	This type of response is only executed under predetermined conditions. When the risk does occur, there will be sufficient warning to implement the response plan, such as missing a milestone or a task gaining higher priority with the seller.
» **Avoidance** is when the project team acts to eliminate the threat or protect the project from its impact. In this case, the project team will attempt to remove the threat, extend the schedule, change the project schedule, or reduce the scope.	» **Exploitation** is appropriate with high-priority opportunities where the organization wants to make sure the opportunity is realized, such as using a more talented resource to increase the chances that a task completes sooner.	» **Exploit** high-priority opportunities where the organization wants to make sure the opportunity is realized, such as using a more talented resource to increase chances that a task completes sooner.	
» **Transference** involves shifting ownership to a third party, such as payment of insurance premiums so that if the risk occurs, its impact will be minimized.	» **Sharing** involves transferring ownership to a third party. Examples of sharing actions include partnerships, teams, and joint ventures.	» **Sharing** involves transferring ownership to a third party. Examples of sharing actions include partnerships, teams, and joint ventures.	
» **Mitigation** is action taken to reduce the probability the risk will occur, such as designing redundancy into the system that may reduce the impact of failure.	» **Enhancement** is used to increase the probability or impact of an opportunity. Examples of enhancing opportunities are increasing resources such as fast-tracking and crashing to finish faster.	» **Acceptance** acknowledges the existence of the threat. However, no action is taken.	
» **Acceptance** acknowledges the existence of the threat. However, no action is taken.	» **Acceptance** acknowledges the existence of the opportunity. However, no action is taken.		

Project Procurement Management

Process	Inputs	Tools and Techniques	Outputs
12.1 Plan Procurement Management	Project Charter Business documents » Business case » Benefits management plan Project management plan » Scope management plan » Quality management plan » Resource management plan » Scope baseline Project documents » Milestone list » Project team assignments » Requirements document » Requirements traceability matrix » Resource requirements » Risk register » Stakeholder register OPA EEF	Expert judgments Data gathering Market research Data analysis » Make or buy analysis » Source selection analysis Meetings	Procurement management plan Procurement strategy Procurement statement of work Source selection criteria Make-or-buy analysis decision Independent cost estimates Change requests Project documents updates » Milestone list » Project team assignments » Requirements document » Requirements traceability matrix » Resource requirements » Risk register » Stakeholder register OPA updates Procurement documents Bid documents

Process	Inputs	Tools and Techniques	Outputs
12.2 Conduct Procurements	Procurement management plan » Scope management plan » Requirements management plan » Communications management plan » Risk management plan » Procurement management plan » Configuration management plan » Cost baseline Product documents » Lessons learned register » Project schedule » Requirements documentation » Risk register » Stakeholder register Procurement documents » Bid documents » Procurement statement of work » Independent cost estimates » Source selection criteria Seller proposals OPA EEF	Expert judgment Advertising Bidder conferences Data analysis » Proposal evaluation Interpersonal and team skills » Negotiation	Select sellers Agreements Change requests Project management plan updates » Requirements management plan » Quality management plan » Communications management plan Risk management plan » Procurement management plan » Cost baseline » Scope baseline » Schedule baseline Project documents updates » Lessons learned register » Requirements documentation » Requirements traceability matrix » Resource calendar » Risk register » Stakeholder register OPA updates

Process	Inputs	Tools and Techniques	Outputs
12.3 Control Procurements	Project management plan » Requirements management plan » Risk management plan » Procurement management plan » Change management plan » Schedule baseline Project documents » Assumptions log » Issues log » Lessons learned register » Milestone list » Quality report » Requirements documentation » Requirements traceability matrix » Risk register » Stakeholder register Agreements Procurement documentation Approved change requests Work performance data OPA EEF	Expert judgments Claims administration Data analysis » Performance reviews » Earned value analysis » Trend analysis Inspection Audits	Closed procurements Work performance information Procurement documentation updates Change requests Project management plan updates » Risk management plan » Procurement management plan » Schedule baseline » Cost baseline Project documents updates » Lessons learned register » Milestone list » Resource requirements » Requirements traceability matrix » Risk register » Stakeholder register OPA updates

Remarks about PROCUREMENT MANAGEMENT

Point of total assumption is the cost point in which the seller assumes 100% of the risk of additional cost increases.

PTA = ((Ceiling Price - Target Price)/buyer's Share Ratio) + Target Cost

Table of contract types, and risk			
Contract Types Versus Risk			
High ------------ Buyer's risk------------------ Low			
CPPC	CPFF	CPIF	FPI
Cost plus percentage	Cost plus fixed fee	Cost plus incentive fee	Fixed price incentive
Low ------------ Seller's risk-------------------- High			

Project Stakeholder Management

Process	Inputs	Tools and Techniques	Outputs
13.1 Identify Stakeholders	Project charter PMP » communications management plan » stakeholder engagement plan Business documents Project documents Agreements Enterprise environmental factors Organizational process assets	Expert judgments Data gathering Data analysis Data representation Meetings	Stakeholder register Change requests PMP updates Project documents updates

Process	Inputs	Tools and Techniques	Outputs
13.2 Plan Stakeholder Engagement	Project charter Project management plan Resource management plan Communications management plan Risk management plan » Projects documents » Assumptions log » Change log » Issue log » Project schedule » Risk register » Stakeholder register Agreement s OPA EEF	Expert judgments Data gathering » Benchmarking » Data analysis » Assumptions » Constraint analysis » Root cause analysis » Data representation » Prioritization/ ranking » Mind mapping » Stakeholder engagement matrix Meetings	Stakeholder engagement plan

Process	Inputs	Tools and Techniques	Outputs
13.3 Manage Stakeholder Engagement	Project Management Plan » Communications management plan » Risk management plan » Change management plan » Stakeholder engagement plan Project documents » Change log » Issues log » Lessons learned register » Stakeholder register OPA EEF	Expert judgments Communication skills » Feedback Interpersonal and team skills » Conflict management » Cultural awareness » Negotiation » Observation/ conversation » Political awareness » Ground rules Meetings	Change requests Project management plan updates » Communications management plan » Stakeholder engagement plan Project documents updates » Change log » Issues log » Lessons learned register » Stakeholder register OPA updates

Process	Inputs	Tools and Techniques	Outputs
13.4 Monitor Stakeholder Engagement	Project Management Plan » Resource Management Plan » Communications management plan » Stakeholder management plan Project documents » Change log » Issues log » Lessons learned register » Project communications » Stakeholder register Work Performance data OPA	Data analysis » Alternative analysis » Root cause analysis » Stakeholder analysis Decision making » Multicriteria decision analysis » Voting Data representation » Stakeholder engagement assessment matrix Communication skills » Feedback » Presentation Interpersonal and team skills » Active listening » Cultural awareness » Leadership » Networking » Political awareness Meetings	Work performance information Change requests Project management plan » Resource management plan » Communications management plan » Stakeholder engagement plan Project document updates » Issue log » Lessons learned register » Risk register » Stakeholder register

Remarks about <u>STAKEHOLDER ENGAGEMENT MANAGEMENT</u>

Stakeholder analysis grid(influence/interest) in Stakeholder management

Stakeholder is an individual, group, or organization that may affect, be affected by, or perceive itself to be affected by a decision, activity, or outcome of a project.

686

Best Exam Tips

Six Tips for Passing the PMP Exam	
The most helpful thing I did was: Study hard and study smart. Study everything to smallest detail. *Leave nothing to chance.* Look for trends and patterns in the PMP material (such *as change requests are outputs in monitoring and control 9/10 times*). Take the mock exam until you pass with an 85% grade or greater consistently.	I read questions following where I was in the project management process *across left to right (initial, planning, execute, m/c or close) then down until I knew where the question was focusing in which process.* I took the exam where I felt most comfortable and when I felt most comfortable. *(Bethesda, md: Sat 12:30pm)* I had a good breakfast, a cup of coffee and a Monster drink, three hours before the exam. *Fuel and energy were not going to be an issue.*

PMBOK® is a registered trademark of Project Management Institute.

Project Management Professional (PMP)® is a registered trademark of Project Management Institute.

Bonus I:

PMP Test and Real-World Templates

PROJECT MANAGEMENT

PROJECT MANAGEMENT

LOREM IPSUM IS SIMPLY DUMMY TEXT OF THE PRINTING AND TYPESETTING INDUSTRY

TIMING

LOREM IPSUM IS SIMPLY DUMMY TEXT OF AND TYPESETTING INDUSTRY

DELEGATION

LOREM IPSUM IS SIMPLY DUMMY TEXT OF THE PRINTING AND TYPESETTING INDUSTRY

PROJECT IDEA

LOREM IPSUM IS SIMPLY DUMMY TEXT OF AND TYPESETTING INDUSTRY

PROJECT PRESENTATION

LOREM IPSUM IS SIMPLY DUMMY TEXT OF THE PRINTING AND TYPESETTING INDUSTRY

PROJECT ANALYSIS

LOREM IPSUM IS SIMPLY DUMMY TEXT OF AND TYPESETTING INDUSTRY

MEETING

LOREM IPSUM IS SIMPLY DUMMY TEXT OF THE PRINTING AND TYPESETTING INDUSTRY

PROJECT CONTROL

LOREM IPSUM IS SIMPLY DUMMY TEXT OF AND TYPESETTING INDUSTRY

WORKFLOW

LOREM IPSUM IS SIMPLY DUMMY TEXT OF THE PRINTING AND TYPESETTING INDUSTRY

RISK MANAGEMENT

LOREM IPSUM IS SIMPLY DUMMY TEXT OF AND TYPESETTING INDUSTRY

Kanban Template

	Sunday	Monday	Tuesday	Wednesday	Thursday	Friday	Saturday
To Do							
Dev							
Testing							
Deployed							
Done							

Project Charter Template

Project Charter			
Project Name			
Project Description			
Project Manager		Date Approved	
Project Sponsor		Signature	
Business Case		Expected Goals/Delivery	
Team Members			
Name	Role		
Risks and Constraints		Milestones	

691

Project Plan Template

No.	Task Details	Owner	Start	Finish	Progress	Status	Risks/Issues	Comments
1	**Project Initiation**							
1.1	Business Case	Ted	12-Feb-16	15-Feb-16	100%	Complete		
1.2	Funding Approval	Ted	15-Feb-16	18-Feb-16	90%	Complete		Funding approved.
1.3	Resource Planning	Ted	19-Feb-16	24-Feb-16	100%	Complete		
1.4	Schedule Planning	Ted	25-Feb-16	27-Feb-16	100%	Complete		
1.5	Arrange Kick off Meeting	Ted	1-Mar-16	5-Mar-16	100%	Complete		Some concerns raised about the scope
2	**Analysis**							
2.1	Business Requirement Specification	Zuber	5-Mar-16	10-Mar-16	65%	Concern	Delay in business input	Reminder sent to SME
2.2	Functional Requirement Specification	Zuber	10-Mar-16	15-Mar-16	90%	On Track		
2.3	Technical Requirement Specification	Zuber	15-Mar-16	20-Mar-16	45%	On Track		
2.4	Requirement Walkthrough	Zuber	20-Mar-16	23-Mar-16	25%	On Track		
2.5	Requirements Sign Off	Zuber	23-Mar-16	25-Mar-16	35%	Concern	Last minute changes.	Can delay the entire project.
3	**Design**							
3.1	High Level Design	Jo	25-Mar-16	27-Mar-16	5%	Delayed	Unplanned leaves	
3.2	Detailed Design	Jo	27-Mar-16	28-Mar-16		Pending		
3.3	Design Walkthrough	Jo	1-Apr-16	5-Apr-16		Pending		
3.4	Design Sign Off	Jo	5-Apr-16	10-Apr-16		Pending		
4	**Development**							
4.1	Build Component 1	Sean	11-Apr-16	19-Apr-16		Pending		
4.2	Unit Testing Component 1	Sean	20-Apr-16	24-Apr-16		Pending		
4.3	Build Component 2	Zac	11-Apr-16	19-Apr-16		Pending		
4.4	Unit Testing Component 2	Zac	20-Apr-16	24-Apr-16		Pending		
4.5	Integration Testing	Sean/Zac	25-Apr-16	28-Apr-16		Pending		
5	**Testing**							
5.1	Create Test Plan	Zen/Sam	28-Apr-16	5-May-16		Pending		
5.2	Create Test Cases	Zen/Sam	10-May-16	15-May-16		Pending		
5.3	Execute Test Case Round - 1	Zen/Sam	16-May-16	25-May-16		Pending		
5.4	Record Defects Round - 1	Zen/Sam	25-May-16	1-Jun-16		Pending		
5.5	Fix Defects	Sean/Zac	2-Jun-16	5-Jun-16		Pending		
5.6	Execute Test Case Round - 2	Zen/Sam	10-Jun-16	15-Jun-16		Pending		
5.7	Record Defects Round - 2	Zen/Sam	16-Jun-16	18-Jun-16		Pending		
5.8	Draft Testing Report	Zen/Sam	19-Jun-16	20-Jun-16		Pending		

Risk Register Template

ID	Risk Description	Identified Date	Identified by	Risk Owner	Impact of Risk	Location	Rating	Action Plan	Solution Date	Status

Requirements Traceability Matrix

Project Name								
Cost Center								
Project Description								
ID	Associate ID	Requirements Description	Business Needs	Project Objectives	WBS deliverables	Project Design	Product Development	Test Cases
001	1.0							
	1.1							
	1.2.1							
002	2.0							
	2.1							
	2.2.1							

Resources Template

Building	Room #	Last Name	First Name	M/F	Email Address	Cell number

Issues Log Template

Project Name									
Project Manager									
Issue ID	Date Reported	Description	Impact	Priority	Discovered by	Owner	Action/ Resolution	Status	Dated Closed
2									

693

4									

Lessons Learned Template

Incident/Risk	Lesson Learned	Action Item	Owner	Status

Stakeholders Register Template

Project Title:				Date Prepared			
Name	Role	Contact Information	Requirements	Expectations	Influence	Classification	

Communications Point-of-Contact Template

		Contact List		
Name	Organization	Phone	Email address	Notes

Bonus II:

PMP Flash Cards

Activity	Actual Cost (AC)
Activity Code	Apportioned Effort
Accuracy	Assumption
Activity Label	Alternative Analysis
Adaptive Lifecycles	Analogous Estimating

The realized cost incurred for the work performed on an activity during a specific time period.

A distinct, scheduled portion of work performed during the course of a project.

An activity where effort is allotted proportionately across certain discrete efforts and not divisible into discrete efforts.

An alphanumeric value assigned to each activity that enables classifying, sorting, and filtering.

A factor in the planning process considered to be true, real, or certain, without proof or demonstration.

Values that are close to the true or target value

A technique used to evaluate identified options in order to select the options or approaches to use to execute and perform the work of the project.

A phrase that names and describes an activity

A technique for estimating the duration or cost of an activity or a project using historical data from a similar activity or project.

The processes within their iterations can be going on in parallel used in application areas where there is rapid change.

Change requests	Work performance data
Baseline	Budget at Completion (BAC)
Avoidance	Benefits Management Plan
Backward Pass	Bidder Conferences
Balanced Matrix	Bottom-up Estimating

The raw observations and measurements identified during activities being performed to carry out the project work.

A formal proposal to modify a document, deliverable, or baseline.

The sum of all budgets established for the work to be performed.

The approved version of a work product that can be changed using formal change control procedures and is used as the basis for comparison to actual results.

Includes the target benefits of the project, such as net present value calculations and the time frame for realizing the benefits.

A risk response strategy whereby the project team acts to eliminate the threat or protect the project from its impact.

Are the meetings between buyer and prospective seller prior to proposal submittal.

Is a critical path method technique for calculating the late start and late finish dates by working backward through a schedule model from the project end date.

A method of estimating project duration or cost by aggregating the estimates of the lower-level components of the work breakdown structure (WBS).

Is a two-dimensional management structure (matrix) in which employees are assigned to two organizational groups.

Brainstorming	Change Control
Change Control Board	Change Control System
Code of Accounts	Communications Management Plan
Work performance report	Configuration Management System
Constraint	Contingency Plan

A process whereby modifications to documents, deliverables, or baselines associated with the project are identified, documented, approved, or rejected.

Uses the combined creative efforts of the project team, experts, and consultants to develop the quality management plan.

A set of procedures that describes how modifications to the project deliverables and documentation are managed and controlled.

A formally chartered group responsible for reviewing, evaluating, approving, delaying, or rejecting changes to the project, and for recording and communicating such decisions.

A component of the project, program, or portfolio management plan that describes how, when, and by whom information will be administered and disseminated.

A numbering system used to uniquely identify each component of the work breakdown structure.

A collection of procedures used to track project artifacts and monitor and control changes to these artifacts.

The physical or electronic representation of work performance information compiled in project documents, intended to generate decisions, actions, or awareness.

A document describing actions that the project team can take if predetermined trigger conditions occur.

A factor that limits the options for managing a project, program, portfolio, or process.

Contingency Reserve	Control Account
Corrective Action	Cost Baseline
Cost Management Plan	Cost Performance Index (CPI)
Cost Variance (CV)	Crashing
Critical Chain Method	Critical Path

A management control point where scope, budget, actual cost, and schedule are integrated and compared to earned value for performance measurement.

Time or money allocated in the schedule or cost baseline for known risks with active response strategies.

The approved version of work package cost estimates and contingency reserve that can be changed using formal change control procedures and is used as the basis for comparison to actual results.

An intentional activity that realigns the performance of the project work with the project management plan.

A measure of the cost efficiency of budgeted resources expressed as the ratio of earned value to actual cost.

A component of a project or program management plan that describes how costs will be planned, structured, and controlled.

A schedule compression technique used to shorten the schedule duration for the least incremental cost by adding resources.

The amount of budget deficit or surplus at a given point in time, expressed as the difference between the earned value and the actual cost.

The sequence of activities that represents the longest path through a project, which determines the shortest possible duration.

A schedule method that allows the project team to place buffers on any project schedule path to account for limited resources and project uncertainties.

Critical Path Activity	Critical Path Method
Data Date	Decision Tree Analysis
Decomposition	Defect Repair
Deliverable	Discrete Effort
Duration	Early Finish Date

A method used to estimate the minimum project duration and determine the amount of scheduling flexibility on the logical network paths within the schedule model.

Any activity on the critical path in a project schedule.

A diagramming and calculation technique for evaluating the implications of a chain of multiple options in the presence of uncertainty.

A point in time when the status of the project is recorded.

An intentional activity to modify a nonconforming product or product component.

A technique used for dividing and subdividing the project scope and project deliverables into smaller, more manageable parts.

An activity that can be planned and measured and that yields a specific output.

Any unique and verifiable product, result, or capability to perform a service that is produced to complete a process, phase, or project.

In the critical path method, the earliest possible point in time when the uncompleted portions of a schedule activity can finish based on the schedule network logic, the data date, and any schedule constraints.

The total number of work periods required to complete an activity or work breakdown structure component, expressed in hours, days, or weeks.

Early Start Date	Earned Value (EV)
Earned Value Management	Effort
Enterprise Environmental Factors (EEF)	Estimate at Completion (EAC)
Estimate to Complete (ETC)	Fast Tracking
Finish-to-Finish	Finish-to-Start

The measure of work performed expressed in terms of the budget authorized for that work.

In the critical path method, the earliest possible point in time when the uncompleted portions of a schedule activity can start based on the schedule network logic, the data date, and any schedule constraints.

The number of labor units required to complete a schedule activity or work breakdown structure component, often expressed in hours, days, or weeks.

A methodology that combines scope, schedule, and resource measurements to assess project performance and progress.

The expected total cost of completing all work expressed as the sum of the actual cost to date and the estimate to complete.

Conditions, not under the immediate control of the team, that influence, constrain, or direct the project, program, or portfolio.

A schedule compression technique in which activities or phases normally done in sequence are performed in parallel for at least a portion of their duration.

The expected cost to finish all the remaining project work.

A logical relationship in which a successor activity cannot start until a predecessor activity has finished.

A logical relationship in which a successor activity cannot finish until a predecessor activity has finished.

Fixed Formula Method	Forward Pass
Free Float	Functional Organization
Gantt Chart	Lag
Late Finish Date	Late Start Date
Lead	Lessons Learned

A critical path method technique for calculating the early start and early finish dates by working forward through the schedule model from the project start date or a given point in time.

A method of estimating earned value in which a specified percentage of the budget value of a work package is assigned to the start milestone and the remaining percentage is assigned when the work package is complete.

An organizational structure in which staff is grouped by areas of specialization and the project manager has limited authority to assign work and apply resources.

The amount of time that a schedule activity can be delayed without delaying the early start date of any successor or violating a schedule constraint.

The amount of time whereby a successor activity will be delayed with respect to a predecessor activity.

A bar chart of schedule information where activities are listed on the vertical axis, dates are shown on the horizontal axis, and activity durations are shown as horizontal bars placed according to start and finish dates.

In the critical path method, the latest possible point in time when the uncompleted portions of a schedule activity can start based on the schedule network logic, the project completion date, and any schedule constraints.

In the critical path method, the latest possible point in time when the uncompleted portions of a schedule activity can finish based on the schedule network logic, the project completion date, and any schedule constraints.

The knowledge gained during a project which shows how project events were addressed or should be addressed in the future for the purpose of improving future performance.

The amount of time whereby a successor activity can be advanced with respect to a predecessor activity.

Level of Effort	Logical Relationship
Management Reserve	Matrix Organization
Milestone	Milestone Schedule
Most Likely Duration	Near-Critical Activity
Near-Critical Path	Network Logic

A dependency between two activities or between an activity and a milestone.

An activity that does not produce definitive end products and is measured by the passage of time.

An organizational structure in which the project manager shares authority with the functional manager temporarily to assign work and apply resources.

Time or money that management sets aside in addition to the schedule or cost baseline and releases for unforeseen work that is within the scope of the project.

A type of schedule that presents milestones with planned dates.

A significant point or event in a project, program, or portfolio.

An activity with a total float that is deemed to be low based on expert judgment.

An estimate of the most probable activity duration that takes into account all of the known variables that could affect performance.

All activity dependencies in a project schedule network diagram.

A sequence of activities with low float which, if exhausted, becomes a critical path sequence for the project.

Network Path	Node
Opportunity	Optimistic Duration
Organizational Breakdown Structure	Organizational Enabler
Organizational Process Assets (OPA)	Organizational Project Management (OPM)
Organizational Project Management Maturity	Parametric Estimating

A point at which dependency lines connect on a schedule network diagram.

A sequence of activities connected by logical relationships in a project schedule network diagram.

An estimate of the shortest activity duration that takes into account all of the known variables that could affect performance.

A risk that would have a positive effect on one or more project objectives.

A structural, cultural, technological, or human-resource practice that the performing organization can use to achieve strategic objectives.

A hierarchical representation of the project organization, which illustrates the relationship between project activities and the organizational units that will perform those activities.

A framework in which portfolio, program, and project management are integrated with organizational enablers in order to achieve strategic objectives.

Plans, processes, policies, procedures, and knowledge bases specific to and used by the performing organization.

An estimating technique in which an algorithm is used to calculate cost or duration based on historical data and project parameters.

The level of an organization's ability to deliver the desired strategic outcomes in a predictable, controllable, and reliable manner.

Path Convergence	Path Divergence
Percent Complete	Performance Measurement Baseline
Performing Organization	Pessimistic Duration
Phase Gate	Planned Value (PV)
Portfolio	Portfolio Balancing

A relationship in which a schedule activity has more than one successor.

A relationship in which a schedule activity has more than one predecessor.

Integrated scope, schedule, and cost baselines used for comparison to manage, measure, and control project execution.

An estimate expressed as a percent of the amount of work that has been completed on an activity or a work breakdown structure component.

An estimate of the longest activity duration that takes into account all of the known variables that could affect performance.

An enterprise whose personnel are the most directly involved in doing the work of the project or program.

The authorized budget assigned to scheduled work.

A review at the end of a phase in which a decision is made to continue to the next phase, to continue with modification, or to end a project or program.

The process of optimizing the mix of portfolio components to further the strategic objectives of the organization.

Projects, programs, subsidiary portfolios, and operations managed as a group to achieve strategic objectives.

Portfolio Charter	Portfolio Management
Portfolio Management Plan	Portfolio Manager
Precedence Diagramming Method	Predecessor Activity
Preventive Action	Probability and Impact Matrix
Procurement Management Plan	Product Life Cycle

The centralized management of one or more portfolios to achieve strategic objectives.

A document issued by a sponsor that authorizes and specifies the portfolio structure and links the portfolio to the organization's strategic objectives.

The person or group assigned by the performing organization to establish, balance, monitor, and control portfolio components in order to achieve strategic business objectives.

A document that specifies how a portfolio will be organized, monitored, and controlled.

An activity that logically comes before a dependent activity in a schedule.

A technique used for constructing a schedule model in which activities are represented by nodes and are graphically linked by one or more logical relationships to show the sequence in which the activities are to be performed.

A grid for mapping the probability of occurrence of each risk and its impact on project objectives if that risk occurs.

An intentional activity that ensures the future performance of the project work is aligned with the project management plan.

The series of phases that represent the evolution of a product, from concept through delivery, growth, maturity, and to retirement.

A component of the project or program management plan that describes how a team will acquire goods and services from outside of the performing organization.

Program	Program Charter
Program Evaluation and Review Technique (PERT)	Program Management
Program Management Office (PMO)	Program Management Plan
Program Manager	Progressive Elaboration
Project	Project Budget

A document issued by a sponsor that authorizes the program management team to use organizational resources to execute the program and links the program to the organization's strategic objectives.

Related projects, subsidiary programs, and program activities managed in a coordinated manner to obtain benefits not available from managing them individually.

The application of knowledge, skills, and principles to a program to achieve the program objectives and to obtain benefits and control not available by managing program components individually.

A technique used to estimate project duration through a weighted average of optimistic, pessimistic, and most likely activity durations when there is uncertainty with the individual activity estimates.

A document that integrates the program's subsidiary plans and establishes the management controls and overall plan for integrating and managing the program's individual components.

A management structure that standardizes the program-related governance processes and facilitates the sharing of resources, methodologies, tools, and techniques.

The iterative process of increasing the level of detail in a project management plan as greater amounts of information and more accurate estimates become available.

The person authorized by the performing organization to lead the team or teams responsible for achieving program objectives.

The sum of work package cost estimates, contingency reserve, and management reserve.

A temporary endeavor undertaken to create a unique product, service, or result.

Project Calendar	Project Charter
Project Life Cycle	Project Management
Project Management Office (PMO)	Project Management Plan
Project Manager	Project Phase
Project Schedule	Project Schedule Network Diagram

A document issued by the project initiator or sponsor that formally authorizes the existence of a project and provides the project manager with the authority to apply organizational resources to project activities.

A calendar that identifies working days and shifts that are available for scheduled activities.

The application of knowledge, skills, tools, and techniques to project activities to meet the project requirements.

The series of phases that a project passes through from its start to its completion.

The document that describes how the project will be executed, monitored and controlled, and closed.

A management structure that standardizes the project-related governance processes and facilitates the sharing of resources, methodologies, tools, and techniques.

A collection of logically related project activities that culminates in the completion of one or more deliverables.

The person assigned by the performing organization to lead the team that is responsible for achieving the project objectives.

A graphical representation of the logical relationships among the project schedule activities.

An output of a schedule model that presents linked activities with planned dates, durations, milestones, and resources.

Project Scope	Project Scope Statement
Projectized Organization	Quality Management Plan
Work performance information	Verified Deliverable
Residual Risk	Variance at Completion (VAC)
Weak Matrix	Resource Leveling

The description of the project scope, major deliverables, assumptions, and constraints.

The work performed to deliver a product, service, or result with the specified features and functions.

A component of the project or program management plan that describes how an organization's policies, procedures, and guidelines will be implemented to achieve the quality objectives.

An organizational structure in which the project manager has full authority to assign work and apply resources.

Completed project deliverables that have been checked and confirmed for correctness through the Control Quality process.

The performance data collected from controlling processes, analyzed in comparison with project management plan components, project documents, and other work performance information.

A projection of the amount of budget deficit or surplus, expressed as the difference between the budget at completion and the estimate at completion.

The risk that remains after risk responses have been implemented.

A resource optimization technique in which adjustments are made to the project schedule to optimize the allocation of resources and which may affect critical path.

In this form of organization, the functional manager retains most of the power; they "own" the people and resources. In a weak/functional matrix, the project manager is not very powerful.

Variable Costs	Waterfall Model
Resource Smoothing	Responsibility Assignment Matrix
Risk	Risk Acceptance
Risk Appetite	Risk Avoidance
Risk Breakdown Structure	Validate Scope

Is a relatively linear sequential design approach as progress flows in largely one direction through the phases of conception, initiation, analysis, design, construction, testing, deployment, and maintenance"

Are expenses that change in proportion to the level of activity of a business, such as the purchase of more or less raw material

A grid that shows the project resources assigned to each work package.

A resource optimization technique in which free and total float are used without affecting the critical path.

A risk response strategy whereby the project team decides to acknowledge the risk and not take any action unless the risk occurs.

An uncertain event or condition that, if it occurs, has a positive or negative effect on one or more project objectives.

A risk response strategy whereby the project team acts to eliminate the threat or protect the project from its impact.

The degree of uncertainty an organization or individual is willing to accept in anticipation of a reward.

The process of formalizing acceptance of the completed project deliverables.

A hierarchical representation of potential sources of risk.

Risk Enhancement	Risk Exploiting
Risk Exposure	Risk Management Plan
Risk Mitigation	Risk Owner
Risk Register	Risk Sharing
Risk Threshold	Risk Tolerance

A risk response strategy whereby the project team acts to ensure that an opportunity occurs.

A risk response strategy whereby the project team acts to increase the probability of occurrence or impact of an opportunity.

A component of the project, program, or portfolio management plan that describes how risk management activities will be structured and performed.

An aggregate measure of the potential impact of all risks at any given point in time in a project, program, or portfolio.

The person responsible for monitoring the risk and for selecting and implementing an appropriate risk response strategy.

A risk response strategy whereby the project team acts to decrease the probability of occurrence or impact of a threat.

A risk response strategy whereby the project team allocates ownership of an opportunity to a third party who is best able to capture the benefit for the project.

A repository in which outputs of risk management processes are recorded.

The degree of uncertainty that an organization or individual is willing to withstand.

The measure of acceptable variation around an objective that reflects the risk appetite of the organization and stakeholders.

Risk Transference	Rolling Wave Planning
Schedule Baseline	Schedule Compression
Schedule Management Plan	Schedule Model
Schedule Model Analysis	Voting
Schedule Performance Index (SPI)	Transference

An iterative planning technique in which the work to be accomplished in the near term is planned in detail, while the work in the future is planned at a higher level.

A risk response strategy whereby the project team shifts the impact of a threat to a third party, together with ownership of the response.

A technique used to shorten the schedule duration without reducing the project scope.

The approved version of a schedule model that can be changed using formal change control procedures and is used as the basis for comparison to actual results.

A representation of the plan for executing the project's activities, including durations, dependencies, and other planning information, used to produce a project schedule along with other scheduling artifacts.

A component of the project or program management plan that establishes the criteria and the activities for developing, monitoring, and controlling the schedule.

Is used to select for best response involving project team members when discussing cost estimates.

A process used to investigate or analyze the output of the schedule model in order to optimize the schedule.

Involves shifting ownership to a third party, such as payment of insurance premiums so that if the risk occurs, its impact will be minimized.

A measure of schedule efficiency expressed as the ratio of earned value to planned value.

Tender	Training
Scope Management Plan	S-Curve Analysis
Secondary Risk	Sponsor
Staffing Management Plan	Stakeholder
Stakeholder Engagement Plan	Start-to-Finish

Is necessary for team members close to the needed skill set but missing a certain tool or discipline.

Notice invites bids for a project or to accept a formal offer such as a takeover bid. Tender usually refers to the process whereby governments and financial institutions invite bids for large projects that must be submitted by a finite deadline.

A technique used to indicate performance trends by using a graph that displays cumulative costs over a specific time period.

A component of the project or program management plan that describes how the scope will be defined, developed, monitored, controlled, and validated.

An individual or a group that provides resources and support for the project, program, or portfolio, and is accountable for enabling success.

A risk that arises as a direct result of implementing a risk response.

An individual, group, or organization that may affect, be affected by, or perceive itself to be affected by a decision, activity, or outcome of a project, program, or portfolio.

A component of the resource management plan that describes when and how team members will be acquired and how long they will be needed.

A logical relationship in which a successor activity cannot finish until a predecessor activity has started.

A component of the project or program management plan that identifies the strategies and actions required to promote productive involvement of stakeholders in project or program decision making and execution.

Start-to-Start	Successor Activity
Summary Activity	Threat
Three-Point Estimating	To-Complete Performance Index (TCPI)
Total Float	Trigger Condition
Variance Analysis	Team Charter

A dependent activity that logically comes after another activity in a schedule.

A logical relationship in which a successor activity cannot start until a predecessor activity has started.

A risk that would have a negative effect on one or more project objectives.

A group of related schedule activities aggregated and displayed as a single activity.

A measure of the cost performance that is achieved with the remaining resources in order to meet a specified management goal, expressed as the ratio of the cost to finish the outstanding work to the remaining budget.

A technique used to estimate cost or duration by applying an average or weighted average of optimistic, pessimistic, and most likely estimates when there is uncertainty with the individual activity estimates.

An event or situation that indicates that a risk is about to occur.

The amount of time that a schedule activity can be delayed or extended from its early start date without delaying the project finish date or violating a schedule constraint.

A document that records the team values, agreements, and operating guidelines, as well as establishing clear expectations regarding acceptable behavior by project team members.

A technique for determining the cause and degree of difference between the baseline and actual performance.

WBS Dictionary	Weighted Milestone Method
What-If Scenario Analysis	Work Breakdown Structure (WBS)
Work Package	Workaround
Project Reporting	Project Team Assignments
Virtual teams	Project Team

A method of estimating earned value in which the budget value of a work package is divided into measurable segments, each ending with a milestone that is assigned a weighted budget value.

A document that provides detailed deliverable, activity, and scheduling information about each component in the work breakdown structure.

A hierarchical decomposition of the total scope of work to be carried out by the project team to accomplish the project objectives and create the required deliverables.

The process of evaluating scenarios in order to predict their effect on project objectives.

An immediate and temporary response to an issue, for which a prior response had not been planned or was not effective.

The work defined at the lowest level of the work breakdown structure for which cost, and duration are estimated and managed.

Contain the project team directory and the roles and responsibilities of team member recorded in the project plan.

Report that contains the deliverables, requirements, tasks, start date, finish date, duration, resources and percentage complete of the project and tasks.

A set of individuals who support the project manager in performing the work of the project to achieve its objectives.

Groups of people with a shared goal who fulfill their roles with little or no time spent meeting face to face.

Prompt Lists	Quality Report
Prototypes	Recognition and Rewards
Purchase Order (PO)	Representations of Uncertainty
Quality	Request for Information (RFI)
SWOT	Request for Proposal (RFP)

A project document that includes quality management issues, recommendations for corrective actions, and a summary of findings from quality control activities and may include recommendations for process, project, and product improvements.

Are predetermined lists of categorized risks to help guide meetings.

Are needed to show team members how important they are to the project and to say thanks for a job well done.

A method of obtaining early feedback on requirements by providing a working model of the expected product before actually building it.

Such as representations of risk in duration, cost, or resource requirement use a probability distribution such as triangular, normal, lognormal, beta, uniform, or discrete distributions.

This type of contract is used to buy commodities.

A type of procurement document whereby the buyer requests a potential seller to provide various pieces of information related to a product or service or seller capability.

The degree to which a set of inherent characteristics fulfills requirements.

A type of procurement document used to request proposals from

prospective sellers of products or services. In some application areas, it may have a narrower or more specific meaning.

Analysis of strengths, weaknesses, opportunities, and threats of an organization, project, or option.

Request for Quotations (RFQ)	**Reserve Analysis**
Requirements Documentation	**Time and Materials contracts (T&M)**
Requirements Management Plan	**Resource Breakdown Structure (RBS)**
Requirements Traceability Matrix	**Resource Calendar**
Supportive PMOs	**Strong Matrix or Project Matrix**

An analytical technique to determine the essential features and relationships of components in the project management plan to establish a reserve for the schedule duration, budget, estimated cost, or funds for a project

A type of procurement document used to request price quotations from prospective sellers of common or standard products or services. Sometimes used in place of request for proposal and, in some application areas, it may have a narrower or more specific meaning.

Use this type of contract when the scope is incomplete or not determined. T&Ms are also used when the deliverable is "labor hours."

A description of how individual requirements meet the business need for the project

A hierarchical representation of resources by category and type

A component of the project or program management plan that describes how requirements will be analyzed, documented, and managed

A calendar that identifies the working days and shifts upon which each specific resource is available.

A grid that links product requirements from their origin to the deliverables that satisfy them.

The project manager has most of the power, resources, and control over the work. The functional manager is there to add support and technical expertise and to look after HR issues

Provide a consultative role to projects by supplying templates, best practices, training, access to information, and lessons learned from other projects

Resource Management Plan	Activity List
Resource Optimization	Rolling Wave Planning
Source selection criteria	Rough Order of Magnitude
Risk Categorization	Scatter Diagrams
Start to Start (SS)	SIPOC (suppliers, inputs, process, outputs, customers) diagram

A documented tabulation of schedule activities that shows the activity description, activity identifier, and a sufficiently detailed scope of work description so project team members understand what work is to be performed.

A component of the project management plan that describes how project resources are acquired, allocated, monitored, and controlled.

An iterative planning technique in which the work to be accomplished in the near term is planned in detail, while the work in the future is planned at a higher level.

A technique in which activity start and finish dates are adjusted to balance demand for resources with the available supply.

Is when a project is at or near its birth stage and someone asks what it may cost for the project, the project manager may give the sponsor or senior management a rough order of magnitude, which is -25% to + 75%.

A set of attributes desired by the buyer which a seller is required to meet or exceed to be selected for a contract.

Allows you to analyze the relationship between two variables.

Organization by sources of risk (e.g., using the RBS), the area of the project affected (e.g., using the WBS), or other useful category (e.g., project phase) to determine the areas of the project most exposed to the effects of uncertainty.

Is a visual tool for documenting a business process from beginning to end.

Is a logical relationship in which a successor activity cannot start until a predecessor activity has started.

Start to Finish (SF)	Schedule Variance (SV)
Schedule Data	Scope Baseline
Share Risk	Scope Creep
Schedule Network Analysis	Sequence Activities
Seller Proposals	Tuckman's Ladder

Which measures the difference between the earned value (EV) (the value of work actually performed) and the planned value (PV), so SV = EV – PV

Is a logical relationship in which a successor activity cannot finish until a predecessor activity has started.

The approved version of a scope statement, work breakdown structure (WBS), and its associated WBS dictionary, that can be changed using formal change control procedures and is used as abasis for comparison to actual results.

The collection of information for describing and controlling the schedule.

The uncontrolled expansion to product or project scope without adjustments to time, cost, and resources

Involves transferring ownership to a third party. Examples of sharing actions include partnerships, teams, and joint ventures.

A technique to identify early and late start dates, as well as early and late finish dates, for the uncompleted portions of project activities

A technique to identify early and late start dates, as well as early and late finish dates, for the uncompleted portions of project activities

Describes the stages of team formation and development. These stages are: 1. Forming- The team meets and learns about the project. 2. Storming - The team begins to address the project work. 3. Norming - The team begins to work together. 4. Performing - The team is efficient and works through issues. 5. Adjourning - The team completes the work and

Formal responses from sellers to a request for proposal or other procurement document specifying the price, commercial terms of sale, and technical specifications or capabilities the seller will do for the requesting organization that, if accepted, would bind the seller to perform the resulting agreement.

Create your own flashcard

(Front)

Create your own flashcard

(Back)

Glossary

Activity	A distinct, scheduled portion of work performed during the course of a project.
Accuracy	Values that are close to the true or target value
Activity Code	An alphanumeric value assigned to each activity that enables classifying, sorting, and filtering.
Activity Label	A phrase that names and describes an activity
Activity List	A documented tabulation of schedule activities that shows the activity description, activity identifier, and a sufficiently detailed scope of work description so project team members understand what work is to be performed.
Actual Cost (AC)	The realized cost incurred for the work performed on an activity during a specific time period.
Adaptive Lifecycles	The processes within their iterations can be going on in parallel used in application areas where there is rapid change.
Alternative Analysis	A technique used to evaluate identified options in order to select the options or approaches to use to execute and perform the work of the project.
Analogous Estimating	A technique for estimating the duration or cost of an activity or a project using historical data from a similar activity or project.
Apportioned Effort	An activity where effort is allotted proportionately across certain discrete efforts and not divisible into discrete efforts.

Assumption	A factor in the planning process considered to be true, real, or certain, without proof or demonstration.
Avoidance	A risk response strategy whereby the project team acts to eliminate the threat or protect the project from its impact.
Backward Pass	A critical path method technique for calculating the late start and late finish dates by working backward through the schedule model from the project end date.
Balanced Matrix	Is a two-dimensional management structure (matrix) in which employees are assigned to two organizational groups.
Baseline	The approved version of a work product that can be changed using formal change control procedures and is used as the basis for comparison to actual results.
Benefits Management Plan	Includes the target benefits of the project, such as net present value calculations and the time frame for realizing the benefits.
Bidder Conferences	Are the meetings between buyer and prospective seller prior to proposal submittal.
Bottom-up Estimating	A method of estimating project duration or cost by aggregating the estimates of the lower-level components of the work breakdown structure (WBS).
Brainstorming	Uses the combined creative efforts of the project team, experts, and consultants to develop the quality management plan.
Budget at Completion (BAC)	The sum of all budgets established for the work to be performed.
Change Control	A process whereby modifications to documents, deliverables, or baselines associated with the project are identified, documented, approved, or rejected.

Change Control Board	A formally chartered group responsible for reviewing, evaluating, approving, delaying, or rejecting changes to the project, and for recording and communicating such decisions.
Change Control System	A set of procedures that describes how modifications to the project deliverables and documentation are managed and controlled.
Change requests	A formal proposal to modify a document, deliverable, or baseline.
Code of Accounts	A numbering system used to uniquely identify each component of the work breakdown structure.
Communications Management Plan	A component of the project, program, or portfolio management plan that describes how, when, and by whom information will be administered and disseminated.
Configuration Management System	A collection of procedures used to track project artifacts and monitor and control changes to these artifacts.
Constraint	A factor that limits the options for managing a project, program, portfolio, or process.
Contingency Plan	A document describing actions that the project team can take if predetermined trigger conditions occur.
Contingency Reserve	Time or money allocated in the schedule or cost baseline for known risks with active response strategies.
Control Account	A management control point where scope, budget, actual cost, and schedule are integrated and compared to earned value for performance measurement.
Corrective Action	An intentional activity that realigns the performance of the project work with the project management plan.
Cost Baseline	The approved version of work package cost estimates and contingency reserve that can be changed using formal change control procedures and is used as the basis for comparison to actual results.

Cost Management Plan	A component of a project or program management plan that describes how costs will be planned, structured, and controlled.
Cost Performance Index (CPI)	A measure of the cost efficiency of budgeted resources expressed as the ratio of earned value to actual cost.
Cost Variance (CV)	The amount of budget deficit or surplus at a given point in time, expressed as the difference between the earned value and the actual cost.
Crashing	A schedule compression technique used to shorten the schedule duration for the least incremental cost by adding resources.
Critical Chain Method	A schedule method that allows the project team to place buffers on any project schedule path to account for limited resources and project uncertainties.
Critical Path	The sequence of activities that represents the longest path through a project, which determines the shortest possible duration.
Critical Path Activity	Any activity on the critical path in a project schedule.
Critical Path Method	A method used to estimate the minimum project duration and determine the amount of scheduling flexibility on the logical network paths within the schedule model.
Data Date	A point in time when the status of the project is recorded.
Decision Tree Analysis	A diagramming and calculation technique for evaluating the implications of a chain of multiple options in the presence of uncertainty.
Decomposition	A technique used for dividing and subdividing the project scope and project deliverables into smaller, more manageable parts.
Defect Repair	An intentional activity to modify a nonconforming product or product component.

Deliverable	Any unique and verifiable product, result, or capability to perform a service that is produced to complete a process, phase, or project.
Discrete Effort	An activity that can be planned and measured and that yields a specific output.
Duration	The total number of work periods required to complete an activity or work breakdown structure component, expressed in hours, days, or weeks.
Early Finish Date	In the critical path method, the earliest possible point in time when the uncompleted portions of a schedule activity can finish based on the schedule network logic, the data date, and any schedule constraints.
Early Start Date	In the critical path method, the earliest possible point in time when the uncompleted portions of a schedule activity can start based on the schedule network logic, the data date, and any schedule constraints.
Earned Value (EV)	The measure of work performed expressed in terms of the budget authorized for that work.
Earned Value Management	A methodology that combines scope, schedule, and resource measurements to assess project performance and progress.
Effort	The number of labor units required to complete a schedule activity or work breakdown structure component, often expressed in hours, days, or weeks.
Enterprise Environmental Factors (EEF)	Conditions, not under the immediate control of the team, that influence, constrain, or direct the project, program, or portfolio.
Estimate at Completion (EAC)	The expected total cost of completing all work expressed as the sum of the actual cost to date and the estimate to complete.
Estimate to Complete (ETC)	The expected cost to finish all the remaining project work.

Fast Tracking	A schedule compression technique in which activities or phases normally done in sequence are performed in parallel for at least a portion of their duration.
Finish-to-Finish	A logical relationship in which a successor activity cannot finish until a predecessor activity has finished.
Fixed Formula Method	A method of estimating earned value in which a specified percentage of the budget value of a work package is assigned to the start milestone and the remaining percentage is assigned when the work package is complete.
Forward Pass	A critical path method technique for calculating the early start and early finish dates by working forward through the schedule model from the project start date or a given point in time.
Free Float	The amount of time that a schedule activity can be delayed without delaying the early start date of any successor or violating a schedule constraint.
Functional Organization	An organizational structure in which staff is grouped by areas of specialization and the project manager has limited authority to assign work and apply resources.
Gantt Chart	A bar chart of schedule information where activities are listed on the vertical axis, dates are shown on the horizontal axis, and activity durations are shown as horizontal bars placed according to start and finish dates.
Lag	The amount of time whereby a successor activity will be delayed with respect to a predecessor activity.
Late Finish Date	In the critical path method, the latest possible point in time when the uncompleted portions of a schedule activity can finish based on the schedule network logic, the project completion date, and any schedule constraints.

Late Start Date	In the critical path method, the latest possible point in time when the uncompleted portions of a schedule activity can start based on the schedule network logic, the project completion date, and any schedule constraints.
Lead	The amount of time whereby a successor activity can be advanced with respect to a predecessor activity.
Lessons Learned	The knowledge gained during a project which shows how project events were addressed or should be addressed in the future for the purpose of improving future performance.
Level of Effort	An activity that does not produce definitive end products and is measured by the passage of time.
Logical Relationship	A dependency between two activities or between an activity and a milestone.
Management Reserve	Time or money that management sets aside in addition to the schedule or cost baseline and releases for unforeseen work that is within the scope of the project.
Matrix Organization	An organizational structure in which the project manager shares authority with the functional manager temporarily to assign work and apply resources.
Milestone	A significant point or event in a project, program, or portfolio.
Milestone Schedule	A type of schedule that presents milestones with planned dates.
Most Likely Duration	An estimate of the most probable activity duration that takes into account all of the known variables that could affect performance.
Near-Critical Activity	An activity with a total float that is deemed to be low based on expert judgment.
Near-Critical Path	A sequence of activities with low float which, if exhausted, becomes a critical path sequence for the project.
Network Logic	All activity dependencies in a project schedule network diagram.

Network Path	A sequence of activities connected by logical relationships in a project schedule network diagram.
Node	A point at which dependency lines connect on a schedule network diagram.
Opportunity	A risk that would have a positive effect on one or more project objectives.
Optimistic Duration	An estimate of the shortest activity duration that takes into account all of the known variables that could affect performance.
Organizational Breakdown Structure	A hierarchical representation of the project organization, which illustrates the relationship between project activities and the organizational units that will perform those activities.
Organizational Enabler	A structural, cultural, technological, or human-resource practice that the performing organization can use to achieve strategic objectives.
Organizational Process Assets (OPA)	Plans, processes, policies, procedures, and knowledge bases specific to and used by the performing organization.
Organizational Project Management (OPM)	A framework in which portfolio, program, and project management are integrated with organizational enablers in order to achieve strategic objectives.
Organizational Project Management Maturity	The level of an organization's ability to deliver the desired strategic outcomes in a predictable, controllable, and reliable manner.
Parametric Estimating	An estimating technique in which an algorithm is used to calculate cost or duration based on historical data and project parameters.
Path Convergence	A relationship in which a schedule activity has more than one predecessor.

Path Divergence	A relationship in which a schedule activity has more than one successor.
Percent Complete	An estimate expressed as a percent of the amount of work that has been completed on an activity or a work breakdown structure component.
Performance Measurement Baseline	Integrated scope, schedule, and cost baselines used for comparison to manage, measure, and control project execution.
Performing Organization	An enterprise whose personnel are the most directly involved in doing the work of the project or program.
Pessimistic Duration	An estimate of the longest activity duration that takes into account all of the known variables that could affect performance.
Phase Gate	A review at the end of a phase in which a decision is made to continue to the next phase, to continue with modification, or to end a project or program.
Planned Value (PV)	The authorized budget assigned to scheduled work.
Portfolio	Projects, programs, subsidiary portfolios, and operations managed as a group to achieve strategic objectives.
Portfolio Balancing	The process of optimizing the mix of portfolio components to further the strategic objectives of the organization.
Portfolio Charter	A document issued by a sponsor that authorizes and specifies the portfolio structure and links the portfolio to the organization's strategic objectives.
Portfolio Management	The centralized management of one or more portfolios to achieve strategic objectives.
Portfolio Management Plan	A document that specifies how a portfolio will be organized, monitored, and controlled.

Portfolio Manager	The person or group assigned by the performing organization to establish, balance, monitor, and control portfolio components in order to achieve strategic business objectives.
Precedence Diagramming Method	A technique used for constructing a schedule model in which activities are represented by nodes and are graphically linked by one or more logical relationships to show the sequence in which the activities are to be performed.
Predecessor Activity	An activity that logically comes before a dependent activity in a schedule.
Preventive Action	An intentional activity that ensures the future performance of the project work is aligned with the project management plan.
Probability and Impact Matrix	A grid for mapping the probability of occurrence of each risk and its impact on project objectives if that risk occurs.
Procurement Management Plan	A component of the project or program management plan that describes how a team will acquire goods and services from outside of the performing organization.
Product Life Cycle	The series of phases that represent the evolution of a product, from concept through delivery, growth, maturity, and to retirement.
Program	Related projects, subsidiary programs, and program activities managed in a coordinated manner to obtain benefits not available from managing them individually.
Program Charter	A document issued by a sponsor that authorizes the program management team to use organizational resources to execute the program and links the program to the organization's strategic objectives.
Program Evaluation and Review Technique (PERT)	A technique used to estimate project duration through a weighted average of optimistic, pessimistic, and most likely activity durations when there is uncertainty with the individual activity estimates.

Program Management	The application of knowledge, skills, and principles to a program to achieve the program objectives and to obtain benefits and control not available by managing program components individually.
Program Management Office (PMO)	A management structure that standardizes the program-related governance processes and facilitates the sharing of resources, methodologies, tools, and techniques.
Program Management Plan	A document that integrates the program's subsidiary plans and establishes the management controls and overall plan for integrating and managing the program's individual components.
Program Manager	The person authorized by the performing organization to lead the team or teams responsible for achieving program objectives.
Progressive Elaboration	The iterative process of increasing the level of detail in a project management plan as greater amounts of information and more accurate estimates become available.
Project	A temporary endeavor undertaken to create a unique product, service, or result.
Project Budget	The sum of work package cost estimates, contingency reserve, and management reserve.
Project Calendar	A calendar that identifies working days and shifts that are available for scheduled activities.
Project Charter	A document issued by the project initiator or sponsor that formally authorizes the existence of a project and provides the project manager with the authority to apply organizational resources to project activities.
Project Life Cycle	The series of phases that a project passes through from its start to its completion.
Project Management	The application of knowledge, skills, tools, and techniques to project activities to meet the project requirements.

Project Management Office (PMO)	A management structure that standardizes the project-related governance processes and facilitates the sharing of resources, methodologies, tools, and techniques.
Project Management Plan	The document that describes how the project will be executed, monitored and controlled, and closed.
Project Manager	The person assigned by the performing organization to lead the team that is responsible for achieving the project objectives.
Project Phase	A collection of logically related project activities that culminates in the completion of one or more deliverables.
Project Reporting	Report that contains the deliverables, requirements, tasks, start date, finish date, duration, resources and percentage complete of the project and tasks.
Project Schedule	An output of a schedule model that presents linked activities with planned dates, durations, milestones, and resources.
Project Schedule Network Diagram	A graphical representation of the logical relationships among the project schedule activities.
Project Scope	The work performed to deliver a product, service, or result with the specified features and functions.
Project Scope Statement	The description of the project scope, major deliverables, assumptions, and constraints.
Project Team	A set of individuals who support the project manager in performing the work of the project to achieve its objectives.
Project Team Assignments	Contain the project team directory and the roles and responsibilities of team member recorded in the project plan.
Projectized Organization	An organizational structure in which the project manager has full authority to assign work and apply resources.

Prompt Lists	Are predetermined lists of categorized risks to help guide meetings.
Prototypes	A method of obtaining early feedback on requirements by providing a working model of the expected product before actually building it.
Purchase Order (PO)	This type of contract is used to buy commodities.
Quality	The degree to which a set of inherent characteristics fulfills requirements.
Quality Management Plan	A component of the project or program management plan that describes how an organization's policies, procedures, and guidelines will be implemented to achieve the quality objectives.
Quality Report	A project document that includes quality management issues, recommendations for corrective actions, and a summary of findings from quality control activities and may include recommendations for process, project, and product improvements.
Recognition and Rewards	Are needed to show team members how important they are to the project and to say thanks for a job well done.
Representations of Uncertainty	Such as representations of risk in duration, cost, or resource requirement use a probability distribution such as triangular, normal, lognormal, beta, uniform, or discrete distributions.
Request for Information (RFI)	A type of procurement document whereby the buyer requests a potential seller to provide various pieces of information related to a product or service or seller capability.
Request for Proposal (RFP)	A type of procurement document used to request proposals from prospective sellers of products or services. In some application areas, it may have a narrower or more specific meaning.
Request for Quotations (RFQ)	A type of procurement document used to request price quotations from prospective sellers of common or standard products or services. Sometimes used in place of request for proposal and, in some application areas, it may have a narrower or more specific meaning.

Requirements Documentation	A description of how individual requirements meet the business need for the project
Requirements Management Plan	A component of the project or program management plan that describes how requirements will be analyzed, documented, and managed.
Requirements Traceability Matrix	A grid that links product requirements from their origin to the deliverables that satisfy them.
Reserve Analysis	An analytical technique to determine the essential features and relationships of components in the project management plan to establish a reserve for the schedule duration, budget, estimated cost, or funds for a project.
Residual Risk	The risk that remains after risk responses have been implemented.
Resource Breakdown Structure (RBS)	A hierarchical representation of resources by category and type
Resource Calendar	A calendar that identifies the working days and shifts upon which each specific resource is available.
Resource Leveling	A resource optimization technique in which adjustments are made to the project schedule to optimize the allocation of resources and which may affect critical path.
Resource Management Plan	A component of the project management plan that describes how project resources are acquired, allocated, monitored, and controlled.
Resource Optimization	A technique in which activity start and finish dates are adjusted to balance demand for resources with the available supply.
Resource Smoothing	A resource optimization technique in which free and total float are used without affecting the critical path.
Responsibility Assignment Matrix	A grid that shows the project resources assigned to each work package.

Risk	An uncertain event or condition that, if it occurs, has a positive or negative effect on one or more project objectives.
Risk Acceptance	A risk response strategy whereby the project team decides to acknowledge the risk and not take any action unless the risk occurs.
Risk Appetite	The degree of uncertainty an organization or individual is willing to accept in anticipation of a reward.
Risk Avoidance	A risk response strategy whereby the project team acts to eliminate the threat or protect the project from its impact.
Risk Breakdown Structure	A hierarchical representation of potential sources of risk.
Risk Categorization	Organization by sources of risk (e.g., using the RBS), the area of the project affected (e.g., using the WBS), or other useful category (e.g., project phase) to determine the areas of the project most exposed to the effects of uncertainty.
Risk Enhancement	A risk response strategy whereby the project team acts to increase the probability of occurrence or impact of an opportunity.
Risk Exploiting	A risk response strategy whereby the project team acts to ensure that an opportunity occurs.
Risk Exposure	An aggregate measure of the potential impact of all risks at any given point in time in a project, program, or portfolio.
Risk Management Plan	A component of the project, program, or portfolio management plan that describes how risk management activities will be structured and performed.
Risk Mitigation	A risk response strategy whereby the project team acts to decrease the probability of occurrence or impact of a threat.
Risk Owner	The person responsible for monitoring the risk and for selecting and implementing an appropriate risk response strategy.

Risk Register	A repository in which outputs of risk management processes are recorded.
Risk Sharing	A risk response strategy whereby the project team allocates ownership of an opportunity to a third party who is best able to capture the benefit for the project.
Risk Threshold	The measure of acceptable variation around an objective that reflects the risk appetite of the organization and stakeholders.
Risk Tolerance	The degree of uncertainty that an organization or individual is willing to withstand.
Risk Transference	A risk response strategy whereby the project team shifts the impact of a threat to a third party, together with ownership of the response.
Rolling Wave Planning	An iterative planning technique in which the work to be accomplished in the near term is planned in detail, while the work in the future is planned at a higher level.
Rough Order of Magnitude	Is when a project is at or near its birth stage and someone asks what it may cost for the project, the project manager may give the sponsor or senior management a rough order of magnitude, which is -25% to + 75%.
Scatter Diagrams	Allows you to analyze the relationship between two variables.
Schedule Baseline	The approved version of a schedule model that can be changed using formal change control procedures and is used as the basis for comparison to actual results
Schedule Compression	A technique used to shorten the schedule duration without reducing the project scope.
Schedule Data	The collection of information for describing and controlling the schedule.

Schedule Management Plan	A component of the project or program management plan that establishes the criteria and the activities for developing, monitoring, and controlling the schedule.
Schedule Model	A representation of the plan for executing the project's activities, including durations, dependencies, and other planning information, used to produce a project schedule along with other scheduling artifacts.
Schedule Model Analysis	A process used to investigate or analyze the output of the schedule model in order to optimize the schedule.
Schedule Network Analysis	A technique to identify early and late start dates, as well as early and late finish dates, for the uncompleted portions of project activities
Schedule Performance Index (SPI)	A measure of schedule efficiency expressed as the ratio of earned value to planned value.
Schedule Variance (SV)	Which measures the difference between the earned value (EV) (the value of work actually performed) and the planned value (PV), so $SV = EV - PV$
Scope Baseline	The approved version of a scope statement, work breakdown structure (WBS), and its associated WBS dictionary, that can be changed using formal change control procedures and is used as a basis for comparison to actual results.
Scope Creep	The uncontrolled expansion to product or project scope without adjustments to time, cost, and resources
Scope Management Plan	A component of the project or program management plan that describes how the scope will be defined, developed, monitored, controlled, and validated.
S-Curve Analysis	A technique used to indicate performance trends by using a graph that displays cumulative costs over a specific time period.
Secondary Risks	A risk that arises as a direct result of implementing a risk response.

Seller Proposals	Formal responses from sellers to a request for proposal or other procurement document specifying the price, commercial terms of sale, and technical specifications or capabilities the seller will do for the requesting organization that, if accepted, would bind the seller to perform the resulting agreement.
Sequence Activities	The process of identifying and documenting relationships among the project activities.
Share Risk	Involves transferring ownership to a third party. Examples of sharing actions include partnerships, teams, and joint ventures.
SIPOC (suppliers, inputs, process, outputs, customers) diagram	Is a visual tool for documenting a business process from beginning to end.
Source selection criteria	A set of attributes desired by the buyer which a seller is required to meet or exceed to be selected for a contract.
Sponsor	An individual or a group that provides resources and support for the project, program, or portfolio, and is accountable for enabling success.
Staffing Management Plan	A component of the resource management plan that describes when and how team members will be acquired and how long they will be needed.
Stakeholder	An individual, group, or organization that may affect, be affected by, or perceive itself to be affected by a decision, activity, or outcome of a project, program, or portfolio.
Stakeholder Engagement Plan	A component of the project or program management plan that identifies the strategies and actions required to promote productive involvement of stakeholders in project or program decision making and execution.
Start to Finish (SF)	Is a logical relationship in which a successor activity cannot finish until a predecessor activity has started.

Start to Start (SS)	Is a logical relationship in which a successor activity cannot start until a predecessor activity has started.
Start-to-Finish	A logical relationship in which a successor activity cannot finish until a predecessor activity has started.
Start-to-Start	A logical relationship in which a successor activity cannot start until a predecessor activity has started.
Strong Matrix or Project Matrix	The project manager has most of the power, resources, and control over the work. The functional manager is there to add support and technical expertise and to look after HR issues
Successor Activity	A dependent activity that logically comes after another activity in a schedule.
Summary Activity	A group of related schedule activities aggregated and displayed as a single activity.
Supportive PMOs	Provide a consultative role to projects by supplying templates, best practices, training, access to information, and lessons learned from other projects
SWOT	Analysis of strengths, weaknesses, opportunities, and threats of an organization, project, or option.
Team Charter	A document that records the team values, agreements, and operating guidelines, as well as establishing clear expectations regarding acceptable behavior by project team members.
Tender	Notice invites bids for a project or to accept a formal offer such as a takeover bid. Tender usually refers to the process whereby governments and financial institutions invite bids for large projects that must be submitted by a finite deadline.
Threat	A risk that would have a negative effect on one or more project objectives.

Three-Point Estimating	A technique used to estimate cost or duration by applying an average or weighted average of optimistic, pessimistic, and most likely estimates when there is uncertainty with the individual activity estimates.
Time and Materials contracts (T&M)	Use this type of contract when the scope is incomplete or not determined. T&Ms are also used when the deliverable is "labor hours."
To Complete Performance Index (TCPI)	A measure of the cost performance that is required to be achieved with the remaining resources in order to meet a specified management goal, expressed as the ratio of the cost to finish the outstanding work to the remaining budget.
Total Float	The amount of time that a schedule activity can be delayed or extended from its early start date without delaying the project finish date or violating a schedule constraint.
Training	Is necessary for team members close to the needed skill set but missing a certain tool or discipline.
Transference	Involves shifting ownership to a third party, such as payment of insurance premiums so that if the risk occurs, its impact will be minimized.
Trigger Condition	An event or situation that indicates that a risk is about to occur.
Tuckman's Ladder	Describes the stages of team formation and development. These stages are: 1. Forming- The team meets and learns about the project. 2. Storming - The team begins to address the project work. 3. Norming - The team begins to work together. 4. Performing - The team is efficient and works through issues. 5. Adjourning - The team completes the work and is released.
Validate Scope	The process of formalizing acceptance of the completed project deliverables.
Variable Costs	Are expenses that change in proportion to the level of activity of a business, such as the purchase of more or less raw material

Variance Analysis	A technique for determining the cause and degree of difference between the baseline and actual performance.
Variance at Completion (VAC)	A projection of the amount of budget deficit or surplus, expressed as the difference between the budget at completion and the estimate at completion.
Verified Deliverable	Completed project deliverables that have been checked and confirmed for correctness through the Control Quality process.
Virtual teams	Groups of people with a shared goal who fulfill their roles with little or no time spent meeting face to face.
Voting	Is used to select for best response involving project team members when discussing cost estimates.
Waterfall Model	Is a relatively linear sequential design approach as progress flows in largely one direction through the phases of conception, initiation, analysis, design, construction, testing, deployment, and maintenance"
WBS Dictionary	A document that provides detailed deliverable, activity, and scheduling information about each component in the work breakdown structure.
Weak Matrix	In this form of organization, the functional manager retains most of the power; they "own" the people and resources. In a weak/functional matrix, the project manager is not very powerful.
Weighted Milestone Method	A method of estimating earned value in which the budget value of a work package is divided into measurable segments, each ending with a milestone that is assigned a weighted budget value.
What-If Scenario Analysis	The process of evaluating scenarios in order to predict their effect on project objectives.
Work Breakdown Structure (WBS)	A hierarchical decomposition of the total scope of work to be carried out by the project team to accomplish the project objectives and create the required deliverables.

Work Package	The work defined at the lowest level of the work breakdown structure for which cost, and duration are estimated and managed.
Work performance data	The raw observations and measurements identified during activities being performed to carry out the project work.
Work performance information	The performance data collected from controlling processes, analyzed in comparison with project management plan components, project documents, and other work performance information.
Work performance report	The physical or electronic representation of work performance information compiled in project documents, intended to generate decisions, actions, or awareness.
Workaround	An immediate and temporary response to an issue, for which a prior response had not been planned or was not effective.

Index

About the Author

Darron Clark is skilled in training, mentoring, and leading teams to achieve established goals. Darron is also recognized for strengthening the overall capability of globally dispersed teams that are managing critical projects, environments, and systems.

Darron has served as vice president of infrastructure and technical project manager, managing and leading medium-size technological projects in accordance with service-level agreements, contract requirements, and company policies, procedures, and guidelines.

Darron has extensive qualifications in collaborating with businesses, leaders, and teams to define, plan, and guide the on-time and within-budget delivery of implementation, upgrades, and tuning projects across enterprise environments.

Darron's strong skills in innovation, automation, and problem-solving are in introducing new processes, standards, and technologies to ensure optimal performance and availability of critical data. He has a proven ability to adapt quickly to challenges and to changing business environments.